technology,
innovation,
AND
educational change

A GLOBAL PERSPECTIVE

A Report of the Second
Information Technology
in Education Study
MODULE 2

Robert B. Kozma, Editor

With contributions from:

JOKE M. VOOGT

WILLEM J. PELGRUM

RONALD D. OWSTON

RAYMOND MCGHEE

RICHARD M. JONES

RONALD E. ANDERSON

A PROJECT OF THE INTERNATIONAL ASSOCIATION
FOR THE EVALUATION OF EDUCATIONAL ACHIEVEMENT (IEA)

Published by the International Society for Technology in Education

Technology, Innovation, and Educational Change

A GLOBAL PERSPECTIVE

A REPORT OF THE SECOND INFORMATION TECHNOLOGY IN EDUCATION STUDY: MODULE 2

A Project of the International Association for the Evaluation of Educational Achievement (IEA)

Robert B. Kozma, Editor

Director of Publishing
JEAN MARIE HALL

Acquisitions Editor
MATHEW MANWELLER

Production Editor
TRACY COZZENS

Copy Editor
RON RENCHLER

Book Design and Layout
KIM McGOVERN

Cover Design
SIGNE LANDIN

International Society for Technology in Education (ISTE)
480 Charnelton Street
Eugene, OR 97401-2626
Order Desk: 1.800.336.5191
Order Fax: 1.541.302.3778
Customer Service: orders@iste.org
Books and Courseware: books@iste.org
Permissions: permissions@iste.org
World Wide Web: www.iste.org

First Edition
ISBN 1-56484-230-4

ABOUT ISTE

The International Society for Technology in Education (ISTE) is a nonprofit professional organization with a worldwide membership of leaders in educational technology. We are dedicated to promoting appropriate uses of information technology to support and improve learning, teaching, and administration in PK–12 education and teacher education. As part of that mission, ISTE provides high-quality and timely information, services, and materials, such as this book.

The ISTE Publishing Department works with experienced educators to develop and produce classroom-tested books and courseware. We look for content that emphasizes the use of technology where it can make a difference—making the teacher's job easier; saving time; motivating students; helping students who have unique learning styles, abilities, or backgrounds; and creating learning environments that would be impossible without technology. We believe technology can improve the effectiveness of teaching while making learning exciting and fun.

Every manuscript and product we select for publication is peer reviewed and professionally edited. While we take pride in our publications, we also recognize the difficulties of maintaining quality while keeping on top of the latest technologies and research. Please let us know which products you would find helpful. We value your feedback on this book and other ISTE products. E-mail us at **books@iste.org**.

ISTE is home of the National Educational Technology Standards (NETS) Project, the National Educational Computing Conference (NECC), and the National Center for Preparing Tomorrow's Teachers to Use Technology (NCPT[3]). To learn more about NETS or request a print catalog, visit our Web site at **www.iste.org**, which provides:

- Current educational technology standards for PK–12 students, teachers, and administrators

- A bookstore with online ordering and membership discount options

- *Learning & Leading with Technology* magazine and the *Journal of Research on Technology in Education*

- *ISTE Update*, online membership newsletter

- Teacher resources

- Discussion groups

- Professional development services, including national conference information

- Research projects

- Member services

ABOUT THE AUTHORS

EDITOR

Robert B. Kozma. Dr. Kozma is an emeritus principal scientist and Fulbright senior specialist at the Center for Technology in Learning at SRI International. Among the more than 30 projects he has directed are a project for the World Bank to evaluate the impact of networked computing in high schools in six countries in Africa and South America, the evaluation of the Virtual High School project (which offers high school courses via the Internet throughout the United States), and research and development in the use of ICT to improve science learning, especially in chemistry. He has consulted with the Ministries of Education in Thailand, Chile, and Singapore on the use of ICT to support education reform. He has authored or coauthored more than 40 articles, chapters, encyclopedia entries, and books. His work has appeared in such publications as *Learning and Instruction, Journal of the Learning Sciences, Review of Educational Research, Cognition and Instruction, Annual Review of Psychology, Journal of Higher Education, Education and Urban Society, Journal for Research in Science Teaching, Journal of Research on Computing in Education, Computers in Human Behavior, Academic Computing, Computers and Composition, Educational Technology Research and Development,* and *International Encyclopedia of Education.*

CONTRIBUTORS

Joke M. Voogt. Dr. Voogt is associate professor at the Faculty of Educational Science and Technology at the University of Twente. Her research focuses on innovative uses of information and communication technologies in the curriculum. Her national and international research projects have included an examination of computer-assisted lab work; the use of Web environments to support staff development; case studies of innovative uses of information technology in primary, secondary, and teacher education; SITES Module 1; evaluation of technology-rich learning practices in teacher education; and several technology projects with Russian teacher education colleges. Her work has appeared in several books and international research journals, including *Computers in Education, Educational Technology Research and Development, Journal of In-service Education, International Encyclopedia of Educational Technology,* and *International Encyclopedia for the Social and Behavioral Sciences.*

Willem J. Pelgrum. Dr. Pelgrum is senior researcher at the Center for Applied Educational Research at the University of Twente in The Netherlands. His main experience is in the field of large-scale international comparative assessments. He has been National Research Coordinator for the IEA's Second International Mathematics Study and the Second International Science Study. He has been International Coordinator for SITES Module 1 (1997–1999) and for the IEA Computers in Education Studies conducted in 1989 and 1992. He conducted an extensive training project for researchers in Central and East Europe and was involved in several consultancy visits. He also performed several studies for the European Commission in the areas of educational monitoring and ICT. He was the coordinator of the European network for educational research on assessment, effectiveness, and innovation. His work has appeared in several books and international research journals, including *Studies in Educational Evaluation, Computers in Education, International Journal of Educational Research*, and *Prospects*.

Ronald D. Owston. Dr. Owston is professor of education and founding director of the Institute for Research on Learning Technologies at York University in Toronto. He has spoken at numerous national and international conferences and has published in variety of fields, including technology in education, program evaluation, and teacher development. His work has appeared in *Research in the Teaching of English, Journal of Computer-Based Instruction, Journal of Information Technology in Teacher Education, Journal of Computer Assisted Learning, Journal of Research on Computing in Education*, and *Educational Researcher*. In 1998 he coauthored *The Learning Highway: Smart Students and the Internet* (Key Porter) and published *Making the Link: Teacher Professional Development on the Internet* with Heinemann. His recent projects include the evaluation of Web-based learning at the postsecondary and continuing education levels, a multisite longitudinal study on how teachers and young children use notebook computers in their classrooms, and the application of online learning to teacher professional development.

Raymond McGhee. Dr. McGhee is a research social scientist in SRI International's Center for Education Policy. He has participated in a variety of state, national, and international evaluation projects examining technological and curricular innovation in schools and universities. With support from the National Science Foundation, Dr. McGhee has conducted numerous case studies examining curricular reform and faculty professional development activities in science, mathematics, engineering, and technology education at universities in the United States. He has also participated in case study research analyzing the school and community contexts supporting professional development related to the use of educational technology in public schools in several U.S. states. Dr. McGhee currently serves as the director of a program evaluation assessing the impact of information technology and training on secondary school students and teachers in eight countries for the World Links Organization.

Richard M. Jones. Dr. Jones is project manager for National, International, and Special Projects with the Education Quality and Accountability Office (EQAO) in Toronto. Prior to this, Dr. Jones was the director of the Assessment and Evaluation Branch with the Saskatchewan Department of Education. His responsibilities included designing and implementing initiatives related to student evaluation, program evaluation, curriculum evaluation, provincial learning assessment, education indicators, and national and international testing. In recent years, he has authored numerous articles on these topics. During 3 years in the Middle East, he served as deputy project manager and administrative manager for an American-based consulting firm. He coordinated provincial learning assessment activities and was assistant director of the provincial and scholarship examination program during 3 years with the Student Assessment Branch of the B.C. Ministry of Education. He has several years of teaching experience at the elementary, secondary, community college, and university levels in Ontario, British Columbia, and Africa.

Ronald E. Anderson. Dr. Anderson is a professor of sociology at the University of Minnesota in Minneapolis, where he has been on the faculty since 1968. Anderson has authored more than 80 articles, coauthored or edited 8 computer-related books, and coordinated the development of at least 50 instructional software packages. Professor Anderson is coeditor of the *Social Science Computer Review* and is regional editor for the *Journal of Computer Assisted Learning*. He is on the editorial boards of the *Journal of Educational Computing Research* and *Education and Information Technologies*. As the United States' National Research Coordinator for the IEA Computers in Education study, he secured a large grant from the National Science Foundation to conduct that assessment in 1992. With Henry Becker he received funding for the "Teaching, Learning and Computing," which included a nationwide survey of K–12 schools and teachers in 1998. Dr. Anderson has served as cochair of the International Steering Committee for the Second International Technology in Education Study (SITES) Modules 1 and 2.

ACKNOWLEDGMENTS

The authors would like to express their deep appreciation to the large number of people who made this project possible. First, we would like to acknowledge the support of the International Association for the Evaluation of Educational Achievement (IEA) for sponsoring this study and especially the efforts of Hans Wagemaker, IEA's executive director, and Barbara Malak-Minkiewicz, IEA's manager of membership relations. We would like to thank those who made special contributions, including the Ministry of Education of Demark, the Ministry of Education of France, the Dutch Science Foundation of The Netherlands, the Ministry of Education and Church Affairs of Norway, the National Institute for Educational Research of Japan, and both the National Science Foundation and the Department of Education of the United States. We would also like to give special acknowledgement to the Ford Foundation and to an anonymous contributor.

The project would not have been possible without the hard work and excellent ideas of the National Research Coordinators (NRCs) from the 28 participating countries (see Appendix A for a list of names). These people made contributions to the design of the international study, collected data in their countries, and wrote up the case reports. We particularly appreciate the gracious hospitality of our hosts for various project meetings: Inge Bryderup (Copenhagen), Catherine Regnier (Poitiers), Richard Jones and Catherine Sim (Toronto), Yoke Chun Tham (Singapore), and Marja Kankaanranta (Jyvaskyla). The project also greatly benefited from the members of the International Steering Committee, cochaired by Tjeerd Plomp (The Netherlands) and Ronald Anderson (United States). Members of the committee included Ryo Watanabe (Japan), Nancy Law (China Hong Kong), Fred-Arne Oedegaard and Jan Peter Stromsheim (Norway), and Chris Dede (United States). We appreciate their support, many thoughtful ideas, and many hours of donated labor.

We would also like to thank our colleagues and staff at each of our institutions for all of their work. At SRI International this includes Martha Agreda, Andy Freedman, Jeff Huang, Amy Lewis, Pamela Jennings, John Rollin, Yukie Toyama, Cheryl Villavicencio, and Wenming Ye. We very much appreciate the work of our colleagues from SRI who reviewed an early draft of this manuscript: Barbara Means, Roy Pea (also at Stanford University), and Margaret Riel. At the University of Twente, we would like to thank Gerard Doornekamp and Charles Matthijssen for their efforts.

We would also like to express our appreciation to our family and friends for their patience and support during the many long hours of work and trips away from home. We would especially like to acknowledge Shari Malone; Kristi Webster McGhee; Connie Jones and family; Anke Owston; Gonnie Marnette; Sietske Pelgrum; and Jan, Maaike, Karin, and Luuk Heitink.

FOREWORD

echnology, Innovation, and Educational Change—A Global Perspective provides a unique, invaluable resource for education policy, practice, and research. Sponsored by the International Association for the Evaluation of Educational Achievement (IEA), the Second Information Technology in Education Study (SITES) Module 2 collected and analyzed 174 case studies from exemplary implementation sites across 28 countries. This research documents the myriad ways in which the integration of learning technologies into instruction enabled deep content, sophisticated pedagogy, and impressive student outcomes. For policy makers, the cases collectively inform an understanding of how conditions necessary for the successful integration of learning technologies vary—and are uniform—across subject areas, grade levels, teaching philosophies, cultures, and other contextual factors in classroom settings. For practitioners, the individual cases referenced in this report illustrate the rich menu of technology-based educational innovations this study provides to the field. For scholars, this large group of case studies collected with comparable methods and equivalent data types forms a rich repository for comparative analysis that can elucidate the relative roles of message, medium, and communicative method in empowering learning.

As the authors of the report describe, at the start of the 21st century our civilization is shifting from loosely coupled, mature agricultural and industrial economies to a profoundly interconnected, knowledge-based global marketplace (Dertouzos & Gates, 1998). Driven by advances in information technology, this economic evolution is the largest leap from yesterday's workplace to tomorrow's in the last two centuries, since the dawn of the industrial revolution (Thurow, 1999). In response, all forms of societal institutions are altering slowly but radically—even schools (Dede, 2000). Since one of goals of education is to prepare students for work and citizenship, schools are attempting to change their policies, practices, and curriculum to meet the challenge of making pupils ready for a future quite different than the immediate past (Tucker & Codding, 1998). Students need to master higher-order cognitive, affective, and social skills not central to mature industrial societies but vital in a knowledge-based economy (Drucker, 1994). These include "thriving on chaos" (making rapid decisions based on incomplete information to resolve novel situations); the ability to collaborate with a diverse team—face-to-face or across distance—to accomplish a task; and creating, sharing, and mastering knowledge through filtering a sea of quasi-accurate information (Peters, 1997).

As this report documents, parallel to the ways in which information technology has improved effectiveness in medicine, finance, manufacturing, and numerous other sectors of society, advanced computing and telecommunications have the potential to help students master these complex 21st-century skills (President's Committee of Advisors in Science and Technology, 1997). However, technology is not a "vitamin" whose mere presence in schools catalyzes better educational outcomes; nor are new media just another subject in the curriculum, suited primarily for teaching technical literacy with business applications students may encounter as adults. Instead, emerging interactive media are tools in service of richer curricula, enhanced pedagogies, more effective organizational structures, stronger links between schools and society, and the empowerment of disenfranchised learners (Trotter, 1998).

This book helps policy makers, practitioners, and researchers explore these possibilities. The SITES Module 2 cases form a rich archive for comparative analysis that help us consider what alternative combinations of interventions support successful transfer of innovations from one educational context to another. Thus, this research fosters the evolution of two key factors in the use of computers and telecommunications in education: policy frameworks for successful adaptation and models of technology-intensive learning.

Too often, education technology policy focuses solely on increasing the hardware and wires that equip the classroom and connect it with the outside world. While these resources are important, they are not the essential policy issues. In some countries student/computer ratios are 5:1 or lower, but in quite a number of cases in this study, exemplary implementations involved ratios of more than 25:1. This is striking and shows that sophisticated human and organizational capacity for effective technology integration can transcend very limited technological resources.

Another important finding of this report is the effectiveness of policy strategies based on "innovation in chords, rather than individual notes." Coordinated policy is more important than having a high level of technology access. The SITES Module 2 research validates that in order to fully realize technology's capabilities for reinventing teaching, learning, and schooling, policy makers must engage in a complex implementation process that includes sustained, large-scale, simultaneous innovations in curriculum, pedagogy, assessment, professional development, administration, organizational structures, strategies for equity, and partnerships for learning among schools, businesses, homes, and community settings (Dede, 1998). Creating policy frameworks that foster the development of powerful learning technologies, the delineation of conditions for their successful implementation, and the preparation of teachers and schools for effective usage are all crucial for improving students' educational outcomes and educators' ability to innovate in response to the demands of 21st-century civilization.

The book also has much to say to practitioners. A theme that runs through many of the case studies is that computers and telecommunications can support pervasive shifts in patterns of teaching and learning. Teachers and students learning together in communities of practice, distance learning that draws on remote archives and experts, and whole-school reforms that extend horizontally across the curricular domains and longitudinally across grade levels all illustrate a transformative impact of information technologies.

The SITES Module 2 case studies show that sophisticated computers and telecommunications have unique capabilities for enhancing learning. These include the following:

♦ Centering the curriculum on "authentic" problems parallel to those adults face in real-world settings (Cognition and Technology Group at Vanderbilt, 1997)

♦ Involving students in virtual communities-of-practice, using advanced tools similar to those in today's high-tech workplaces (Linn, 1997)

♦ Facilitating guided, reflective inquiry through extended projects that inculcate sophisticated concepts and skills and generate complex products (Schank, Fano, Bell, & Jona, 1994)

♦ Utilizing modeling and visualization as powerful means of bridging between experience and abstraction (Gordin & Pea, 1995)

◆ Enhancing students' collaborative construction of meaning via different perspectives on shared experiences (Chan, Burtis, & Bereiter, 1997)

◆ Including pupils as partners in developing learning experiences and generating knowledge (Scardamalia & Bereiter, 1994)

◆ Fostering success for all students through special measures to aid the disabled and the disenfranchised (Behrmann, 1998)

SITES Module 2 provides rich examples of all these capabilities, illustrating the ways that content, instructional process, and interactive media can work together to enhance learning. In some cases, telecommunications-based access to distant experts and archives was the central capability enabling exciting student outcomes. In other cases, computers made possible a shift from presentational instruction to guided learning-by-doing, collaborative learning, or mentoring, all of which foster students' mastery of curricular knowledge and skills as well as their motivation to succeed. Sometimes, the capabilities of an interactive medium were the key driver for learning, such as the deep reflection enabled by asynchronous threaded discussions as opposed to fast-paced classroom dialogue. This book mines these cases for comparative insights that provide teachers with richer models of how all these factors shape learning, combining in ways that make their whole impact on education much greater than the sum of its parts.

An important insight from this study is that the use of interactive media for student expression is a very powerful means of teaching and learning. Many exemplary implementations center on helping learners "find their voices." This seems particularly powerful when students communicate across cultures or use their expressive capabilities to develop electronic artifacts about culture. Contrary to popular misconceptions, the SITES Module 2 research illustrates that language and fine arts—not just math and science—are empowered by learning technologies.

Another finding is that most of the curriculum changes involved a reorganization of the current content rather than deepening content or moving knowledge and skills earlier in students' developmental progression through grade levels. However, in a few cases, teachers and students used specialized software to increase the depth of students' understanding of specific subjects. In another set of cases, information and communications technology (ICT) tools and digital resources helped break down the barriers across the subject disciplines. And in some cases, ICT was integrated throughout the curriculum and the school, and ICT environments were structured to help students take on the responsibilities of lifelong learning. Where significant curriculum change occurred, it was often supported by a local vision of educational change, strong local leadership, and resources for schoolwide improvement. In the long run, computers and telecommunications may enable students to do work three or more grade levels ahead of what our current expectations are, or to understand material now thought to be too difficult to be included in the curriculum. But for this to happen, we need the integration of technology into classroom instruction, strong local leadership, and coordinated national policies.

For researchers, this study provides an excellent example of how to conduct a large-scale, international qualitative study. Collecting comparable case studies and developing the coding schemes that adequately categorize and differentiate the complex patterns of teaching and learning processes across these cases is extremely difficult. The enormous effort the investigators devoted to this study's design, execution, and analysis has resulted in findings of a depth and rigor rare in large multicountry educational research.

Of course, it is also important to understand the methodological limitations that necessarily constrain any such large-scale study. The study cites strong positive outcomes of technology-based innovation for students and teachers. But these conclusions are compromised by the strong vested interest of the students, teachers, and administrators who reported these outcomes—a limitation acknowledged by the authors. Different types of research designs are needed to establish a formal causal relationship, or at least stronger correlations, between wise usage of learning technologies and better educational outcomes.

However, evaluating the effectiveness of current and emerging learning technologies is complex because such an assessment is possible only when the conditions for successful implementation are met. An analogy to medical technologies can be made, using the contrast between an immunization and a controlled longitudinal administration of antibiotics. To be effective, the immunization needs only to take place. In contrast, the antibiotics must be taken at the prescribed dosage, at the prescribed time intervals, for the prescribed amount of time. If these conditions for success are not met, the antibiotics may well be ineffective, even though this medical technology is a powerful intervention when used properly.

The conditions for success of learning technologies in schools are much more complex than for the use of antibiotics in medicine. Moreover, the beliefs, attitudes, and values of users are vital to the effectiveness of learning technologies—as opposed to medical technologies such as immunizations and antibiotics. Education is more like public health than medicine and presents challenges similar to public health in moving basic research findings into everyday practice. One reason that frequent pronouncements are made about the ineffectiveness of learning technologies is that preparing schools and teachers to use learning technologies well is a challenging process. Many of the critics of educational technology are citing implementation methods equivalent to grinding up antibiotics and smearing them over one's body, or taking the entire dose at once, or worshiping the pills rather than using them.

Had international business been discouraged by similar early ineffective applications of information technology in those organizational settings and given up on desktop computers and the Internet before learning to create their conditions for success in a corporate context, a vital component of the last decade's economic prosperity would have been lost. While it is important for us to conduct rigorous research on the outcomes of technology use, it is also important for us to move forward with our policies and practices. This book helps us do that.

— CHRIS DEDE

Wirth Professor of Learning Technologies
Harvard Graduate School of Education

JANUARY 2003

CONTENTS

1 ICT and Educational Change: A Global Phenomenon

Robert B. Kozma

2 Study Procedures and First Look at the Data

Robert B. Kozma

3 ICT and Innovative Classroom Practices

Robert B. Kozma and Raymond McGhee

4 ICT and the Curriculum

Joke Voogt and Willem J. Pelgrum

5 School Context, Sustainability, and Transferability of Innovation

Ronald D. Owston

6 Local and National ICT Policies

Richard M. Jones

7 Stellar Cases of Technology-Supported Pedagogical Innovations

Ronald E. Anderson

8 Summary and Implications for ICT-Based Educational Change

Robert B. Kozma

Appendixes

CHAPTER 1

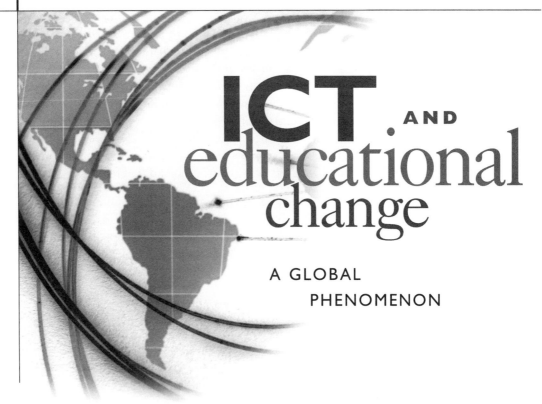

ICT . AND educational change

A GLOBAL PHENOMENON

By Robert B. Kozma

INTRODUCTION

Over the past several decades we have witnessed a fundamental economic transformation. Economists generally acknowledge that a profound shift has occurred in the role that knowledge and technology play in driving productivity and economic growth (Stiglitz, 1999), a phenomenon referred to as the "knowledge economy" (Organization for Economic Co-operation and Development [OECD], 1996). From this perspective, knowledge is both the engine and the product of economic growth (OECD, 1999). The production, distribution, and use of new knowledge and information are major contributors to increased productivity and the creation of new, high-paying jobs. Associated improvements in manpower qualifications and institutional capabilities are, in turn, major sources of new knowledge and innovation.

A parallel, linked development—sometimes called the "information society" (European Commission, 2000)—is the broader social transformation resulting from the convergence of computers and communication technologies and their assimilation throughout society. As information and communications technologies (ICT) become an integral part of our work places, schools, and homes, they are changing the way we live, work, play, communicate, and learn (President's Information Technology Advisory Committee [PITAC], 1999). The information society refers to the potential that these technologies have to make education and health care more widely available, foster cultural creativity and productivity, increase democratic participation and the responsiveness of governmental agencies, and enhance the social integration of individuals with different abilities and of different cultural groups.

ICT provides the tools needed by the knowledge economy and the information society. These tools allow us to create, collect, store, and use this new knowledge and information. They enable us to connect with people and resources all over the world, to collaborate in the creation of knowledge, and to distribute and benefit from knowledge products.

These economic and social transformations have significant implications for employees of the knowledge economy and citizens of the information society. The knowledge economy is characterized by an increased proportion of the labor force engaged in handling and producing information rather than producing more tangible goods (OECD, 1996, 2001a). The employment demand is high for workers with advanced skills in the use of information, including the use of ICT. Employers pay high wages for workers who are able to search for and select relevant information, interpret and analyze data, work with distributed teams, and learn new skills as needed. Particularly prized is the ability to use information to solve problems and create new knowledge. Similarly, citizens of the information society must be able to use ICT to access information about education, health care, and government services (European Commission, 2000). They must be creative producers of cultural artifacts, and they must be able to communicate effectively with others, particularly those of different backgrounds. These social and economic developments also require that people be able to acquire new skills in response to changing circumstances, assess their own learning needs and progress, and learn throughout their lifetime—they must become "lifelong learners" (OECD, 2001a).

These economic and social changes are global in scope. Since the end of the Cold War, there has been a dramatic increase in the opening of trade; a rise in influence of multinational corporations and intergovernmental agencies; a growth in the international movement of money, ideas, goods, and (to a lesser extent) people; and an increase in both economic competitiveness and interdependency among nations (Soros, 2002; Stiglitz, 2002). To a large extent, globalization has built upon and contributed to the pervasive use of ICT.

However, while these developments are global they have not equally benefited all nations and groups of people (Soros, 2002; Stiglitz, 2002; United Nations Development Program [UNDP], 1999). There is a significant digital divide among peoples of the world. For example, Thailand has more cell phones and New York has more Web sites than exist in the entire African continent (UNDP, 1999). English is the language of nearly 80% of all Web sites, yet less than 10% of people worldwide speak it. These discrepancies attest to the global challenges we face, as well as to the potential benefits we may enjoy, in living in the knowledge economy and information society.

ICT AND EDUCATIONAL CHANGE

With these economic and social developments as a backdrop, interest has been growing in the role that ICT can play in improving education and changing schools (European Commission, 2001b; President's Committee of Advisors on Science and Technology [PCAST], 1997). Some researchers (Bransford, Brown, & Cocking, 2000) posit that a number of features of new technologies are consistent with principles of the science of learning and hold promise for improving education. New technologies can bring exciting curricula based on real-world problems into the classroom and provide scaffolds and tools to enhance learning. The interactivity of technologies is cited as a key feature that enables students to receive feedback on their performance, test and reflect on their ideas, and revise their understanding. Networked technology can enable teachers and students to build local and global communities that connect them with interested people and expand opportunities for teacher learning.

However, Bransford, Brown, and Cocking (2000) caution that the positive impact of technology does not come automatically; much depends on how teachers use ICT in their classrooms. On the one hand, in a national study in the U.S., Wenglinski (1998) found a negative relationship between the frequency of use of school computers and school achievement. Similar findings have come from international data (Pelgrum & Plomp, 2002). On the other hand, Wenglinski (1998) found that certain types of technology use had a positive effect on achievement. For example, Wenglinski found that the use of computers for learning games in the 4th grade was positively related to math achievement. He also found that teachers' professional development in the use of ICT and its use in the 8th grade to teach higher-order thinking skills were positively related to math achievement. More recent analyses of U.S. data show a positive relationship between science achievement and the use of computer learning games in the 4th grade, the use of simulations in the 8th grade, and the use of computers to collect, download, and analyze data in the 12th grade (NCES, 2001).

Nor does the positive impact of technology automatically affect all groups and nations equally. There is a digital divide in education as well. For example, as of 1998 there was approximately one computer for every 9 lower secondary students in Canada but only one for every 133 students in Lithuania and only one for every 210 students in Cyprus (Pelgrum & Anderson, 1999). Furthermore, only 25% of schools in South Africa have a telephone line (UNDP, 1999).

There are also disparities within countries. For instance, non-Hispanic children in the U.S. are more likely to have home use of computers and the Internet than are Black or Hispanic children (U.S. Census Bureau, 2001). Among American children 3 to 17 years old, 77% of White non-Hispanics and 72% of Asians lived in households with computers, while only 43% of Black children and 37% of Hispanic children lived in households with computers at the time of the study.

In response to large-scale economic and social changes and to the potential of ICT for improving education, many countries have begun to formulate policies that apply ICT in order to improve schools. Countries ranging from Chile (Ministerio de Educación, Republica de Chile, 1998) to Finland (Ministry of Education, Finland, 1999) and from Singapore (Ministry of Education, Singapore, 2002) to the United States (U.S. Department of Education, 2000) have all set national goals and policies that identify a significant role for ICT in improving their education systems and reforming their curricula. For example, in the late

1990s the Ministry of Education in Singapore formulated a vision called Thinking Schools, Learning Nation in response to the twin forces of globalization and technological change. The intent was to reformulate what was taught and how it was taught in Singaporean schools to emphasize such thinking skills as problem solving and critical thinking. Singapore's "Master Plan for IT in Education," which was recently updated (Ministry of Education, Singapore, 2002), supports this vision through the integration of ICT into the entire education system—curriculum, assessment, instruction, professional development, and the school culture—to support the development of students' ability to think flexibly and innovatively, cooperate with others, and make sound judgments. In 1996, the U.S. Department of Education released a report called "Getting America's Students Ready for the 21st Century: Meeting the Technology Literacy Challenge," which presented a vision for the 21st century in which all students would be technologically literate and better prepared for the demands of the new American economy. The report presented challenges to the nation's states and schools to train all teachers to use technology in their classes, to provide all classrooms with modern computers and Internet access, and to integrate technology into the curriculum. In 1999, the U.S. Department of Education revised the national educational technology plan. New challenges included the need to increase student technology literacy skills and use technology to help students achieve high academic standards (U.S. Department of Education, 2000). The Ministry of Education in Finland has created a vision of the Finnish information society (Ministry of Education, Finland, 1999) whose main thrust is to develop and use the opportunities inherent in ICT to improve the Finnish people's quality of life, knowledge, international competitiveness, and interaction. Finland's National Information Strategy supports this vision by providing schools and teachers with the necessary infrastructure, technical support, teacher training, and technologically enriched environments and innovative learning and teaching materials.

Multinational organizations, too, such as the OECD (2000) and the European Commission (2001b), have identified an important role for ICT in education. They agree on the need to prepare students for lifelong learning in the information society of the 21st century. Reports issued by UNESCO (Blurton, 1999) and the World Bank (1998) advocate the use of these technologies to promote international socioeconomic progress and educational change, both inside and outside the classroom. The World Bank has made significant investments in networked computers in 24 developing countries (Kozma & McGhee, 1999; McGhee & Kozma, 2000), with the intent of closing the digital divide between industrialized and developing countries.

Evidence indicates that these policy investments around the world have resulted in a dramatic increase in the number of computers in schools and classrooms and the access that teachers and students have to the Internet (Anderson & Ronnkvist, 1999; European Commission, 2001b; NCES, 2001; Pelgrum & Anderson, 1999). But what changes do these increases portend for the world's teachers and students? How do these changes fit with the needs and demands of the knowledge economy and information society?

A number of researchers have speculated on how technology-rich classrooms might look (Kozma & Schank, 1998; OECD, 2001a, 2001b; Riel, 1998). They envision a future in which schools have completed the transformation from the industrial age to the information age, a future in which ICT is integrated throughout society in general and in schools in particular. In this vision of the future, the increased flow of information is associated with more autonomous learning environments, environments rich with people and information that support student learning. This future can be characterized by several shifts:

- From the teacher as initiator of instruction for the whole class to the teacher as a guide who helps students find their appropriate instructional path and evaluate their own learning.

- From teachers working in isolation to teachers collaborating with their colleagues on joint plans and projects.

- From students as passive individual learners to students as active learners working in teams to create new knowledge and solve problems.

- From schools isolated from society to schools integrated into society.

- From parents uninvolved in their children's schooling to parents who are actively involved.

ICT enables these innovations by supporting teacher and student activities and by connecting students and teachers to each other and to a vast array of human and informational resources around the world.

The distinction between this emerging educational paradigm and traditional notions about education constitutes an overarching construct for this study of innovative pedagogical practices that use ICT. But in contrast to those with futuristic visions, most teachers in most schools are still caught in the traditional education paradigm and make limited use of ICT. For a variety of reasons, many teachers do not use technology even when it is available (Cuban, 2001). A study by Anderson and Ronnkvist (1999) showed that in the U.S., where Internet-connected classroom computers are quite plentiful, relatively few teachers actually incorporate ICT into their teaching. Becker, Ravitz, and Wong (1999) found that although more than 70% of U.S. teachers assign computer work to students at least occasionally, only about one third do so regularly. According to the European Commission (2001a), about 70% of the primary teachers and 60% of the secondary teachers in the European Union use computers in their teaching. However, less than half (34% primary, 42% secondary) use the Internet.

Nonetheless, evidence indicates that at least a small number of innovative teachers in each country have integrated ICT into their teaching and use it to make significant changes in their classrooms (Pelgrum & Anderson, 1999). These innovations are the focus of this study. We ask the following questions: What are these innovative teachers and students doing differently in their classrooms? Are they using ICT to change the curriculum and what students learn? What school-based organizational practices, national policies, and other contextual factors support and sustain these changes? How can the innovative practices of a few become the common practices of the many? What can policy makers, administrators, and other teachers learn from these innovations? These are the basic questions that motivated the Second Information Technology in Education Study (SITES) Module 2.

THREE SITES MODULES

SITES is a study in three modules, authorized by the International Association for the Evaluation of Educational Achievement (IEA). SITES Module 2—the focus of this book—is a series of qualitative studies that identify and describe innovative pedagogical practices that use technology. Module 2 was a 3-year study, which started in 1999 and concluded in 2002, with data collected in 2001. Module 2 builds on Module 1 and will contribute to Module 3. Conducted between 1997 and 1999, Module 1 included a survey of principals and technology coordinators at a sample of schools in 26 countries. The focus of Module 1 was on ICT resources in schools and the extent to which schools have adopted and implemented pedagogical practices that are considered important to education in the information society. Scheduled for 2002–2006, Module 3 will include a follow-up survey of principals and technology coordinators. It will also survey teachers and students and will assess students on their use of ICT skills to solve problems in science and math. A more complete description of Modules 1 and 2 is given in the following two sections.

SITES MODULE I

SITES Module 1 was a comparative international study designed to help countries estimate their current positions relative to other countries in the educational use of ICT. The study established baselines against which developments could be judged in subsequent years. Moreover, the comparative data were intended to help national policy makers reflect upon improvements that might be considered for the near future.

The study was designed as a survey of principals and technology coordinators from a representative sample of schools in each of the participating countries. A total of 26 countries participated, from Europe, North America, South America, Africa, and Asia. Schools were sampled at one or more of three levels in the education system: primary, lower secondary, and upper secondary education. The data collection for the study took place between November 1998 and February 1999. The coordination center of the study was located at the University of Twente in The Netherlands and was directed by Dr. Willem J. Pelgrum, who was also on the International Coordinating Committee (ICC) of SITES Module 2. Results of the study were published by Pelgrum and Anderson (1999) and are summarized here.

Module 1 addressed four main questions:

- To what extent does the school management offer a supportive climate for the use of ICT in the school?

- What ICT infrastructure (equipment, software, access to the Internet, and the like) is available in schools?

- What staff development and support services exist with regard to ICT?

- To what extent have schools adopted objectives and practices that reflect a focus on autonomous learning strategies?

In general, Module 1 found that school principals tended to have a positive attitude toward ICT usage in their schools. To a variety of questions related to principals' attitudes about the impact of ICT on achievement, the relevance of the Internet, the impact of ICT on school management, the contribution of ICT to lifelong learning, and so forth, principals as a group responded positively worldwide. Nevertheless, principals in some countries differed in the extent of their positive responses. For example, lower secondary school principals in Singapore had a mean score of 91 while those in Israel had a mean score of 88, on a theoretical range scaled from 0 to 100, where a higher score means more favorably disposed toward ICT. Principals in Hungary had a mean score of 70, while those in Japan had a mean score of 66, the lowest score of any country. A majority of school principals also reported that they had adopted ICT policies of various sorts in their schools, such as plans for equipment replacement, staff development, software acquisition, equity of access, and Internet use. However, in many countries a substantial number of principals admitted that they had not yet realized these goals.

With regard to the ICT infrastructure in schools, the study examined, across countries, the ratio of students to computers used for instruction. This ratio indicates the number of students in a school per computer. A ratio of 20 to 1 (20:1), for instance, means that if all students wanted to use the equipment at the same time, 20 students would have to share one computer. As noted previously, as of February 1999 (the end of the data-collection period) the student-computer ratios for lower secondary schools ranged from approximately 9:1 in Canada and 12:1 in Denmark and Singapore to 133:1 in Lithuania and 210:1 in Cyprus. While 13 of the 24 countries that responded at the lower secondary level had a student-computer ratio of 30:1 or less, the other 11 countries had higher—sometimes much higher—ratios. Nonetheless, it is clear that this ratio has come down significantly over the past several years. When similar data collected in 1995 as part of the Third International Mathematics and Science Study (TIMSS) (Beaton, Mullis, Martin, Gonzales, Kelly, & Smith, 1996) were compared to the SITES Module 1 data, Norway dropped from a ratio of approximately 55:1 to 9:1 in the Module 1 study, while Thailand dropped from 206:1 to 62:1. Substantial declines in this ratio occurred in every country that participated in both studies.

SITES Module 1 also examined the extent to which schools had access to the Internet for instructional purposes. Again, there were significant differences among countries. In Singapore and Iceland, 100% of the lower secondary schools had access, while the figure was 98% in Canada and 96% in Finland. Only 11% of the lower secondary schools in Cyprus and 4% of those in Russian had access.

While the ICT-related problem most often mentioned by principals was a lack of equipment, the second most often mentioned problem was teachers' insufficient knowledge and skills regarding ICT. The majority of schools reported that they had a policy goal of training all teachers in the use of ICT, but this goal had been achieved in only a minority of schools in most countries. As for the computer coordinators (or those persons who answered the technical questionnaire), a majority across countries responded that they were adequately prepared with regard to general applications (such as word-processing, database, and spreadsheet software). But the percentage was much lower with regard to the instructional aspects of ICT (for instance, didactical integration and applications of subject-specific software).

Perhaps the most significant goal of SITES Module 1 was to examine the extent to which countries were changing their approach to pedagogy and to look at the contribution that ICT was making to this change. Principals were asked a number of questions about the type of pedagogical practices being used in their schools. A factor analysis was run on the responses to these questions, and two factors were created, one called *emerging practices* and the other called *traditional practices*. The emerging practice factor was formed from eight items listed in Table 1.1, while the traditional practice factor was formed from three items. In brief, the emerging practices included those that made students active in and responsible for their own learning, involved them in cooperative or project-based learning, engaged them in the search for information, and allowed them to work at their own pace and determine when to take a test. Traditional practices were those where the development of skills was emphasized, where all students were working on the same materials at the same pace, and where teachers kept track of all student activities and progress.

Table 1.1

TYPES OF PEDAGOGICAL PRACTICES EXAMINED IN SITES MODULE 1

QUESTION

To what extent is each of the following aspects of teaching and learning present in your school? (Response alternatives were "not at all," "to some extent," or "a lot" for each of the following practices.)

Responses indicating "emerging practices" (not specified as such in the survey)

- Students developing abilities to undertake independent learning
- Teachers providing weaker students with additional instruction
- Teaching and learning organized so that differences in entrance level, learning pace, and learning route are taken into account
- Students learning to search for information, process data, and present information
- Students being largely responsible for controlling their own learning progress
- Students learning and/or working at their own pace during lessons
- Students involved in cooperative and/or project-based learning
- Parts of school subjects combined with one another (multidisciplinary approach)

Responses indicating "traditional practices" (not specified as such in the survey)

- Emphasis in learning on the development of skills
- Students working on the same learning materials at the same pace and/or sequence
- Teachers keeping track of all student activities and progress

---

Many schools around the world indicated that the emerging pedagogical practices were present to a large extent in their schools. However, as with other indicators, there were also large differences in pedagogical practices among countries. For example, on a theoretical scale score from 0 to 100, Norway, with a score of 71, scored the highest on emerging pedagogical practices in its lower secondary schools, while Denmark and Hungary scored 69. China Hong Kong scored 36 and Japan scored 29, the lowest. In regard to traditional practices, Thailand scored 75 and Luxembourg scored 72, while Norway scored 43.

Principals were also asked whether ICT had contributed to the realization of the various emerging pedagogical practices in their schools. In Denmark, 62% of the lower secondary school principals responded affirmatively. The figure was 58% in Israel, and 56% in Canada, Hungary, and Slovenia. The figure was much lower in China Hong Kong (40%), the French Belgium community (37%), and Japan (31%).

In summary, SITES Module 1 showed that many school principals considered ICT to be important in their schools and that many of them had developed local policies regarding its use. It also demonstrated that the participating countries had made significant investments in computers in schools. In many countries, the student to computer ratio was below 30:1 and had been falling significantly over the past few years. A large investment had also been made to connect schools to the Internet. Module 1 data also indicated that this investment had started to pay off, at least in some schools in some countries, as teachers began to use ICT to change their pedagogical approach to be more student-centered.

SITES MODULE 2

SITES Module 2 was an in-depth exploration of the relationship between ICT use and innovative pedagogical practices in classrooms. It built on Module 1 in that it looked at primary and lower and upper secondary classrooms to examine in more detail the emerging pedagogical practices reported by principals and technology coordinators in Module 1. Module 2 was a qualitative study of innovative pedagogical practices that use technology (i.e., "innovations"). A total of 28 countries participated in the study, from North America, South America, Europe, Asia, and Africa. National Research Coordinators (NRCs) from each country played a key role in contributing to the design of the international study and conducting the national study in their own country. (See Appendix A for a list of the countries and NRCs.)

The NRCs in each country formed national panels that used common selection criteria, modified by national context, to identify innovative classrooms, as locally defined. The national research teams used a common set of methods and instruments to collect data and to analyze the pedagogical practices of teachers and learners, the role that ICT plays in these practices, and the contextual factors that support and influence them.

This book is based on the analysis of the 174 case reports generated by these research teams. This large body of cases—unique in both its size and its manner of selection—allowed the International Coordinating Committee (ICC)—the authors of this book—to examine a wide range of ICT-based pedagogical practices that countries considered to be innovative. Our analysis has provided us with many reasons to be hopeful about the use of ICT to support educational change and the movement of schools toward an information society. But we also have identified a number of significant challenges that must be addressed if this future is to be realized.

The goals of SITES Module 2 were to:

- ◆ Identify and provide rich descriptions for innovations that are considered valuable by each country and that might be considered for large-scale implementation or adoption by schools in other countries.

- ◆ Provide information to national and local policy makers that they can use to make decisions related to ICT and the role it might play in advancing their country's educational goals and addressing educational needs and problems.

- ◆ Provide teachers and other practitioners with new ideas about how they can use ICT to improve classroom practices.

- ◆ Add to the body of research knowledge and theory about the contexts and factors, within and across countries, that contribute to the successful and sustained use of innovative technology-based pedagogical practices.

ADVANTAGES OF AN INTERNATIONAL STUDY

The issues that frame this study are global. Otherwise, the goals of the study could be accomplished within the context of any individual country. But the international nature of this study enables each country to identify other countries comparable to itself in terms of economics, technological advancement, history, or culture. Each country can then assess the usefulness to its own schools of ICT innovations by studying the usefulness of those technologies in other comparable countries.

Some countries, such as Singapore and Finland, are engaged in significant national efforts to implement ICT in schools and use these resources to change education. Although few countries may currently be in a position to conduct such large-scale national efforts, findings from these countries can help others plan for a future in which technology is more affordable and pervasive. But even modest innovations may be worthy of adoption in other countries. Using the 174 case studies in SITES Module 2, each country has the opportunity to examine a wide variety of classroom practices in other countries that may not exist in its own schools yet may be relevant to the future of its educational system. In this sense the world is a laboratory of ICT-related educational experiments. The successful ones may stimulate new initiatives in countries where these experiments have not yet taken place.

Furthermore, the broad range of participating countries allows us to look at trends and patterns that may cut across national and cultural boundaries. The international, comparative nature of this study allows researchers and policy makers to see ways in which ICT may be changing education worldwide. Education, like the economy, is becoming global. One goal of SITES Module 2 is to see whether a common international vision is emerging on how information technology can best be incorporated into teaching and learning. Yet the qualitative nature of the study allows us to explore the ways in which common trends or visions can be reshaped to accommodate national cultural, political, and historical factors.

CONCEPTUAL FRAMEWORK

We frame our study with prior empirical and theoretical work. This framework does not constitute a theory—with multiple variables and causal mechanisms—that is to be tested by our findings. Neither the design nor the procedures of our study are appropriate for this purpose. Ours is a qualitative, analytic study, not a theory-validation study. Rather, our framework specifies a set of factors and general relationships that detail and give context to the primary focus of our study: innovative pedagogical practices that use technology. We used these factors and relationships to help us generate research questions and guide the construction of our instruments, data collection protocols, and analyses. While we do not start with a theory, our findings may allow us to elaborate on the framework in a way that advances it toward a testable theory.

A broad and varied body of literature provides a conceptual framework of the factors that may influence the use of technology in the classroom and its impact on educational outcomes. Our framework relies on literature from comparative education, school improvement and reform, technology and education, evaluation, cultural psychology, and the adoption and diffusion of innovations. In this section we survey key ideas from these literatures and outline a framework that articulates the relationships that underlie and give rise to the research questions of the study.

In our framework, innovative pedagogical practices are embedded in a concentric set of contextual levels that effect and mediate change. Pedagogical practices consist of patterned sets of goals, materials, activities, and people engaged in classroom teaching and learning. The levels that surround these practices are the classroom (micro level), the school or local community (meso level), and state, national, and international entities (macro level). At each level there are actors and factors that mediate change. According to the literature, the successful implementation of innovative practices depends not only on the characteristics of the innovation but also on factors such as classroom organization and personal characteristics of the teachers and students (micro level), the school organization and personal characteristics of administrators and community leaders (meso level), and national and state policies and international trends (macro level). We assume an integral, transactional relationship between successful technology-based innovations and this extended set of personal, pedagogical, curricular, and organizational factors that constitute the context of their use (De Corte, 1993; Kozma, 1994; Salomon, 1991). As Dede (1998) points out, the essential conditions for the successful use of learning technologies in schools include complementary shifts in curriculum, pedagogy, assessment, professional development, administration, organizational structures, and partnerships between schools, businesses, homes, and community. Causality among these factors is not unidirectional; rather, successful practices depend on the ways the factors at these various levels fit together and reinforce each other. Classroom practices are affected by school organization and national policies, but school organization and national policies can also be shaped by successful innovations in the classroom. Consequently, the process by which innovations are adopted and diffused is also relevant to the research of Module 2. The prospective interrelationships among factors in our conceptual framework are illustrated in Figure 1.1.

MICRO LEVEL

The focus of attention in SITES Module 2—and the center of the diagram in Figure 1.1—is the change in ICT-supported pedagogical practices that effect classroom learning. Plomp, Brummelhuis, and Rapmund (1996) define classroom learning as a process in which four components interact: (1) the teacher, (2) the student, (3) curriculum content and goals, and (4) instructional materials and infrastructure—in the case of SITES, the ICT infrastructure. We are particularly interested in how innovative pedagogical practices can be enabled and constrained by the capabilities of computer-based technologies, capabilities related to the representation, generation, storage, processing, and communication of information (Kozma, 1991, 1994). These capabilities may support teacher and student information-related activities, such as searching for and organizing information, analyzing data, representing ideas, simulating complex systems, and communicating with others in ways that previously have not been practical or even possible. They may also enable new ways of teaching and learning—new activities, new products, and new types of learning.

Figure 1.1

SITES MODULE 2 CONCEPTUAL FRAMEWORK

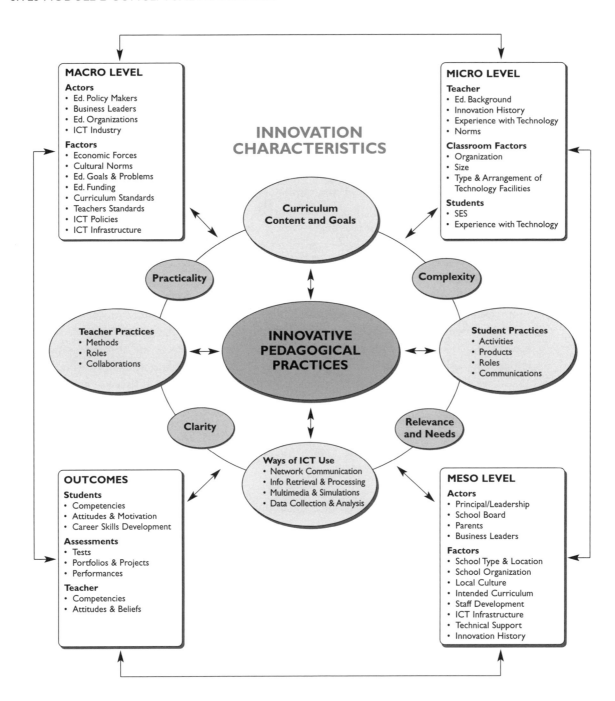

Classroom research (Means & Olson, 1997; Means, Penuel, & Padilla, 2001; Sandholtz, Ringstaff, & Dwyer, 1997; Schofield & Davidson, 2002) has documented a strong association between technology-based practices and changes in curriculum and pedagogy. For example, in many countries the use of educational technology is part of an instructional shift toward constructivist approaches to teaching and learning within a context of school improvement or reform (Pelgrum & Anderson, 1999). Instead of focusing solely on increasing the acquisition of facts related to specific subject areas, teams of students are engaged in solving complex, authentic problems that cross disciplinary boundaries. Instead of dispensing knowledge, teachers set up projects, arrange for access to appropriate resources, and create organizational structures and support that can help students succeed. This approach moves the concept of learning beyond the rote memorization of facts and procedures (and the notion of mind as a mental filing cabinet) to learning as a process of knowledge creation. It envisions a learning process in which students set their own goals, plan their learning activities, and monitor their current levels of mastery and understanding—what is sometimes referred to as "metacognition" (Bransford, Brown, & Cocking, 2000)—in preparation for lifelong learning. It moves concepts of school beyond the notion of place where knowledge is imparted to one of classrooms, organizations, and societies as knowledge-building communities (Bereiter, 2002; Brown & Campione, 1994; Scardamalia & Bereiter, 1994). These practices are more consonant with the requirements of a knowledge economy and information society than current, traditional didactic practices.

The knowledge economy and the information society also have implications for the curriculum. The traditional role of ICT in the curriculum has been that of a minor subject, sometimes called *informatics* or *computer literacy*. Research studies have begun to document a more integrated curricular role for ICT (Means & Olson, 1997; Means, Penuel, & Padilla, 2001; Sandholtz, Ringstaff, & Dwyer, 1997; Schofield & Davidson, 2002). Increasingly, ICT is being incorporated into various subjects in the curriculum and across subjects. Many teachers see ICT as a resource, often assessed by standardized tests, to help them teach the standard curriculum (Law, Yuen, Ki, Li, Lee, & Chow; 2000; Schofield & Davidson, 2002). But other teachers are coming to see ICT as a way of changing what is taught and how it is assessed. These teachers are using ICT within the context of complex tasks, conducted within a multidisciplinary context and extended blocks of time, and with performance-based assessment (Means & Olson, 1997). Such changes in the nature and organization of student work correspond to changes in the organization of work in the knowledge economy, where individuals work in teams, are flexible and creative, and apply problem-solving and continuous learning skills (OECD, 2001a).

This earlier theoretical and empirical work focuses Module 2 research on the extent to which classrooms around the world that are judged to be innovative are engaged in these constructivist, knowledge-building practices that integrate ICT into the curriculum and change assessments. Our national research teams interviewed teachers and students, observed classrooms practices, and looked at classroom materials to assess the extent to which technology was being used to support students' problem solving, communication, collaboration, and knowledge creation in multidiscipline contexts. At the micro level, we also looked at the ways in which ICT use is supporting new roles and practices of teachers and students, new goals for the curriculum, and new resources that become available. For example, we analyzed a primary English class in Singapore (Case SG002) where teachers developed materials and posted them on their local area network. Students accessed the lessons, searched for information on the Internet, solved problems, and posted their work on the Web. The better pieces of work were selected for publishing in a virtual gallery. We also examined an upper secondary school in the Czech Republic (Case CZ002) in which ICT was integrated into geography; history; Czech, German, and English languages; and civics. Students designed Web pages for local villages; these pages contained histories of the villages, descriptions and photos of places of interest, lists of social events, maps, transportation connections, and other information considered important to the municipalities.

MESO LEVEL

At the meso level, it is well known that innovation and change within organizations benefit from leadership and a supportive organizational environment (van den Akker, Keursten, & Plomp, 1992; Fullan, 2001a, 2001b; Rogers, 1995; Senge et al., 2000). Hence, innovative practices are likely to be part of an environment in which the school management is in favor of the practice, the practice is supported by the school organization, the practice fits in the curriculum, and the practice is part of the teacher's routine. In some countries, technology may be introduced as part of school improvement or reform—it contributes to "a systematic, sustained effort aimed at change in learning conditions and other related internal conditions in one or more schools" (Van Velzen et al., 1985, p. 48). These efforts often involve coordinated changes in curriculum, instructional strategies, and learning focus for both teachers and students that place different demands on resource allocation and use (Louis & Miles, 1991). School improvement studies emphasize the central role of context and school culture in mediating change (Dalin, 1973, 1978, 1994; Fullan, 2001a, 2001b; Fuller & Clarke, 1994; Huberman, 1992; McLaughlin, 1993; Stoll & Fink, 1996). Furthermore, parental and community involvement is important to school change. Children of involved parents—especially students from low-income families and ethnic minorities—earn higher grades and have higher test scores (Henderson & Berla, 1994). Schools also perform better when parents are involved.

The literature suggests that the extent to which innovation succeeds, is sustained, and is transferred depends, in part, on the extent to which certain of its characteristics fit with the characteristics of the school environment (meso level). Specifically, innovations are likely to be more successful if they are relevant to some need or problem that is articulated in the environment. Their success is measured based on the extent to which it is clear how the innovation can be implemented within this context and on the extent to which the complexity is manageable and the implementation is practical, all within the demands and limitations of the environment (Fullan, 2001b).

Consequently, in SITES Module 2 we looked at factors related to school support and community involvement. Our national research teams interviewed technology coordinators, principals, and district administrators about their ICT policies and the resources provided to support teachers' efforts. When appropriate, they also interviewed parents and other community members. In one project (Case CA002), we saw a primary school principal in Canada who worked with teachers and the school council to raise support for the widespread use of ICT throughout the school. We also saw a project in the Philippines (Case PH005) where an integrated-science teacher developed Web-based materials to support her students' explorations and where parents provided financial and moral support.

MACRO LEVEL

At the macro level, classroom practices can be influenced by state or national policies and international trends in areas such as curriculum and assessment, professional development, and telecommunications. A number of countries that participated in this study have national policies that articulate a major role for ICT in education. In several countries, such as Thailand, Chile, and Norway, some of these policies are connected to educational reform. Some policies are more focused on the improvement of student achievement, such as those in Australia and the United States. Still others are linked to the development of ICT capacity, such as those in Denmark and the Czech Republic. Some educational policies are highly centralized, such as those in Singapore, while others, such as those in Finland, are decentralized. However, in all these countries policies were developed with the intent to influence practices in schools and classrooms. A variety of programs were created to support the implementation of these policies, from the installation of equipment and networks to the development of materials and the training of teachers.

Research has found that there is often a gap between national or state and provincial policies and the classroom practices that they are meant to influence (Cohen & Hill, 2001; McLaughlin, 1990). However, practices are more likely to be affected when there is coherence among curriculum, assessment, instructional materials, and instructional guidance and when teachers have opportunities to learn policies in connection with specific, practice-oriented materials, strategies, and activities.

At the macro level, our framework guided the examination of national and local policies related to ICT and educational change. We also asked teachers and administrators about the extent to which these policies influenced their school- and classroom-based practices. In the analysis of our case studies, we looked at how these national and local policies influenced the innovative practices they reported. For example, we studied a case in Thailand where a lower secondary science teacher developed Web-based materials to stimulate student thinking, analysis, and discussion (Case TH005). This was done in the context of Thailand's National Education Act, which advocates learner-centered education and a significant role for ICT in the support of such education. We also examined the case of a Dutch primary school where all the students created their own Web pages linked to the school's home page in the context of a national policy focused on developing the country's ICT capacity (Case NL003). We also found cases that were not obviously influenced by national policies but where teachers were nonetheless successful.

Beyond the national or provincial domains, current theories of comparative education (Arnove & Torres, 1999) identify a fundamental tension that affects contemporary educational change. This is a dialectical tension between massive global forces that affect social relations and institutions across national boundaries, such as the emergence of the knowledge economy and information society—and the accommodation of these forces to local cultural, political, and historical factors. Thus, the transnational, economically driven pressures to increase educational quality and efficiency play out differently in the United States, England, and Australia (Berman, 1999) than in Asia (Su, 1999), Eastern Europe (Bucur & Eklof, 1999), or Africa (Samoff, 1999). These global forces are modified and, in some cases, even transformed in the process by which international trends are reshaped to local ends. At the end of this book, we return to the theme that began this chapter and summarize how various countries are using and modifying ICT-based educational change to respond to global developments. We consider the implications these developments have for the future policy directions of national, multinational, and nongovernmental organizations.

RESEARCH QUESTIONS

The factors specified by our conceptual framework suggest a number of specific questions that we pursued in our research. We felt that the answers to these questions would meet the goals set for our study and help us understand the nature of the emerging pedagogical paradigm established in SITES Module 1 (Pelgrum & Anderson, 1999) and its connection to broader sets of contextual factors at the classroom, school, and national levels. Specifically, our research questions involved four different areas.

ICT AND INNOVATIVE CLASSROOM PRACTICES

What are the ICT-based pedagogical practices that countries consider to be innovative? How are these innovative practices similar and different from one country to another?

What new teacher and student roles are associated with innovative pedagogical practices using technology? How are these innovations changing what teachers and students do in the classroom? How do they affect patterns of teacher-student and student-student interactions?

How do these practices change the classroom? In what ways does the use of ICT change the organization of the classroom, extend the school day, break down the walls of the classroom, and involve other actors (such as parents, scientists, or business people) in the learning process?

What capabilities of the applied technologies support innovative pedagogical practices? How do these capabilities shape the practices they support?

ICT AND THE CURRICULUM

How do these practices change curriculum content and goals? What impact do these practices have on student competencies, attitudes, and other outcomes? Have they changed what students are learning and what teachers need to learn? Have they changed the ways student outcomes are assessed?

ICT IN THE SCHOOLS

What contextual factors are associated with the use of these innovations? Which factors seem to be present across different innovative pedagogical practices? Which ones are associated with different practices? What are the implications of contextual factors for the sustainability and transferability of these innovations?

What are the barriers to using ICT in these innovative ways? How are teachers overcoming these barriers? How do they cope with limited resources?

ICT POLICIES

Which local policies related to staff development, student computer fees, facilities access, technical support, and other issues appear to be effective in supporting these innovations?

Which national telecommunications policies related to such things as school Internet access, equipment purchase, teacher training, and student Internet use seem to be effective in supporting these innovations?

STRUCTURE OF THE BOOK

In this book, we address the research questions and report on the results of SITES Module 2. Chapter 2, "Study Procedures and First Look at the Data," describes the study design and methodology. We describe the details of how we worked with national research teams to select the cases for study, collect data, monitor the quality of the study, and analyze the data. We also take a first look at the data from our 174 case studies. Overall, the data support the SITES Module 1 findings: Teachers and students are using ICT as part of larger changes in the roles and activities of the classroom. In the large majority of cases, teachers were engaged in advising and guiding students, and students collaborated with other students to search for information, design or create products, and publish or present their results. As a result of the innovations, many teachers acquired new ICT and pedagogical skills and many students acquired ICT skills, subject knowledge, and collaborative skills. Various ICT tools and applications were used in support of these practices.

In Chapter 3, "ICT and Innovative Classroom Practices," we extend our examination of micro-level factors to focus on the range of pedagogical practices associated with ICT use. While there are many commonalities across cases and countries, we wanted to see if we could tease apart certain patterns of practice among the cases. In Chapter 3 we identify seven clusters of cases organized around characteristic patterns of teacher, student, and ICT practices. We identify two clusters in particular—the Information Management Cluster and the Student Collaborative Research Cluster—that seem to focus most on changes in pedagogy and that are associated with a number of other changes in the classroom. We also look at models of practice that organize these clusters.

In Chapter 4, "ICT and the Curriculum," we identify changes in the curriculum that are associated with technology use. We examine cases in which ICT is associated with curricular changes within specific subjects (such as math or physics) and with changes in two or more subjects that are integrated thematically, as well as throughout the school, where ICT is used in all or nearly all subjects. We look at changes in the curriculum as it is planned, as it is enacted, and as it is experienced in the classroom. We also examine the impact of ICT on student and teacher outcomes and the ways student outcomes are assessed.

In Chapter 5, "School Context, Sustainability, and Transferability of Innovation," we turn to the meso-level context for pedagogical and curricular innovation using ICT. We examine innovations that have been in place for a while and have been used elsewhere to identify the essential and contributing factors that support the sustainability and transferability of ICT-based innovations or that lower the barriers to ICT use.

In Chapter 6, "Local and National ICT Policies," we discuss the range of policies that schools and countries have designed to address the potential of ICT for improving education, specifically as they support educational reform, improve student achievement, and build ICT capacity in schools. We discuss the connection—or often disconnection—between these policies and the innovations that we studied.

In Chapter 7, "Stellar Cases of Technology-Supported Pedagogical Innovations," we look beyond our cross-case analysis to examine a set of cases that the NRCs identified as particularly unique and noteworthy. We examine these not in the context of how they related to the general set of cases or to trends across these cases, but on their own merits. We describe these cases and look at what makes them particularly interesting and worthy of consideration.

Finally, in Chapter 8, "Summary and Implications for ICT-Based Educational Change," we conclude our analysis by reviewing our findings and discussing their implications for classroom practice, policy, and future research on the impact of ICT on schooling, teaching, and learning.

CHAPTER 2

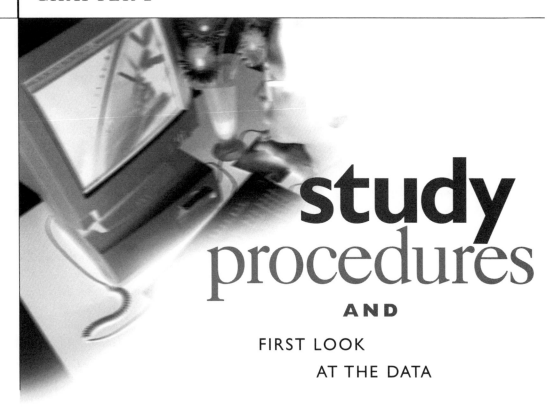

study
procedures
AND
FIRST LOOK
AT THE DATA

By Robert B. Kozma

INTRODUCTION

As a study sponsored by the International Association for Evaluation of Educational Achievement (IEA), the Second Information Technology in Education Study (SITES) Module 2 generally followed the procedures outlined in the *Technical Standards for IEA Studies* (Martin, Rust, & Adams, 1999). However, these guidelines were developed primarily for quantitative studies that use representative samples for purposes of international comparison. These procedures had to be modified significantly for SITES Module 2, since this study was designed primarily as a qualitative study of innovative technology-based pedagogical practices.

The purpose of the study was to explore the notion of the emerging pedagogical paradigm identified in SITES Module 1 (Pelgrum & Anderson, 1999). Specifically, we were charged with identifying and examining innovative practices of the sort identified in Module 1. The study was not meant to examine typical practices or representative cases, nor was it meant to be comparative, in the statistical sense of the term. Consequently, we had to develop many of our own procedures for this very different purpose.

We did, however, start with the standard organizational structure and arrangements of an IEA study. The study, which was authorized by the IEA General Assembly, was designed and supervised by an international team of researchers that constituted the International Coordinating Committee (ICC), located at Center for Technology in Learning at SRI International. The ICC was composed of Robert Kozma (the International Study Director) and Raymond McGhee from SRI International, Ronald Owston from York University, Richard Jones from the Educational Quality and Accountability Office (both in Canada), and Willem (Hans) Pelgrum and Joke Voogt at the Twente University in The Netherlands. These members of the ICC are the authors of this book.

This team received advice and guidance from the SITES International Steering Committee (ISC), cochaired by Ronald Anderson of the University of Minnesota and Tjeerd Plomp from Twente University. The members of this committee are listed in Appendix A.

The study could not have been conducted without the efforts and advice of the National Research Coordinators (NRCs) from the 28 participating countries (see Appendix A) and the research teams that they lead. The NRCs participated in every aspect of the project. They helped design the study and the instruments, collected the data, and wrote up the case reports. They also wrote national reports based on an analysis of their own cases. The project built on the initial design work of Ronald Anderson, with a planning grant from the U.S. National Science Foundation. The assistance of the NRCs began with a meeting in April 1999 in Prague, Czechoslovakia, where the initial design of the study was detailed. The design was refined at another meeting in Copenhagen, Denmark, in October 1999. In March 2000, we met with the NRCs in Poitiers, France, where we discussed the procedures for forming the national panels and for establishing selection criteria. We also reviewed drafts of the data collection instruments. In September 2000, we met again in Toronto, Canada, and reviewed the guidelines and procedures for writing the case reports. We met in Singapore in June 2001 to review procedures for the cross-case analysis. Finally, we met with the NRCs in Jyvaskyla, Finland, where they reviewed initial drafts of this report and gave us feedback.

The study also could not have been conducted without the support of its sponsors. The study was funded by the participating countries, with special funding from the countries of Denmark, France, Japan, The Netherlands, Norway, and the United States (both the Department of Education and the National Science Foundation), as well as the Ford Foundation and an anonymous donor. Individual countries funded their own national research teams.

In this chapter, we look at the design of the SITES Module 2 study. We discuss methodologies related to the study and describe the procedures we used to identify cases, collect data, and analyze the cases. Those readers less interested in the technical aspects of the study may want to skip to the later section of this chapter entitled "A First Look at the Data," where we summarize our results. These results are analyzed in more detail in subsequent chapters.

MIXED QUALITATIVE AND QUANTITATIVE METHODOLOGIES

The advantage of qualitative research approaches over more quantitative methods, such as surveys or experiments, is that they provide detailed information on people, programs, or events in a natural context (Creswell, 1998; Yin, 1994). Qualitative methods are also used to identify and describe the complex interactions and interrelationships among factors within a system. These advantages have a strong affinity for the kinds of assumptions and questions that have been identified for SITES Module 2. As specified in the research questions listed in Chapter 1, we are interested in identifying and describing innovative, information and communication technologies (ICT)–based pedagogical practices, looking at how they might vary from one country to the next, describing the new roles and activities they offer to teachers and students, and analyzing how ICT might support these and other aspects of classrooms and schools. In addition, we are interested in the ways these classroom phenomena interact with other factors at the school, local, and national level. These interests draw us to a methodology that emphasizes richness of detail and context.

This is not to say that quantitative approaches cannot also provide answers; we take a very inclusive position on the qualitative-quantitative paradigm wars of the 1980s (Gage, 1989; Howe & Eisenhart, 1990). Indeed, it is generally felt that these wars were unproductive, other than to advance the notion that neither approach alone has all the answers and each has significant limitations (Tashakkori & Teddlie, 1998). Many educational researchers have come to a pragmatic perspective that draws on both paradigms. Many take the position that it is the research question that drives the methodology and that scientific claims often are significantly strengthened when they are subject to testing by multiple methods (Shavelson & Towne, 2001).

Qualitative and quantitative methods can be used together to capture the richness, complexity, and interdependence of events, actions, and conditions in the real classroom (Tashakkori & Teddlie, 1998). SITES adopted this mixed approach in several ways. First, SITES uses quantitative and qualitative methods in a serial fashion. SITES Module 1 was a quantitative study that involved national surveys of representative samples of school principals and technology coordinators. SITES Module 2 consists of case studies designed to complement Module 1 by picking up the findings established in that study and developing them in more detail. In turn, SITES Module 3 (scheduled for 2003–2006) returns to quantitative methods by surveying principals, technology coordinators, teachers, and students in order to determine the trend of the Module 1 results and the degree to which the Module 2 findings can be generalized. Module 3 will also include an assessment of student ICT skills as they are used to solve problems in science and math.

Furthermore, we have used a mixed model (Tashakkori & Teddlie, 1998) within SITES Module 2, the study reported here. We used a naturalistic design for the study rather than an experimental or survey design, but we collected both quantitative and qualitative data. We interviewed administrators, teachers, and students and conducted classroom observations; but we also readministered some items of the Module 1 surveys. In addition, we used both quantitative and qualitative analytic methods. Given the large number of cases generated by SITES Module 2, we used quantitative analyses to identify major trends. We then used both qualitative and quantitative methods to conduct a detailed, cross-case analysis. We analyzed selected cases to pursue these trends.

But at its core, SITES Module 2 remained a qualitative study. Its primary focus in the 28 participating countries was on 174 case studies of innovative pedagogical practices in which technology was used. The unique challenge of SITES Module 2 was to adapt a methodology normally associated with a single researcher in an intimate field setting by scaling it to the requirements of international comparative research, where a large amount of data are collected and research must accommodate the constraints of many teams and countries, diverse social and cultural contexts, and a range of policy needs. This chapter describes our approach to this challenge.

CASE STUDY METHODOLOGY

The term *case study* is formally defined as an exploration of a bounded system over time through detailed, in-depth data collection from multiple sources of information rich in context (Creswell, 1998). The several approaches to case study methodology differ in their goals and purpose (Creswell, 1998; Miles & Huberman, 1994; Stake, 1995; Yin, 1994). Among them are the *instrumental* and *intrinsic* approaches (Stake, 1995). A case can aid in understanding a more general question, issue, or problem (instrumental), or it can be studied for its own special (intrinsic) qualities. In an intrinsic study, the case is selected for its special or unique status relative to the purpose of the study; and the analysis describes the people, events, and issues that characterize it. The analysis focuses on patterns or themes that are consistent within the case and account for what happened—what Stake (1995) calls "petite generalizations." In an instrumental case study, the focus of the analysis is on the underlying issues, relationships, and causes that can be used to generalize beyond the case—what can be learned about an underlying issue or research question. Cases are selected for this purpose. The methodology used to analyze these cases emphasizes the categorization and aggregation of data rather than the special complexities of a specific case. The analysis might involve a single case or multiple cases. For the latter, a cross-case analysis is typically done in which common themes are identified that unite and/or distinguish the cases.

In SITES Module 2, we have, for the most part, been interested in the cases we study for how they can help us answer our research questions rather than for their uniqueness. Consequently, the study took a primarily instrumental approach; the results of this approach are presented in Chapters 3–6. In this regard, the cross-case analysis of the 174 cases in this study identified important similarities and differences within and across countries that were useful in answering the research questions. In this regard, it would have been far more difficult to answer these questions with just one or two cases per country. On the other hand, some cases we encountered were worthy of special note, based on their own merit. In addition to the research questions addressed by the cross-case analysis, we asked the researchers in each country if they would like to identify a "stellar" case. These cases and the reasons they were nominated are featured in Chapter 7, where we use the intrinsic approach to case study.

Case study approaches can also differ in their orientation toward theory. Studies can employ a specific theoretical analytic framework, they can result in the generation of theory, they can test theory, or they can be atheoretical (Yin, 1994). In SITES Module 2 we do not begin with a particular theory of classroom innovation, but we do use a conceptual framework (described in Chapter 1) that identifies important factors to be included in the construction of instruments and the analysis of data. While contributing to theory is not inconsequential to the purpose of the study, the knowledge generated by SITES Module 2 is primarily in the service of policy and practice. The focus of the project is on the creation, implementation, sustainability, transferability, and effectiveness of technology-based practices that can improve educational systems and on the contextual factors that influence these processes.

While case study approaches differ in purpose and analysis, common to all is a focus on "the case" and on a set of techniques commonly used to study cases. With all these approaches, the researcher collects data from multiple sources of information, such as observations, interviews, and documents. The common goal of the analysis is to thoroughly understand the case: what is happening and why, and what are the issues or problems. With any of these variations in analysis, an effort is made to describe the context of the case in detail. The description and analysis of the context may be used to limit the findings and/or account for them. The conclusions are validated through the triangulation of findings across these various data sources (Miles & Huberman, 1994; Stake, 1995). The resulting report contains a detailed description of the case, themes that emerge from the analysis, assertions, and perhaps vignettes that illustrate the themes or assertions in terms of the particulars of the case. Given the research questions posed by SITES Module 2, the conclusions are drawn from an analysis across a large number of cases from many countries. This fact presented us with a number of unique procedural challenges, which we address in the following sections.

PROCEDURES FOR SITES MODULE 2

Creswell (1998) and Merriam (1998) identify a number of procedural issues that must be addressed in any case study. These issues have to do with the specification of the central research questions, the selection of cases, the collection of data, the write-up of the case report, quality assurance, and data analysis. The central questions of SITES Module 2 are articulated in Chapter 1. In the following sections, we describe our procedural approach and address issues related to the remaining components of case study methodology.

An overarching consideration in our approach was the international context of this study. The project involved the participation of researchers (NRCs) from 28 participating countries. The NRCs and their teams were brought together by the common goals and purposes of the study, but they also brought their own concerns and constraints relative to national policy needs. Indeed, these national considerations were a major substantive focus of the study. Consequently, the ICC had to find a balance between the standardization required of an international comparative study and the need to accommodate national contexts, goals, and needs. In pursuit of this balance, the ICC collaborated with the NRCs to establish a common set of study procedures, instruments, and guidelines. These were articulated in a researchers' handbook. This handbook was distributed to the NRCs in hard copy and posted electronically on the project Web site, where it was modified and updated periodically. These policies, procedures, instruments, and guidelines were used as a common set of standards for the purpose of monitoring quality. At the same time, these procedures were devised in a way that accommodated national concerns.

The SITES Module 2 study was also conducted in coordination with a series of international case studies sponsored and independently designed by the Organisation for Economic Cooperation and Development (OECD). The SITES Module 2 study director collaborated with the director of the OECD study to sharpen the distinctions between the two studies, to make them complementary, and to reduce the potential conflicts and redundancies for countries that wanted to participate in both studies. It was decided that the appropriate distinction was the size of organizational units. The SITES Module 2 study would focus on innovative classroom practices using ICT, while the OECD study would focus on the use of ICT to support innovative schools (Venezky, 2002). As part of the coordination, 18 countries participated in both studies (see Appendix B.1 for a list of the countries). In some countries, the same research teams conducted both studies; in others they were conducted by different teams. In some countries, some cases were used for both the SITES Module 2 and OECD studies. The international research teams for the two studies coordinated the instruments and data collection to reduce the burden on these schools as much as possible.

Despite the coordination, there may have been some confounding across the two studies in the 18 countries that participated in both studies, especially those where the studies were conducted by the same research team. There was some discussion among the SITES Module 2 NRCs from these countries about the possibility that the cases selected for both studies may have focused on school-side innovation more than in countries that participated only in SITES Module 2. Also, the reports on these cases may have fewer details about classroom practices, since more classrooms within a school were covered by the investigations. However, we believe that any such confounding may indeed reflect the priorities of the countries that decided to participate in both studies.

CASE SELECTION

The first task of case study research is to bound the case (Stake, 1995). Within these boundaries, the case is defined and cases are selected for the purposes of the study. As mentioned in Chapter 1, the conceptual framework for SITES Module 2 bounds the case by layers of context that surround classroom practices in primary and secondary education. Within these boundaries, the focus of this study is on innovative pedagogical practices using technology (i.e., "innovations"). Pedagogical practices are those organized or patterned sets of activities or interactions used by teachers and students to support and promote learning. Given this purpose for SITES Module 2, it is the classroom and its associated context that define the system for the study rather than, say, innovative national or international projects such as GLOBE (www.globe.gov) or iEARN (www.iearn.org).

However, we were looking for practices that are innovative, so we allowed for the possibility that a form of innovation might involve multiple classrooms, practices outside the classrooms, or large-scale programs or projects such as GLOBE or iEARN. In such situations, the case would focus on a specific classroom and school but could be extended to include several classrooms in which the same innovation was used. The case could also be extended to include activities outside the classroom (e.g., student work at home or in museums), as long as these remote activities were coordinated with those in the classroom.

Once the boundaries and unit of analysis are specified, the criteria for selecting the case must be defined (Miles & Huberman, 1994; Stake, 1995; Yin 1994). Unlike the random sampling of quantitative studies intended to represent a larger population, the selection of cases in qualitative research is purposive. Cases are selected to meet the goals of the study. In SITES Module 2, the cases were not meant to represent "typical" classroom practices but those that were "innovative." The selected cases were intended to represent the aspirations of each country rather than represent what was already going on in many classrooms. Our goal was to identify the kinds of ICT-enabled practices that each country valued and wanted to hold up to others in their country and to the world. Consequently, it was important that the selection process be credible and the selected cases be highly compelling.

With this requirement in mind, the ICC worked with the NRCs to specify a process and set of criteria by which each country identified the cases that were most worthy of examination. Central to this effort was a balance between international standardization and local considerations; the selection criteria had to have both international and local elements. We decided that the use of national panels would be the mechanism for selecting innovative cases, establishing their credibility, and addressing local considerations.

National Panels

To assist in the selection process and to increase the credibility of the cases selected, the NRC in each country established a national panel. The panel worked with the NRC to perform the following functions:

- Review the international criteria, provide a national definition for the term *innovative*, and propose any modifications of the international criteria that would be appropriate for the national context

- Develop a site selection process for SITES Module 2

- Propose cases for consideration

- Select cases for SITES Module 2 based on the criteria

- Provide support and advice to the NRC on the conduct of the case studies and the development of case study reports for SITES Module 2

In creating the national panels, NRCs were advised to include an appropriate blend of experts in educational technology and representatives of education stakeholder groups that might be drawn from the following:

- Education-based technological organizations

- Primary and/or secondary school teachers

- School board central office personnel or school administrators

- Educational researchers specializing in the field

- Ministries of education or equivalents (e.g., specialists in curricula or instructional technologies)

The NRCs reported on the compositions of their panels; the ICC reviewed their reports and occasionally suggested modifications. For example, one country proposed an original panel composed primarily of Ministry of Education staff members. The ICC suggested that teachers and university faculty members be added, and such members were incorporated into the panel. An analysis of the final composition of the 28 national panels showed that they consisted of a total of 241 members. The average size of the panel was 8 members, ranging from 5 (Italy) to 18 (United States). A majority of the panel members (126) were professors or researchers at universities or research institutes. A smaller number (46) were from education ministries. Yet another significant group was drawn from schools: principals and other administrators (24), computer coordinators (7), teachers (16), and even a few students (3). Several countries included professionals from technology companies, other businesses, or NGOs (21).

NRCs provided a number of reasons for selecting the particular members. In general, they selected members who represented a range of educational stakeholders, including those who were experts in the use of educational technology, those familiar with innovative pedagogical practices related to ICT, and those who had an excellent overview of the current status and trends in ICT use in schools in the country.

The NRCs informed panel members of the goals and design of the study and prepared them for their work. This involved providing them with the following information:

- Background information about SITES Module 2 and its relationship to Module 1 and Module 3

- The role and charge of the panel

- The tasks and time frame of the panel's work

- Relevant policy statements or national white papers related to educational goals and ICT educational policies

- Guidelines developed by the ICC to structure the work of the panel, along with any supplemental guidelines developed by the NRCs

With this information and the collective experience and expertise of the panel members, the national panel was charged to review the international selection criteria, recommend modifications in these criteria to accommodate local concerns and priorities, and provide a local definition for the term *innovative*.

In establishing these criteria, the ICC recommended that each panel draw on these resources:

- Their own country's curriculum and policy documents related to the use of information technology in schools

- Studies of practices that other countries have defined as innovative

- The SITES Module 1 database of "satisfying practices" that were identified by the principals who responded to the survey

- The advice of relevant constituencies in their country, such as teacher federations, parent associations, business leaders, school districts, government bureaus, universities, and other appropriate community and national organizations

- Reactions and comments on draft criteria from the previously mentioned constituencies

Selection Criteria

The ICC worked with the NRCs to specify criteria for selection. The discussion began with the kinds of pedagogical practices that were identified in Module 1. Broadly speaking, these practices involve changes in what teachers and students do and learn in the classroom. The practices are intended to provide students with skills and competencies they need as they extend their learning throughout their lives in the information society of the 21st century.

From this start, we worked with the NRCs to elaborate on the criteria. During the discussion, concern was expressed that while common criteria were needed to assure that the research questions were addressed and that there was some level of comparability from country to country, there was also a need for the criteria to be sensitive to the unique circumstances and cultural differences in each country. Consequently, we established both a common set of *international* criteria and provisions for a *local* accommodation.

The international criteria were as follows:

- The innovation should show evidence of significant changes in the roles of teachers and students, the goals of the curriculum, assessment practices, and/or the educational materials or infrastructure.

- Technology must play a substantial role. Technology should not merely replace previous practices but make a significant contribution to change. In other words, the technology should provide an added value to the pedagogical practice and this contribution should be articulated clearly.

- Preferably, there would be evidence that the innovation was associated with positive student outcomes. This evidence might be documentation (such as increased achievement scores, diminished gaps in achievement between groups, increased enrollment in rigorous courses, increased graduation rates) that shows that the intended goals and objectives were attained or that shows a desirable impact on an important indicator, such as student learning, enrollment, or completion rate. In general, multiple forms of supporting evidence would make a stronger case than a single form. Teacher outcomes were also a consideration.

- The innovation should be sustainable and transferable. The emphasis here was on potential. It was an important goal of this study to identify innovations that had been sustained and transferred; but the focus is on innovation, so the sustainability and transferability of the new practices may not yet be proven. In these cases, there should be evidence or reasons to believe that the new practices actually could be sustained and transferred.

Among the first four criteria, the first two were considered essential and the second two preferable. Cases that met more of the criteria were given priority. Beyond these four international criteria was a fifth local one:

- The practice must be innovative, as locally defined.

Innovative is a difficult concept to specify and operationalize. The notion of newness embedded in the term demands that a study of innovation be open to the unanticipated. Furthermore, innovation often depends on the cultural, historical, or developmental context within which it is observed—what is innovative in one country may not be in another. Consequently, we did not want to overspecify the definition of innovation and wanted to provide for significant local input into what would be considered innovative. We constituted a process whereby each national panel would define innovation. We also gave the panels a range of examples to consider that were drawn from the findings of Module 1. These included practices that:

- Promoted active and independent learning in which students took responsibility for their own learning, set their own learning goals, created their own learning activities, and/or assessed their own progress and/or the progress of other students.

- Provided students with competencies and technological skills that allowed them to search for, organize, and analyze information, and communicate and express their ideas in a variety of media forms.

- Engaged students in collaborative, project-based learning in which they worked with others on complex, extended, real-world problems or projects.

- Provided students with individualized instruction customized to meet their needs in terms of different entry levels, interests, or conceptual difficulties.

- Addressed issues of equity for students of different genders or ethnic or social groups and/or provided access to instruction or information for students who would not have access otherwise because of geographic or socioeconomic reasons.

- "Broke down the walls" of the classroom, for example, by extending the school day, changing the organization of the class, or involving other people (such as parents, scientists, or business professionals) in the education process.

- Improved social cohesiveness and understanding by having students interact with groups and cultures they would not interact with otherwise.

The first task of the national panel in each country was to review the criteria, propose modifications that might make them more appropriate for the local context, and provide a local definition for innovative pedagogical practices that used technology. These changes were reported to the ICC, shared electronically with other NRCs, discussed, and revised.

Panels in most countries accepted the four international criteria as specified, noting that the criteria were comprehensive enough to encompass their local contexts. However, some countries elaborated on one or more criteria to make them more specific to their needs. For example, Korea, the Philippines, and Thailand specifically mentioned that the teacher's role not only should change but also should specifically shift from that of information source to guide and that the student's role should shift to that of active learner. Thailand further elaborated on this criterion by emphasizing that they were looking for innovations where students collected information by themselves, worked as a group, collaborated with teachers, and evaluated their own learning process. Likewise, Finland pointed out that students in innovative classes should come to recognize different techniques of learning in the classroom. Denmark and Finland noted that emphasis should be placed on cross-curricular projects and improvement of social competencies such as collaboration. Moreover, Korea pointed out that the acquisition of problem-solving skills, as well as ICT skills, was important. Denmark even argued that ultimately the innovative use of ICT might eliminate the categorization of students by age, as well as eliminate standardized timetables and length of lessons.

Several countries contended that student outcomes should be considered broadly to include social competencies (such as collaboration), cognitive processes (such as critical thinking and problem solving), and attitudes. Finland and Norway suggested that traditional assessments may not be appropriate measures of ICT impact and indicated that other assessment forms would be included in their evidence of impact. In addition, several countries (Chile, Finland, Thailand, and the United States) argued that learning results from a complex environment and interactions and therefore innovations should be considered systemically with regard to relationships among technology, pedagogy, curriculum, student learning, and social contexts.

Most of the extended comments related to the local definition of innovation. In their comments, national panels often referenced social or cultural considerations and/or policy statements relating to ICT or education reform. For example, Singapore said that to be innovative, as defined in its national IT Master Plan, a case would have to show evidence of a bringing about a shift toward active, student-centered learning and should either be original or be a significant enhancement to existing practices. In addition, a stronger candidate would have at least one of the following characteristics: it would "break down the walls" of the classroom or improve social cohesiveness by causing students to interact with groups and cultures with whom they would not otherwise interact. Thailand, referencing its National Education Act, indicated that in order to reform the current educational system and advance the information technology society, ICT would need to accelerate changes in the roles of teachers, students, school administrators, and parents in innovative ways.

The Finland panel described a number of potential characteristics for Finland's innovative classrooms. For example, these classrooms should promote active and independent learning in which students take responsibility for their own learning and set their own learning goals and activities. The classrooms also should provide students with competencies to search for, organize, and analyze information, and communicate and express their ideas in a variety of media forms. The classroom also should engage students in collaborative, project-based learning in which they work with others on complex, extended, real-world problems. Educators should break down their own walls, for example, by extending the school day, changing the organization of the class, or involving other people (such as parents, scientists, or business professionals) in the education process.

Some countries (Chinese Taipei, Finland, The Netherlands, Norway, and Singapore) tended to associate innovation strongly with what students learn (e.g., ICT skills, social competencies, interpersonal skills) and with the students' motivation and willingness to learn. Others focused more on how teaching and pedagogical practices should change in certain ways, for example, by providing individualized instruction, particularly for weak students (Denmark); by providing critical insights for future practices of schools (Norway); and by instilling changes in teachers' classroom management skills, assessment skills, and the nature and content of their work (Slovak Republic).

Some countries added their own criteria for selecting cases. For instance, the Czech Republic and Norway indicated that the selected group should represent the widest possible spectrum of case models. The United States specified that the selected schools should represent students from diverse backgrounds. Denmark and Finland stipulated that schools should demonstrate collaboration among classroom teachers, teacher colleges, and student teachers. Norway also included practices that used ICT outside of school. Canada emphasized regional and language representation to include both English- and French-speaking populations.

These variations in the criteria for case selection—particularly the local definitions of innovative—are important, for they demonstrate the priorities of the participating countries. In turn, the cases in this study that were selected using these criteria represent the priorities and aspirations of the country.

Selection of Cases

The most important work of the national panels was to engage in the following four-step process to select the cases for study in their countries:

1. Identify prospective cases by building an inventory of potential innovative pedagogical practices using technology (i.e., "innovations")

2. Collect any additional information needed to make the selection of innovations

3. Nominate these cases for review by the ICC

4. Select the final innovations for inclusion in the SITES Module 2 study

First, NRCs used a variety of sources to build an inventory of potential innovations. The ICC suggested two approaches to this task: the NRCs could actively search for potential innovations, or schools and teachers could nominate them. In searching for potential innovations, the NRCs could use a variety of sources, including the following:

◆ The Module 1 database (for the countries involved in SITES Module 1)

◆ Lists of existing awards to schools or teachers for innovative uses of technology

◆ National journals for practitioners that listed or described outstanding schools or teachers who use technology

◆ A search of the World Wide Web to identify schools that were engaged in innovative practices and described on the Web

◆ Information provided by recognized experts or organizations in the country

◆ Calls for nominations in newspapers, practitioner journals, government bulletins, or the Web

A search for potential innovations often resulted in the identification of good possibilities but incomplete information on them. Sometimes, additional information was needed that often was available only at the school level. In these cases, NRCs often collected preliminary data before making the final selection. The ICC provided a nomination form to structure the information for each nomination.

As a result of this process, 220 cases were initially nominated by the NRCs. These nominations were reviewed and discussed with the ICC.

Ultimately, the national panels had to reduce their selections to no more than 12 cases for inclusion in the international study, although countries could choose to select more cases for inclusion in a national study that could be done outside SITES Module 2, at the country's option. A maximum of four cases could be selected from primary, lower secondary, and upper secondary grade levels. Grade levels were defined by each country according to the way the terms are used in their context. If more than 12 innovations were competitive, the national panels sometimes established an additional screening process to reduce the number and make the final selection. In this regard, the final selection of innovations was guided by a number of pragmatic considerations in addition to the international and local criteria discussed previously. Some of these factors were:

◆ The feasibility of collecting data on the teaching-learning practice during the period of the study.

◆ The willingness of schools and teachers to participate in SITES Module 2.

◆ The desire to represent a diversity of curriculum domains or a variety of ICT applications.

◆ The need to reflect regional variety within a country.

Nominated cases could be removed at any time, based on additional information gained about them. After the NRCs had completed their case reports, 174 case reports were received. The number of cases ranged from 1 (Japan) to 12 (Germany) and averaged about 6 cases per country.

INSTRUMENTATION AND DATA COLLECTION

Qualitative methodologists advocate the use of multiple sources and types of data in case study research (Creswell, 1998; Hamel, 1993; Merriam, 1998; Miles & Huberman, 1994; Yin, 1994). Multiple types of data, such as interviews and observations, and multiple sources of data, such as interviews with multiple respondents or observations over several sessions or in several classrooms, enable the data to be triangulated and thereby increase confidence in the conclusions drawn.

In SITES Module 2, the ICC constructed draft instruments that were reviewed with the NRCs. To ensure comprehensiveness, the items on these instruments were mapped onto the study's goals, research questions, and conceptual frameworks. The following instruments and data sources were included:

◆ Interviews with administrators, technology coordinators, and innovative teachers

◆ Focus group discussions with other teachers (i.e., those not directly involved in the innovation), students, and, where relevant, parents and other community members

◆ An administration of selected items from the SITES Module 1 survey of principals and technology coordinators

◆ Classroom observations that described teacher and student behaviors, seating arrangements, resource allocation, and so forth

◆ Documents or archival or historical data, such as project proposals, program materials, evaluations, curriculum guides, software, reports, assessment instruments, teacher-generated lesson plans and instructional materials, and students' products, including reports and projects

The members of the ICC team pilot tested these instruments in a single case in each of their three respective countries: the United States, Canada, and The Netherlands. It took two researchers approximately 1 week to collect these data. The ICC in turn shared their experiences with the NRCs. Based on this discussion, the instruments were revised and a set of administration protocols were developed. These were subsequently field tested in 17 countries and revised again. The instruments and protocols were also coordinated with the OECD case study project in order to reduce the burden of data collection on schools that were studied for both projects.

These instruments and protocols were translated into the appropriate languages by the NRCs and used to collect data on their selected case studies. The technical reports submitted by the NRCs after their field work identified no significant deviations from the data collection protocols.

THE CASE REPORT

There is no standard format for a case report in the methodological literature (Creswell, 1998). Rather, as with most other aspects of qualitative research, the format depends on the purpose of the research study. While in many case study research projects much of the analysis is done in the course of writing the case report (Creswell, 1998; Miles & Huberman, 1994), the focus of SITES Module 2 was on the analysis of a range of cases across countries. A further consideration was the large number of cases anticipated and the demands this would make on the limited resources of the researchers responsible for the cross-case analysis (i.e., the ICC). This had four implications for the contents and format of the case reports:

1. Since the cases would be analyzed by researchers other than those originally conducting the case study, the cases had to contain all of the information about the case that would be needed for its analysis.

2. The cases had to address comprehensively the research questions that would be included in the cross-case analysis.

3. The information needed to address specific questions in a format that could be located quickly within a case.

4. The reports needed to be of modest length to accommodate the limited resources of both the ICC and the NRCs, who had to write up the cases and often translate them into English from their native tongues.

The ICC, along with the project's technical advisor, Yvonna Lincoln, explored two alternative approaches to the case write-up that might deal with these requirements: the *narrative approach* and the *data matrix approach*. The narrative approach is the most common format for a case study. This approach uses a structured prose write-up organized around our conceptual framework. While narrative reports generally vary in the balance between description and analysis (Creswell, 1998), the emphasis in the SITES Module 2 narrative approach was on description, with conclusions about the local situation drawn from and warranted by these descriptions. The data matrix approach is, perhaps, unique to SITES Module 2. It used a "slot-filling" approach to assure comprehensiveness of the data. This format was structured by a series of questions, organized around the conceptual framework, that required short answers describing the case and presenting evidence relative to a particular aspect of the framework. Guidelines for both approaches were developed and shared with the NRCs.

When the NRCs in 17 countries field tested the draft instruments and protocols, they had the option of using either the narrative or data matrix approach in writing their case reports. All reports were submitted in English. The resulting reports were analyzed by the ICC; 12 were in the narrative format and 6 were in the data matrix format. (One country submitted reports in both formats.) The ICC's analysis of the field-tested case reports identified several problems, including the following:

◆ As a group, the case reports were too long to be easily read or to accommodate the limited resources available for analyzing the cases.

- The reports often lacked descriptive details of the classroom practices of interest.

- The research questions were not always comprehensively addressed.

- The claims made or conclusions drawn from a case were too often insufficiently warranted.

- Trendy terms (such as "teacher as advisor") were overused and were not defined or explained; the same was true of terms whose meanings varied from country to country.

- There were instances of apparent pro-innovation bias, with positive qualities and effects attributed to ICT on insufficient grounds.

Some of these problems were associated more with one report format than with the other. For example, reports in the data matrix format often lacked descriptive detail, while the reports in the narrative format were often not comprehensive or sufficiently backed by warrants. In response to the analysis of the pilot case studies, the ICC revised case report guidelines and presented these to the NRCs. In response to feedback from the NRCs, the ICC developed a final version of the instruments and guidelines for writing up cases that addressed the identified issues. The final approach was a combination of the earlier narrative and data matrix approaches, which took advantage of the strengths of each approach and minimized the associated problems.

The report guidelines described a two-step process for writing the reports and addressing the problems identified in the field studies. In the first step, researchers used a data matrix (which had been mapped onto the conceptual framework) to reduce and organize the data collected by various instruments. Only the portion of the data matrix that pertained to class-room practice was translated and submitted as part of a case report. The second step involved the conversion of the matrix to a case narrative. The narrative report template followed a standard, highly structured format, again based on the conceptual framework. This template included sections on the meso-level context (such as the school background and culture), the macro-level context (such as policies related to educational reform and ICT), and the micro-level context (such as curriculum content and goals, teacher and student practices and outcomes, the ways ICT was used and the problems encountered, and the sustainability and transferability of the innovation).

These guidelines recommended a 10-page narrative for each case, a glossary that defined special terms, and the portion of the data matrix pertaining to classroom practice. The guidelines specified a standard set of sections for the report that corresponded to the conceptual framework and research questions. Each section had recommended word limits. In this regard, more words were allocated to the sections on curricular goals and teacher and student practices and outcomes than to sections on context, sustainability, and transferability. Consequently, the ICC had access to more detailed information on classroom practices and curricular goals than on the school and policy contexts. Again, all these documents were to be presented in English. In total, more than 200 documents related to 174 cases were submitted to the ICC for the international analysis. (The narrative report and the data matrix were often combined in a single document.)

QUALITY MONITORING

Qualitative methodologists (Creswell, 1998; Miles & Huberman, 1994) have addressed issues associated with standards and the verification of qualitative research. According to these standards, good qualitative research studies are those in which the following occurs:

- The data collection and analysis are driven by the research questions.

- The data collection and analysis techniques are auditable and are competently and uniformly applied by all researchers.

- Researchers are neutral and free from unacknowledged bias.

- Assertions are warranted by detailed descriptions and triangulated by multiple data sources, particularly when there is conflicting data within a case.

One of the primary responsibilities of the ICC in SITES Module 2 was to monitor the quality of the research conducted in the participating countries. The following five activities were used to assure quality throughout the project:

- The ICC monitored and coordinated the NRCs' formation of the national panels, their modification of the criteria for case selection, and their selection of cases.

- The ICC mapped all instruments, protocols, and guidelines onto the research questions and the conceptual framework.

- The ICC held workshops for the NRCs on both data collection and data analysis to ensure the uniform application of these techniques.

- The case report guidelines and templates were structured to ensure the comprehensiveness of the presentation and the warranty of assertions.

- The NRCs exchanged their first case reports with a "friendly critic" (a fellow NRC), as well as with the ICC, for review and discussion relative to the guidelines for the reports and the issues identified in the field tests, such as the comprehensiveness of the presentation, potential bias, and warranty of assertions.

In addition, the ICC coordinated its own efforts and analyses through periodic meetings and conference calls. The coordination included establishing common guidelines for coding, including discussion of and agreements on analytic approaches. This distributed, collaborative effort was supported by functionality built into the project Web site. This Web site was designed to support the downloading of guidelines and instruments, the uploading of progress and case reports, the sharing of materials among and between NRC and ICC members, and the monitoring of progress. NRCs used the Web site to submit reports that documented each phase of the implementation of the research design. The ICC used this system of reports to monitor each step and to coordinate efforts among members of the group.

DATA ANALYSIS

Tashakkori and Teddlie (1998) describe a mixed model of research that combines qualitative and quantitative approaches within different phases of a study. This model allows for a combination of qualitative and quantitative analytic methods in service of the purposes of the study. Such a combination might allow for the "quantitization" of qualitative data and the use of statistical analyses to look for patterns in the data. This analysis could be combined with more traditional qualitative techniques that examine the details of selected cases. This mixed model is particularly well suited for the purposes and conditions of SITES Module 2.

The goal of our analysis of the cases was to understand innovative pedagogical practices using technology, how these innovations changed what it is that teachers and students do, the roles ICT plays in supporting them, and how the innovations are associated with various outcomes and contextual conditions. The mixed model is both necessitated by and takes advantage of the fact that we had 174 case studies to analyze.

In the first step of our analysis, the ICC devised a cover sheet to characterize the cases (see Appendix B.2). This cover sheet consisted of a 27-item scheme derived from the research questions and conceptual framework. The cover sheet characterized cases along variables such as grade level and subject area. But more importantly, we used the macro, meso, and micro components of the conceptual framework to identify specific factors that could characterize the kind of practices that constitute an innovation and the contextual factors that might be associated with it. Specifically, we included the types of curricular changes, teacher classroom activities, student classroom activities, types of technology used, and reported impact. We also created a set of guidelines that elaborated on the meaning of the codes to support common coding practices with the ICC.

Each of the 174 cases was read by one of the members of the ICC and coded via the cover sheet coding scheme. A particular coding was based on the statements made in the case reports that were backed by evidence from the data. These data were often comments made by administrators, teachers, or students or observations made by the researchers, and were cited in the case reports. The ICC coding of the cases was conservative. If statements were not sufficiently warranted, ICC members asked the NRCs for clarification or requested additional data from them to support the statements. It should be noted, however, that evidence related to student outcomes was rarely hard data or test scores. More often it was in the form of comments or inferences made by administrators, teachers, or students based on their experiences or inferences made by the researchers based on their observations and interviews, without extensive support.

To increase the quality of ICC coding, the NRCs reviewed the codes. The coding guidelines were shared with the NRCs, along with the codes and questions for each case. In response to the questions, the NRCs sometimes augmented the case reports to include additional details from the data or provided additional warrants for claims they made. If the NRCs suggested that certain ICC codes needed to be changed, they were asked to provide evidence that would support their claims. The ICC then made the changes that were warranted by the NRCs' comments or additional data.

The second step of the analysis was more quantitative. The ICC used appropriate statistical techniques to analyze the data from the cover sheets. Here, we looked for specific trends and patterns across cases. The specifics of these analyses varied with the research questions addressed; they are described in detail in subsequent chapters. For example, in Chapter 3 a cluster analysis was used to sort the cases into groups with different patterns of teacher, student, and ICC practices.

The quantitative analysis resulted in a third step, again drawing on qualitative methods. We selected subsets of cases that corresponded to the trends and patterns identified in the quantitative analysis. *ATLAS ti*, a qualitative analysis software package, was used to code specific portions of these cases. Again, the scheme used to code the passages of the cases was based on the research questions and conceptual framework. The codes were parallel to but much more detailed than those used to code cases during the first step of our analysis. ICC members practiced using *ATLAS ti* and the coding scheme on a common set of cases. We met to review our codes and coordinate our coding practices. We divided the different research questions among members of our group and divided up the detailed coding effort accordingly. While we all started with a common set of codes, each ICC member created additional detailed codes, as necessary, that corresponded to the research question being addressed. For example, as described in Chapter 3, additional codes were added to provide more detail about teacher, student, and ICT practices in the classroom.

Each ICC member subsequently analyzed these more detailed codings, using qualitative methods such as the constant comparative method, Boolean analysis, and network analysis (Creswell, 1998; Miles & Huberman, 1994; Ragin, 1987; Strauss & Corbin, 1994) that are supported by the software tools in *ATLAS ti*. The analytic approach varied for each research question; each approach is described in subsequent chapters. For example, in the analysis of classroom practices (described in Chapter 3), we used the cover sheet codes to identify different patterns of teacher, student, and ICT classroom activities. The detailed code list was used to identify specific instances of these practices in portions of selected cases. Using *ATLAS ti* to search for certain combinations of these codes allowed us to cite examples of these patterns in specific cases and contrast them with alternative patterns of teacher, student, and ICT practices. For example, in Chapter 3, cases that were sorted into different clusters were compared on the detailed teacher, student, and ICT classroom practices that were the basis for the clustering.

A FIRST LOOK AT THE DATA

As mentioned previously, the ICC members read all 174 of the cases and characterized them using a cover sheet coding scheme based on the project's conceptual framework. Appendix B.2 shows the distribution of the cases across various descriptors; here we elaborate on these findings.

The group of cases were quite evenly divided among primary, lower secondary, and upper secondary grades, with about 35% of the cases at each level. The fact that several cases examined innovations that crossed two grade levels accounts for the fact that these percentages sum to more than 100. At the meso level, most innovations were linked to local ICT policies or plans at the school; however, 37% of the cases made no such link. School principals were very supportive of the innovations; more than 30% were directly involved in the innovations and another 64% were supportive without being directly involved. However, very few other members of the community were involved. Parent participation was reported in only 9% of the cases, business and industry participated in nearly 13% of the cases, and scientific or higher education institutions participated in 9% of the cases. The largest number of cases that involved some kind of outside participation were those that included students or teachers from other schools; 20% of the cases involved this kind of participation. Of the 174 cases, 57% had no outside involvement.

At the macro level, 61% of the cases made some kind of link with a national educational policy or a state or provincial policy in countries with decentralized education systems. Even more of the cases—73%—made a link with a national ICT policy or plan. On the other hand, relatively few of the innovations—approximately 38%—were part of a national, state, or regional project. Only 10% were part of an international project. Again, a majority— 55%—were not part of an outside project, according to the case reports.

The case reports elaborated most on micro-level factors—the classroom curriculum, assessment, teacher and student practices and outcomes, and the ways ICT was used to support these practices. A large number of cases were in the sciences, with 25% in biological or life sciences, 14% in earth sciences, and 13% in physics. Another 21% were in mathematics. Languages accounted for another large group, with 32% of the cases involving the mother tongue and 24% involving foreign languages. A smaller group of cases were in the social sciences (14% in geography, 16% in history, and 13% in civics) or creative arts (20%). It is an interesting finding that only 21% of the cases involved computer education or informatics as a subject area and that only 8% were focused on vocational studies. This confirms that ICT has become integrated throughout the curriculum, at least in this set of innovative cases. Indeed, many of these ICT-based innovations involved multidisciplinary projects (28%) or multiple subject areas, with 37% of the reports involving several subject areas and 32% involving nearly all of the subject areas in the school. In only 29% of the cases was the innovation limited to a single subject area.

The reorganization of the subject areas seems to be the primary curricular impact of the innovations. More than 68% of the cases mentioned changes of this sort, while 36% mentioned changes in the allocation of time for specific topics, and 37% mentioned new kinds of curricular goals, such as the development of metacognitive skills or communications skills. Only 27% of the cases specifically mentioned changes in the standard curriculum content. More than 60% of the cases reported the use of nonstandard assessments such as portfolio assessment, self-assessment, or peer assessment.

The largest amount of space in the case reports was reserved for descriptions of teacher and student practices and outcomes. A large number of the reports (74%) stated that the activities of the teacher changed as a result of the innovation. An even larger number of cases—nearly 90%—described teachers who were engaged in advising and guiding their students' work. These practices, and the corresponding role of the teacher as advisor or guide, are certainly consonant with constructivist notions expressed in the literature and the findings in SITES Module 1. On the other hand, a large number of cases also described more traditional practices, such as creating structure (81%) and monitoring or assessing student performance (76%), although only 25% reported that the teacher engaged in lecturing as part of the innovation. Approximately 24% of the cases described teachers' collaborations with students.

A large number of cases—nearly 59%—reported that teachers collaborated with other teachers as part of their innovation. But only 23% reported that teachers collaborated with other actors outside the class.

The reported impact on teachers was primarily in the development of their ICT skills (63% of the cases) and pedagogical skills (57% of the cases). Another group of cases— 35%—reported that teachers acquired collaborative skills as a result of the innovation.

Student activities changed even more than those of teachers; 84% of the cases reported such changes as a result of the innovation. The largest number (83%) reported that students collaborated with each other. Students in a large majority of these innovations were actively engaged in constructivist activities, such as searching for information (74%), publishing or presenting the results of their work (66%), or designing or creating products (61%). Only 26% of the cases reported that students collaborated with actors outside the classroom. An even smaller number—13%—reported that students were engaged in drill-and-practice tasks.

The stated impact of the innovation on students was quite broad. The largest number of cases claimed that students acquired ICT skills as a result of the innovation. A large majority of cases claimed students developed positive attitudes toward learning or school (68%), acquired new subject matter knowledge (63%), or acquired collaborative skills (63%). Fewer than half of the cases reported that students acquired metacognitive skills (38%), communication skills (40%), information-handling skills (29%), or problem-solving skills (19%) associated with learning for the 21st century. A surprising number of these cases (19%) also reported negative outcomes.

Very few of the innovations were specifically targeted or beneficial to special student groups. Approximately 12% of the cases stated a special benefit to low-ability or at-risk students. Even fewer cases reported benefits to other groups, such as students of low socioeconomic status (8%), ethnic or language minorities (6%), students with learning disabilities (5%), gifted students (5%), or girls (3%).

What kinds of technology did teachers and students use and what role did ICT play in supporting these innovations? A large majority of the innovations used productivity tools (78%), Web resources (71%), and e-mail (68%). Many cases (52%) reported the use of multi-media software. Some used Web design tools (34%). Very few used specialized educational software, such as simulations and microcomputer-based laboratories (13%). In almost all of the cases (94%) computers were used in regular school settings such as the classroom, library, or computer laboratory. In a relatively small number of cases (28%) technology was used outside of the school.

The case reports stated that software packages were often used to create products or presentations (80%), Web browsers or CD-ROMs were used to search for information (77%), and e-mail was used to support communication (55%). In far fewer cases, teachers used ICT to plan or organize instruction (26%) or to monitor or assess student work (22%). In a small number of cases ICT was used to support student collaboration (17%), and simulations or modeling software packages were used for research or experimentation (13%).

NRCs were asked to make statements about the value that ICT added to the innovation, based on the data they collected. By far, the most often cited contributions of ICT were to support student practice that would not otherwise be possible or likely (77%) or to contribute to student outcomes (66%). Fewer cases mentioned that ICT provided resources that would not otherwise be available (46%), supported teacher practices (33%), or supported student learning processes by providing feedback or monitoring progress (31%). It was relatively rare that cases mentioned a contribution that ICT made to supporting education reform (25%), saving money (21%), or contributing to teacher outcomes (17%). Only 6% reported that ICT contributed to the involvement of parents in the innovation.

A variety of factors were cited as problems that interfered with these innovations. Problems related to equipment and other resources were mentioned in 62% of the cases. Teacher-related or organizational issues were mentioned in 41% of them. Unfortunately, few solutions were found to the problems that plagued these teachers and others who try to integrate ICT into their pedagogy. Only 16% of the cases mentioned solutions to the equipment or resource issues most often cited as problems. Nonetheless, 78% of the innovations had been sustained over some period of time, and 44% had been transferred to other classes either within the school or to those in other schools.

SUMMARY

In this chapter we have reviewed approaches to qualitative research that pragmatically draws on both qualitative and quantitative traditions and methods in service of the research purposes of SITES Module 2. We have described our approach to the design of the study and the procedures for implementing this design. With this approach we address a unique challenge of SITES Module 2—to take a methodology (case study) normally associated with a single researcher in an intimate field setting and appropriately scale it to the demands and constraints of large-scale international research.

In our approach to the study, we define the unit of analysis (the case) as an innovative pedagogical practice that uses technology (i.e., an "innovation"). We bound the case by several contextual layers specified in our conceptual framework. We build on this definition, and on the research questions and conceptual framework, to describe a set of procedures for the study of the cases: case selection, instrument construction, data collection, the organization of the case reports, quality monitoring, and data analysis. The procedures included the formation of a national panel in each of the 28 participating countries. A total of 241 people participated in these panels, including university professors, educational ministry staff members, technology experts, business people, school principals, technology coordinators, teachers, and even a few students. These people reviewed an international set of criteria for selecting innovative cases, appropriately modified the criteria to fit national considerations, and provided a national definition for the term *innovation*. The international criteria required that cases bring about significant changes in the classroom, use technology in a central way, have measurable impacts on teachers and students, be sustainable and transferable, and meet local standards of innovativeness. The national panels used these criteria and a specified process to conduct an extensive search for innovations in their countries and to rigorously review nominees. The result of this process was the identification of 174 cases in which technology supported innovative changes in classrooms. This large number of cases gave us a unique view of the range of practices that countries considered to be innovative. These cases do not represent typical practice in the participating countries, but we believe they represent the aspirations that these countries have for the kinds of practices and outcomes they would like to see in most of their classrooms in the future.

We then describe the process by which research teams in each country studied these innovations. The teams conducted structured interviews with school principals, technology coordinators, and innovative teachers. Principals and technology coordinators also filled out survey questionnaires. The process also included focus group discussions with other teachers, students, and, on occasion, parents and other community members, as well as structured classroom observations and document analysis. This data collection often took two researchers 1 to 2 weeks to complete for each case.

Each case write-up presented the data in a structured manner in keeping with the study's conceptual framework and included a narrative case report for each innovation. The process resulted in the submission of more than 200 documents related to the 174 cases included in the international study. This set of 174 case reports (and their associated documents) was the source of the database for our international analysis.

We described the results of the first step of our analysis (the creation and analysis of cover sheets to characterize the cases). Overall, the cases ranged across grade levels. Most innovations were linked to local schools' ICT policies; the large majority of them benefited from the support or active participation of the school principal. Most were also linked to national education or ICT policies.

The cases also ranged across the curriculum, including mathematics and science, social studies, language, and creative arts. Relatively few were focused on informatics or vocational studies. A large majority of the innovations involved multidisciplinary projects or multiple subjects; the projects often involved many or even all of the subject areas in the school. Nonstandard assessments were used in many classrooms, but reorganization seems to be the primary curricular impact of the innovations. Relatively few cases made substantive changes to the curriculum content.

Teacher and student practices found in this study confirm the findings from SITES Module 1 related to the emerging pedagogical paradigm. The large majority of teachers in this study were engaged in advising and guiding students. But many also engaged in more traditional practices, such as creating structure and monitoring student progress. A large majority of the cases described students who were collaborating with other students to search for information, design or create products, and publish or present their results. The cases claimed that as a result of the innovations many teachers acquired new ICT and pedagogical skills and many students acquired ICT skills, subject knowledge, and collaborative skills. In some cases, students also acquired metacognitive skills, communication skills, information-handling skills, or problem-solving skills. Very few cases benefited students with special needs, such as at-risk students or students of low socioeconomic or minority status.

The types of ICT typically used in the cases included productivity tools, Web resources, e-mail, and multimedia software. Students used software to create products or presentations, they used Web or CD-ROM resources to search for information, and they used e-mail to support communication. Occasionally, teachers used ICT tools to plan or organize instruction or monitor student progress. The added advantage claimed for ICT in these reports included the support of student activities and outcomes and, to a lesser extent, the support of teacher practices that would not have otherwise been possible or likely. These classroom changes occurred despite problems related to equipment, teacher issues, and organizational issues. Few of these problems were solved, and teachers were left to cope with them. Nonetheless, the innovations were often sustained and occasionally transferred to other classrooms in the school or elsewhere.

While it is clear from our initial analysis that ICT is supporting major pedagogical and assessment changes within classrooms and, to a large extent, breaking down the barriers between the subject disciplines, in only a few cases around the world did these innovative uses of ICT help to break down barriers between schools. That is, while many students and teachers collaborated with each other in these innovations, most of this collaboration went on within the classroom or the school building. Few teachers and students collaborated with their peers in other schools. A minority of projects were part of a national, regional, or international program. A few used ICT outside of the school, a few involved scientists or higher education institutions, and only a very few involved parents.

In Chapters 3–6, we look at these trends in more detail. In Chapter 3 we identify and analyze patterns of teacher, student, and ICT classroom practices. In subsequent chapters we analyze the impact on curriculum, assessment, and student and teacher outcomes, and consider contextual factors related to sustainability and transferability and local and national policies.

CHAPTER 3

ICT AND innovative

CLASSROOM

PRACTICES

By Robert B. Kozma and
Raymond McGhee

INTRODUCTION

A central purpose of the Second Information Technology in Education Study (SITES) Module 2 was to describe and analyze the range of innovative pedagogical practices in participating countries that use information and communication technologies (ICT). We began with the finding of SITES Module 1 (Pelgrum & Anderson, 1999) and other studies (Ravitz, Becker, & Wong, 2000) that schools in many countries are now beginning to change classroom practices in ways that were called, in SITES Module 1, the "emerging pedagogical paradigm."

This phrase was used to describe new practices, including those that make students active in and responsible for their own learning, that involve them in cooperative or project-based learning, that engage them in the search for information, and that allow them to work at their own pace and determine when to take a test. (See Chapter 1 for a complete discussion of these points.)

In this chapter we draw on a base of 174 case studies to look at these new classroom practices in more detail. Specifically, we address the following research questions:

What are the ICT-based pedagogical practices that countries consider to be innovative? How are these innovative practices similar and different from one country to another?

What new teacher and student roles are associated with innovative pedagogical practices using technology? How are innovations changing what teachers and students do in the classroom? How do they affect patterns of teacher-student and student-student interactions?

How do these practices change the classroom? In what ways does the use of ICT change the organization of the classroom, extend the school day, break down the walls of the classroom, and involve other actors (such as parents, scientists, or business people) in the learning process?

What capabilities of the applied technologies support innovative pedagogical practices? How do these capabilities shape the practices they support?

ICT AND CLASSROOM PRACTICE

While this chapter focuses on ICT and changes in classroom pedagogical practices, pedagogical change was not the focus of many early applications of ICT. Rather, the focus was on using computers to make traditional education more effective or efficient. Early writings on this new technology characterized educational computing in terms of tutorial, tool, and "tutee" functions of ICT (Taylor, 1980). While these categories defined different roles for technology, rarely was a role articulated for the teacher, let alone one that involved changes in the teaching methods, curricular goals, or patterned social interactions supported by the computer. For example, in its role as tutor the computer would patiently take an individual student through a series of activities, providing information, asking the student questions, and providing feedback and reinforcement. This approach to the educational use of ICT did not challenge the prevailing educational model. The approach was based on the assumption that student learning depended on what was done to the student, whether by the teacher or the computer. Students were to be provided with information and their responses corrected. Computers used in this way could supplement a teacher's traditional, direct instruction.

Similarly, computer tools did not challenge the traditional classroom model. In this approach, tools such as word processors or spreadsheets supported the work of students as they produced some classroom product. This application of computers, an artifact of the new uses of ICT that were making their way into businesses at the time, had relatively few implications for pedagogical change. The products that students produced with these new tools were often electronic versions of term papers, lab reports, and other products. These often were produced—albeit, perhaps more efficiently—within the standard pedagogical paradigm. The ways in which the use of these tools fit into a broader pattern of classroom practices was typically not specified.

The most direct challenge to normal classroom pedagogy came from the "tutee" function of ICT. Deriving from the work of Seymour Papert (1980), the tutee function centered on a new set of activities that students would do with the computer. In this approach, students used the LOGO programming language to "teach" a computer to move a cursor on the screen, draw diagrams, and do other things. Explicit in this approach was the notion that learning resulted not from what was done or said to the students but from the students' active construction of objects and products that were personally meaningful to them. Papert drew on the cognitive theory of European psychologist Jean Piaget to develop a notion of education that he subsequently termed "constructionism" (Harel & Papert, 1991) and that others termed "constructivism" (Bransford, Brown, & Cocking, 2000). When these notions were imported to the computer, it became not a tool for productivity but a tool of expression, exploration, and inquiry. Such notions fit well with emerging conceptions of students as knowledge producers (Brown & Campione, 1994; Scardamalia & Bereiter, 1994).

While this represented a fundamental shift in the educational use of technology, Papert (1980) did not explicitly articulate an alternative role for the teacher or a set of pedagogical practices that would accompany this use, nor did he discuss how the use of computer was to be integrated into the broader fabric of the classroom. Nonetheless, two implications were implicit: (1) learning did not depend on information provided to the student by the teacher (or the computer) and (2) since the computer did not take an active role in guiding the students' activities, someone else needed to provide this type of support. Consequently, the role of the teacher would need to change from lecturer to guide, providing students with opportunities to learn and structuring their constructive activities with the computer.

Over the past two decades, technology has evolved and the number of computers in schools has grown significantly (Pelgrum & Anderson, 1999). Schools and classrooms are now wired to the Internet, and the use of the World Wide Web is common. Teachers and students have accrued a significant amount of experience in the classroom use of these technologies, and classroom research studies have begun to identify sets of practices that have evolved around the use of ICT. For example, Means and Olson (1997) conducted case studies of 8 schools and a network-based program that involved 462 schools in the United States, all of which used technology to support educational reform. The study included both urban and suburban schools in both low- and high-income areas. The technologies used ranged from productivity tools and multimedia to e-mail and collaborative knowledge-building environments. The study identified a number of classroom practices associated with the use of these technologies, practices that supported educational reform. While not all schools were engaged in all of these practices, the researchers found that as a group, teachers in these schools used technology to provide students with authentic, challenging tasks, and students worked collaboratively in heterogeneous groups on multidisciplinary projects for extended blocks of time. The roles of both teachers and students changed such that students were more actively involved in determining their own learning tasks and teachers supported and guided these activities. To some degree, assessment techniques also changed; student assessments were likely to be based on the body of the student's work as collected in portfolios. Technology played an important role in supporting these practices by enabling students to search for information, collect and analyze data, produce reports and other products, and communicate with others.

A UNESCO-sponsored international study conducted between 1988 and 1992 looked at 23 classrooms in 16 countries where teachers of students between the ages of 9 and 10 were known by the researchers to be "doing good things" with computers (Collis, 1993). The researchers used a common theoretical perspective and a common set of instruments and protocols to interview principals and teachers and to observe classroom practices. A majority of the researchers reported that students displayed higher-level thinking behaviors while using ICT. The higher-level skills included analyzing problems, evaluating their own actions, and formulating appropriate questions. Both researchers and classroom teachers reported that students developed new strategies for working with peers, were highly motivated in their learning, and became more self-confident in their work.

More recently, a team of researchers in China Hong Kong studied 18 computer-using schools in association with SITES Module 1 (Law, Yuen, Ki, Li, Lee, & Chow, 2000). They found that while in some schools teachers integrated ICT into their traditional, didactic role, other teachers saw the introduction of ICT as an opportunity to move from the role of key provider of information to one in which they supported the learning of students. Practices related to this role were observed in an upper secondary English class where teachers used ICT in conjunction with a social-constructivist approach to learning and in a lower secondary class where teachers used it as part of a problem-based learning approach to math.

Schofield and Davidson (2002) studied the results of a 5-year program to implement network-based computing in 25 schools in a major U.S. city. Their research focused on case studies of 5 of these schools. They found that the use of technology was associated with changes in classroom roles and curricular practices. Specifically, teacher-student interactions improved, students became more autonomous, and students took on the roles of contributors, technical consultants, and tutors. Curriculum resources expanded, learning activities allowed students to use knowledge in more realistic ways, and people external to schools participated in curricular activities—people such as adult tutors and students and teachers in other schools.

Case studies of classroom practices using technology have typically been used to evaluate the impact of a single program or examine schools in a single country. Cross-country studies that involve this methodology—especially those that use standardized protocols in each country—are rare in the literature. Nonetheless, findings from SITES Module 1 (Pelgrum & Anderson, 1999) suggest that the innovative classroom practices described in the previously mentioned studies should exist in many countries around the world.

SITES Module 2 sought to pursue this possibility. In the following sections, we investigate questions related to innovative teacher and student classroom practices associated with the use of ICT. As mentioned in Chapter 2, research teams in 28 participating countries used a standard set of protocols to identify and select cases to study. They used a common set of instruments and guidelines to observe classrooms, analyze documents, and interview administrators, teachers, parents, and students to collect data. They used a common template to write up the results of each case study. The International Coordinating Committee (ICC) used this set of 174 cases as the source for its database in addressing questions related to changes in teacher and student roles, changes in classroom practices, and the role that ICT played in these changes.

ANALYTIC APPROACH

Chapter 2 summarized the findings from our initial analysis of the data. In the large majority of cases, teachers and students were engaged in practices different from those that dominate the traditional classroom. This initial analysis suggests a number of significant common trends that cut across the cases we studied. Teachers in these innovative cases are taking on new roles, with teachers in 90% of the cases advising students and 80% creating structure for student activities. Students are, in turn, more deeply involved in their own learning. In 83% of the cases students collaborated with other students, in 74% they searched for information, in 61% they designed or created products, and in 66% they published or presented the results of their work. Very few teachers were observed lecturing, and in very few cases were students involved in drill-and-practice exercises. These trends are themselves important findings that establish a set of common practices across participating countries. However, our goal was to look more deeply at these practices to see if they coalesced into distinguishable patterns that might form different models of ICT use in support of educational change.

In understanding the relationship between the use of ICT and classroom practices, we wanted to analyze the previously described trends. We also wanted to differentiate among various uses of ICT and their associated patterns of teacher and student practices. We wanted to individually identify cases that might typify these different patterns and help us understand the interrelationships between ICT use and classroom activities by teachers and students. Finally, we wanted to understand the relationships between these patterns and other contextual and outcome variables at the micro, meso, and macro levels.

At the same time, we had to approach this analytic task within the constraints of the project budget and staff time. A common approach to the cross-case analysis of qualitative reports is to code cases and sort them into common and contrasting groups that emerge during the analysis process (Glaser & Strauss, 1967; Ragin, 1987; Strauss & Corbin, 1990). With a small number of cases and a few coding themes, this sorting is usually done by hand. This process is often carried out by a single researcher or a small, close-knit team. In SITES Module 2, we had 174 cases, 27 themes with 143 codes (see Appendix B.2), and an ICC that was distributed across three countries and two continents. The magnitude of the sorting task (and limitations on time and budget) demanded a combination of quantitative and qualitative approaches (Tashakkori & Teddlie, 1998). In this section, we describe the analytical process we used to accomplish this task. Those readers interested only in our results can turn directly to the next section and read about the patterns of ICT use and innovative classroom practices identified by our analyses.

STEP 1: CODING OF CASES

As mentioned in Chapter 2, we used a three-step approach to the analysis. In the first step, members of the ICC read all 174 cases and used a 27-item "cover sheet," which was based on the conceptual framework described in Chapter 1, to code them (see Appendix B.2). Using this cover sheet and common coding guidelines, the ICC categorized each case by such characteristics as grade level, subject area, type of curricular change involved, teacher classroom activities reported, student classroom activities reported, type of technology used, reported impact, and so on. To ensure reliability, the ICC shared its codings for each case, along with any questions requesting clarification, with the National Research Coordinators (NRCs). Changes were made in codes that NRCs could warrant either with existing data in the case report or with additional information that they appended to the case.

STEP 2: CLUSTER ANALYSIS

In the second step, we looked for patterns within the cases. Our goal in this analysis was to find coordinated practices that meaningfully distinguished one set of cases from others. Such patterns might allow us to understand how certain teaching practices fit together with certain activities by students using technology, and how these practices might differ from one set of cases to another. With such a large number of cases and codes, it would have been very difficult to find such coordinated, yet discriminating, patterns through manual sorting, especially when conducted by a distributed team within a constrained budget and time schedule. Consequently, we performed a cluster analysis as an efficient way to create coordinated patterns from this large data set. Cluster analysis is an interpretive quantitative procedure; there is no single solution to the analysis and the outcome selected from the various ones generated is the one that is most satisfying relative to the goals of the analysis. This quantitative approach is particularly compatible with the qualitative nature of this study.

Since our focus was on innovative pedagogical practices using technology, we analyzed only those cover sheet codes that related to teacher activities, student activities, ICT practices, and the technologies used (items 13, 16, 19, and 22 in Appendix B.2). We used k-means clustering (a SAS FASTCLUS procedure) on these variables to see how the cases might aggregate in meaningful ways. This procedure is intended for use with large data sets of 100–100,000 observations. It combines an effective method for finding initial clusters with an iterative algorithm for minimizing the sum of squared distances from the cluster means. Observations that are very close to each other are usually assigned to the same cluster, while observations that are far apart are assigned to different clusters.

This approach to cluster analysis begins with the prespecification of the desired number of clusters. We did a series of analyses, specifying 4, 5, 6, 7, and 8 clusters, to see which might produce the best solution. The choice among these solutions is subjective. We based our choice on the relative definition and discrimination of the clustering, that is, the extent to which a particular division created meaning within groups and differentiation between groups, relative to other divisions. We found the 8-cluster solution most satisfying. The solutions with fewer clusters did not seem to create enough coherence within groups.

As part of the analysis, the procedure forces each of the cases into membership in one cluster or another, based on its closeness to the means of other group members. Cases that fail to meet a minimum criterion for closeness are considered outliers and are not assigned to a group. The program then provides the group mean value for each cluster on each of the variables included in the analysis. By comparing the group means of the clusters, one can identify the cluster that has the highest mean for each variable. By identifying the set of variables for which a cluster had the highest group mean or had a higher group mean than the overall mean, one can create a profile of important variables associated with each cluster. A particular pattern of high-scoring variables is, in effect, the definition of each cluster.

Table 3.1 displays the pattern of means for the clusters. The overall means are the percentage of all cases that engaged in the corresponding practice or ICT use, according to the cover sheet codes. The means in each cell are the percentage of cases in each cluster that were engaged in these practices. We shaded the cells with the highest group means for each variable—dark for the cluster with the highest means and a lighter shade for means above the overall mean but not the highest. For purposes of contrast, we did not shade the means for group with averages above the overall mean but below 50%. We used the patterns of high-scoring means to assign each of the clusters with descriptive titles.

One cluster was distinguished only by the fact that it did not score above the overall mean on any of the variables. This we called the "Undefined Cluster"—27 cases fell into this cluster. Given its character, we chose not to examine it or its cases in any more detail.

Table 3.1

PATTERNS OF PRACTICES FOR DIFFERENT CLUSTERS

	CLUSTER AND OVERALL MEAN PERCENT								
Practices	Tool Use (n = 14)	Student Collaborative Research (n = 14)	Information Management (n = 22)	Teacher Collaboration (n = 19)	Outside Communication (n = 27)	Product Creation (n = 35)	Tutorial (n = 12)	Undefined (n = 27)	Overall Means (n = 174)
TEACHER PRACTICE									
Lecture	21	71	0	37	18	31	17	15	25
Advise	86	100	95	90	96	100	83	63	90
Create structure	0	100	100	90	89	100	75	59	80
Design materials	7	78	91	90	56	34	75	41	58
Monitor	64	100	95	90	89	57	75	52	76
Collaborate w/students	14	0	9	100	15	17	17	22	24
Collaborate w/colleagues	50	43	73	95	74	43	75	29	59
Collaborate w/outside	0	14	9	42	41	14	25	18	23
Drill and practice	14	0	14	16	0	8	82	4	13
STUDENT PRACTICE									
Conduct research	28	86	68	47	56	17	17	11	39
Search for information	86	93	100	89	81	80	17	37	74
Solve problems	14	57	73	47	26	3	42	30	33
Analyze data	21	36	23	26	26	14	0	22	22
Publish results	64	64	95	79	85	83	0	30	66
Create products	64	50	68	74	67	86	42	26	61
Collaborate w/others	93	100	91	95	89	83	50	74	83
Collaborate w/outside	50	0	4	53	56	11	0	22	26
Assess themselves	14	43	54	32	26	34	8	15	30
Pick own tasks	21	28	45	89	30	40	33	33	40
ICT PRACTICE									
Tutor	43	7	36	5	0	0	100	7	18
Communicate	78	78	86	63	96	26	0	26	55
Search for information	93	93	95	84	85	94	33	37	77
Create products	93	86	100	100	78	100	58	30	80
Collaborate	0	50	32	10	33	8	0	4	17
Simulate/research	0	50	0	37	0	0	0	22	13
Monitor	14	43	86	5	18	3	17	4	22
Plan	14	78	100	5	15	3	8	7	26
ICT USED									
Laptop	14	43	18	16	7	17	0	11	16
LAN	28	100	73	21	18	51	33	15	41
E-mail	100	100	95	89	100	43	17	22	68
Web resources	93	93	95	63	85	77	17	41	71
Productivity tools	100	93	100	89	81	86	67	37	78
Web design tools	21	50	45	37	44	48	17	4	34
Collab environment	7	0	14	0	33	6	0	0	9
Multimedia	64	86	73	68	26	68	25	15	52
Simulations	7	36	0	37	0	0	0	22	13
Tutorials	36	0	36	5	0	3	100	11	18
Course management	0	7	23	0	7	2	0	4	6

Highest cluster mean

Cluster mean at or above overall mean and above 50%

It should also be noted that 4 of the cases (SG006, FI005, PH001, and CN003) could not be assigned to any of the clusters by the procedure; we considered these cases to be outliers. In contrast to the Undefined Cluster, whose members hung together as a group based on patterns of low-occurring practices, the outliers had practices that did not fit closely to those in any particular cluster. Two of these cases (CN003 and FI005) were selected by the NRCs from the respective countries as "stellar cases." These cases are described in Chapter 7.

Table 3.2 provides brief descriptions of each of the clusters other than the Undefined Cluster. One could ask whether this partitioning of the cases is particularly valid. As mentioned previously, cluster analysis is an interpretive methodology in which the partitioning of the data is valid to the extent that it assists in the meaningful interpretation of the cases. This is the step to which we turn next. However, another way to validate the partitioning is to determine the extent to which the clusters also related in meaningful ways to other variables not included in the original analysis. In this regard, we crossed cluster membership with a large number of other variables coded on the cover sheets. These relationships are displayed in Tables C.4–C.23 in Appendix C. A number of significant relationships emerged that are consistent with the characteristics of the clusters. While this may be an overly quantitative approach to analyzing qualitative data, it adds to the validity of the cluster analysis and to the understanding of the clusters, as described in the section entitled "Patterns of Innovative Pedagogical Practices Using Technology."

STEP 3: CODING WITHIN CASES

In the third step in our analysis, we examined a subset of cases in more detail, which allowed us to better understand what the clusters meant and how the corresponding practices looked in the classroom. Since the ICC did not have the resources to analyze all 174 cases in detail, we used the output of the cluster analysis to make this task more manageable and meaningful. The cluster analysis listed all cases in each cluster in the order of their closeness to the geometric center of the cluster (i.e., its "centroid"). In this regard, the cases closest to the centroid in some sense typify the cluster.

We selected at least 30% of the cases in each cluster for closer examination. The cases we selected were from among the half closest to the centroid. This selection protocol allowed us some latitude in selecting cases that maximized the representation of the various countries participating in the study. The protocol gave us 47 cases across the 7 clusters. We selected 10 cases from the Product Creation Cluster, 7 from the Information Management Cluster, 8 from the Outside Communication Cluster, 6 from the Teacher Collaboration Cluster, and 5 cases each from the Tutorial, Tool Use, and Student Collaborative Research Clusters—these are the minimum numbers we chose to code for any cluster. However, we did not further analyze any of the cases in the Undefined Cluster or outliers. These coded cases covered 27 of the 28 countries. Only Russia was unrepresented in our detailed analysis; its two cases were both in the Undefined Cluster.

We used a fine-grained coding scheme—again based on our conceptual framework and parallel to those used for the coding sheets—to characterize practices described in the 47 cases. The coding scheme was used along with *ATLAS ti*, a software package designed to facilitate qualitative analysis. With this package, we coded specific passages of selected cases. For the purposes of this analysis, we focused our coding primarily on the sections of the case reports that related to the practices of teachers and students and their use of ICT.

Table 3.2
DESCRIPTIONS OF PRACTICES FOR DIFFERENT CLUSTERS

Clusters	ICT USED		ICT PRACTICES		STUDENT PRACTICES		TEACHER PRACTICES	
	High	Highest	High	Highest	High	Highest	High	Highest
Tool Use (n = 14)	Web resources, multimedia	E-mail, productivity tools		Communicate, search for information, create products	Collaborate with others; search for information, create products			
Student Collaborative Research (n = 14)	Web resources, productivity tools	Laptops, LANs, e-mail, Web design tools, multimedia	Communicate, search for information, create products	Collaborate, simulate research	Search for information, solve problems	Conduct research, analyze data, collaborate with others	Design materials	Lecture, advise, create structure, monitor
Information Management (n = 22)	LAN, e-mail, multimedia	Web resources, productivity tools, course management tools	Communicate	Search for information, create products, monitor, plan	Conduct research, create products, collaborate with others	Search for information, solve problems, publish results, self-assess	Advise, monitor, collaborate with colleagues	Create structure, design materials
Teacher Collaboration (n = 19)	E-mail, productivity tools, multimedia	Simulations	Communicate, search for information	Create products	Search for information, publish results, create products, collaborate with others, collaborate outside	Pick your own tasks	Advise, create structure, design materials, monitor	Collaborate with students, collaborate with colleagues, collaborate with outside actors
Outside Communication (n = 27)	Web resources, productivity tools	E-mail, collaborative environments	Search for information	Communicate	Conduct research, search for information, publish results, create products, collaborate with others	Collaborate with outsiders	Advise, create structure, monitor, collaborate with colleagues	
Product Creation (n = 35)	Web resources, productivity tools, multimedia		Search for information	Create products	Search for information, collaborate with others, publish results	Design products		Advise, create structure
Tutorial (n = 12)		Tutorials		Tutor		Drill and practice	Design materials, collaborate with colleagues	

Data from the data matrix portion of the report (i.e., backup information) was coded if additional information was necessary.

The analysis of these codes allowed us to examine the similarities and differences of specific instances of pedagogical practices and ICT use within and across cases that typified each cluster. In this way, we could provide details illustrating how practices fit together within clusters and how these patterns might be different from those of cases in other clusters. The collection of these details allowed us to elaborate on the practices that made these clusters distinctive, as well as those that were common across clusters. For example, we looked at the various instances where teachers were creating structure in the Student Collaborative Research Cluster to see how these instances might relate to the ways students were conducting research projects in this cluster. We looked at how students created products in the Product Creation Cluster to see if they were similar to or different from student activities in the Tool Use Cluster.

PATTERNS OF INNOVATIVE PEDAGOGICAL PRACTICES USING TECHNOLOGY

Based on our detailed analysis of 47 of the 174 case reports, we can provide descriptive profiles of the seven patterns of innovative pedagogical practices that emerged from the cluster analysis. While many commonalities cut across clusters, our intent in this section is to draw contrasts that might highlight certain combinations of practices, relative to those in other clusters. We provide selected cases from the 47 that we coded to illustrate the key distinctions.

TOOL USE CLUSTER

The title of this cluster—Tool Use—is drawn from the fact that as a group the cases in this cluster were distinguished most by various technologies and the ways they were used rather than by distinctive patterns of teacher or student pedagogical practices. Of course, teaching and student practices were exhibited in these cases, but the ties that bound the cases together was the emphasis on the extensive use of technology and the lack of emphasis on specific teacher practices. As seen in Table 3.1, all of the cases in this cluster used e-mail and productivity tools such as word processors, spreadsheets, and presentation software. Web resources and multimedia were also heavily used. These tools were used to communicate, search for information, and create products. Several student practices were also more common in these cases than others, including collaborating or working in groups to search for information or create products.

A case from a secondary school in the United States (US019) illustrates these characteristics (Box 3.1). In this technology-rich school, students used a variety of ICT tools in courses across the curriculum, including language arts, math, science, and social studies.

Box 3.1 THIN CLIENT TECHNOLOGY AND WHOLE LANGUAGE LEARNING

Located in one of the most densely populated municipalities in the eastern United States, this secondary school serves more than 1,200 students, the vast majority of whom speak Spanish as their native language and come from families with low income levels. Through the school's 500 plus computers (230 of which were thin client terminals) and high-speed DSL connections, all the school's students, teachers, and administrators had anytime-anywhere access to the school district's intranet. The use of the thin client terminals in the classroom permitted students to work independently or in groups. Students made presentations, critiqued their own work, and learned from each other. Students and their parents could also store and retrieve student assignments from any Web browser at any time. One student remarked that "you can access the server from home. So that's pretty neat because you get to work at school and save your work, and then come home and finish it."

US019

A case from a Canadian high school (CA003) was another example of the technocentric focus of this cluster. The use of technology involved a wide variety of projects that supported education and enriched the learning environment. Rather than being isolated in a particular project or subject area, technology was integrated throughout the school. For example, the ICT used in this school included 250 Pentium 400 computers located in seven computer labs, and 1 computer in each classroom in the school. All students at all grade levels used technology throughout the curriculum. Technology was used daily as a facilitative tool for learning and for various school activities. Examples of how ICT was integrated throughout the curriculum include assignments posted on the Web, from which students could select projects and resources listed with links; assignments e-mailed to staff members for grading; a chat room set up prior to exams so students could study collaboratively; math software to supplement the curriculum; science simulations to replace experiments; human anatomy software for use in physical education; e-mail dialogue with schools in other parts of the world, allowing a comparison of viewpoints; music experimentation with Musical Instrument Digital Interfaces (MIDI); video and sound editing connected to live performances in the theatre; and yearbook, newsletters, and desktop-publishing projects created by a media club.

"If you're doing a group project, you can send projects over the Web. You can send information over the Web, you can give notes over the Web, you can notify them over the Web."

—STUDENT, CA003

Another case emphasizing the technology focus of the innovation was from an upper secondary institution in England (UK006). The school offered a 2-year online course leading to formal accreditation in ICT. The course required students to spend 3 hours each week working on the program. Two of those hours were completed at school after the end of the school day under the supervision of an IT teacher. Students had to work for an additional hour on their own time, either at home or at school. All students had one-to-one access to a PC and worked independently at their own pace, although they had to submit the assignments for each unit by a specified deadline. Students had access to course materials through the school intranet, at home via the Internet, or at home using a CD-ROM.

Another characteristic of this cluster was that students often collaborated with other students in their class (in 93% of the cases), searched for information (86% of the cases), and designed products (64% of the cases). ICT was used to support searches for information (93% of the cases), the creation of products (93% of the cases), and communication (79% of the cases). Web resources were often used (93% of the cases), as was multimedia (64% of the cases). An example of this use of Web resources is an upper secondary religious school in The Netherlands (NL017), the "stellar case" from this country. Project Codename Future was a cross-curricular, Web-based project taught by a team of teachers and carried out over a 7-week period. The project replaced earlier textbooks with Web resource material in three subjects (information technology, geography, and a subject called "care") and addressed students' independent study skills (i.e., investigations, collaboration, presentation). Students used a log book as a guide that described various phases of the project and offered a choice of up to 30 social themes that might be pursued in their research. Using the log book and working in pairs, students developed an action plan, posed research questions, and collected information by searching the Internet. They communicated by e-mail with their peers and interviewed others in person or by telephone. After the information was synthesized, the students attempted to answer questions related to the issue they had studied, using PowerPoint for their presentations.

STUDENT COLLABORATIVE RESEARCH CLUSTER

As the name implies, cases in the Student Collaborative Research Cluster are characterized primarily by collaborative student research projects. The most distinguishing characteristics of this cluster are that students in these cases worked in pairs or groups with other students in their class (in all of the cases), most often doing research (in 86% of the cases) and occasionally collecting and analyzing data (36% of the cases). These practices occurred most often in cases in this cluster, relative to those in all other clusters. Often cases in this cluster described students' activities as they searched for information (93% of the cases) and solved problems (57% of the cases). Exploring Live Physics (CN005) is an example of this pattern of practices (Box 3.2). Here, groups of students in a China Hong Kong secondary school engaged in Internet-based explorations of physics phenomena, guided by their teachers.

Another example of this pattern of student practices is a Grade 7 multimedia development project in an Australian primary school (AU002). Students in this school participated in research activities associated with the Jason project—a series of real-life, Internet-based science explorations designed for students (www.jasonproject.org). The students followed Jason researchers as they explored the geology and biology of a group of isolated islands in Hawaii, traced the migration paths of the diverse peoples who settled these islands, and explored the cultural tapestry of modern Hawaii. Students in this school were presented with two research questions and were required to select one of them as their research topic. Students used Inspiration, an idea-organizing tool, in their initial research planning and PowerPoint to construct the final presentations of their completed research. They also used iMacs to produce movies for their presentations. Operating in teams, students divided their time between the different tasks needed to construct their team's movie. Some used the computers to refine the script; others worked outside with a digital video camera to shoot footage for their project. Several more groups used iMacs to edit video material they had taken earlier.

| Box 3.2 | EXPLORING LIVE PHYSICS |

In Exploring Live Physics, groups of Hong Kong secondary students were given authentic physics problems to work on. For example, one group of students investigated the causes of the Challenger explosion. Another group examined physical issues related to the idea of faster-than-light travel. Students used information on the Internet to study their topics and construct a proposal for more detailed research, which was presented to the rest of the class members for their comments. Over the 3-month period of the project, student groups completed their investigations and gave final presentations to their classmates. As part of their project, students had to decide what kinds of information they needed. They planned how to work collaboratively and share the workload. They analyzed the topic, searched for relevant information, organized presentation materials, and finally made their presentation to the class. The Internet and productivity tools were used extensively.

The teacher provided guidance when necessary by interacting with students via e-mail. The teacher stated, "As teachers, we are providing a suitable environment for students to learn in and giving them directions. Students need to choose which directions they are going and each student had their individuality. The role of teacher is that of a coach or facilitator who gives guidance to the students."

CN005

Science was not the only topic addressed by innovations in this cluster. For example, another project in China Hong Kong called Creanimate (CN006) involved lower secondary students in explorations in creative art. In this project, groups of students used the Internet to search for pictures and information about different species of animals and used the graphics package Picture It to morph the pictures in order to create new animal species for some fictitious ecological settings.

Even though the focus in these cases was on student practices, teachers played an important role in this cluster. These are quite different from the group of cases in the Tool Use Cluster, where teacher practices were not emphasized. In all cases in the Student Collaborative Research Cluster teachers supported their students by structuring their activities, giving advice, and monitoring student progress. For example, while students in the Australian multimedia development project (AU002) generated ideas and worked on their presentations, their teacher helped refine their choices. One of the teachers commented, "I'm obviously the one guiding what the kids are doing, but it's negotiating on what it is, where do we need to go from here, what is it you want to learn." The school's principal observed, "Because the students in general are quite engaged in what they're doing, the teacher can afford to sit down with a couple of kids and do something a bit more deeply rather than the crowd control that often happens when the task is less engaging."

Teachers in the Student Collaborative Research Cluster often lectured or otherwise provided content (in 71% of the cases). For example, the teacher in a lower secondary biology project in Chinese Taipei (TW005) usually introduced concepts to be taught with a PowerPoint presentation, along with related videos from the school's video server, thus visualizing the concepts. These presentations then launched student research projects on various topics, such as the human digestive system. Students would analyze data collected on the Internet.

"Each group needs to decide who is doing the presentation, who is collecting information, and who is organizing the data before they actually set out to do the project."

—TEACHER, TW005

If students encountered problems they were unable to solve, they could ask the teacher in the class or post questions to their Internet discussion group to request help. The students' research was structured by worksheets that the teacher prepared for each topic; students filled out the worksheets with the information they collected. This was similar to another practice in the Student Collaborative Research Cluster, where teachers designed materials in 79% of the cases.

As in the Tool Use Cluster, Web resources and productivity tools were often used in the Student Collaborative Research Cluster, where both types of tools were used in 93% of the cases. ICT often supported the search for information (in 93% of the cases), creation of products (86% of the cases), planning of activities (79% of the cases), and communication (79% of the cases). In all of the cases, students used LANs and e-mail. In an Australian multimedia development project (AU002), a biology project in Chinese Taipei (TW005), and a creative art class in China Hong Kong (CN006), students frequently used multimedia hardware or software (86% of the cases). Occasionally, Web design tools (50% of the cases) and laptops (43% of the cases) were used, which was more often than in any other cluster. Also, ICT practices occasionally included the use of simulations or modeling to support research and students' collaboration (50% of the cases for both types of ICT practices).

As has been noted, there were certain similarities between the Student Collaborative Research Cluster and the Tool Use Cluster (and several other clusters) in the common use of ICT tools and certain ICT practices. But there were also significant differences, primarily related to teacher and student practices. The distinctive practices in the Student Collaborative Research Cluster were associated, in turn, with several other factors not included in the analysis that formed these clusters. Specifically, cases in the Student Collaborative Research Cluster were more likely to mention changes in the organization of curriculum content (see Table C.13.3, Appendix C) and the allocation of curriculum time (Table C.13.4, Appendix C) than were cases in the Tool Use Cluster or most other clusters. Perhaps because of the greater emphasis on teacher practices in the Student Collaborative Research cluster, cases in this cluster were more likely to mention the acquisition of new pedagogical skills as a positive outcome for teachers (Table C.16.1, Appendix C). Students, too, were more likely to benefit from positive outcomes, according to case reports. Cases in this cluster were more likely to mention students' acquisition of new ICT skills (Table C.18.2, Appendix C), new problem-solving skills (Table C.18.4, Appendix C), and collaborative skills (Table C.18.6, Appendix C).

Reports for cases in the Student Collaborative Research cluster were also more likely to claim that ICT added value to the innovation, such as supporting changes in student practice (Table C.21.1, Appendix C), supporting changes in the curriculum (Table C.21.6, Appendix C), providing resources that would not otherwise be available (Table C.21.8, Appendix C), supporting student learning processes (Table C.21.10), inhibiting undesirable activities or outcomes (Table C.21.11, Appendix C), and changing the time or structure of the classroom (Table C.21.9, Appendix C). With regard to these factors, practices in the Student Collaborative Research Cluster, as in the Information Management Cluster (discussed next), seem to have an affect on the normal structure of the classroom. That is, these innovations seemed to restructure the way students worked together, the organization of the curriculum, and the class day.

The association between membership in the Student Collaborative Research Cluster and other variables not included in the cluster analysis validates the importance of the pattern of practices in this cluster vis-à-vis other clusters. These associations also help to elaborate on the meaning of the Student Collaborative Research Cluster.

INFORMATION MANAGEMENT CLUSTER

Another cluster rich in innovative teacher, student, and ICT practices is one we termed the Information Management Cluster. This term was selected to describe the complex set of teacher and student activities in this cluster that involved searching for, creating, managing, organizing, and using information for teaching and learning. The Virtual Gallery Project (SG002) (Box 3.3) provides a good example of the practices in this cluster. In this primary school, both teachers and students in an English class used a sophisticated set of network-based tools to locate information, create products, and share this information with others.

Box 3.3   VIRTUAL GALLERY PROJECT

The Virtual Gallery (SG002) was a resource repository where teachers in a Singaporean primary school posted their lesson materials and instructions and pupils posted their work. These resources, once published online, were accessible from home by teachers and their pupils in a given class, as well as teachers and pupils from other classes.

The software system used for the project consisted of several components. The administrative component included online facility booking, public announcements, an online school calendar, electronic forms, and a forum. The academic component provided teachers and students with free server space to store their projects, free Web mail accounts, a Web page generator, and an interactive quiz generator.

In an English class using the Virtual Gallery, teachers sat together to plan the resources and search for relevant Web sites for pupils to visit. They put these resources together into lesson packages and published them on the Virtual Gallery. Pupils accessed the lesson instructions through the system, searched for information on the Internet, completed worksheets, and posted their work on the Web with the help of the system's Web page generator. The teachers walked among pupils, clarifying the lesson and encouraging and helping their students. Teachers gave comments and feedback on the pupils' online work. Some of the better pieces of work were selected for publishing on the repository.

SG002

As in the Student Collaborative Research and Product Creation Clusters and in contrast to the Tool Use Cluster, all of the teachers in the Information Management Cluster played the important role of structuring student activities. In addition, teachers in this cluster frequently provided advice to their students (95% of the cases) and monitored and assessed their students' work. ICT was used to assess students in 86% of the cases in this cluster. For example, in the Virtual Gallery Project (SG002), the English teachers circulated among their students while the students were working with online materials to provide them with any help or clarification they needed. Teachers also provided the students with online feedback in response to the work that students posted.

In a project called Honcho Time (JP003), an integrated study period in a Japanese primary school, teachers served as a sounding board for students who were choosing a topic or theme for their multimedia projects. Teachers then served as advisors while the project was actually executed. Questions from the teachers tended not to be directive but encouraged students toward a certain decision.

Even more frequently than in the Student Collaborative Research Cluster, teachers in the Information Management Cluster prepared instructional materials (in 91% of the cases). An example of this practice occurred in an integrated science course in a Philippines primary school (PH005). During her summer vacation, one of the teachers used the objectives of the lesson to guide her conceptualization of the instructional materials, which she planned to present using PowerPoint. Her intent was to concretize her teaching through the use of vivid images of science concepts created by computer graphics. She wanted to use animations to bring to life what would otherwise be routine verbalizations and generalizations of science concepts. While developing the materials, she made a variety of decisions about such issues as the content to include, the Web sites students would visit, the graphics to use to concretize the concepts, how the slides would be presented, which colors to apply for an eye-catching presentation, when and where to integrate the voice over, what questions to ask to stimulate student thinking, what student activities to give as an application of learning, and how student learning would be assessed. The preparation for each PowerPoint presentation took 2 or 3 days. Then the teacher conducted a dry run of the presentation to preview the material and asked colleagues to provide feedback.

"Along the way, the students also learn the strategies used to search for desired information from available sources. They learn by doing and they present their work in different formats."

—PRINCIPAL, TH005

Teachers in the Information Management Cluster often worked in collaboration with their colleagues (in 73% of the cases). For example, teachers in a Korean lower secondary school (KR003) collaborated with the technical coordinator in searching for and creating teaching-learning materials in math, social studies, science, and physical training in order to improve learning in these classes. The teachers conducted teaching-learning analyses in which they considered the learning tasks (e.g., concepts, arrangement and rules, problem solving) and identified the best materials for each task. They collected materials by looking for Web sites related to each subject and carefully selected contents that were applicable to the middle school curriculum. They also constructed their own materials. The physical education teachers created materials by recording certain motions of gymnasts with a video camera. Then they translated these scenes to MPEG files and edited them. A total of 12 gymnastic motions were then converted into movies and loaded onto the school home page. The teachers added titles and explanations for each of the movements into the database.

This case in Korea is typical of a majority of the cases in this cluster in that the innovation cut across all or almost all of the subjects in the school (Table C.11, Appendix C).

Unique to the Information Management Cluster was the teachers' use of ICT to plan and organize instruction (all cases in this cluster). In addition, teachers in 23% of the cases used ICT course management tools. For example, a primary School of the Future in Israel (IL003) was built on an educational concept that views ICT as a means to empower students, redefine the relationship between students and knowledge, facilitate learning skills acquisition, and improve academic achievement. Teachers in this school were involved in an ongoing effort to update curricula. Most of the communication between staff members was by e-mail and the school Web site. The accessibility of information and the customary procedures enabled daily updates, which were easy to follow. The principal said:

> At the end of each week, I send messages to the teachers, including reference to the past week and announcements concerning the following week, in which I embed ideological principles relating to the uniqueness of the school. ... This enables a culture of sharing, among all staff members, not only subgroups. At the middle of the week, by turn, each teacher e-mails a case report, and other teachers respond to the described event.

The school's academic advisor commented about the teachers and their work:

> Maybe the most evident achievement is that the teachers have become a learning community. Not only students, but also teachers, learn in this school all the time. The school norms have become academic in nature, in that you can inquire about anything, doubt anything. You have to work hard, prepare and plan, keep track of processes via documentation, and explain steps you take.

Students in the Information Management Cluster were also focused on the use of information in their studies. As in the Student Collaborative Research, Teacher Collaboration, and Outside Communication Clusters, students in the Information Management Cluster searched for information (in all cases), often in collaboration with others in their class (90% of the cases). In 95% of the cases, ICT supported the search for information. Productivity tools were used in all cases in this cluster, as they were in all the cases in the Tool Use Cluster. Students and teachers used e-mail in 95% of the cases, and ICT was used to support student communication in 86% of the cases.

For example, student use of information was an important focus in a general science class in a Thai boys' school (TH005). The lower secondary science teacher in this case developed Web-based materials on the topic "light bulbs, lamps, and electrical wires," in which he provided both science content and tests. Questions were used to stimulate student thinking, analysis, and discussion. To participate in these activities, students used Web sites the teacher recommended and Web sites the students themselves located. They carried out online searches of the Web-based materials the teacher prepared, as well as other materials they located. Working in groups, students helped one another with their assignments and made joint decisions on the activities to be carried out. Later, the teacher led a discussion by asking questions that helped the students analyze the information they obtained and interpret the data to draw conclusions. For the students, ICT served as a research tool to search for information on Web sites and as a productivity tool to prepare reports. Then they used ICT as a communication tool to submit their work on the school's Web site. They also used a bulletin board to share interesting science stories with other students. Students used Internet Explorer to access the school's and other Web sites, and Microsoft Word and Power-Point to prepare and present their reports. The teacher used Microsoft Word, FrontPage, HTML, and PowerPoint.

Students in the Information Management Cluster also designed products (in 68% of the cases) and published or presented the results of their work (95% of the cases). ICT was used to support the creation of products or presentations in all the cases in the Information Management Cluster. Web resources were used in 95% of the cases, and both LANs and multimedia were used in 73% of the cases. Similar to students in the Student Collaborative Research Cluster, students in the Information Management Cluster conducted research projects in 68% of the cases and solved problems in 73% of the cases. However, unique to the Information Management Cluster was the relatively high incidence of students assessing their own work and that of other students (54% of the cases).

An example of student research and product creation in the Information Management Cluster is the Theme Day Project at a private upper secondary school located in Pretoria, South Africa (ZA008). Here, groups of students were instructed to act as entrepreneurs who had received a fictitious 10 million Rand budget to invest in and manage a wine farm in the Western Cape province of South Africa. Before the purchase was made, students were required to justify their decision to "company Head Quarters" (HQ), which was represented by the teacher facilitators. To do so, students had to research the farm and select one grape cultivar that would thrive under the climatic conditions and on the topography of the farm. The students had to report their choices of the cultivars to HQ in a 200-word report. They had to draw a map of their own farms, on which they indicated the location of the cultivars in relation to the geographical features, including the Manor house, sheds, distillers, work quarters, quarters for the workers, and so forth. The students also designed bottle labels that would be pasted on their wine bottles. After studying the social, cultural, and economic context of winemaking and the various cultivars, the students presented a 100-word description of the history of wine in South Africa, using any South African official language other than English. They also produced a 150-word description of the winemaking process. The students were required to produce and design a mechanism for removing grapes from bunches without damaging the grapes, a bag for carrying grapes, a greenhouse or shed that would accelerate the growth of grapes, a model for crushing grapes, and a new corkscrew. The students then responded to broadcasts sent by HQ regarding the price of the wine they planned to produce. Using a profit-and-loss sheet, they reported their projected profit and loss via HQ to the shareholders. During the day, HQ sent regular announcements to the groups, warning them about pests and potential disasters such as hail damage, and informing them about fertilizers for improving yields. Students had to respond to these messages quickly so as to minimize loss and maximize their profits. To conduct their research, students used computers networked and linked to the school's intranet. In creating their products and reporting to HQ, students used word processing, graphics, PowerPoint, Web Builder, spreadsheets, and videoconferencing. The project teachers reported that without ICT, Theme Day would not have existed.

As in the Student Collaborative Research Cluster, the rich set of innovative pedagogical practices that constitute the Information Management Cluster is associated with a number of other variables. Cases in the Information Management Cluster were more likely than cases in other clusters to be associated with changes in the organization of curriculum content (see Table C.13.3 in Appendix C) and the allocation of curriculum time (Table C.13.4, Appendix C). They were also more likely than cases in other clusters to mention teachers' acquisition of new pedagogical skills (Table C.16.1, Appendix C). For example, the science teacher in the Thai case (TH005) learned many new learner-centered teaching strategies that brought him recognition from the other teachers in the school. In addition, cases in this cluster were more likely than cases in other clusters to report teachers' acquisition of collaborative skills (Table C.16.3, Appendix C).

As in the Student Collaborative Research Cluster, cases in this cluster were more likely than cases in other clusters to mention student acquisition of new ICT skills (Table C.18.2, Appendix C), new problem-solving skills (Table C.18.4, Appendix C), and collaborative skills (Table C.18.6, Appendix C). The principal in the school where the Singapore Virtual Gallery project (SG002) was conducted said, "If the future is still a digital age then the kids are very well prepared for it because they start the subject at an early age. We are actually creating a lot of kids who are very sophisticated in ICT at a very young age." In addition, the cases in this cluster were more likely to mention student acquisition of communication skills (Table C.18.3, Appendix C) and information-handling skills (Table C.18.5, Appendix C). For example, a teacher in the Theme Day Project (ZA008) reported that the benefits students derived from the project included "teamwork, communication, self-directed learning, self-monitoring, and lifelong learning."

Given all the positive outcomes for this cluster, it is perhaps ironic that the Information Management Cluster was also more likely to be associated with various problems (Table C.18.9, Appendix C). Negative comments were made in 50% of the cases. Some of these comments had to do with the amount of time that students spent with computers. A parent of a student in the Thai physics project (TH005) said, "I agree [with his father] where health is concerned. There was a period of time when my son didn't see any friends because as soon as he got home he went straight to the computer and just planted himself in front of it." A student in the Honcho Time Project (JP003) said, "I can't cooperate with my friends. I work alone on the computer." However, a student in the Singapore Virtual Gallery Project (SG002) complained that there was "not enough time spent on the computers." And a teacher in that project commented, "You get parents who do not allow the children to access the Internet at home. That's why we tell parents as much as we can, [to allow the children] to work on the computer even on weekends and holidays."

Despite the negative comments on some outcomes in these cases, the particular pattern of teacher, student, and ICT practices in the Information Management Cluster seem particularly significant in ways that we will return to at the end of the chapter. Reports in this cluster often claimed that significant value was added by the innovations. As in the Student Collaborative Research Cluster, cases in this cluster were likely to say that ICT added value, such as support for changes in student practice (Table C.21.1, Appendix C), resources that would not otherwise be available (Table C.21.8, Appendix C), changes in the time or structure of the classroom (Table C.21.9, Appendix C), support for student learning processes (Table C.21.10, Appendix C), and inhibition of undesirable activities or outcomes (Table C.21.11, Appendix C). In addition, cases in this cluster were more likely than cases in other clusters to state that ICT supported innovative teacher practices (Table C.21.2, Appendix C) and educational reform.

TEACHER COLLABORATION CLUSTER

The emphasis in the cases in the Teacher Collaboration Cluster was on teachers' collaboration with students (in all cases) and with their colleagues (95% of the cases). Also, teachers often designed instructional materials or activities (90% of the cases). An example of this pattern of practices is the Hypertext Development project (SK003) (Box 3.4). In this project, informatics teachers in an upper secondary school trained students in the development of hypertext; the students subsequently worked with teachers in other subject areas to develop materials that were used by other students in the school. As in this case, the majority of cases in this cluster were from upper secondary schools (Table C.4.3, Appendix C).

Box 3.4   THE HYPERTEXT DEVELOPMENT PROJECT

The Hypertext Development project, which took place in an upper secondary school in the Slovak Republic, focused on students with an interest in computer science and further university study. This innovation was started by two informatics teachers who created hypertext educational materials for programming courses. Later they began to develop these educational materials together with students. First, students learned how to create hypertexts, using HTML code, scripting languages, and text, graphic, and sound editors. Then the students worked individually or in teams on projects over the next 3 to 5 months on a selected topic. They applied their skills to work with teachers to develop hypertext materials in other areas such as mathematics, physics, the Slovak language, and history. Topics were selected in collaboration between teachers and students. The finished projects were presented on the school Web page for use by other students. During the project, subject matter and informatics teachers acted as consultants, managers, and supervisors of the students; at the same time they also acquired new learning. As one teacher commented, "It is certainly an enormous benefit. I learn something from the students as well, and the fact that everybody asks how to do this or that keeps me filling up my knowledge. It satisfies me when I can acquire something for me, too."

SK003

Similarly, student-teacher collaboration was part of the Information, Technology, and Media Program (FI003), a line of study in an upper secondary school in Finland. This program was composed of 26 different courses from which every student had to choose 16 courses. The program included technical courses such as programming, data structures, and multimedia, as well as nontechnical courses such as creative writing, social psychology, and media criticism. The students in the program became so highly skilled that a collaborative culture evolved in which students assisted teachers in their use of ICT. Teachers also worked with faculty at the University of Turku and local companies to find practice positions for students. This kind of collaboration between teachers and outside actors applied to 42% of the cases in this cluster, more than in any other clusters.

Teachers often collaborated with each other in this cluster. An example of this peer collaboration took place in an upper secondary French technical school (FR006). A cross-disciplinary team of teachers of geography, physics, and biology-geology developed course materials that engaged students in the analysis of satellite images available on Internet sites by means of software created for this purpose (TITUS). In this case, groups of students applied physical principles linked to remote detection, studied meteorological phenomena representation and ecological problems, and compared representation tools (topographical and geological maps, variable digital images, and so forth). As in this case, the cases in the Teacher Collaboration Cluster were more likely than those in other clusters to involve physics (Table C.12.2, Appendix C) or earth science (Table C.12.5, Appendix C).

In another case, two fine arts teachers in a Lithuanian secondary school (LT001) worked with each other and the school's informatics teacher to incorporate ICT into the course as a way to make it more attractive and interesting to students. The teachers integrated ICT into their own teaching by using it in their lectures and classroom discussions. But they also had students use a variety of ICT tools to develop their own creative art projects. The school's informatics teachers helped students acquire ICT skills and with the school's librarians helped students find materials related to their class projects.

The level of teacher collaboration in this cluster seemed to have its payoff in positive teacher outcomes. Cases in this cluster were more likely than in any other to mention teachers' acquisition of collaboration skills (Table C.16.3, Appendix C).

The art projects of these Lithuanian students illustrate another pattern of practice in this cluster, pertaining to the collaborative creation of student products. As in other clusters (but not the Tutorial Cluster), students in a majority of cases in the Teacher Collaboration Cluster collaborated with each other (in 95% of the cases), searched for information (90% of the cases), designed products (74% of the cases), and published results (79% of the cases). In 90% of the cases, students picked their own tasks. However, unlike the Student Collaborative Research and Information Management clusters, case reports in this cluster were less likely to mention that students conducted research projects and solved problems.

An example of students' collaborative product creation is from a Canadian primary school (CA002), which Canada selected as its "stellar case." (These cases are described in Chapter 7). This school was designed around a vision of autonomous, authentic, and engaged student learning integrated into everyday practice. The use of ICT was widespread in the school but varied in the degree to which it was embedded in student-directed practices. In some classes, students took the lead in developing questions that then became themes for major student projects that continued over several weeks. In other classes, students worked on shorter-term projects the teachers determined. Most commonly, students worked together on projects. Students either shared the same grade for a project or both teacher and students partitioned the grade according to what each student contributed to the project. Students used ICT to work with advanced, professional-level graphics, multimedia, and presentation tools, including Microsoft Office, Astound, PhotoShop, and Internet Explorer. Children as young as 7 and 8 years old developed animations to accompany stories they wrote, coded HTML for pages they created for the school's Web site, or used search engines to locate current population data on the Internet and then entered the data into a spreadsheet to explore population growth in a region.

As in the Outside Communication Cluster, many cases in the Teacher Collaboration Cluster mentioned that students collaborated with outside actors (53%). (This practice was not typical in other clusters.) An example of this collaboration occurred in a lower secondary school in Norway (NO006), the "stellar case" from that country. In this case, a group of students used technologies such as the Internet, word processing, graphics software, and digital video to create a Web site about a 2000–2001 expedition to Antarctica made by two female explorers, one Norwegian and one American. The students searched for information about the expedition on the Internet as well as at the library. They also met with one of the explorers before and after the expedition and spoke with her during the expedition via e-mail and satellite telephone. Furthermore, the students exchanged information with local journalists who were following the expedition. The teacher described his motivation for doing the project:

> I wanted to further expand the use of ICT towards internationalization. … [The students] meet people; they get contact with students in other countries … and in this project there was a possibility to communicate through satellite to Antarctica, to follow something that actually is going right now, then the students are sort of in the first row on this arena and following it.

In the same vein, one female student commented, "I think it is very exciting to hear how they [the explorers] can get messages, and also about the technical part, how we can get messages from them, where they are."

The places where students worked seemed more flexible in this cluster. Cases were more likely to mention that the innovation took place in the school but outside the regular classroom (Table C.20.2, Appendix C). In this regard, practices in this cluster are beginning to break down the walls of the classroom.

"There is so much information that teachers cannot know everything. Students can be more skillful in some areas than teachers."

—TEACHER, FI003

As in several other clusters, instructors in the Teacher Collaboration Cluster often advised their students, created structure for their activities, and monitored their progress (in 90% of the cases for all of these factors). For example, in the Lithuanian art class (LT001), the fine arts teacher discussed selected topics with students, reviewed their projects, discussed the evaluation criteria, and consulted with students on issues related to fine arts and ICT use. In one of the French science classes (FR006), the teacher was observed helping students with their activities. He worked with only one or two students at a time, discussing their misunderstandings or forgotten manipulations and helping them to search appropriate information. The teacher did not operate the software for the students but helped them in their use of it. He went from group to group answering questions and consulting in this manner. If some questions were of interest to the entire group, he addressed the whole class or had them all come to see a point of detail on the screen of the group where the questions appeared.

ICT served various roles in this cluster. As in the Product Creation and Information Management Clusters, ICT was used to create products in all of the cases. Unlike other clusters, however, simulations or microcomputer-based laboratories were used in 37% of the cases, the highest use of this technology among any of the clusters. Both e-mail and productivity tools were used in 90% of the cases, and multimedia was used in 68% of the cases. ICT supported the search for information in 84% of the cases and communication in 63% of the cases.

OUTSIDE COMMUNICATION CLUSTER

The most distinctive characteristic of the Outside Communication Cluster was the relatively high incidence of students working with others outside the classroom. This was mentioned in 56% of the cases, the highest of all clusters. In support of this collaboration with outsiders, cases in the cluster are characterized by the use of e-mail, the Internet, conferencing software, or listservs. This was true in all cases in this cluster. In 96% of the cases communication was supported by the use of e-mail or other communication tools. Collaboration software environments were used in 33% of the cases. Other frequently used technologies included Web resources (85% of the cases), productivity tools (82% of the cases), and local area networks (73% of the cases). ICT was frequently used to support students in their search for information (85% of the cases). This use of technology to support communication and collaboration is illustrated by a case in South Africa (ZA004), where primary students used e-mail and videoconferencing to communicate with students in other countries and track sailors in an around-the-world yacht race (Box 3.5).

Box 3.5　ICT-ENABLED PARTICIPATION IN THE BT GLOBAL CHALLENGE YACHT RACE

Students at a South African girls' primary school participated in a cross-disciplinary project that encompassed English, art, history, geography, math, and home economics. The project followed an around-the-world yacht race. ICT played a central role. The teacher commented, "Technology fits in with everything I teach because technology in today's society is absolutely part and parcel of everything we do." Students used e-mail and videoconferencing to communicate with the yacht's crew and with students in other countries throughout the race. Although only one computer was connected to the Web and the teacher had to download materials to a local server, students used these resources to learn about the geography, history, and weather conditions in the areas where yachts sailed. For math, they calculated sailing distances and times and plotted the ship's position on a map. They also made high-energy nutritious biscuits, using spreadsheets to compile data for food comparisons. Students used productivity tools to create electronic souvenir cards and software to compose questions they used to interview the crew when the boat visited Cape Town. The students presented the crew with their homemade biscuits and their electronic souvenir cards.

ZA004

Another example of these uses of technology is a case in Denmark (DK007), where students in a primary school used the First Class conferencing system to interact with primary students in a school in the Faeroe Islands, a self-governing division of Denmark located near Iceland. A joint project with the theme of "springtime" took place over a 3-week period. Working in teams, students explored various conceptualizations of springtime in both the Danish mainland and the Faeroese environments with students living in a different geographic, climatic, and cultural context.

As in this Danish case, communication outside the school was often used to help students understand other peoples and cultures. Perhaps this is why cases in this cluster were more likely to involve foreign languages than cases in other clusters (Table C.12.7, Appendix C).

Another example of the use of ICT to communicate with students in other cultures is a project in an upper secondary school in Germany (DE010). This school participated in an international project with five other schools from across Europe. The objective of the project, entitled The New Millennium: Hopes and Fears, was to promote intercultural understanding as well as ICT knowledge. Parts of the project dealt with life in the 21st century and international comparisons of the consumer behaviors of adolescents in Great Britain, Finland, France, and Poland. The innovation was extensively supported by ICT; some student projects depended completely on it, since they were based on the fast exchange of information or products between the schools. The students used computers for word processing, Internet research, creation of presentations, communication, exchange of project results between schools, and documentation of the project on the Internet. As a result, the students started to work in a more self-directed manner and the teachers assumed consulting and supporting roles.

Sometimes this outside communication allowed students to collaborate with their peers in other schools, as in the preceding cases; but at other times it allowed students to connect with other actors outside of school, as in a case in Norway (NO009). This upper secondary school is situated in a small rural community in the west of Norway. In this case, groups of students were "hired" as consultants by one of the enterprises in the municipality or the municipality itself. For example, one of the groups was asked by an electrical engineering firm whether the firm should lease or buy cars. Another group consulted for the municipality after the group was asked to look closely at the social and environmental consequences of having a power plant in the local area. ICT was an important tool for their work. E-mail was used for student-teacher, student-student, teacher-company, and student-company communication. The Internet was used to prepare presentations and documentation, along with software including Word, PowerPoint, and Multimedia Lab. Excel was used for calculations and as a modeling and simulation tool.

"You have to collaborate when you are in working life. You have to collaborate with your colleagues. With collaboration I really think you learn that other people can contribute where you do not have so much competence, and then you can contribute in another area."

—STUDENT, NO009

As in this case in Norway, students in the Outside Communication Cluster often collaborated with students in their own class (89% of the cases) as well. Students in this cluster, as they did in other clusters, searched for information (82% of the cases), designed products (67% of the cases), conducted research (56% of the cases), and published results (85% of the cases). Also as in other clusters, teachers frequently provided advice to their students (96% of the cases), created structure for student work (89% of the cases), and monitored and assessed student work (89% of the cases). Teachers in this cluster frequently collaborated with their colleagues (74% of the cases).

The nature of teacher and student collaborations in the Outside Communication Cluster is illustrated by a case in Catalonia, Spain (ES005). This case involved collaboration among teachers in five primary schools in a rural school district. Teachers from these schools got together under the leadership of one of their school principals and created a project called ARRELS (Roots), which engaged students in collecting information about their local villages and posting that information on the Web. Teams of students in each school worked on parallel research projects about their villages. Topics included history, monuments, and the village square, among others. Students took digital photos, interviewed their grandparents, and shared their experiences with students in the other schools. They used word processing, e-mail, and digital photography to communicate with each other and to publish their reports on the Web in the Catalan language. Some of the Catalan songs and folktales recorded from their grandparents were quite old and in danger of being lost to the culture. Teachers provided pupils with instructions so that they could work independently. Once the students got started, the teachers moved from group to group, helping students solve problems and reason out solutions.

The patterns of innovative practice in this cluster, particularly the outside communication, began to break down the walls of the school and involve others in the students' education. These results contrast with those in the Student Collaborative Research and Information Management clusters, where collaboration took place primarily inside the school. Cases in the Outside Collaboration Cluster were more likely to report the involvement of teachers and students from other schools (Table C.6.2, Appendix C), the involvement of scientific or higher education institutions (Table C.6.3, Appendix C), and participation in a national, state, or regional project (Table C.10.1, Appendix C). Conversely, these cases were less likely to have no outside involvement (Tables C.6.6 and C.10.3, Appendix C).

PRODUCT CREATION CLUSTER

As the name implies, the Product Creation Cluster is distinguished primarily by the design of digital products. In 86% of the cases, students were involved in the design or creation of products. In all of the cases in this cluster, students and teachers used software packages to create products or presentations. This is exemplified by the practices in a Czech secondary school (CZ002), where students developed Web pages for local communities (Box 3.6).

A community's Web page created by Czech students.

Another example is a group of primary schools in Italy (IT001) that published an electronic newspaper in which the majority of articles were written by students. This was the "stellar case" from Italy. The articles in this electronic newspaper were written with the everyday activities of the school in mind. Students used text and pictures to plan, edit, critique, and produce the newspaper, putting it all on the Internet. Published 14 times during the school year, the newspaper consisted of 12 different sections, including sections on breaking news, science news, news from faraway countries, news about books, and a self-help section providing advice on a variety of topics. Teachers helped prepare students to write each article and supervised its assembly. The students worked in groups to write drafts of the articles, and the school's ICT coordinator supervised article preparation for the Internet using FrontPage software. This newspaper was read by the students' families and the local community, as well as by students at other schools in the international community.

Box 3.6 PROJECT REGION

In a Czech secondary school (CZ002), students participated in a Web design project that presented a wide range of information on 60 Czech villages and municipalities. The task was to design the Web pages for the villages; these pages would contain all the materials that should be available to the public by law. The presentations should also include maps of the villages and surrounding area, transportation connections, lodging options, the histories of the villages, descriptions of places of interest (with photographs), lists of social events, decrees, minutes of the meetings of local councils, and other information considered important to the municipality. Students had to search for most of their sources of information via the Internet and outside the school, in cooperation with people working for various local institutions, such as local councils, libraries, archives, and museums. The information collected from a village was then assessed at school, and those items deemed most appropriate for the Web site were selected for use on the village's Web page. In addition to creating an information source that benefited the local community, participation in this project helped create cross-curricular links between the information technology and other subjects, such as geography, history, Czech language, civics, German, and English.

CZ002

Cases in this cluster were also often characterized by students searching for information (80% of the cases) and publishing results (83% of the cases). These student activities can be illustrated by the case of students in an upper secondary school in Latvia (LV002). Students in this school used ICT to search the Internet and study the geography of different countries. The use of ICT was not a part of the geography curriculum in Latvia, but the geography teacher in this school had recently integrated ICT into his classes in order to expand his students' knowledge of regional and world geography. In this case, students collected information from the Internet and developed multimedia presentations to share and communicate what they had learned. The geography teacher collaborated with the head of the media center to plan and organize how students would work together to gather information on the topics they chose. Students exercised a great deal of autonomy in making decisions about the form and content of their work, as well as in deciding how to tackle a particular problem. The teacher was also available to provide assistance to students if asked. Students mostly worked individually, but they freely exchanged information with their peers about their work assignments and their information search strategies.

Teachers also played an important role in the Product Creation Cluster. In all cases, teachers both advised students and created structure for their activities. Teachers in these roles supported and guided students in their efforts to design, plan, and organize themselves so as to effectively use technology to create products. These supporting teacher practices are illustrated in the "stellar case" from France, in which a French secondary school (FR005) sponsored a school trip to Italy. The trip was designed to allow students to search for information and write a fictional historical scenario in French. In preparation for the trip, students participated in a series of Web search activities designed to help them answer a series of questions based on texts and illustrations on European history. Students searched the preselected site to find answers to the questions, while the teacher provided instruction and monitored student progress. The teachers' major activities focused on ensuring that student activities ran smoothly. Teachers directed students to work with their peers, posed questions, provided technical advice and guidance when needed, and monitored the completion of the projects.

Productivity tools were used in 86% of these cases. The Web was used in 77% of the cases, and multimedia resources were used in 69% of the cases. A case from the United States (US009) illustrates the central role these technologies played in this cluster. In a lower secondary school, innovative practices were used in a number of subjects, including social studies, science, English, and mathematics. Students in the classes worked in pairs on inquiry-oriented assignments and projects, using productivity tools such as Microsoft Office and Web and multimedia resources the teachers had previously collected. During class time, teachers circulated through the room and answered students' questions, stopping at times to redirect students' attention, keep students on task, or provide needed clarification. If a pair of students located an especially relevant Web site or reached an insight into the work at hand, the teacher asked the group to share it with the rest of the class. Students used Word and PhotoShop to write up what they had found and then created a PowerPoint presentation for their final products.

In a case in a Dutch primary school (NL003), all 160 students created their own Web pages on the school's home page, integrating text, graphics, and audio into the Web sites. The innovation did not address a particular subject but aimed instead at teaching the students basic ICT skills with which they could make Web pages and add drawings, photos, sounds, and music. These Web sites contained information about the students, as well as stories, poems, and other written artifacts. The students worked in pairs or individually, depending on the number of students in a class and the number of computers. They also collaborated to solve problems arising during the development and design of their Web pages and gave each other feedback on the design and the content of their respective pages. As in other cases within this cluster, the teachers in this case engaged in a range of supporting behaviors but ultimately left the students with the responsibility of determining the design and content of their Web pages.

TUTORIAL CLUSTER

Cases containing the use of tutorials constituted another cluster with a unique set of common practices. In all cases within the Tutorial Cluster, tutorial or drill-and-practice software was used to support instruction. Students in all these cases used software packages that allowed them to work independently and receive feedback on their performance. An example of this use of ICT is in a primary math class in Catalonia, Spain (ES004) (Box 3.7). This case is typical in that cases in this cluster were more likely to be at the primary level (Table C.4.1, Appendix C) and more likely to be in math (Table C.12.1, Appendix C).

Box 3.7	USING A MATHEMATICS SOFTWARE PROGRAM TO PERFORM MENTAL CALCULATIONS

In the region of Catalonia in Spain, a mathematics software program called CLIC was developed by the local school administration as an extra resource for teaching basic arithmetic to students in a rural primary school. Students, with the oversight of a technology teacher, used the software 1 hour per week in the technology lab to develop their competence in mental calculations. The learning activities were divided into three blocks of increasing difficulty. Teachers programmed the activities so that in every packet pupils found different types of activities presented in different ways. Review and consolidation exercises followed after the packets were completed. Students worked independently on their assigned packets, while teachers provided assistance to those who needed it. The CLIC software program notified students of the percentage of correct answers; students could advance only if their performance was higher than 70%. With this software program, teachers at this primary school provided students with customized instruction at differing levels of difficulty. As a result, students were able to manage their own process of learning and advance at their own pace.

ES004

Another example of a primary math application of tutorial software is a case in the Slovak Republic (SK010). Here the teacher modeled the use of the software. Students used the software to experiment with different methods of counting and practiced multiplication and division operations. In addition to receiving feedback from the software on their performance, students were also monitored and given oral assessments by their teacher.

In the case of a primary school in Chile (CL010)—the "stellar case" for Chile—the teacher planned and prepared classroom activities that provided math content as well as the particular skills students needed to use the software package. Later, using exercise guides, students visited the computer lab accompanied by the teacher and divided into groups to work together on solving problems on the computer or to work at the classroom tables with their learning guides. The teacher also provided assistance to students in order to help them understand how to use the software to solve problems. Remarking on the students' experience of independent learning, the school principal explained the purpose of the activities:

The main objective of the experience is that the kids become capable of solving problems on their own. The teacher should not simply tell them how to solve a problem in such a way and then students just copy it down. The idea is that the student discovers how to arrive at the result, that students develop logical, sequential reasoning and are capable of resolving situations that may arise.

Language arts was another subject area addressed by some of the cases in this cluster. In a German primary school (DE012), teachers worked together in using English language software programs to complement student work in spelling or English vocabulary acquisition. Students spent at least one lesson-hour per day using the software to complete different assignments in the weekly plan. Students decided what task they would perform and when to complete the assignment.

Teachers in 75% of the cases in this cluster collaborated with colleagues and designed materials. An example of these teacher activities can be seen in the case of a primary school in China Hong Kong (CN010) that used drill-and-practice software to support autonomous learning activities. Developed by a research team at a local university in a government-supported project, this software was designed to help students understand the use of punctuation marks in the Chinese language. The software was designed to address a lack of teaching resources available for teaching Chinese punctuation, which teachers often overlooked. Using a PowerPoint slide presentation designed by three teachers at the school, instructors followed a prearranged sequence of giving students a pretest, presenting information about the rules of Chinese punctuation, and having the students work individually with the software before taking a posttest.

SIMILARITIES AND DIFFERENCES AMONG CLUSTERS

"The system is drifting away from frontal teaching, and students thereby have more opportunities of assuming responsibility for their behavior."

—TEACHER, DE012

The intent of our cluster analysis was to try to emphasize the distinctions among cases in their patterns of innovative practices. Consequently, we selected a statistical analysis that forced cases into one cluster or another. But while we emphasize the distinctiveness of the clusters in the preceding section, we should also comment on their similarities. There is considerable overlap among these clusters and the differences among them are primarily a matter of degree. In reading the cases, it would have been much more difficult to put a case indisputably in one cluster but not in another through manual sorting. For example, the Project Codename Future case (NL017) has many characteristics, such as students working together in pairs to develop action plans, pose research questions, and collect information by searching the Internet, which could have caused us to put it into the Student Collaborative Research Cluster. The Norwegian case (NO006) where students communicated with explorers crossing Antarctica was assigned to the Teacher Collaboration Cluster by cluster analysis, but it shares many characteristics with the Outside Communication Cluster.

While relatively small differences in patterns may account for the cluster assignments of some cases, a major finding of the study is that there is widespread use of a number of practices in these innovative cases, such as the teacher acting as an advisor and students collaborating with each other and using technology to search for information. Table 3.1 displays these similarities. For example, not only do all of the cases in the Product Creation Cluster involve the use of ICT to create products, but this practice also was exhibited in all of the cases in the Teacher Collaboration Cluster and the Information Management Cluster. In addition, 93% of the cases in the Tool Use Cluster and 86% of the cases in the Student Collaborative Research Cluster involved the use of ICT to create products.

While the Teacher Collaboration Cluster had the highest percentage of cases in which teachers collaborated with students (100%), colleagues (95%), and outside actors (42%), the Outside Communication, Information Management, and Tutorial Clusters also had a higher percentage of cases reporting colleague collaboration than the group of cases as a whole. Even when the mean percentages for clusters were lower than the overall mean, the incidence of certain practices was sometimes still quite high. For example, in 86% of the cases in the Tool Use Cluster, teachers provided students with advice, even though the mean for all cases was 90%. While the overall mean for within-class student collaboration was 83% and all of the cases in the Student Collaborative Research Cluster involved this practice, even in the Tutorial Cluster (the cluster with the lowest incidence of the practice) students collaborated with others in their class in 50% of the cases.

MODELS OF INNOVATIVE PEDAGOGICAL PRACTICES

Given the considerable overlap in practice, we looked at the patterns of similarities and differences among clusters to see if there was a core set of teacher, student, and ICT practices that might tie the clusters together and help characterize the use of ICT in these innovative classrooms from around the world. Starting with the patterns of highest and high cluster means listed in Table 3.1, we regrouped the variables in ways that brought the most frequently occurring patterns closest to the center of the chart. This reorganization is displayed in Table 3.3.

We used these analyses along with the results of the cluster analysis to combine considerations of commonality and distinctiveness. Table 3.3 shows how several teacher, student, and ICT practices cut across clusters. At the same time, it makes it easier to visualize the differences among clusters. We consider the shared practices that cut across clusters to be the basis for what could be called models of innovative pedagogical practices that use technology.

We found a core set of nine teacher, student, and ICT practices that are shared by many of the clusters. All of these practices were exhibited together more often than average in four of the clusters—the Student Collaborative Research Cluster, the Information Management Cluster, the Teacher Collaboration Cluster, and the Outside Communication Cluster. In this core model, teachers advise students, structure their activities, and monitor their progress. Students collaborate with others in their class and search for information. Teachers and students use e-mail and productivity tools. ICT supports the search for information and

Table 3.3

MODELS OF INNOVATIVE PEDAGOGICAL PRACTICES USING TECHNOLOGY

CLUSTERS						
Tool Use	**Student Collaborative Research**	**Information Management**	**Teacher Collaboration**	**Outside Communication**	**Product Creation**	**Tutorial**
			Outside Collaboration			
			Students collaborated outside.			
		Students created products and published results.				
		Teachers collaborated with peers and designed materials.				
	Students conducted research and solved problems.					
	Teachers advised students, structured their activities, and monitored their progress.					
	Students collaborated with others in their class and searched for information.					
	ICT supported the search for information and communication.					
	E-mail and productivity tools were used.					
	ICT supported product creation.					
	Multimedia, Web resources, and local area networks were used.	Product				
	ICT supported planning.					

Teacher Practices

Student Practices

ICT Used

communication with others. We call this core set of practices the Student Collaboration Model. Some of these practices were also exhibited more often than average in other clusters, except for the Tutorial Cluster. For example, the cases in the Product Creation Cluster often reported that students worked collaboratively to find information and that teachers advised students and structured the students' activities. But cases in this cluster were less likely than other cases to report that teachers monitored and assessed student progress. Again, this distinction is a matter of emphasis because 57% of the cases in this cluster did report these practices. But only in those clusters within the Student Collaboration Model were all of the practices present in large numbers of cases.

In addition to this core set of practices, other patterns augmented the Student Collaboration Model in some clusters to create several other additive models of pedagogical practices. In the Student Collaborative Research and Information Management clusters, students conducted research projects and solved problems. Teachers often designed materials. In addition to students collaborating in their use of e-mail and productivity tools to search for information, students used multimedia, Web resources, and local area networks to plan and create products. We refer to these patterns as the Student Research Model. Again, parts of this model were also exhibited in some other clusters. Specifically, the use of multimedia to create products was common in the Tool Use, Teacher Collaboration, and Product Creation Clusters.

Another pattern, which we call the Product Model, was shared by the Information Management and Teacher Collaboration Clusters. More often in these clusters than in other clusters, students created products and published or presented results. Similarly, teachers collaborated with their peers and designed instructional materials. Multimedia was used in addition to the e-mail and productivity tools of the core model, and this ICT supported the creation of products. The pattern of student creation and publication of products also occurred in the Outside Communication Cluster and, of course, the Product Creation Cluster. On the other hand, teachers typically did not collaborate with peers to design materials in the Product Creation Cluster. They often did in the Tutorial Cluster, while students did not. Consequently, these clusters do not quite fit the Product Model.

Finally, in the Teacher Collaboration and Outside Communication Clusters, students collaborated with others outside the class in what we call the Outside Collaboration Model. These are the only two clusters where student collaboration with outside actors occurred in more than 50% of the cases. In this model, students collaborated with outsiders in addition to the student practices of the Student Collaboration Model and the Product Model. That is, they collaborated with students both inside and outside the class; they searched for information; and they created and published products. Teachers also collaborated with peers in this model.

Further analysis showed that certain clusters and models were associated with a number of important teacher and student outcomes, as described in the case reports and coded on the cover sheets. Both the Information Management and the Student Collaborative Research Clusters—those clusters that participated in both the core Student Collaboration Model and the Student Research Model—were more likely to report the acquisition of new pedagogical skills by teachers (Table C.16.1, Appendix C). In addition, the Information Management Cluster was more likely to be associated with the acquisition of collaborative skills by teachers (Table C.16.3, Appendix C), as was the Teacher Collaboration Cluster.

Student acquisition of ICT skills (Table C.18.2, Appendix C), problem-solving skills (Table C.18.4, Appendix C), and team or collaborative skills (Table C.18.6, Appendix C) was also highly associated with the Collaborative Student Research and Information Management Clusters. Beyond this, the Information Management Cluster was also associated with student acquisition of communication skills (Table C.18.3, Appendix C) and information-handling skills (Table C.18.5, Appendix C), as described in the case reports.

As for other factors, cases in the Information Management and Student Collaborative Research Clusters were more likely to be involved in changes in the organization of the curriculum content (Table C.13.3, Appendix C) and the reallocation of curriculum time (Table C.13.4, Appendix C); in this respect, these cases brought down barriers within the curriculum. Cases in the Information Management Cluster were more likely to involve all subjects or at least a few, while cases in the Product Creation and Outside Communication Clusters were likely to involve just a few different subjects (Table C.11, Appendix C). The Student Collaborative Research Cluster was most likely to involve only one subject.

Cases in the Outside Communication Cluster brought down the barriers of the school walls. These cases were more likely to involve teachers and students from other schools (Table C.6.2, Appendix C), as well as actors from scientific or higher education institutions (Table C.6.3, Appendix C). They were also more likely to be involved in national, state, or regional projects (Table C.10.1, Appendix C). Finally, in regard to policy the Information Management and Student Collaborative Research Clusters were more likely to be associated with school ICT policies or plans (Table C.5, Appendix C), while those in the Outside Communication Cluster were less likely to be associated with school ICT policies or plans.

SIMILARITIES AND DIFFERENCES AMONG COUNTRIES

As mentioned in Chapter 2, SITES Module 2 was designed to be sensitive to national goals, priorities, and perspectives. In setting up the selection process, national panels reviewed and occasionally proposed modifications to international criteria. They also provided local definitions of "innovativeness." By intent, the selection of cases in SITES Module 2 was meant to reflect these local definitions of innovative practices.

In response to these opportunities, some countries narrowed the international criteria to make them more sensitive to local considerations. For example, with respect to the international criterion that ICT use should be associated with changes in the classroom, Korea, the Philippines, and Thailand all specifically mentioned that the teacher's role should shift from that of information source to guide and that the student's role should shift to that of active learner. Thailand further stated that it was looking for innovations where students collected information by themselves, worked as a group, collaborated with teachers, and evaluated their own learning process. Finland and Denmark placed emphasis on cross-curricular projects and the improvement of social competencies such as collaboration. They further stipulated that schools should demonstrate collaboration between classroom teachers, teacher colleges, and student teachers. Norway included practices that used ICT outside school in its criteria for selection.

Some countries specifically linked their definitions and selections to national policies. For example, Singapore said that to be innovative, as defined in its national Master Plan for IT in Education, a case must show evidence of a shift toward active, student-centered learning;

and it should either be original or significantly enhanced beyond existing practices. Thailand, referencing its National Education Act, indicated that in order to reform the current educational system and advance the information technology society, ICT would need to accelerate changes in the roles of teachers, students, school administrators, and parents in innovative ways.

Other countries interpreted the criteria broadly. For example, both the Czech Republic and Norway indicated that the selected group should represent the widest possible spectrum of different case models.

Given these opportunities to interject local considerations into the selection process, it is particularly impressive that so many trends cut across a wide range of cases from countries with diverse cultural backgrounds. This global commonality is a major finding of SITES Module 2.

Nonetheless, there were some important differences in the way cases were distributed across clusters for some countries. Cases for some countries were rather evenly distributed across clusters. For example, China Hong Kong's 8 cases, the U.S.'s 9 cases, and Israel's 10 cases were distributed across 6 clusters for each country. Norway's intent was to maximize the diversity of its 11 cases, so they were distributed across 7 clusters.

But the cases for some countries were concentrated in one or two clusters. For example, 4 of Finland's 6 cases were assigned to the Outside Communication Cluster, and 2 were assigned to the Teacher Collaboration Cluster, which most certainly reflects Finland's emphasis on collaboration in its criteria. Two other clusters—the Information Management Cluster and the Student Collaborative Research Cluster—were assigned cases from a fairly small group of countries that focused their practices in specific ways. Of Singapore's 6 cases, 3 were assigned to the Information Management Cluster and 1 to the Student Collaborative Research Cluster. (One of the cases was an "outlier.") The 5 cases from the Philippines were divided between the Information Management Cluster (3) and the Student Collaborative Research Cluster (2). All 3 of Chinese Taipei's cases fell in the Student Collaborative Research Cluster, and all 5 of Thailand's cases were assigned to the Information Management Cluster.

It is worth noting that the kinds of pedagogical practices found in the cases from these Asian countries are quite different from those reported in SITES Module 1. In Module 1, Asian countries generally scored lower than other countries on an index of emerging pedagogical practices, while they scored high on an index of traditional practices. Both the criteria proposed by Asian countries and the cases selected with these criteria would suggest that there are major developments occurring in Asian countries with regard to the use of ICT and pedagogical practices more like the emerging practices found in Module 1.

In these Asian countries and some others, the pattern of practices upon which the cluster sorts were based seemed to correspond in general ways to policies and programs that promoted not only technology in the schools but also technology-based changes in pedagogy or curricula. For example, the Ministry of Education in Finland has created a vision of the Finnish Information Society (Ministry of Education, Finland, 1999) that stresses, among other things, the "knowledge and skills needed to reform pedagogical practices in schools, especially with regard to collaborative teaching and learning, networking, and team work" (Kankaanranta & Linnakyla, in press). The Masterplan for IT in Education in Singapore connects the use of ICT to broader educational goals for its Thinking Schools, Learning

Nation vision. As Yeo, Kan, and Tham (in press) note, "Through the use of ICT, the younger generation will be equipped with learning skills, creative thinking skills, and communication skills." The National Education Act in Thailand specifies that instructional strategies should change the role of teachers and students to make students the center of the learning process (Ministry of Education, Thailand, 1999). We will return to the discussion of these national policies in Chapter 6.

SUMMARY AND CONCLUSIONS

Let us return to the research questions that began our chapter. The questions we addressed were:

What are the ICT-based pedagogical practices that countries consider to be innovative? How are these innovative practices similar and different from one country to another?

What new teacher and student roles are associated with innovative pedagogical practices using technology? How are innovations changing what teachers and students do in the classroom? How do they affect patterns of teacher-student and student-student interactions?

How do these practices change the classroom? In what ways does the use of ICT change the organization of the classroom, extend the school day, break down the walls of the classroom, and involve other actors (such as parents, scientists, or business people) in the learning process?

What capabilities of the applied technologies support innovative pedagogical practices? How do these capabilities shape the practices they support?

In answering these questions, we found much evidence of the "emerging pedagogical paradigm" found earlier by Pelgrum and Anderson (1999). But we also found some significant, if sometimes subtle, distinctions within this paradigm. Our detailed analysis allowed us to identify different patterns or clusters of classroom practices, different pedagogical models that employ ICT, and different factors and outcomes associated with these clusters and models.

INNOVATIVE PRACTICES AND NATIONAL DIFFERENCES

Twenty-eight countries from Europe, Asia, North America, South America, and Africa participated in SITES Module 2. These countries applied a common set of international criteria to select innovative cases from among their schools. The innovativeness of these cases was defined locally, yet there were many commonalities across cases and countries. In general, countries picked cases in which teachers changed their roles to become advisors and guides, while students took more active roles in their own learning, often in collaboration with other students. They used the Internet and productivity tools to search for information, communicate with others, and create products. The occurrence of these practices in Asian countries is particularly worthy of note, since Asian countries rarely exhibited the "emerging pedagogical paradigm" in SITES Module 1.

This commonality across cases and countries is a major finding of the study. Yet we do not want to overstate our results. Given the methods used for case selection, our findings do not represent typical practices across a majority or even a large number of schools in the countries that participated in our study. Rather, these cases appear to represent a common global vision of how ICT can and perhaps should change what is happening in classrooms and schools. These cases can serve as models for other schools and teachers.

Beyond this common vision, subtle but important differences in emphasis sometimes existed between countries. Some countries emphasized the use of technology to support the development of collaborative skills and teamwork. Other countries emphasized the development of creative thinking skills or student-centered pedagogy. These priorities influenced the cases that were selected as innovative practices.

NEW ROLES AND PRACTICES FOR TEACHERS AND STUDENTS

Our results provide evidence that supports findings from earlier case studies that changes in teacher and student roles and practices often occur with the use of ICT in the classroom (Law, Yuen, Ki, Li, Lee, & Chow, 2000; Means & Olson, 1995; Pelgrum & Anderson, 1999; Schofield & Davidson, 2002). Across the 174 cases in our study, teachers in a large majority of these innovative schools stepped back from their role of knowledge provider to advise students and create structure for their students' activities, as indicated by our coding of the cover sheets. Our cluster analysis also found that these teacher practices commonly occurred along with a pattern of certain student and ICT practices. In four of the seven clusters—Student Collaborative Research, Information Management, Teacher Collaboration, and Outside Communication—these new teacher practices corresponded to student practices in which students collaborated with others in their classes and searched for information. E-mail and productivity tools were used, and ICT supported the search for information and communication. We call this core set of practices the Student Collaboration Model. There was a relatively small and distinct set of practices associated with the use of ICT for tutoring and drill and practice. The common occurrence of the Student Collaboration Model across many cases from different countries is another major finding of this study.

In addition, this core model was augmented by other sets of coordinated practices in some clusters. In the Product Model both teachers and students created products. Typically, teachers collaborated with their colleagues in this effort and students published the results of their work. They used the multimedia, e-mail, and productivity tools of the core model, and this ICT supported product creation. In two of the clusters, students also conducted research and solved problems while using multimedia, Web resources, and local area networks to support product creation and planning. We called this set of practices the Student Research Model. Two clusters represented the Outside Collaboration Model, in which students collaborated with outside actors and other students in the class to create products and publish results. Teachers also collaborated with peers in this model.

While many of the clusters shared the core set of teacher and student roles and practices, this core pattern alone seemed insufficient when it came to teacher and student outcomes. It was when this core model was augmented by other practices that certain teacher and student outcomes were more likely to be reported in the cases. The Student Collaborative Research and Information Management Clusters—those clusters that combined both the core Student Collaboration Model and the Student Research Model—were associated with teacher acquisition of new pedagogical skills. These clusters were also associated with student acquisition of ICT skills, problem-solving skills, and team or collaborative skills.

The Information Management and Teacher Collaboration Clusters—those exhibiting the Product Model along with the core Student Collaboration Model—were associated with teacher acquisition of collaborative skills. Beyond this, the Information Management Cluster—the only cluster to participate in both the Student Research and Product Models as well as the core Student Collaboration Model—was associated with student acquisition of communication skills and information-handling skills, as reported in the case studies. This provides a more variegated set of practices for teachers and policy makers to consider, depending on their goals for educational change.

CHANGES IN THE CLASSROOM

Across cases and clusters, we noticed significant patterns in the reorganization of the classroom. Student group work was widely observed and was at the core of the Student Collaboration Model. Often these groups and their projects cut across subject domains. Very few instances were reported of students sitting in rows, working individually on computers in a single subject domain. Student collaboration with others in the use of e-mail and productivity tools to search for information and communicate with others seems to be part of the new, worldwide consensus. In this regard, ICT is beginning to break down some of the traditional barriers within the classroom—barriers between students, between subject areas, and between teachers and students.

But for the most part this change in classroom structure stayed within the classroom. Only in two clusters—Teacher Collaboration and Outside Communication—was there a large number of cases in which teachers and students connected and collaborated with others outside the classroom. But even in these clusters, the communication was almost exclusively with other teachers and students. Overall, few innovations involved participation in national and international programs. There were very few cases in which teachers and students used ICT to collaborate with scientists, professors, and business people. There were far fewer yet that connected parents to the classroom. It seems, by and large, that the schoolhouse walls are still firmly in place, even in the most innovative classrooms in the world.

THE ROLE OF ICT

Finally, we address the question of the role of ICT in support of these innovative practices. We found that ICT played a central role in the innovations that were submitted to the study. This should not be surprising; it was one of the international criteria for selecting cases. But in the large majority of cases, it was not innovative technologies that were used. The dominant technologies used in these classes were commonly available ones, such as productivity tools, e-mail, and the Web. Few cases used simulations, microcomputer-based laboratories, collaborative environments, or course management systems. In the large majority of cases, teachers used *ordinary* technology to do *innovative* things. It was not the tools that were innovative but the pedagogical practices.

However, certain patterns of ICT use corresponded with certain patterns of innovative teacher and student practices. The core Student Collaboration Model involved the use of e-mail and productivity tools in support of the search for information and communication with others, but these resources seemed insufficient by themselves. The two clusters that combined the core Student Collaboration Model with the Student Research Model were more often associated with claims that ICT added significantly to the innovation. Case reports in the Information Management and Student Collaborative Research Clusters were more likely to describe ICT as supporting changes in student practices, providing direct support for student learning, providing additional resources, changing the time or structure of the classroom, and inhibiting undesirable outcomes.

In these latter clusters—the ones most often associated with many positive teacher and student outcomes—students used networked multimedia and Web resources, e-mail, and productivity tools to conduct research, solve problems, create products, and publish their results. It seems that in these cases, the use of ICT came closest to the kinds of practices envisioned by researchers for technology-rich classrooms (Kozma & Schank, 1998; OECD, 2001a, 2001b; Riel, 1998).

CHAPTER 4

ICT AND THE curriculum

By Joke Voogt and
Willem J. Pelgrum

INTRODUCTION

The massive economic and societal changes that frame this book have implications for the curriculum as well as pedagogy. These changes entail new skills, abilities, attitudes, and habits for employees in the knowledge economy and for citizens of the information society. Consequently, the changes call for new curricular goals and outcomes for students and teachers. Policy papers (European Commission, 2000, 2001b; OECD, 1996, 1999) suggest that beyond knowledge of subject domains—such as science, mathematics, and literature—students need to able to search for and select relevant information; interpret and analyze data; work with diverse, distributed teams; solve problems; create new knowledge and cultural artifacts; and develop capabilities to learn new skills and knowledge as needed. Teachers need to be able to take on new roles and acquire new pedagogical skills that support this kind of student learning.

In addition, information and communication technology (ICT) must take on new roles in schools. While technology has been a subject in the traditional curriculum, the findings discussed in Chapter 3 and other classroom research studies (Means & Olson, 1997; Means, Penuel, & Padilla, 2001; Sandholtz, Ringstaff, & Dwyer, 1997; Schofield & Davidson, 2002) suggest that ICT can be a more integral part of the new curriculum and can support the development of skills that students need for the future.

In this chapter we address the following research questions related to the curriculum:

How are the innovative pedagogical practices in the Second Information Technology in Education Study (SITES) Module 2 related to changes in curriculum content and goals? Have these practices changed what students are learning and what teachers need to know? Have they changed the way student outcomes are assessed? What impact do they have on student competencies, attitudes, and other outcomes?

As in Chapter 3, we want to examine the role that ICT may play in these changes. Specifically, we want to revisit these two questions:

What capabilities of the applied technology support innovative pedagogical practices? How do these capabilities shape the practices they support?

To be able to tackle these questions, we must first conceptualize the term *curriculum*. Marsh and Willis (1999) define *curriculum* as "an interrelated set of experiences that a student undertakes under the guidance of the school." The concept of curriculum, according to this definition, is not just the content and goals of education but also the instructional experiences that are encountered in the classroom and the outcomes that result from these processes. To describe these aspects of the curriculum, Marsh and Willis use the terms *planned curriculum*, *enacted curriculum*, and *experienced curriculum*. The *planned curriculum* describes the content and formal goals that are intended for the schools. Because the focus of SITES Module 2 is on classroom practices, we examine the planned curriculum at the school level. In the conceptual framework for this study, planned goals and content at the national or state level are considered as a context within which school practices operate. For some of the innovations this might imply that changes in the curriculum content and goals could not be made because national and state curriculum requirements were too restrictive. The *enacted curriculum* is the curriculum as it is actually taught or operationalized at the classroom level. It describes whether and how content and goals are implemented. In this chapter, enacted curriculum refers to the organization of the innovations and the concrete student and teacher activities that take place. Since a detailed analysis of teacher and learning activities has been presented in the previous chapter, this chapter describes teacher and student activities only when the description is necessary to an understanding of changes in content and goals. The *experienced curriculum* describes the actual outcomes of education—the knowledge, skills, and attitudes that students have acquired. The outcomes of education are affected not only by goals and instructional processes but also by the way the outcomes themselves are assessed (Black & Wiliam, 1998; Plomp & Loxley, 1993). Therefore, assessment practices are also an indispensable part of the curriculum. Our focus is on classroom assessment rather than national examinations; however, these national exams often shape and constrain how teachers assess students in the classroom.

In this chapter, we examine changes in curriculum content and goals as they relate to the innovative pedagogical practices that are the focus of this study. But we also want to understand the impact of these changes on outcomes for students and teachers, as well as the extent to which assessment practices have been altered because of these changes.

ICT AND THE CURRICULUM

In the knowledge economy and information society, citizens need to be able to search for, analyze, and manage huge amounts of information; they also must be able to use that information to solve complex problems and create new knowledge and cultural products (OECD, 2001). Changes in workplace organization require employees to work collaboratively in teams. The structure of jobs changes quickly and job responsibilities are fluid; the knowledge needed to do these jobs also changes. Many students who are about to start their school careers will, upon graduation, get a job of a sort that does not currently exist. Some of the knowledge that was current when they entered school will be outdated by new discoveries. It is often argued, therefore, that students need to develop lifelong learning skills and that this should be a major goal and outcome of education (European Commission, 2001b). This requires students to develop the capability of setting their own goals, planning their own learning, and evaluating their success, sometimes referred to as metacognitive skills (Bransford, Brown, & Cocking, 2000).

It is also argued that such major changes in society require other approaches to teaching and learning, perhaps even radical reforms in education (OECD, 2001). Instead of pedagogy that focuses mainly on transfer of defined knowledge and skills, new approaches are required that emphasize a more active involvement of students. Voogt and Odenthal (1999) conducted an extensive review of the literature to distinguish features of a curriculum that reflect these changes in society and new visions of teaching and learning. They summarize the characteristics of a curriculum for the knowledge economy and information society as follows:

1. New goals that reflect the demands of the information society imply the need for students to become competent in information management, communication and collaboration, and metacognition.

2. Less structured sources of information will become important as learning materials.

3. The traditional boundaries between subjects need to be bridged. Content should not be divided into isolated facts and topics but offered in an integrated way. In addition, students need to be able to understand relations between concepts instead of being able to just reproduce facts.

4. The current gap between discipline-related content taught in schools and the application of knowledge in real life also needs to be bridged. The curriculum should be centered on authentic problems parallel to those in real-world settings.

5. The boundaries between the school and the outside world need to fade. It is expected that students will spend less time in the classroom and the school. Moreover, instruction in the classroom needs to move from an approach focused on teaching 30 children to one focused on meeting the needs of individual learners.

Changing content and goals implies other ways of assessing students. Instead of measuring the extent to which students are able to reproduce knowledge, assessment must measure students' ability to apply knowledge in realistic settings. Consequently, closed formats of assessment need to be changed to more open formats, such as portfolio and performance assessment. Also, more emphasis must be placed on formative assessment, in place of the current focus on summative assessment.

ICT can contribute to the realization of such a new vision of teaching and learning. First, technology is itself a major factor in the transition to a knowledge economy and information society. Consequently, the application of ICT to manage information and solve problems is an important set of skills. Also, various applications of ICT can support the pedagogical changes that are needed to implement new curricular visions.

Dede (2000) lists the ICT capabilities that can enhance learning and change the curriculum. ICT and multimedia can create authentic problem situations that parallel those in real-world settings. Networked communications can involve students in virtual communities of practice, in which they use advanced tools similar to those in today's high-tech workplaces. ICT learning tools and environments can facilitate guided, reflective inquiry through extended projects in which students can generate complex products and acquire sophisticated concepts and skills. Modeling and visualization software can be a powerful means of bridging experience and abstraction. Collaborative environments can enhance students' joint construction of meaning via different perspectives on shared experiences. Environments designed for special needs can foster success for all students and aid the disabled and the disenfranchised.

The question we address in this chapter is the extent to which the innovative classrooms in our study are currently using the capabilities of ICT to make significant changes in the curriculum. We want to investigate to what extent the innovations studied in SITES Module 2 imply or are associated with changes in curriculum content and goals, what consequences these changes have on student and teacher outcomes, and to what extent assessment practices have changed in response to changes in content and goals.

SELECTION OF CASES

In Chapter 2, we described how the International Coordinating Committee (ICC) of SITES Module 2 conducted an initial analysis of the 174 case reports we received from participating countries. We described how the ICC read the reports and characterized them using a cover sheet coding scheme based on our conceptual framework, also described in Chapter 2.

In our analyses of the cover sheet codes, we found that the innovative practices in this study occurred across all grade levels and across the broad expanse of the curriculum, from mathematics (21% of the cases) and physics (13%) to history (16%), language (32% mother tongue, 24% foreign language), and creative arts (20%). Of the total, 49 cases (28%) were multidisciplinary in nature. As described in the case reports, many cases were involved in curriculum change. Of the total number of cases, 27% described changes in content, 37% described new curricular goals (other than ICT skills or regular subject matter goals), 68% were involved in reorganization of the content, and 36% described a reallocation of time in the curriculum. The cases were fairly evenly divided among those that involved one specific subject (29%), a few subject areas (37%), and many or all subjects in the school (32%).

In addressing the research questions for this chapter, we are primarily interested in changes of curricular goals and content. Consequently, in deciding which cases to focus on in our detailed analysis, we looked at those that reported either a change in curriculum content or new curricular goals, as previously mentioned. Since cases could be involved in both kinds of changes, the subset of the 174 cases that were engaged in curriculum change of interest to us were 91 cases, or 52% of the total.

But we are also interested in the role ICT might play in these changes. Consequently, we looked at the cover sheet coding that characterized the kinds of value that ICT added to the innovation (see Question 22 in Appendix B.2). The two sorts of ICT impact that we used to focus our analysis were those that contributed to changes in the curriculum (in 16% of the cases) and those that contributed to education reform more generally (25% of the cases). The subset of the whole that contributed to either or both of these types of change consisted of 59 cases, or 34% of the total.

To select a group of cases that would allow us to answer both of these questions, we crossed the first subgroup with the second. That is, we wanted to examine those cases that either changed content or introduced new goals, and those where ICT either contributed to curriculum change or education reform. The result is a group of 32 cases, or 18% of the total. We used these cases, listed in Table 4.1, in our detailed analysis for this chapter. We used *Atlas ti* software to code in more detail the segments of the cases that described the curriculum goals and content of the innovations.

Table 4.1

SELECTED CASES FOR ANALYSIS

PRIMARY EDUCATION	LOWER SECONDARY EDUCATION	UPPER SECONDARY EDUCATION
AU002	AU001	CZ00
AU004	DE002	CZ003
CN003	DE003	DE006
CN010	IL013 (plus upper secondary)	DE013
DE007	KR004	DE015
FR001	NO005	FI004
FR002	NO007	FR006
IL001	PH003	IL009
IL003	SG004	NL025
IT001		PH002
NO004		US014
		ZA008

First, it should be noted that this number is in itself a significant finding of our study. As discussed previously in this chapter, it may very well be that teachers in the schools that we studied are limited in the kinds of changes that they can make by the curriculum and examination policies at the national or state level. (The implications of policy for this study are examined in Chapter 6.) But it is significant that only 32 cases out of the 174 submitted by national panels reported significant changes in curriculum content or goals, and that ICT had an impact on curriculum or education reform more generally, as characterized by the cover sheet coding. Consequently, it would appear that these ICT-based innovations from 28 countries around the world are focused primarily on ICT-supported pedagogical practices as described in Chapter 3, rather than ICT-supported curriculum change.

However, our attention to this small number of cases is warranted not just by the fact that they map to our research questions but also by the analysis displayed in Table 4.2. In this analysis we compared the selected cases to nonselected cases on a number of cover sheet codes related to issues we address in this chapter. The table indicates that the selected cases do indeed provide information on outcomes and assessment practices and therefore serve as a good basis for analyzing the research questions of this chapter.

By way of comparison, we are also interested in examining some of the cases that did not meet our selection criteria. Of the 174 cases, 142 did not meet our criteria for one reason or another. The cases of most interest to us were the ones where curriculum changes occurred but ICT did not seem to play a part in those changes. In 59 cases, curriculum change (change in content, change in goals other than subject matter or relative to ICT, or both) was coded, but there were no clear indications that ICT had added value for curriculum change or educational reform. In the context of SITES Module 2, with case selections based on innovation and ICT use, one would expect that if a change in the curriculum was mentioned, it would also be perceived as being supported by ICT. On the other hand, it may be that curricular changes and ICT use co-occur in these cases but there may be no dependency between the two. For example, an innovation may involve curriculum change, but the use of ICT may be focused more on any pedagogical change that also occurs. We randomly selected 28 (50%) of the 59 cases that could throw light on the reason why ICT was not perceived as being supportive of curriculum change.

Another group of interest are those cases in which the curriculum did not change, or in which ICT did not support curricular change or education reform. This was so in 56 cases, according to the cover sheet codes. In these cases, ICT-based innovation did not affect curriculum change. There may be a number of reasons for this. For instance, the innovation may have taken place as an extracurricular activity and therefore did not affect the school curriculum. We randomly selected 23 cases (50%) of the 56 in this group for further examination, making sure (where applicable) that at least 1 case from each country was represented. Consequently, we examined a total of 51 cases beyond those selected as the group that we would draw on to answer our questions.

Table 4.2

COMPARISON OF SELECTED AND NONSELECTED CASES ON OTHER FACTORS
Percent of each group

Questions	ALL CASES (n = 174)	ALL NONSELECTED CASES (n = 142)	SELECTED CASES (n = 32)
Does this case describe changes in the curriculum related to:			
Content	27.0	19.7	59.1
Goals	37.4	29.6	71.9
Organization	68.4	67.6	71.9
Time	36.2	35.2	40.6
Does this case describe alternative assessment procedures:			
Assessment	60.3	42.3	71.9
Does this case describe impacts on teachers in terms of:			
New Pedagogical Skills	56.9	54.9	65.6
ICT Skills	63.2	63.4	62.5
Collaborative Skills	35.1	30.3	56.3
Positive Attitudes	21.3	19.0	31.3
Negative Outcomes	7.5	5.6	15.6
Does this case describe impacts on students in terms of:			
Subject Matter Knowledge	62.6	63.4	59.4
ICT Skills	75.3	73.2	84.4
Communication Skills	39.7	37.3	50.0
Problem-Solving Skills	19.0	16.2	31.3
Information-Handling Skills	28.7	26.1	40.6
Teamwork and Collaborative Skills	62.6	59.9	75.0
Metacognitive Skills	38.5	38.0	40.6
Positive Attitudes	68.4	68.3	68.0
Outcomes for Different Groups	20.1	16.9	34.4
Negative Outcomes	19.0	16.9	28.1
Added Value of ICT			
Added Value for Curriculum Change	16.1	16.2	62.5
Added Value for Educational Reform	24.7	8.5	50.0

APPROACH TO THE ANALYSIS

For the 32 cases in our primary sample, we read the case reports and used *Atlas.ti* to code specific text segments related to curriculum and ICT use. We used two organizing themes to code the data. The first theme was based on the curricular distinctions of Marsh and Willis (1999): planned, enacted, and experienced curricula. We also coded for the added value ICT had for these curricular changes. Within these aspects of the curriculum, we coded for the following kinds of factors:

- Planned curriculum: changes in content and goals of the curriculum

- Enacted curriculum: teacher and student activities; changes in curriculum organization

- Experienced curriculum: changes in assessment practices; teacher and student outcomes

A second organizing theme emerged as we coded the cases. We found quite large differences between cases in terms of the focus of curricular change. A major distinction appeared between schoolwide innovations (involving multiple subjects) and innovations that were more limited in scope. Regarding the latter, a further distinction could be made; a number of cases were oriented on single-discipline-based subjects, while others seemed to be of a cross-curricular nature, using themes instead of academic disciplines to organize the curriculum. The distinctions are as follows:

- Single-Subject Curricular Focus: the innovation is situated within discipline-based subjects; ICT is used primarily to improve students' understanding of subject matter content and concepts.

- Thematic Curricular Focus: the innovation is of a cross-curricular nature; curriculum content is offered through themes; ICT is used to facilitate the implementation of lifelong learning goals.

- Schoolwide Curricular Focus: ICT-supported pedagogical practices are integrated throughout the school curriculum; ICT facilitates the realization of the school's vision on teaching and learning.

In Table 4.3 we present the division of the cases according to these three emerging themes. In the following sections we also use these themes to organize the presentation of the results of our analysis. We describe results for each curricular focus, organized by changes in content and goals (planned curriculum), changes in curriculum organization and instructional method (enacted curriculum), and assessments of student and teacher outcomes (experienced curriculum).

Table 4.3

THREE TYPES OF CURRICULUM FOCUS BY CASE

SINGLE-SUBJECT FOCUS	THEMATIC FOCUS	SCHOOLWIDE FOCUS
(n = 11)	(n = 13)	(n = 8)
CN003	AU001	AU002
CN010	CZ002	AU004
DE006	CZ003	DE003
DE015	DE002	IL003
FI004	DE007	NO004
IL009	DE013	NO005
KR004	FR001	US014
NL025	FR002	SG004
NO007	FR006	
PH002	IL001	
PH003	IL013	
	IT001	
	ZA008	

RESULTS

SINGLE-SUBJECT CURRICULAR FOCUS

Changes in Content and Goals

From the cover sheet coding, 10 of the 11 cases with a single-subject focus reported a change in content; four of them also mentioned a change in goals other than subject matter or ICT-related goals. However, our in-depth analysis showed that most of the innovations in this pattern did not involve new content in the curriculum. Rather, these innovations tended to focus on more in-depth content coverage of curriculum content. Changes in the curriculum were described in terms of goals that emphasized critical thinking or problem solving. In some cases, i.e., the German math innovation (DE015) (Box 4.9) and the innovations from Finland (FI004) (Box 4.3) and Israel (IL009) (Box 4.10), emphasis was also placed on students acquiring the ability to direct their own learning process.

The main reason for introducing the innovation in a lower secondary school in Korea (KR004, Box 4.11) was to develop better understanding of science. The traditional approach in this school, where the teacher presented research results to the students, was replaced by a curriculum where students were actively involved in their own research. Students conducted lab experiments and simulations and wrote up their results. The goal of the innovation was to improve students' ability to solve problems and improve their way of thinking.

Box 4.1   INTERACTIVE TOOLKIT FOR MATHEMATICS

The interactive toolkit for mathematics (ITM) helped ninth-grade students learn concepts in basic analytic geometry. ITM provided students with a new way to create simple geometric figures, explore the relationships among quantities represented in the figures, and make conjectures about these properties. The use of ITM in the innovation was aimed at developing critical thinking in mathematics and made it easier for students to understand mathematical concepts through self-exploratory activities.

PH003

Students used graphic calculators in a German upper secondary math class (DE015) to develop their ability to solve complex, authentic problems. Similar statements were made in the case report of the innovation of a 10th-grade science class from the Philippines (PH002).

In only a few cases was new content added to the curriculum, sometimes replacing old content. The original curriculum content was replaced with new content in the Cyber Art Project from China Hong Kong (CN003) (Box 4.2), a case mentioned in Chapter 3 and described as a stellar innovation in Chapter 7. The innovation was aimed at developing students' aesthetic sense and vision, helping them understand the language of art, developing their creativity in producing visual art, and helping them realize the vision of extending computer art. According to one of the teachers, the art curriculum had changed as a result of the Cyber Art Project; in addition, traditional sketching via computer graphics also became part of the curriculum. Similarly, the use of the computer was new in the German art class (DE006) (Box 4.5).

Box 4.2   CYBER ART PROJECT

Students from primary Grades 4–6 used laptop computers in art lessons and in the Computer Art Club extracurricular activities. The laptops made outdoor sketching possible and the wireless feature enabled students to connect flexibly to the school network while working anywhere, indoors or outdoor, within the school premises. The focus of this innovation was on motivating students' creativity and interest in learning art.

CN003

In the innovation on Chinese punctuation, also mentioned in Chapter 3 (CN010) (Box 4.8), a new curriculum topic was not introduced in the curriculum, but the topic in the innovation was hardly ever taught in China Hong Kong schools because of lack of materials. The software developed in the innovation on Chinese punctuation made it possible to teach the content.

Box 4.3	A WEB DEVELOPMENT COURSE

Upper secondary school students could take a Web course as an elective. The students needed 20 study weeks over 3 years to complete the course. At the end of the course they got a certificate. The goals of the Web course were to provide students with good technical capabilities, improve their capabilities in working with groups and in customer service, and improve their capabilities in understanding business activities. The goals also included helping students to adopt a constructive attitude for rapidly changing circumstances and skills for independent work.

FI004

In the WISE Project (NO007) (Box 4.7), one of the Norwegian cases, the curricular purpose of the innovation was to encourage students to engage in and evaluate science-related content on the Internet. The topics were chosen not because they were part of the curriculum but because they were debated in public and therefore attractive to students. From this perspective one might say that the curriculum content had changed. However, it is not clear from the case report to what extent the innovation replaced formal curriculum content or whether it was just an addition to the curriculum.

Two innovations at the upper secondary level, one in Finland (FI004) and one in Israel (IL009), were extensions to programs of the usual general secondary education curriculum and can therefore be typified as aiming at new curriculum content. In these innovations, courses were offered with the goal of providing students with high-level ICT knowledge and skills. Students took these programs on a voluntary basis. Significant for both programs was that they did not isolate ICT skills from the professional context in which those skills would be used.

Box 4.4	MICROCOMPUTER-BASED PERSONAL SCIENCE LABORATORY

The innovation simulated the conduct of laboratory work of 10th-grade students in a relatively high-tech setting. The goals were to enable the students to learn physics experientially and to facilitate the gathering of data as they conducted experiments using the computer-based Personal Science Laboratory Kits. The innovation was designed for self-paced learning. The goal was the same for all types of learners: to enhance the development of critical-thinking skills through hands-on investigation, in-depth verification, exploration, and discovery of science concepts and processes.

PH002

Changes in Curriculum Activities and Organization

In the majority of the innovations with a Single-Subject Curricular Focus, the curricular goals were realized through certain kinds of classroom activities, either research projects carried out by students (five cases; for a typical example see KR004) or student project work aimed at creating products (four cases; for a typical example see DE006). For example, in the WISE innovation (NO007), students prepared themselves for a debate on an actual topic. They read texts, watched movies, answered questions, and made discussion notes. In the German math class (DE015), students researched complex and authentic math problems.

Box 4.5	WHY THE SCHOOL WAS GIVEN THE NICKNAME "FACTORY"

The innovation took place every week for a period of approximately 4 months, within the framework of the art lessons in an 11th-grade setting. Students had to compare the characteristics of the architecture of their school with those of industrial buildings. They collaborated in small groups. ICT was used for research purposes and for the presentation of the project results on a Web page.

DE006

The students' activities were focused on the collection and processing of information (seven cases), and students drew conclusions or created a product. In addition, problem solving and the manipulation and interpretation of data were important student activities in cases where students conducted research projects. In these cases, the kind of research or the products that were prepared were closely related to the field of study. In the innovations that dealt with science, for instance, such as the Philippine case (PH002) and the Korean case (KR004), students formulated their own hypotheses and carried out experiments. They compared their results, drew conclusions, and presented a report about their findings. Students in the two upper secondary school cases in Finland (FI004) and Israel (IL009) prepared products for real clients. In the Israeli case, for instance, students constructed software for high-tech companies that were located in a nearby industrial area.

Student collaboration was very important in 11 cases. The teachers involved in the innovations considered the interaction between students to be important because it helped students to better understand the concepts they had to deal with. As expressed by the Norwegian teacher from the WISE Project (NO007) (Box 4.7), "I emphasise that the students discuss between each other when they read a text or look at a picture. They need a discussion before they write down the answers."

In many cases with a Single-Subject Curricular Focus, teacher activities involved structuring student work (10 cases), guiding students (10 cases), and monitoring their progress (8 cases). In the Philippine math case (PH003) (Box 4.1), for instance, the teacher started the lesson with a short lecture in which she set goals for the students, reviewed related concepts, and worked with students to address their difficulties. Two other major tasks of the teachers in the cases in this group were to prepare materials and to mediate content. For example, in the Chinese Punctuation Project (CN010), three teachers worked together to design the activities of this innovation. Two of these teachers actually taught the class, and the third teacher developed the software.

Most innovations in this pattern were carried out within the structure of a typical lesson. Sometimes some minor changes in lesson organization had to be made, but in general the innovations did not greatly affect the curriculum planning at the school level. To some extent the Cyber Art Project from China Hong Kong (CN003) was different because extracurricular activities were added to regular art lessons. For the German math class (DE015) the innovation had to be planned during a specific period in the school year.

A lesson typical of innovations with a single-subject focus was organized as follows: after a short introduction from the teacher, the students spent the majority of their time in interaction with the software. The teacher moved through the classroom to help the students when necessary. At the end of the lesson, time was spent with the whole class discussing the findings. Most of the lessons took place in the classroom or the computer lab. During the interaction with the software the students explored concepts (secondary school cases) or practiced skills (primary school cases). One innovation was very different. In the Dutch case on managing animal husbandry (NL025) (Box 4.6) students planned their own time for working on the assignments, which were located in a Web environment.

Box 4.6	COLLABORATIVE LEARNING AND ANIMAL HUSBANDRY

The course on managing animal husbandry was taught to students in Grade 13 at three locations of the school. The students had to do an analysis of the economic aspects of an existing cattle farm and discuss their analysis with students at the other locations. Subject matter and course assignments were placed in an electronic learning environment.

NL025

Changes in Assessment Practices

In most of the 11 cases with a single-subject focus, other ways of assessment were adopted. The only exceptions were the tutorial on Chinese punctuation (CN010), the course on managing animal husbandry (NL025), the German art class (DE006), and the science-learning environment from Korea (KR004).

In the other cases, procedures emphasized formative assessment through feedback from the teacher or through self-assessment and peer assessment. In some innovations, ICT was used to support these assessment strategies. For example, in the Cyber Art Project from China Hong Kong (CN003) students assessed their own artwork and that of other students. ICT was perceived as supportive because the drawings of the students could easily be shown to others and comments could be collected. Moreover, the case report argued that students could easily make improvements based on the comments.

In the Norwegian WISE Project (NO007), the teacher reviewed the online work of the students and provided them with online feedback after each session. The researchers stated in their case report, "In this way the teacher had the opportunity to see the process that lead to a finished product." In the Philippine math case (PH003), students could take a formative test, which was an integrated part of the software.

Box 4.7   WEB-BASED INTEGRATED SCIENCE ENVIRONMENT

The innovation was related to the use of a program called Web-Based Integrated Science Environment (WISE) in an eighth-grade science and environment class. WISE is a free online science-learning environment that was used to provide context, sequence, and support for students as they critically evaluated and engaged with existing content on the Internet.

NO007

The procedures for summative assessment changed in these cases. In the Finnish ICT course (FI004) and the Philippine science case reports (PH002), it was mentioned that portfolios were used for summative assessment next to more traditional assessment procedures, such as lab reports and paper-and-pencil tests. In the Israeli innovation (IL009), a working final project was used for assessment. One of the teachers said,

> I don't grade students and I don't test them either. I constantly explain to them that what I want is that they understand the material, that they know it and internalize it, and this I check. I give them assignments on an application level … and on this application I grade them. The truth is, I tell them, you don't need marks. If you manage to do it on your own, you can grade yourselves.

In the two Philippine cases (PH003 and PH002) it was reported that summative assessment was still based on paper-and-pencil tests but that the content of the assessment had changed due to the focus on critical thinking. For instance, in the math case the researchers reported that "instead of 'the what and the how' questions, the tests measured higher-order thinking skills that focused on 'the why' and on determining relationships, identifying differences, and inferring."

Student Outcomes

In all case reports that had a Single-Subject Curricular Focus, there were indications that the innovation improved subject matter knowledge and/or subject-matter-related skills. This is a particularly distinctive feature of cases in this group and not a surprising one, given that the curricular goals focused on better learning of the subject matter. For instance, by comparing students' pretest and posttest results, teachers of the China Hong Kong innovation on Chinese punctuation (CN010) found that their students made great improvement in their knowledge of Chinese punctuation. The students agreed with their teachers and said that they found themselves more competent in using Chinese punctuation after working with the software. In the Cyber Art Project (CN003), also from China Hong Kong, the students believed that the use of ICT helped them improve their drawing. As one student said, "At the end of each lesson, the teacher will upload our work to the servers and show it to the whole class. We can comment on each other's work, and improvement will be made." Also, the teacher involved in the Korean science project (KR004) mentioned that the reports turned in by the students who were involved in the innovation were more complete than the reports from the other students. The teacher involved in the Norwegian WISE Project (NO007) emphasized that because of the combination of pictures, sound, and text used in the WISE program, it seemed that the students remembered better what they had worked with.

Box 4.8	CHINESE PUNCTUATION

Grade 6 students followed a series of lessons that aimed at helping them learn about punctuation marks in Chinese Language. The teachers made use of self-developed PowerPoint presentations and software developed by the University of Hong Kong. While the students played the role of active learners in the learning process, ICT acted as a tool for demonstration and drill and practice.

CN010

Given the curricular goals of this group, it was a little unexpected that only three case reports—the Philippine math case (PH003), the German math class (DE015), and the Dutch course on managing animal husbandry (NL025)—mentioned that problem-solving skills were an important impact of the innovation. From the perspective of the goals that were aimed at in most cases, namely, providing students with critical thinking skills, one would expect that more case reports would have reported impacts in this domain. Apparently these outcomes were not perceived as separate from subject matter but were included as an integrated part of subject matter.

ICT skills were also mentioned as an important student outcome in all but one of the innovations analyzed in this section (CN003). This finding is also somewhat unexpected, given that the goals of this group of cases were primarily focused on the subject matter. Apparently, student use of ICT as a medium for enhancing the learning of subject matter had the side effect of also contributing to the development of ICT skills. Of course, the two upper secondary cases from Israel and Finland were an exception because their aim was to achieve high-level ICT skills.

Box 4.9	SELF-DIRECTED LEARNING IN MATHEMATICS

About 70 students in 11th- and 12th-grade classes were involved in this innovation, which aimed at self-directed learning in math. The students used a specially designed Web environment with mathematics tasks and a graphic calculator to solve complex but authentic math problems. To reflect on their learning process, the students used a "learning diary."

DE015

In 5 of the 11 cases in this group, students gained collaboration skills as a result of the innovation, according to case reports. In 2 of the upper secondary cases (FI004 and IL009), this was the result of having to work for a client. The researchers in the Finnish case reported that "students learned to know that everybody had their own special skills and abilities." In the Cyber Art Project (CN003) from China Hong Kong and the German math class (DE015), the fact that students helped classmates was seen as an important gain from the innovation. Also in the Philippine science case (PH002), collaboration was seen as an important outcome associated with the innovation. As with ICT skills, collaboration skills were not explicitly mentioned as curricular goals for these cases. However, collaboration took place during instruction in many of these cases, and student acquisition of collaboration skills was perceived as having an important impact by the teachers involved. The acquisition of communication skills was mentioned in 2 case reports.

Box 4.10	THE CENTER FOR LEADERSHIP AND EXCELLENCE IN TECHNOLOGY

The Center for Leadership and Excellence in Technology at this school enabled students in Grades 10–12 to learn in an ICT-enriched environment shaped as an innovative high-tech enterprise. The center cooperated with high-tech factories in the region to develop technological-management reserves. Besides ICT-related courses, the curriculum included courses in subjects such as business entrepreneurship, creative thinking, and planning and producing projects with the support of industrialists.

IL009

Metacognitive skills were mentioned as an impact of the innovation in 5 of the 11 case reports. These skills were seen as an important goal in the German math class (DE015) and the Finnish (FI004) and Israeli cases (IL009). In the German math class the teachers observed that the students had become more independent. They took more responsibility for their learning process and were more able to articulate their learning interests. Metacognitive skills were mentioned as an impact of the innovation even though these skills were not an explicit curricular goal. According to the researchers who studied the Korean science-learning environment (KR004), "The biggest difference that the innovation brought about was that the students changed from receivers who simply swallow presented materials to constructors who create their personal knowledge." Both of the Philippine case reports also mentioned that the students became more self-directed.

The general impression that we got from the analysis of this group of cases is that most students had positive attitudes toward the new approach to teaching and learning. Students experienced the innovation as motivating. The principal of the China Hong Kong school that organized the Cyber Art Project (CN003) said:

> It reduced the sense of failure and increased students' self-competence in doing the artwork. ... This is especially beneficial for low-ability students. Students particularly liked the approach because they could be more active; instead of sitting quietly, they could work on their own with the computer, and this made their learning much more interesting.

| Box 4.11 | LEARNING ENVIRONMENT FOR THE SCIENCE CURRICULUM |

The innovation focused on improving eighth-grade students' abilities to solve problems and ways of thinking in the science laboratory. The students performed hands-on experiments, carried out simulation experiments, searched for information on the Internet, wrote their own research reports, and communicated via the Internet.

KR004

One other case report mentioned that the innovation impacted specific groups of students differently. In the German math class (DE015), teachers attributed the improved performance and understanding of mathematical problems of lower-performing students to the use of the learning diary.

Some negative impacts were mentioned as well. In the Korean case and the German art class (DE005), a problem was that some students visited irrelevant Web sites. According to the researchers of the Dutch case on managing animal husbandry (NL025), some students preferred the traditional way of teaching. They did not like to be responsible for their own learning process. Moreover, because the innovation assumed that students would work in teams, some students felt that not all teammates contributed equally to the results. This latter remark was mentioned in the report on the Philippine science case (PH002).

Teacher Outcomes

In 9 of the 11 cases that had a Single-Subject Curricular Focus, the reports contained indications that the innovation had an impact on the pedagogical skills of the teachers. The fact that teachers focused more on the students' critical thinking seemed to require the use of new pedagogical approaches. In the 2 cases from the Philippines this new approach was part of a specific training that the teachers took before implementing the innovation.

According to eight case reports, much emphasis in the innovations was placed on the need for teachers to learn ICT skills. It was often mentioned that continuous training was needed because of the rapid change in technology. In the Israeli case (IL009) teachers needed to upgrade their competencies regularly. The training did not always consist of formal workshops. One teacher in the Finnish case (FI004) phrased the need for continuous ICT training as follows: "I learn new things from these young people. They have courage to try 'impossible' things and they keep my thinking fresh."

In four innovations the development of collaborative skills was reported as a teacher outcome. Often this was expressed as an indication that collaboration among the teachers increased because of the innovation.

Added Value of ICT

The cases with a Single-Subject Curricular Focus used ICT primarily to improve student understanding of the subject that was being taught. In all these innovations students were supported with specific software or a Web environment specially designed to help them accomplish their tasks. A typical example is one of the cases from the Philippines (PH003). In this innovation, a set of computer-based analytic tools was used in a ninth-grade math class to facilitate the learning of concepts in geometry. The use of ICT made it easy to change variables and show the resultant graphs, which then could be compared. In this way more emphasis could be given to the depth and breadth of the course content. There were indications that students had more opportunities to develop higher-order thinking and reasoning skills, and the curriculum standards were correspondingly enriched. The advantages of these specialized, subject-specific ICT tools were also evident in the German math class (DE015) and the two art projects (CN003 and DE006). In two of the science projects (PH002 and KR004), ICT laboratory kits or simulations helped students conduct experiments and analyze data. In the Norwegian science case (NO007), the WISE environment structured students' examination and construction of scientific arguments. In the Chinese Punctuation Project (CN010), teacher-developed tutorial software supported students' learning of the material.

ICT was also perceived as beneficial to student outcomes. This was particularly so in the Chinese Punctuation Project (CN010), where students increased their test scores as a result of using the tutorial software, and in the Norwegian science course (NO007), where, according to the teacher, the multimedia features of the WISE software helped students remember what they learned. In quite a number of cases, formative assessment became more important and in some of these cases ICT was supportive to this change, as in the math class in the Philippines (PH003) and the Norwegian science course. In two of the upper secondary cases (Finland and Israel) the added value of ICT was obvious, since ICT was the object of study. The added value of ICT for teacher outcomes was also obvious because many teachers acquired ICT skills through their involvement in the innovation.

THEMATIC CURRICULAR FOCUS

Changes in Content and Goals

In the innovations that belong to this curricular pattern, ICT was used in a thematic approach to education. The theme might be a real or simulated event like an around-the-world yacht race or the planning of a wine farm, or it could be centered on the analysis of certain artifacts, such as novels or satellite images. It could be the creation of an artifact such as a Web page or a CD-ROM. In this curriculum group two or more subject areas often were integrated in the themes on which students worked. In some innovations, information science or information literacy was involved. These innovations usually existed within a curriculum that was subject matter oriented.

The cover sheet coding revealed that 11 of 13 cases in this pattern reported a change in the curriculum, other than subject matter or ICT-related goals. Of these cases, 1 also reported a change in content and 2 reported a change in content only. Therefore, it was not surprising that our in-depth analysis found that most cases involved changes in the way content was offered rather than a change in curriculum content per se. Our in-depth analysis revealed that the changes in goals that were reported involved collaborative skills, communication skills, and information handling. These skills were considered important to support independent learning. The acquisition of ICT skills was also an important goal of these innovations, not as an isolated set of skills but as a set of skills that students could apply in a variety of situations.

| Box 4.12 | CINDERELLA IS JUST IN TIME: AUTHENTIC LEARNING IN THE MIDDLE YEARS |

Seventh-grade students were involved in an integrated unit of work drawn from the English and history disciplines and based on the novel *Chinese Cinderella*. Students used online multimedia to investigate and analyze the lives of girls and women in China. The goal of the innovation was to provide a rich interdisciplinary learning environment in which to (1) engage students in an authentic learning context, (2) provide a range of learning tasks for different learning styles, (3) enable independent and collaborative learning, (4) facilitate the development of critical-thinking and literacy skills, (5) fully utilize technology, (6) encourage student-directed interest, and (7) utilize a range of developmental assessment strategies.

AU001

An example of a case with a Thematic Curricular Focus was an Australian innovation in lower secondary education (AU001) (Box 4.12). Two subjects, English and history, were integrated in a project on the novel *Chinese Cinderella*. Students had to research, process, and analyze information and summarize what they had learned. ICT was used for storing unit materials and for encouraging collaboration with other students and with an outside consultant. In this way not only were subject matter goals achieved but information-handling and collaborative skills were also realized.

| Box 4.13 | SMOKE SIGNALS |

Primary and preprimary schools from San Remo worked together in publishing the e-newspaper Segnali di fumo. The articles came from everyday school activities. Writing an article, reading what others had drafted, discussing the different essays, and using a computer to produce, send, or upload hypertext were familiar activities for these pupils. The journal improved the teaching of reading and writing, offering the pupils the opportunity to write, draw, and talk not only with teachers but also with a wider audience. In particular, the project tried to satisfy the need to make the teaching and learning experiences of pupils visible, accessible, and available.

IT001

Another example is Smoke Signals, the e-newspaper from a group of schools in Italy (IT001) (Box 4.13) that was featured in Chapter 3 and appears as a "stellar case" from Italy in Chapter 7. In this innovation primary school students regularly submitted articles to the school's electronic newspaper. Besides helping students acquire ICT skills, a major aim of the innovation was improving students' reading and writing skills. This aim was addressed not only in a single subject but also throughout the whole curriculum. The students wrote articles related to all of the kinds of activities they were involved in within the school, such as an exhibition on prehistoric man, a project on hot air balloons, or a visit to the State Archive. In this case, reading and writing were seen as important communication tools for the students.

The skills that these innovations aimed to improve were seen as important for preparing students for the information society. For instance, teachers in the Israeli primary school that implemented ICT-based projects (IL001) (Box 4.18) felt that these projects were a major means of developing independent learning skills, which were essential for students' adjustment to the information society. In the French innovation on satellite images in upper secondary education (FR006) (Box 4.19), which was also mentioned in Chapter 3, independent learning was a goal of the innovation. This was also the case in the Czech innovation Project Region (CZ002 (Box 4.22), another case described in Chapter 3. The German media competence project (DE002) (Box 4.14) had similar aims. In this innovation, training in the use of ICT was integrated into daily classroom practice. According to the case report, "The implementation of ICT in the classroom is also a major concern because it is believed to have a positive impact on the acquisition of key qualifications students need in order to succeed. One of the objectives is to prepare students for lifelong learning and to develop their competence in teamwork and their social skills."

Box 4.14   FOSTERING MEDIA COMPETENCE FROM GRADE 5 UP

Students from Grade 5 (age 10) and higher were encouraged to try self-directed learning supported by using ICT. The students were enabled to look for information and to creatively design the products they had to make with the use of ICT. The use of the new media was not restricted to certain subjects or topics but served as a link within a framework of interdisciplinary topics. The students practiced skills in self-evaluation and peer evaluation for the process and results of their work. They achieved self-monitoring and self-directed learning to quite a large extent.

DE002

Changes in Curriculum Activities and Organization

In the cases with a Thematic Curricular Focus, the previously mentioned goals were realized primarily through project work. A typical example of such a project is a French innovation, Vendée Globe Junior (FR001) (Box 4.15). Students in this innovation (and in all 12 other cases in this group) had to design and create products. Typical activities for students were searches for information (10 cases) and the publication and presentation of results (10 cases). In 8 cases, collaboration with classmates was important. However, collaboration took place primarily with other students inside the classroom. Collaboration with people outside the classroom happened in only 4 cases. Students assessed their own or their peers' work in 7 cases. In 6 innovations in this group, students picked their own tasks.

In most of the innovations in this group, the students used general ICT applications, such as productivity tools for preparing products and publications (in all cases) and the Internet for searching for information (in 12 cases). In 7 innovations e-mail was used for communication.

| Box 4.15 | VENDÉE GLOBE JUNIOR |

This primary school was actively involved in an ICT project piloted at the regional level. Students had to create a Web site about the solo, around-the-world maritime race "le Vendée Globe," which takes place every 4 years. All students in the school worked in connection with the project, particularly the 9–11 year olds. The innovation consisted of a variety of fieldwork about the race and, more widely, the maritime environment. All the activities resulted in the creation of Web pages on the site "Vendée Junior Globe."

FR001

In several cases, the products students prepared were ICT products, such as Web pages or CD-ROMs. For example, in the Salt Flats Project (IL013) (Box 4.16), the stellar case from Israel, some students were trained as computer trustees. They created Web sites to be used for teaching purposes and supported students and teachers in using ICT. In the Czech Project Region (CZ002), featured in Chapter 3, students worked with officials in local villages to create Web sites that contained information on local history, places of interest, accommodations, and so on.

The major activities for the teachers involved in the innovation were guiding students (in 12 cases) and creating structure (in 12 cases). In 9 of the 13 innovations, teachers monitored student progress. In 7 of the 13 cases, teachers also collaborated with colleagues.

| Box 4.16 | THE SALT FLATS PROJECT |

The Salt Flats Web site contained projects by and for lower and upper secondary school students, a bank of geographical and historical textual and visual materials, learning activities, links to relevant Web sites, and sections for special education and immigrant students. Computer trustees (i.e., students who received high-level training and were involved in many ICT-activities in the school) developed Web sites for the Web learning center. All other students used the Web learning center in projects.

IL013

Since the cases with a Thematic Curricular Focus involved two or more subjects, they often required at least minor adaptations to the curriculum organization. For instance, in the School Library as Media Center Project (CZ003) (Box 4.24), the innovation in an upper secondary school featured in Chapter 7 as a stellar innovation from the Czech Republic, two subsequent lesson periods had to be allocated for the project. In the other Czech innovation in this group, Project Region (CZ002), time had to be made available to allow students to collect information from the villages. Similar adaptations had to be made in the Australian Cinderella Is Just in Time Project (AU001). In other innovations, such as the

French innovation on satellite images (FR006) and the South African Theme Day Project (ZA008) (Box 4.21) in a lower secondary school, a specific period had to be allocated for students to implement the innovations. In the French innovation a 1-week workshop had to be planned, and in the South African innovation a 1-day project was organized four times per year. In the German media class (DE013) (Box 4.17), students took a 2-hour supplementary media course as an elective and joined the school media group. Curricular and extracurricular time was used for the innovation.

Box 4.17 PERSONALITY DEVELOPMENT THROUGH MEDIA-SUPPORTED WORK ON AUTHENTIC PROBLEMS

This innovation aimed at media education through work on authentic problems. The goal was to build a bridge between in-school and extracurricular activities. Projects already undertaken by the group (mainly Grade 10 students) included the publication of a student newspaper, the coproduction of films officially used as teaching material in other schools, and the production and presentation of video films. In the projects, the students dealt with topics related to their own experiences (e.g., problems emerging from equipping schools with computers; self-help projects among students). The strengthening of the student's personality (e.g., self-confidence) was seen as a major result of the innovation.

DE013

Changes in Assessment Practices

We noticed changes in the ways students were assessed in most of the cases in this group. Only one case report, on the French primary school innovation Vendée Globe Junior (FR001), explicitly stated that the system of assessment had not changed. Researchers for the Smoke Signals Project (IT001) said that the assessment practice did not change because the ICT-supported evaluation system had already been used for a long time. The system assessed not only cognitive skills but also social and metacognitive skills.

Several case reports mentioned the use of formative assessment for tracking student progress. In most of the innovations in this pattern, formative evaluation implied that teachers provided feedback to the students. One of the teachers involved in the ICT-based projects of an Israeli primary school (IL001) expressed his view on formative assessment:

> As a result of the innovation, I feel that I guide them more often. The girls do most of the work at home, and at school they show me parts of their work stage by stage, not the final product, and they're under supervision: one page, one topic; I change, reinforce if necessary.

Electronic portfolios were used to keep track of student progress only in the Australian innovation on the Cinderella novel (AU001). In three innovations (AU001, DE002, and CZ002), self- and peer-assessment strategies were applied. In these innovations, teachers still played a major role in assessing students.

Box 4.18   ICT: A BRIDGE TO COMMUNICATION

Skills and knowledge acquired in the ICT projects in this primary school were
implemented in other learning and social situations. Students worked 2 hours
per week on each project: One hour was spent in the classroom focusing on
skills such as planning, writing texts, editing a report, managing a virtual discussion, and so forth. The second hour was for a lesson held in the computer lab,
where the students learned to use ICT for their assignments. In most projects
students worked in groups of two or three. Each project had its own Web
pages, which students and teachers used for communication and the presentation of results. The school considered ICT projects as a major means of
realizing independent learners.

IL001

Summative assessment was mainly based on the products students created. Teachers set the
criteria for the evaluation of the products, except for the Israeli ICT-based projects (IL001)
and the German media class (DE013), where teachers and students agreed upon the evaluation criteria. The criteria for assessing the products addressed not only cognitive
performance but also the ways students solved complex problems, for instance, in the Israeli
innovation (IL001) and the Czech innovation (CZ002).

Although teachers saw the need for other approaches to assessment, they did not always
perceive assessment as an easy task. The teacher involved in the French primary school that
used ICT with very young children (FR002) noticed that "assessment is not maybe as
rigorous as in a 'traditional' way because it is difficult to estimate individual skills through
collective productions." Also, the case report on the Israeli innovation (IL001) stated that
"the assessment culture in the school is still in its initial stages."

Student Outcomes

Of the 13 cases with a Thematic Curricular Focus, 6 mentioned the acquisition of new
subject matter as a student outcome. In the Italian innovation, Smoke Signals (IT001),
results of evaluation tests showed that student learning was improved in the school. Progress
in written and oral expression was noticed in the French innovation Vendée Globe Junior
(FR001). Improvement of students' linguistic skills was reported in the German media class
(DE002). In 3 cases, the Israeli Salt Flats Project (IL013), the French case on satellite
images (FR006), and the South African Theme Day project (ZA008), the learning of subject
matter was not explicitly mentioned as an outcome but was inferred by the researchers
because of the importance of subject-matter-related content in the innovation.

In all but three cases in this group, the students acquired ICT skills as a result of the innovation. These ICT skills were not learned in isolation but were clearly related to tasks that had
to be carried out in the various projects. For instance, the Australian case report (AU001)
stated that "as well as undertaking stimulating tasks, students learned many ICT skills, for
example, how to insert sound and image files, how to create hyperlinks, and how to write
simple computer programs to animate characters." In the South African innovation (ZA008),
the researchers reported that the students gained ICT skills and could transfer them to

real-life situations. One of the French primary school cases (FR002) showed that even very small children (between 5 and 8 years old) were able to use ICT quite proficiently. The case report stated that "they [the students] use electronic mail" and "they seize texts in the screen."

Box 4.19   SATELLITE IMAGES IN SECONDARY SCIENCE

Students used satellite images (remote detection) in three disciplines (geography, physics, and biology-geology). The students acquired an understanding of physical principles linked to remote detection (propagation and reflection of waves, sensors), they studied the representation of meteorological phenomena and ecological problems, and they compared representation tools. Students were involved in multidisciplinary projects where they worked independently.

FR006

There are indications that students acquired collaborative skills in 12 of the 13 cases in this pattern. In some cases the researchers inferred that these skills were acquired because student collaboration was a core student activity (IL001, CZ002, DE007, and CZ003). We noticed that collaborative skills were often mentioned in relation to the acquisition of other skills. For instance, in the French Vendée Globe Junior Project (FR001) the development of collaborative skills was mentioned together with students becoming responsible for their activities. The technical coordinator in the Theme Day project (ZA008) expressed very well the important impact of collaborative and other skills in the preparation of students for the information society:

> They are acquiring so many more skills that can be transferred to life. It is not just meeting the requirements of a matric exam [final exam], they are able to put more tools in the toolbox of life. You are ultimately trying to teach them to cope with life in a technological world, e.g., team building, self-monitoring, all of those form an integral part to support bigger principles such as knowledge management and lifelong learning.

Box 4.20   INTEGRATION OF ICT IN THE LEARNING PROCESS

The construction of knowledge was one of the important aims of a French primary school in a rural area (the school had one class only). Every pupil—from Grade 3 (age 5) onward—participated in the implementation of the aim. Pupils' activities took varied forms: productions of CD-ROMs, creation of Web sites, shooting a film (video cassette), writing novels, electronic communications with the authors of textbooks, and playing interactive games with other classes.

FR002

Box 4.21	THEME DAY

Theme Day was a 1-day cross-curriculum activity to facilitate the teaching and learning of a group of about 100 11th-grade students. The purpose of Theme Day was to equip the students with practical skills they needed in the world after college. The skills identified were lateral thinking, creative thinking, team building, and problem solving. One of these Theme Days, based on the local vineyard industry, was the focus of the innovation. The students were divided into groups. Student groups were instructed to act as entrepreneurs who receive a fictitious R10 million and had to invest in and manage a wine farm in the Western Cape province of South Africa. The structure of the teaching-learning process at Theme Day was based on a series of group activities.

ZA008

Related to collaborative skills, communication skills were often mentioned by the researchers of the innovations. For instance, in the South African Theme Day case report one of the teachers stated, "I think if they [the students] had to go to a firm and do a presentation for that firm they would sell it better than most other people." Similarly, in the Czech Project Region (CZ002), communication with community representatives was important for collecting the necessary information for the Web sites of the villages. One of the students said,

> A student has much more responsibility working on this project. We have to learn to communicate with different people. I like the fact that I can choose the way of work that suits me the best.

Box 4.22	PROJECT REGION

Third-grade students (17 to 18 years old) in a Czech upper secondary school were involved in preparing Web pages for villages and towns in the school district as part of the information technology lessons. Other subjects also were an integrated part of the innovation, including history, civics, geography, and languages. Students designed Web presentations that included materials that should be available to the public by law: maps, transport connections, accommodation, history, places of interest, and so forth. Students had to consult local authorities to get the information they needed for the Web site.

CZ002

The development of students' information-handling skills was mentioned in the case reports of eight innovations. Often these skills were not reported explicitly as a student outcome. Rather, they were inferred by the researchers because the students spent quite some time on searching for information in their projects. This was not always easy for students to do, particularly the younger students, as reported by the German primary school where young students were involved in Internet research (DE007) (Box 4.23). The researchers of this innovation observed that "some students were overwhelmed by the multitude of information. They kept reading for quite a while without being able to find answers for the questions given to them beforehand." However, one of the 10th-grade students from the German media class (DE013) was able to express the importance of information-handling skills very well:

> I find it better. You really can form your own opinion. If you have a book, you have to believe what is written in the book. But when I have five different pieces of information and three are the same but two differ, then I can quietly read through them all and make up my own mind about what to believe and what not to believe.

Box 4.23   MEDIA COMPETENCE THROUGH SUBJECT-RELATED INTERNET RESEARCH

ICT is used in various ways at this primary school. Fourth-grade classes dealt with the topic Guinea Pigs. The children drew information from books and from the Internet. Fifth-grade classes worked on the topic Introduction of the EURO. The students were supposed to answer questions with the help of research on the Internet. The students acquired factual knowledge on a certain topic independently. They searched for necessary information, using a range of available media. They had to determine the usefulness of this information and evaluate the credibility of the source.

DE007

Researchers reported the development of students' metacognitive skills in four cases (AU001, IT001, DE002, and DE013). In the Australian project on *Chinese Cinderella* (AU001), for instance, students learned to reflect on their own learning and developed independent learning habits. In the German media class (DE013) the researchers reported that the students "become more critical about themselves and others (i.e., they hold a clear personal opinion when talking to the teacher and are not afraid to contradict him), and also about public media offerings." Besides these four innovations, we found indications for the development of metacognitive skills in two more innovations (FR001 and FR006). In the French innovation on satellite images, for instance, the researchers found that the students developed independent learning habits, not only within but also outside the innovation.

The development of problem-solving skills was mentioned in case reports on four innovations (IT001, FR006, ZA008, and CZ002). However the case reports did not elaborate on the nature of these skills.

When analyzing the innovations, we found that students gained positive attitudes toward the innovations. The Italian Smoke Signals (IT002) aroused curiosity and motivation among students. In the French case on satellite images (FR006), students were enthusiastic and eager to show the researchers how seriously they worked on their project. This was also the case with the students who worked on the design of House 2012, one of the Czech cases (CZ003).

Box 4.24 SCHOOL LIBRARY AS A MULTIMEDIA CENTER

This innovation was part of a European project on the change of school libraries into multimedia centers. The project had an impact on teacher and student practices throughout the school. Project House 2012 is a good example. It was situated in civics but had cross-curricular links with other subjects. Students (ages 15–16) had to design a house. The students and the teacher decided on the themes that needed to be considered (e.g., construction, mortgage), and teams of students were assigned to work on each theme. The multimedia center was used to collect information and to communicate with students from partner schools in other countries also working on the same project.

CZ003

In some innovations (ZA008 and CZ002), negative impacts on students were also found. These had to do with some students' excessive reliance on others to do the work. For those passive students, the positive impact of the innovation was considerably smaller.

In a few other innovations, different outcomes for different groups of students were mentioned. In the German media competence project (DE002), it was felt that girls took less advantage of the possible uses of ICT. In the Israeli innovation (IL001), parents and teachers felt that the ICT gap between high and low achievers did not decrease. On the other hand, the innovation was perceived as particularly beneficial for immigrant students and special education students in the two Israeli innovations (IL013 and IL001) within this group. In the Israeli Salt Flats Project, for instance, problematic students were assigned to special tasks that seemed to positively influence their behavior.

Teacher Outcomes

In 7 of the 13 innovations, the case reports mentioned development of new pedagogical skills as a teacher outcome. In some cases the researchers inferred the acquisition of new pedagogical skills because of the teachers' intensive experience in working in the innovation (for instance, the teachers' work in the Australian innovation on *Chinese Cinderella*) or because the integration of formal professional development was part of the innovation (as was the case in the Israeli ICT-based projects). In a few cases the acquisition of new pedagogical skills was an explicitly mentioned outcome for teachers. For instance, in the Smoke Signals Project from Italy (IT001) the researchers reported that the use of ICT had led to the development of new pedagogical and teaching strategies and techniques for adaptive teaching.

In 6 of the 13 innovations the acquisition of new ICT skills was mentioned. In most innovations this implied that teachers had to learn how to use new ICT applications. In the Israeli ICT-based projects (IL001), teachers learned much about the use of ICT in their teaching. The researchers of this innovation reported the following: "At first, there were fear and resistance to the change. But with the gradual mastery of relevant [ICT] skills, the level of anxiety lowered and the level of openness grew higher."

The development of teachers' collaborative skills was mentioned in eight innovations. In most innovations the acquisition of collaborative skills was inferred by the researchers who investigated the cases. In six of these innovations teacher collaboration was also mentioned as an important teacher activity.

In general, the teachers involved in the cases had positive attitudes toward the innovation—the teachers commented on the recognition they got from peers and their growing self-esteem. For instance, in the report on Project House 2012, a Czech innovation (CZ003), teachers said that the most important benefit for them was that their input in the projects was recognized by peer teachers from schools abroad. However, the increase in workload was seen as a negative teacher outcome in the Czech Project Region (CZ002).

Added Value of ICT

For the majority of the innovations with a Thematic Curricular Focus, ICT had an added value for the realization of new goals that were seen as important in the information society. In many of the cases, students were engaged in using ICT to search for, analyze, and present information and create knowledge products—the kinds of activities envisioned for employees in the knowledge economy and citizens of the information society. Often these products were themselves digital in format. For example, very young students in a French primary school (FR002) were engaged in producing CD-ROMs and Web sites. Secondary students in the Czech Republic (CZ002) and Israel (IL013) developed Web sites for real clients to use in real situations.

These ICT-based activities supported the learning of skills needed for the information society. The impact on student outcomes was clearly expressed in the case report on the Australian innovation (AU001):

> The innovation effectively demonstrated the power of ICT in helping to develop lifelong learning skills. The innovation allowed students to develop the ability to undertake independent learning; to assemble and integrate information, search for information, process data and present information in different forms; to develop collaborative attitudes to learning by discussing and sharing information; to follow their emerging interests throughout the unit, thus providing opportunities for the students to gain control over their own learning; to work at their own pace and revisit sites as often as they felt it necessary; to obtain feedback on their progress through the tracking of their skill and knowledge development to develop the ICT skills they identified as necessary to complete their products; to use technology to facilitate the achievement of learning outcomes; to reflect on their learning through ongoing evaluation and feedback; and to communicate beyond the immediate classroom environment.

Most of the cases reported that students developed ICT skills, such as the ability to use search engines and productivity tools to gather and use information. These ICT skills were integrated into activities and learning related to subject areas such as literature, science, and civics.

In this regard, ICT supported the crossing of subject matter boundaries that was typical of the group of cases with a Thematic Curricular Focus. Often ICT tools and resources themselves crossed boundaries and allowed students to look at and use information as it is organized in the real world rather than as it is organized in textbooks. For example, students in a French secondary school (FR006) looked at satellite imaging data that had implications for biology, geography, and physics. Students in the Czech Republic (CZ002) used ICT to look for and organize history, civics, and geography information in ways that were useful for citizens and visitors of neighboring villages. Finally, students in South Africa (ZA008) used a variety of ICT tools to conduct the tasks of developing and managing a winery, such as using a spreadsheet to figure budgets and a graphics package to design wine labels.

SCHOOLWIDE CURRICULAR FOCUS

Changes in Content and Goals

Innovations that fell in this pattern involved ICT-supported pedagogical practices that occurred throughout the school. For most of these innovations, ICT was used as an integral part of the curriculum and was implemented throughout the school. In two cases, a designated class in the school served as a pilot project for the rest of the school, although the innovations had not yet been used in the whole school.

An analysis of the cover sheet coding for this group of cases revealed that seven of the eight cases in this pattern concerned a curricular change other than subject matter or ICT-related goals. In five of these innovations, a change in content was also reported. For one innovation, only a change in content was reported. The in-depth analysis of the cases showed that the use of ICT was closely related to the school's vision on teaching and learning. A core characteristic of seven cases in this pattern was the use of the concept *responsibility* in describing the school's vision of teaching and learning. In the eighth case, the concepts were *a search for excellence* and *in-depth, independent learning*. The change in the curriculum was often described in terms of goals that emphasized the importance of developing autonomous learners who would be responsible for their own learning process. These goals were established for the whole school. The goals of the innovation and the school's vision appeared to be closely interwoven. Most of the case reports explicitly stated that the curriculum content being taught was embedded in national curriculum requirements.

| Box 4.25 | MULTIMEDIA DEVELOPMENT TOOLS AND AUTHENTIC TASKS |

The technology-rich environment was seen as a vehicle to achieve innovative approaches to teaching and learning at this primary school. Students had to make critical decisions about their own learning. The school instituted systems that formally recognized the ability of students to play a leading role in the teaching of others, not necessarily restricted to ICT. A predominant application of ICT was the development of multimedia products by students. The innovation is a representation of the school's philosophy and beliefs about how students learn.

AU002

In the five cases that reported a change in curriculum content, the change was related to the way content was organized. Subject matter content was often offered in a cross-curricular way and was embedded in authentic contexts. In addition, in three of the five cases, namely, the two Australian cases (AU002) (Box 4.25) and (AU004) (Box 4.29) and the ICT-Related Project-Oriented Pedagogy innovation from Norway (NO005) (Box 4.30), students and teachers negotiated about the specific projects students would work on in order to cover the content that was described in the national curriculum requirements. From this perspective one might argue that content had changed.

The multimedia project in the Australian primary school (AU002) featured in Chapter 3 is an example of the kind of goals that have been formulated in the innovations that fit in this pattern. According to the researchers, curriculum goals were formulated in which the potential of technologies was used to (1) change and improve the nature and quality of thinking and problem-solving processes, (2) help students to learn more about themselves and their world and to take action in order to make a difference locally and globally, (3) enhance the power and effectiveness of the message being communicated or the position argued, (4) improve students' critical engagement with and analysis of the information being created and explored, (5) improve literacy and numeracy outcomes, (6) improve the independent and collaborative skills of all learners, and (7) help students learn how to learn. In this innovation these goals were embedded in a constructivist approach to teaching and learning. Goals with similar ambitions were articulated in the case reports of the other innovations analyzed in this section, but sometimes they were formulated at a more general level.

Box 4.26	PROJECT I

Project I was a 2-week program for lower secondary education students that transformed normal curriculum class teaching into virtual teaching. Students carried out a variety of activities, such as a search for more information by accessing prescribed URLs, online self-testing quizzes, a discussion forum, games, a dissection video, and posters, all of which were incorporated into the program.

SG004

A characteristic of all these innovations was that goals were explicitly linked to the school's vision of teaching and learning. For example, the second Australian primary school in this group (AU004) (Box 4.29), which was submitted as the stellar case from that country, focused on the creation of a learning community based on a constructivist vision of teaching and learning. Another example is the innovation by the Israeli primary school of the future (IL003) (Box 4.32), which aimed at developing autonomous learners.

The Future High School innovation (US014) (Box 4.31), the stellar case from the United States, is focused on high standards and learning outcomes in order to prepare the students for career and college. To realize these goals students had to take four community college courses and had to complete an internship at a local business. Also, these goals were highly linked to the school's vision, which was, according to the school's mission statement, "to prepare students to excel in an information-based, technology advanced society." In addition to subject-matter-related standards, the development of collaboration skills was also an explicit goal in this case. As stated in the case report, "Collaboration is viewed as an essential set of workplace skills that every future student must cultivate and develop before graduating."

Box 4.27	INTEGRATED USE OF ICT

The goal of this primary school was to create a "student active school." This reform was an integrated part of the implementation of ICT. The students themselves decided when to use ICT and when to use other learning resources. Students worked on several projects at the same time. One such project was called the Internet as an English Textbook. In this project the emphasis was on learning English the practical way.

NO004

An important reason for initiating the innovations in this group seemed to be the desire to increase the motivation of students to learn and to increase students' self-respect, as was the case in the Student Active School from Norway (NO004) (Box 4.27). Also, in the Norwegian innovation on visual communication (NO005, Box 4.30) the goals were centered on the concept of *responsibility*. In this way, the teachers involved in the innovation aimed at developing the students' self-respect. This school worked with many students from families having a low socioeconomic status. An important principle was to find pedagogical approaches to subject areas that could develop each student's potential. The students' competence in visual communication media helped to motivate their interactions with subject matter.

Changes in Curricular Activities and Organization

The goals of these innovations with a Schoolwide Curricular Focus were realized primarily through project work. Students had to design and create products (in seven of eight cases). Typical activities for students included searching for information (all eight cases) and assessing their own and their peers' performance (in six cases). Students collaborated during project work with their classmates (in six cases) but not with actors outside the classroom. The students presented their products to the rest of the class or to other audiences (in six cases), often with the help of ICT. Besides project work, students in six out of eight cases were encouraged to pick their own tasks. Students had to plan these tasks and were held responsible for accomplishing them in time. For instance, in the Norwegian innovation that emphasized the importance of visual communication (NO005), students did not have traditional homework. They were given a plan for a 2-week period and were supposed to complete the assignments autonomously.

Compared to students in the other patterns, the students who participated in the innovations in this pattern had a large variety of ICT tools at their disposal. During the whole school day they could use e-mail for communicating, the Internet for searching for information, software for creating products, and multimedia software and digital video cameras for other activities. In the German laptop class (DE003) (Box 4.28) students even had their own laptops at their disposal.

| Box 4.28 | LAPTOPS IN GRADE EIGHT |

This innovation was a model project that equipped all students of a class with laptops. The aim was to explore the educational opportunities offered by the constant applicability of the laptops as well as a project-oriented vision of teaching and learning. Twenty-four students in an eighth-grade class participated in the innovation. The students used the laptops for writing, preparing presentations, communicating, and doing Internet research. Project-oriented work made up a large part of class time; more conventional teaching methods were also used to a varying extent, depending on the subject and work phase. The students acquired abilities of organizing individual working processes. There was a stronger collaboration among the students in the sense of mutual coordination and counseling.

DE003

To realize the organizational challenges, teachers collaborated, at least in planning. Such teacher collaboration was encouraged and facilitated by the schools. For instance, in the technology-rich Australian school (AU002), teachers were provided with noninstructional time.

Quite often a major change was needed in the organization of the curriculum at the school level to realize the innovations. In some of the innovations curriculum content was organized around a particular area of study for a specific period of time, instead of discrete subjects studied throughout the year. In the Australian innovation on constructivist teaching with ICT (AU004), key learning areas were defined and organized as units of study. The units of study operated on a 2-year cycle of eight school terms. Approximately every 10 weeks students worked with a new unit of study. A unit of study could incorporate any or all of the key learning areas. The units of study included Our Cultural World; Energy; Our Living World; Investigating Our World: The World Through Artists' Eyes; Well Being; Earth and Space; Past, Present, and Future; and Constructing Our World. Similarly, in the Norwegian case on visual communication (NO005) the school year was divided in different periods, each of which had a different focus.

| Box 4.29 | CONSTRUCTIVIST TEACHING WITH ICT |

This primary school provided a seamless outcomes-based curriculum through its programs in English, mathematics, and integrated studies. Students worked in groups on a variety of activities, at least one of which was ICT based. ICT was seen as a powerful tool in motivating and engaging students in their learning. It was used on a daily basis in classrooms across the school. The innovation is integral to the school's vision of teaching and learning.

AU004

Also, classes were arranged differently. In some innovations students from different age levels were in the same class. In other innovations a considerably larger number of students (varying from 40 to 75 students) formed a group that was taught by a team of teachers. In this Norwegian innovation, 40 to 60 students (and four to five teachers) were divided into work-team groups of 4 to 5 students. In the Israeli school of the future (IL003), a group of 75 students was taught by two to three teachers. In this innovation students from two consecutive age levels were in the same class. The same was the case in the Australian innovation on constructivist teaching with ICT (AU004).

In three innovations in this section, the two Norwegian cases (NO004 and NO005) and the Israeli case (IL003), the school interior was changed so that the aforementioned changes could be implemented. In the Israeli School of the Future, the school was divided in "homes," each of which was the size of two classrooms. Each home contained three study environments: the open space teaching area, the computer gallery, and the mini-auditorium. The work teams in the Norwegian case on visual communication (NO005) had their own area in the school, including some rooms for group work. The Student Active School from Norway (NO004) is a school without classrooms in the traditional sense. This school has rooms with big and small working tables and two or three computers at the end of the room. Also, the traditional blackboard has disappeared in this school.

Box 4.30   VISUAL COMMUNICATION AND PROJECT-ORIENTED PEDAGOGY

This school developed project-oriented pedagogy linked to the use of ICT. The innovation took place in a junior secondary school with eighth-grade students. The school emphasized the importance of producing and presenting knowledge by students. To realize this, iMovie was used in student project work. In this way students learned to illustrate their arguments and create understanding for others.

NO005

In one case, the traditional classroom disappeared all together, at least during the period of the innovation. Project I from Singapore (SG004) (Box 4.26) was a 2-week program during which students did not attend school. Rather, the school offered students a virtual learning environment in which they could access Web-based lessons anytime, anywhere, and at their own pace. In addition, students could consult their teacher anytime via e-mail or in face-to-face meetings during specific time slots.

Changes in Assessment Practices

In seven of the eight innovations that were analyzed for this pattern the assessment system differed from a system where grading was predominantly based on marks from written tests. Despite the changes in assessment practices, not all the innovations in this section completely abolished traditional exams and paper-and-pencil tests. In the Future High School in the United States (US014) and the Israeli School of the Future (IL003), paper-and-pencil tests coexisted with other forms of assessment. In the Norwegian Student Active School (NO004), the practice of using tests continued. In one innovation, the German laptop class (DE003), the assessment system was still very much in development. The teachers and students in this innovation were not satisfied with the current assessment practice. The teachers desired a more intensive involvement of the students in the assessment processes than had hitherto been the case, and the students complained about the lack of transparency in the evaluation standards.

Box 4.31	FUTURE HIGH SCHOOL

The aim of this school was to create independent learning opportunities for upper secondary school students. Project- and problem-based learning was used as a way to give students relevant academic work in a format they might encounter in a technology-rich work environment. ICT played a central role in supporting project-based and problem-based learning activities.

US014

In the assessment systems of all the innovations, formative and summative assessment was integrated. The students' products formed a major element of the evaluation of student performance. In Project I from Singapore (SG004), researchers claimed that the innovation led to more variety in assessment modes, such as the use of creative games and poster designs.

In a number of the innovations in this pattern these products were part of a digital portfolio where other assessment results, such as results from reflective journal writing and self-assessment and peer assessment, were kept. Using portfolios to keep track of student performance was, according to the teachers, possible only with the help of ICT. A teacher from the Norwegian innovation on visual communication (NO005) said, "The point is that the computer makes it easier to organize the student portfolio and send documents between the students and the teachers." An important advantage of portfolios was that students themselves could keep track of their progress.

In all but two cases—the Israeli School of the Future (IL003) and the German laptop class (DE003)—a mix of student and teacher assessment existed. The way this was organized differed among the cases. In the Australian multimedia project (AU002), for instance, students developed and agreed upon rubrics for assessing the results of a science project. In the Norwegian Student Active School (NO004), students had to write a logbook at the end of each week describing how they worked, what subjects they worked on, and what they could do better.

Student Outcomes

General academic accomplishments related to subject matter were reported by the Norwegian Student Active School, the German laptop class, the Australian school on constructivist teaching with ICT (AU004), the Future High School in the United States (US014), and the Israeli School of the Future (IL003). For instance, the graduates of the college/career school in the United States were particularly well prepared to pursue postsecondary studies. The school counselor stated that more than 95% of the students continued education after graduation.

Another example came from the school advisor of the Israeli School of the Future. He reported findings that showed that the average grades on math, language skills, and civics of students from the innovation were higher than those of students from neighborhood schools. Similarly, an evaluation of the performance of students in the German innovation (DE003) showed that the students in the laptop class performed better than students from the same grade level in the other classes. Student outcomes related to subject matter areas were not reported very explicitly or in great detail. An exception was the Norwegian Student Active School (NO004), where the English teacher perceived gains in English-speaking skills, particularly among weaker students.

Improvements in team and collaborative skills of students were mentioned in seven of the eight innovations. Students developed communication skills along with the collaborative skills they learned. These gains are very understandable, since students in many of the innovations in this pattern had to work in teams when they created their products. The researchers of the U.S. innovation (US014) reported that collaboration is viewed as an important workplace skill; therefore, students had to assess themselves and their peers on their team skills. The researchers of the Australian innovations (AU002 and AU004) stressed the fact that students mentored other students, which they took as evidence that students had developed their collaborative skills. Researchers of several of the cases inferred that students had developed communication skills from the fact that the students had presented their products to an audience.

Box 4.32   SCHOOL OF THE FUTURE

This primary school was planned and built as an advanced schooling model. Its goal was to develop autonomic learners by refining the teachers' sensitivity to students' needs, providing flexibility of time and space, broadening teaching methods and fields of interest, encouraging cooperation with parents and the community, and using resources beyond school boundaries. Computers were implemented in most subjects, enabling the development of a variety of learning methods. ICT-supported learning processes were performed throughout the day, covering about 30% of the lessons.

IL003

All case reports indicated that students had improved their ICT skills. In the Israeli School of the Future (IL003), students were tested on their ICT skills at the end of the sixth grade. The students showed a good command of all basic ICT applications, such as word processing, spreadsheets, and presentation and communication software. At the Future High School in the United States (US014), students were required to take a 1-year multimedia design class and had to pass computer applications competencies in Microsoft Office before graduation. Parents and teachers at the school identified an increase in ICT skills as a result of participation in the school's project-based learning approach. Researchers in the other innovations provided much less explicit information about student development of ICT skills. For instance, the researchers involved in the Student Active Primary School (NO004) noticed that "the students seemed to have a computer literacy that is quite good for a 10 year old." And in the innovation on visual communication (NO005), the researchers concluded that students were quite proficient in using the ICT that they needed in their project, after having followed special training at the start of the school year.

The development of problem-solving skills was reported for three innovations in this pattern. The researchers inferred a gain in these skills from the activities the students carried out. For example, students in the Australian innovation on constructivist teaching with ICT (AU004) had to work out, for a clay animation, how to move a car made of clay through the air.

In only three innovations did students develop information-handling skills. The low number of cases reporting this outcome was unexpected, since students searched for information in nearly all the cases. However, the search for information may have been only a small part of all the activities that students were involved in when carrying out their projects. The three innovations in which the researchers claimed that students developed information-handling skills were the German laptop class (DE003), the Israeli School of the Future (IL003), and the Norwegian innovation on visual communication (NO005). However, these outcomes were inferred by the researchers and evidence was not explicitly provided in the case reports. For instance, the researchers of the Norwegian innovation stated that the students developed information-handling skills because they had to account for the information they had used.

Metacognitive skills were reported as a student outcome by the researchers in the three of the case reports (NO005, US014, and DE003). In the Norwegian case on visual communication one of the students said, "Because we do things ourselves, there are no teachers who stand and point and tell you what you should do. You get to choose yourself and sort of what you think is best." In the case report on a college and career school in the United States, the researchers wrote that students developed personal management skills. In the German innovation the teachers regarded the ability of the students to organize and execute work processes (e.g., mutual coordination, selection of sources of information, implementation of results in presentations, time scheduling) as the major positive effect of the innovation. But we were surprised that only three case reports in this pattern reported gains in this area, given that all the innovations with a Schoolwide Curricular Focus stated goals that strongly emphasized the responsibility of students for their own learning. Also, the majority of the innovations emphasized such student activities as picking their own tasks (six cases) and assessing their own and their peers' performance (six cases). These kinds of activities could be interpreted as preparing students for acquiring metacognitive skills.

A general finding was that students were motivated to learn by participating in the innovation. This impression was shared by teachers, parents, and students. For instance, in the Australian case on constructivist teaching with ICT (AU004), the researchers wrote the following in the case report:

> The innovation fosters positive attitudes to learning. Technology plays an important role in engaging and challenging students. Parents and staff commented that students are very happy and highly motivated. This was evident in the classes we observed.

Other affective outcomes related to positive attitudes were also reported. For instance, researchers in the aforementioned Australian case (AU004) reported that the innovation had an impact on student self-esteem. This was also mentioned in one of the Norwegian cases

(NO005). These impacts were considered beneficial, particularly for weaker students, as was noted in the Norwegian case report: "Poor-performing students seem to take advantage of this way of working." However, concern was raised about the impact of the Israeli School of the Future (IL003) on weaker students. One of the fathers asserted that "using these methods, if you are a weak student, you are lost."

Teacher Outcomes

Intensive professional development activities, both formal and informal, were an integral part of most innovations to support the teachers' implementation of changes. According to the researchers of the innovations, these professional development activities contributed to the impact of the innovation on teachers and resulted in positive attitudes. The informal professional development activities were often related to collaboration between teachers in planning the innovation or through team teaching. As a result of these activities, teachers gained collaborative skills, which was reported in six of the eight cases. The report on one of the Australian innovations (AU004) described an example of such collaboration between teachers. New teachers at this school teamed up with experienced, like-minded teachers who acted as mentors. This approach increased the new teachers' understanding of and commitment to the school's philosophy of teaching and learning. An example of formal professional development came from the Israeli School of the Future (IL003). In this school, ICT and pedagogical training based on needs was provided to the teaching staff by a special staff member.

An increase in the ICT skills of teachers was implied in all innovations reported in this pattern. In a few innovations (NO005 and US014), this increase had to do with teachers learning new computer applications. In other cases, ICT training was part of the professional development activities supporting the innovation (NO004, SG004, and IL003). In the Israeli School of the Future (IL003), for instance, all teachers mastered ICT skills and one third of them were experts on working in ICT-enriched environments.

In five cases an outcome of the innovation was the development of the pedagogical skills of teachers. For instance, in the Singapore Project I (SG004) teachers learned how to design online lessons, which contributed to their development of new pedagogy associated with the use of ICT. It also contributed toward the mastery of ICT skills. In the Australian innovation on constructivist teaching with ICT (AU004), teachers were able to use many more teaching strategies than usual and to teach far more effectively. In the German laptop class (DE003), the researchers reported that teachers developed the "ability to let go" of the traditional roles of teachers and rigid curricular specifications.

In one of the innovations from the United States (US014), a negative teacher outcome was mentioned. Several of the teachers in this innovation had left the school due to burnout. The school principal saw this as the result of the intensive nature of the innovation:

> It was a burnout model without doubt, but I don't think that that should be a surprise to anybody. We're modeled after a high-tech start up. And if you really look at a high-tech start up, there are three cycles to it, and it's built on burnout.

Added Value of ICT

ICT had a more integrated role in the cases that had a Schoolwide Curricular Focus than in the other patterns. It is perceived as a critical tool in supporting the realization of the school's vision of teaching and learning. This is clearly expressed by the principal of the technology-rich Australian primary school (AU002). She believed that within a technology-rich environment it is possible to question current pedagogy and continually ask how it could be improved:

> I think in the settings where I've been where technology hasn't been such a focus I would say that it has at times been more difficult to challenge some of the pedagogy. The technology has meant that the pedagogy can't remain the same.

These comments are mirrored by the principal in the Singapore case (SG004), who said,

> We can integrate IT as a way of life. We want the whole community, both teaching and nonteaching staff, as well as all the boys, to realize that IT is a tool to facilitate the way we work, study, and play, as best as we can.

In the Future High School (US014), ICT played a central role in supporting school reform and project-based learning. According to the researchers, the role of ICT was seen as a tool or a resource and not so much as a catalyst for the reform itself. One of the teachers in the U.S. innovation highlighted the leveraging role of ICT by saying,

> I guess when you look at the broader projects that happen in all of our courses, I think those could happen in another setting with less technology, but I think the presence of technology makes us more efficient and makes our students more efficient learners.

ANALYSIS OF CASES NOT SELECTED

Our analysis thus far has focused on the relationship between ICT-based innovations and curricular change; but, as mentioned, relatively few cases (only 32) met our criteria of both changing curriculum and connecting this change to ICT. As important as these cases are, it is also important to know something about the larger group of cases where ICT-supported curriculum change did not occur. We examined a subset of these cases to address the following questions:

1. For cases that did not report curriculum changes in content or new goals (i.e., other than ICT- or subject-related goals), can we gain knowledge about the reasons for this lack of change?

2. If the reported cases of curriculum changes (in content or new goals) did not associate these changes with ICT, can we understand why ICT was not perceived as having added value in support of these changes?

With regard to the first question, we examined 23 of the cases that did not contain indications of curriculum change. A first observation from this examination is that for most of these cases, explicit statements were made about the lack of curriculum content change; often statements were made that the content of the curriculum was the same as before. The reasons for this were mainly twofold: (1) the innovation concerned only pedagogical change or (2) the innovation took place as an add-on to the existing curricula (e.g., extracurricular, optional, elective).

It is interesting to observe that in a vast majority of these cases the innovation was perceived as being beneficial for creating more student-centered pedagogical approaches. Also, a very substantial number of cases contain explicit statements that ICT is indispensable for running the innovation. A conclusion that emerges from the data is that new kinds of curricular goals and content (such as in information management skills and collaboration skills) appear to be unanticipated effects of the innovation rather than being established as new goals at the start.

With regard to the second question, we examined 28 of the cases where curriculum change occurred but was not associated with the added value of ICT. In many of these cases, explicit statements were made that ICT was indispensable for implementing the innovation. However, the contribution of ICT was praised in terms of its support for pedagogy rather than curriculum change.

SUMMARY AND CONCLUSIONS

In this chapter, our focus has been on technology-supported curriculum change. We wanted to see the extent to which the 174 cases submitted to the study exhibited the kinds of changes that were implied by the policy documents used to justify the introduction of ICT into schools. These policy documents cited the new skills required of employees of the knowledge economy and citizens of the emerging information society. These skills involved the management of information, the solution of complex problems, collaboration in teams, and the skills required to learn new knowledge and skills as needed. The ability to use a wide range of ICT tools and digital resources is both required for and facilitates the learning of these other skills.

Specifically, we addressed these questions:

> *How are the innovative pedagogical practices in SITES Module 2 related to changes in curriculum content and goals? Have these practices changed what students are learning and what teachers need to know? Have they changed the way student outcomes are assessed? What impact do they have on student competencies, attitudes, and other outcomes?*
>
> *What capabilities of the applied technology support innovative pedagogical practices? How do these capabilities shape the practices they support?*

In our analysis of the cover sheet codes that characterized the 174 cases, we found that only 27% described new content and 37% described new goals of the sort implied by economic and social changes. We found that only 32 cases, 18% of the total, described one of these forms of curricular change and claimed that technology contributed either to curriculum change or, more generally, to education reform. This is itself a major finding of the study.

The primary focus of the chapter was on the 32 cases in which curriculum change occurred and was supported by ICT. We felt that an analysis of these cases might give us some insights into how the use of ICT in schools might contribute to even larger changes associated with curriculum and educational reform.

We found that the cases fell into three patterns—those with a Single-Subject Curricular Focus, those with a Thematic Curricular Focus that cut across several subject areas, and those with a Schoolwide Curricular Focus. We analyzed cases in each of these groups in order to understand the changes in content and goals (the planned curriculum), the major classroom activities of students and teachers and how these might reorganize the curriculum (the enacted curriculum), and the student and teacher assessment practices and outcomes (the experienced curriculum). In addition, we examined the contribution that ICT made to these changes. Our findings are summarized in Table 4.4 and in the following sections.

CHANGES IN CONTENT AND GOALS

Our in-depth analysis of the case reports that described ICT-supported curriculum change showed that the change was less often related to new content and more often related to new goals or to offering existing content in a different way. These changes in goals differed among the three patterns. The cases with a Single-Subject Curricular Focus often described improvements in the teaching of content and concepts. The cases described a more in-depth coverage of current content. The goals of the innovations were the improvement of students' understanding of the subject matter and mentioned the need to develop problem-solving and critical-thinking skills.

Cases with a Thematic Curricular Focus described new goals that were considered important for the information society. The innovations in this pattern often referenced information management and lifelong learning goals. In order to realize these goals, curriculum content was delivered in a different way, and cross-curricular and thematic approaches to the curriculum were adopted.

In cases with a Schoolwide Curricular Focus, the realization of new goals was an important aim, with a strong emphasis on fostering students' responsibility for their own learning. In this group, students were often given opportunities to work on themes in projects as well as independent work on subject-matter-related knowledge. Particularly in this Schoolwide Curricular group, the aim of the innovation was strongly aligned with a vision of the school that held in high regard students' independence and responsibility for their own learning.

CHANGES IN CURRICULAR ACTIVITIES AND ORGANIZATION

In all three curricular patterns, student activities were rather similar—students created products or carried out a research project. (This was more often the case when there was a Single-Subject Curricular Focus.) In most cases across the three groups, students collaborated during their project work and had to search for information. In cases with a Single-Subject Curricular Focus students were often involved in tasks requiring problem solving. In the other two patterns, students published or presented results. In a number of cases, students were involved in self-assessment or peer assessment. In many innovations with a Schoolwide Curricular Focus, students picked their own tasks.

In all three groups, teachers advised and guided students while providing structure and keeping track of students' progress. In the cases with a Schoolwide Curricular Focus teacher collaboration was common. In cases with a Single-Subject Curricular Focus, teachers also mediated content and prepared materials (sometimes ICT-based) for students.

Table 4.4

ICT AND THE CURRICULUM: OVERVIEW OF RESULTS

Curriculum Component	Dimensions	SINGLE-SUBJECT CURRICULAR FOCUS (n = 11)	THEMATIC CURRICULAR FOCUS (n = 13)	SCHOOLWIDE CURRICULAR FOCUS (n = 8)
Planned curriculum	*Change in content and goals*	The aim was to realize a better and more in-depth knowledge of (often existing) content of academic subjects.	The aim was to introduce new goals that were considered important in preparing students for lifelong learning in the information society.	The aim was to create environments that foster students' responsibility for their own learning. This aim was closely connected to the school's vision of teaching and learning.
Enacted curriculum	*Student and teacher activities*	Students carried out research projects or created products in which they collaborated with others; students searched for information and were involved in problem solving.	Students created products in which they collaborated with others; students searched for information and presented results; they assessed their own and their peers' performance.	Students picked their own tasks.
			Teachers advised students, structured their activities, and monitored their progress.	
		Teachers designed materials and mediated content.		Teachers collaborated.
	Change in curriculum organization	No major changes occurred in the organization of the curriculum at the school level; there were large variations in the time that was allocated to the innovation.	Subject boundaries were crossed, which implied that the school curriculum had to be adapted somewhat; there were large variations in the time allocated to the innovation.	There were major changes in the organization of the curriculum (e.g., mixing grade levels, large groups, team teaching); students participated in the innovation during the whole school day and throughout the year.
Experienced curriculum	*Assessment practices*	Teachers put more emphasis on formative assessment.		New assessment systems were adopted in which students played an active role.
		ICT did not provide much support for assessment practices, but portfolio assessments looked promising.		
	Student outcomes	Reported in almost all or all cases: • Subject matter knowledge • ICT skills • Positive attitudes	Reported in almost all or all cases: • Collaborative and communication skills • Positive attitudes	Reported in almost all or all cases: • Collaborative and communication skills • ICT skills • Positive attitudes
		Reported in most cases: • Collaborative skills • Metacognitive skills	Reported in most cases: • ICT skills • Information handling	Reported in most cases: • Subject matter knowledge
	Teacher outcomes	Reported in almost all or all cases: • Pedagogical skills • Positive attitudes	Reported in almost all or all cases: • ICT skills • Positive attitudes	Reported in all or almost all cases: • Collaborative skills • ICT skills • Positive attitudes
		Reported in most cases: • ICT skills	Reported in most cases: • Pedagogical skills • Collaborative skills	Reported in most cases: • Pedagogical skills
	Added value ICT	Specialized software supported the learning of specific subject goals.	Generalized productivity tools and digital resources helped break down discipline barriers and promote information-handling skills.	ICT was integrated throughout the curriculum and school to support the school's vision and to foster students' responsibility for their own learning.

Despite the similarity in learning activities, the organization of innovative projects was very different in each group. In cases with a Schoolwide Curricular Focus, students participated in the innovation during the whole school day. For these students, the concept of *school* was identical with the innovation. In the other two patterns, the time that was allocated to the innovation varied considerably and was sometimes difficult to estimate because the innovations ranged from those that were completely integrated into a subject and ran throughout the year to innovations that took only 1 day. In cases with a Thematic Curricular Focus, subject boundaries were crossed, which often had implications for the organization of content.

CHANGES IN ASSESSMENT PRACTICES

In all three curricular patterns, changes in assessment practices were observed. In only a small number of innovations the case report explicitly stated that there were no changes in assessment practices. In cases with a Single-Subject Curricular Focus and a Thematic Curricular Focus, changes in the assessment practices meant that more emphasis was placed on formative than on summative assessment only. In many of the cases, this implied that teachers gave feedback more often during the execution of the activities. In some innovations students also were active in the assessment process. Students assessed their own or their peers' work, in addition to being assessed by the teacher. Changes were also observed with regard to summative assessment. For instance, summative assessments often focused on students' products rather than only on paper-and-pencil tests. Teachers often felt that these new assessment practices were still in an initial stage. In the Schoolwide Curricular Focus new assessment systems were adopted in which formative and summative assessment were integrated and, in some cases, supported by ICT. In general, however, ICT did not often support assessment practices, although when it did, electronic portfolios were used and seen as particularly promising.

STUDENT AND TEACHER OUTCOMES

A word of caution is needed with regard to the findings concerning student and teacher outcomes. First, only a very few case reports referenced objective data as evidence for the outcomes. The objective evidence that was presented related mostly to subject-matter-related outcomes. In most case reports, the impact of the innovation on teachers and students was described in terms of perceived outcomes, based on opinions from teachers, students, the school principal, or parents. In many case reports, the researchers inferred the impact of the innovation on students and teachers, based on their observations and interviews. Often we felt that these inferences were based on the fact that students or teachers carried out specific activities, rather than on concrete, demonstrated outcomes.

We will first focus on the outcomes related to students. A general finding was that throughout the three patterns students were very positive about the innovations. Students were motivated by the innovation, and the innovation improved their self-esteem. From our analysis we may also infer that the acquisition of ICT skills was an important student outcome in all three patterns, although a little less so for cases with a Thematic Curricular Focus. It was unexpected that the acquisition of ICT skills appeared so important for cases with a Single-Subject Curricular Focus because these skills were not part of the goals that were pursued. Second, it is noteworthy that in all three patterns ICT skills were not learned separately from the context in which the students needed to use them.

A third common impact was the acquisition of collaborative skills in all three patterns, although it was a little less in cases with a Single-Subject Curricular Focus. It must be noted that in cases with a Thematic Curricular Focus and a Schoolwide Curricular Focus the acquisition of communication skills was often mentioned in relation to collaborative skills. This probably had to do with the fact that the students involved in the innovations in these patterns had to make presentations of their project work. While collaboration was not a specific aim for cases with a Single-Subject Curricular Focus, the intensive collaboration of students in project work (either research projects or the creation of products) may explain why this outcome was mentioned in a substantial number of these cases.

While there were many similarities across the curricular groups, we also found differences. For instance, subject matter knowledge was an important student outcome in cases with a Single-Subject Curricular Focus, as well as in those with a Schoolwide Curricular Focus, although somewhat less so. Of course, this could be expected in cases with a Single-Subject Curricular Focus because the reason for using ICT was to improve the teaching of content. The subject matter outcomes in cases with a Schoolwide Curricular Focus were often in compliance with national curriculum requirements. Since cases with a Thematic Curricular Focus emphasized the acquisition of new goals, we expected that student outcomes in these areas would have been identified more often than they were. However, the acquisition of information-handling skills in the cases in this group was not unexpected because information handling was seen as an important skill for lifelong learning.

The emphasis on students' responsibility for their learning process, an important aim of the innovations in the Schoolwide Curricular Focus, increased our expectations about the acquisition of metacognitive skills in this pattern. However, this student outcome was hardly mentioned in this group of cases. On the other hand, it was more surprising to find this outcome mentioned often in cases with a Single-Subject Curricular Focus.

The innovations had impacts not only on students but also on the teachers who were involved. A common outcome for teachers in all three patterns was the development of a positive attitude toward the innovation, particularly because of the recognition they got from colleagues in the school. Another common impact was the acquisition of ICT skills, often because teachers had to learn new software applications. The development of pedagogical skills was an important teacher outcome in many innovations in all three patterns but appeared particularly important in the innovations with a Single-Subject Curricular Focus.

The acquisition of collaborative skills was seen as an important outcome in cases with a Thematic Curricular Focus and those with a Schoolwide Curricular Focus. In the latter group, the development of collaborative skills was explicitly related to the formal and informal strategies for professional development that the school had incorporated in order to support the implementation of the innovation.

ADDED VALUE OF ICT

Given the way the cases were selected for the analysis in this chapter, we could expect a clear role for ICT in supporting curriculum change. Our analysis showed that this role differed to some extent among the three curricular patterns. In cases with a Single-Subject Curricular Focus, specialized software and subject-specific Web environments supported a more in-depth coverage of curriculum content that seemed to foster student understanding of subject matter. In this regard, one may argue that ICT improved the existing curriculum.

In the two other patterns, the added value of ICT was more explicitly related to educational reform. In cases with a Thematic Curricular Focus, this reform was related to more general societal change—students needed to master new goals in order to be prepared for the information society. Students in these cases used generalized productivity tools and digital resources that cut across disciplinary boundaries and helped students acquire the information-handling skills that can prepare them for these societal changes. In cases with a Schoolwide Curricular Focus, ICT was integrated throughout the curriculum to help students take more responsibility for their own learning.

ICT-SUPPORTED CURRICULUM CHANGE

By and large, the innovative pedagogical practices that were submitted to this study did not involve ICT-supported curriculum change. Instead, the emphasis was on changes in teachers' and students' classroom practices, as described in Chapter 3. When technology-supported curriculum changes did occur, they were rather modest.

However, in a small number of cases ICT supported change in curriculum and assessment. In some cases, teachers and students used specialized software to increase the depth of students' understanding of specific subjects. In another set of cases, ICT tools and digital resources helped break down the barriers across the subject disciplines. In a few cases, ICT was integrated throughout the curriculum and the school, and ICT environments were structured to help students take on the responsibilities of lifelong learning. The innovations in these cases were supported by a local vision of educational change.

In Chapter 5 and 6, we discuss the local school contexts and local policies that can foster and support change. However, as we mentioned previously in this chapter, curriculum change is often limited by national policies that determine the content to be taught and the way it is assessed. From the cases that we analyzed in this chapter, it appears that national policies are not yet in place that can mobilize ICT in support of curriculum change and education reform. Without such national policies, it is likely that ICT will have a minimal impact on education. We return to the discussion of national policies in Chapter 6.

Students from the Philippines collaborate on an innovative project.

CHAPTER 5

school context, sustainability, AND TRANSFERABILITY OF INNOVATION

By Ronald D. Owston

INTRODUCTION

Pedagogical innovation—whether involving technology or not—is shaped by a complex interaction of the innovation with contextual factors such as school and school district policy, leadership, cultural norms and values, teacher attitudes and skills, and student characteristics. In this chapter, we examine the school contexts in which pedagogical innovations based on information and communication technology (ICT) are situated, with the goal of addressing the following research questions:

What are the contextual factors associated with the use of these innovations? Which factors seem to be present across different innovative pedagogical practices? Which factors are associated with different practices? What are the implications of contextual factors for the sustainability and transferability of these innovations?

What are the barriers to using ICT in innovative ways? How are teachers overcoming these barriers? How do they cope with limited resources?

The organizing theme in this set of questions is the sustainability and transferability of innovative pedagogical practices: the significant contextual factors—and the interrelationships among them—that contribute to, or inhibit the continuation of, an innovation and its transfer to other classrooms and schools. Addressing these factors is the crucial challenge faced by policy makers interested in scaling up a successful innovation, as well as by teachers and school administrators who want to adopt an innovation locally.

We will respond to these questions by proposing a conceptual model of sustainability derived from an analysis of a subset of cases in this study and by discussing the elements in that model and their interrelationships. Following this, we will discuss the underlying factors identified in our analyses of cases that appear to promote the transferability of innovations. In order to frame our research, we first need to consider the literature on innovation and the change process, and, in particular, factors relating to the sustainability and transferability of educational innovations.

INNOVATION AND THE CHANGE PROCESS

Significantly changing educational practice is a long, arduous process. Michael Fullan (2001a), who has studied and written extensively about the change process, estimates that an elementary school can be turned around from a poor-performing school to a good or better one within 3 years, a high school can be reformed in 6 years, and a school district in about 8 years. Even at that, he adds, the number of examples of schools and school districts that have been transformed is discouragingly small given the intense efforts that have been devoted to educational reform over the last several decades. Moreover, reform efforts that have focused specifically on using ICT by and large have fared no better in producing fundamental changes in teaching and learning, nor have they achieved the productivity gains often promised by their leaders (Cuban, 2001).

In those schools and districts that have succeeded, however, sustaining the innovation has been fragile, so much so that if one or two key people leave, the success can be reversed almost overnight. The heart of the dilemma appears to be an infrastructure that is "weak, unhelpful, or working at cross purposes" (Fullan, 2001a, p. 18). By *infrastructure* Fullan means the next layers above the unit of focus in the school system. For example, teachers cannot sustain change if they are working in an unsupportive school culture, schools cannot continue to be transformed if they are part of an unhelpful district, and districts cannot significantly change if they are part of a state or country that is not helping to sustain reform. Peter Senge, in his book *Schools That Learn*, emphasizes the need for all levels of the system to work together for change to succeed: "Classrooms can only improve in a sustainable way if the schools around them improve" and "schools depend on the districts and communities of which they are a part" (Senge et al., 2000, p. 6).

Educational change itself is typically viewed as a three-stage process (Fullan, 2001a). First is *initiation*, the process leading up to and including the decision to initiate or adopt the innovation or reform. During the next phase, *implementation*, the innovation is put into practice, a process that may extend over several years depending on its complexity. The third phase, variously called *continuation*, *routinization*, or *institutionalization*, is when the innovation becomes part of the regular practice at the school and no longer stands out as something special. Although change is described as involving these three phases, the reality is that it rarely proceeds smoothly as a linear process. More often than not, decisions are made or events occur at one phase that will cause a return to the previous stage. These changes will, in turn, then have to work their way through the remaining stages again.

SUSTAINING EDUCATIONAL CHANGE

Of particular interest is the final stage that leads to an innovation being continued or sustained. Fullan (2001a) describes three groups of factors that affect the implementation and sustainability of educational change: characteristics of the change, local characteristics, and external factors.

Characteristics of the Change

The first group of factors, which concerns the nature of the change or innovation itself, consists of four characteristics: need, which deals with the fit between the innovation and district or school needs; clarity of the goals and means of achieving them; complexity, which concerns the extent and difficulty of the change for those implementing it; and quality and practicality, which is about how good the innovation is and how attainable it is. Rogers (1995), who has studied for four decades the nature of innovations and their rate of adoption, suggests that there are five factors related to the nature of innovations and their rate of adoption: relative advantage, or the degree to which an innovation is perceived as better than the idea it supersedes; compatibility, or the extent to which it is consistent with existing values, experiences, and needs of adopters; complexity, or how difficult it is to use and understand; trialability, or the degree to which it can be experimented with on a limited basis; and observability, or the degree to which the results of the innovation are visible to others. Despite their extensive writings on the change process and the similarities between their analyses of the nature of innovations, neither Fullan nor Rogers cites each other's work. Fullan's concepts of complexity and need are similar to Rogers's concepts of complexity and compatibility, respectively; however, they diverge in their views on the remaining factors. Therefore, innovation leaders would be wise to attend to all characteristics to increase the likelihood of sustaining an innovation: need, complexity, clarity, quality, practicality, relative advantage, trialability, and observability.

Local Characteristics

Fullan's (2001a) second group of factors affecting implementation and sustainability deals with four characteristics related to the school environment where the innovation takes place: community, school district, principal, and teachers. Community support, which includes parents and the school board, can be very influential in districtwide reform, depending on the role those participants choose to play, which could range from complete apathy to direct involvement. Parental involvement appears to be especially critical to ensuring success, provided that parents and teachers work together while recognizing the complementary role they play in the children's lives (Fullan, 2001a). Indeed, there is evidence that children whose parents are involved in their schooling tend to perform better (Henderson & Berla, 1994).

Support from the local school district's central administration (or an equivalent higher-level administrative unit in countries where schools are not organized into districts) is essential for innovation to be sustained if it is a districtwide endeavor. The success of the innovation appears to be directly related to the actions taken by the district's leaders in demonstrating support, as opposed to mere verbal endorsements, and to the district's record in successfully managing change. If the innovation is in a single school or individual classroom, then district support is often much less essential. In addition, it is clear that neither top-down mandated change strategies nor solely classroom-based grassroots strategies will be very successful in the long run. Combined strategies which capitalize on the center's strengths (to provide perspective, direction, incentives, networking, and retrospective monitoring) and local capacity (to learn, create, respond to, and feed into overall directions) are more likely to achieve the greatest at sustaining innovation (Fullan, 1994).

Third, school principals are viewed as key in implementing and sustaining schoolwide change because they are in the best position to shape such matters as organizational goals and work structures, understand teacher concerns about the innovation, and provide needed infrastructure. Fullan (2001a) contends that principals must demonstrate active rather than passive involvement in the innovation (for example, by attending teacher workshops) in order to understand issues, problems, and needs related to the innovation. In his book *The Fifth Discipline*, Senge (1990) differs with the traditional Western notion of effective leaders being visionaries "who set the direction, make the key decisions, and energize the troops" (p. 340). He maintains that effective leaders are designers, who create the learning processes for people in the organization to deal productively with the critical issues they face; stewards, who oversee the purpose and direction of the organization; and teachers, who help others in their organization develop a systematic understanding of its purpose and where it is heading.

Finally, teachers, acting both as individuals and collectively with their colleagues, are absolutely vital in sustaining innovation, as school innovation clearly stands or falls depending on what teachers choose to do in the classroom (Elmore, Peterson, & McCarthy, 1996; Fullan, 2001a). Among teachers, collegiality, open communication in the school, trust, support, and high job satisfaction and morale are vital. Schools that focus on team learning foster a culture that values these attributes (Senge et al., 2000). A major part of team learning is teacher professional development, but not the traditional notion of professional development that permeates most schools, where one-shot workshops and outside authorities "deliver" professional development to teachers, because this kind of professional development offers those teachers very limited growth opportunities. Rather, professional development that is long term, school based, collaborative, focuses on students' learning, and linked to curricula tends to be most effective (Hiebert, Gallimore, & Stigler, 2002). ICT-specific professional development should involve hands-on technology use by teachers, a variety of learning experiences, ongoing technical assistance and support, and learning curriculum-specific software applications (North Central Regional Education Laboratory [NCREL], 2002).

External Factors

Outside forces, including the various levels of government, schools of education, philanthropic foundations, lobby groups, private enterprise, and research organizations, comprise Fullan's (2001a) third set of sustainability-related factors. The relationship of the outside influences on the innovation is often complex, yet essential to analyze in order to fully understand the influences on school innovation. Five characteristics of the external environment that appear to either favor or frustrate public organizations in sustaining innovation were delineated by Light (1998) in his study of 26 public organizations, including schools, that successfully sustained their innovations. First is turbulence, or the level of uncertainty that besets most public institutions today. Shocks, such as budget crises, resignation of key advocates, or changes in policy, are a second factor. Organizations tend to become accustomed to turbulence; however, shocks demand their immediate focus and attention. Third is support and encouragement for innovation—the degree to which the external environment greets new ideas is directly linked to their survival. Schools may receive this support through government policies or plans that support particular kinds of innovation. The fourth factor is collaboration with other organizations in the same field. Contrary to the tendency to innovate in isolation, organizations that collaborate frequently end up being more successful in sustaining innovation. Slack, the level of resources available for discretionary investment, is the final factor. The availability of some unrestricted funds to spend on an innovation may well determine whether the idea will survive.

TRANSFERRING INNOVATIONS

Once an innovation has been successfully sustained, the natural question that arises is "How do we go to scale?" In other words, how can an innovation be transferred from one setting to other settings, which may be other classrooms within a school, other schools, or even other countries? This question is at the heart of our book because one of the main goals of conducting an international research project is to learn from the broad range of experiences of others and adapt those ideas to our local settings where appropriate. What is clear is that successful practices most likely will not transfer spontaneously just because they are successful elsewhere. Nor will they transfer by simple policy shifts or exhortations from people with money because the problems of scaling up are deeply rooted in the incentives and cultural norms of the institutions adopting the innovation (Elmore, 1996). The dilemma that many adopters of innovations face is that they focus on the products of other people's reforms. A successful innovation in one place is partly a function of good ideas, but, more important, it is largely a function of the conditions under which those ideas flourished. Therefore, the challenge in transferring an innovation is to replicate in the new setting the conditions that spawned the original innovation, not the innovation itself (Fullan, 1999).

The challenge of replicating the conditions that produce an innovation becomes exacerbated because, as Elmore (1999) found, the more the innovation requires altering the core teaching and learning practices in a school, the less likely the chances are that it will be adopted successfully. The alteration of these core practices becomes a process of fundamentally changing the culture of a school, a process that Fullan (1999) calls "reculturing," to distinguish it from "restructuring," which focuses on reforming the organizational structures. A synthesis of a decade of research on scaling reforms initiated under the New American Schools program found that before actually implementing an innovation schools first must focus on developing their capacity for implementing the innovation (Berends, Bodilly, & Kirby, 2002). Also identified by the study as critical for scaling innovations were teacher support and sense of teacher efficacy; strong and specific principal leadership abilities; clear communication and ongoing assistance on the part of innovation developers; and stable leadership, resources, and support from the district. To this Elmore would add that incentive structures for teachers must be changed. This may be accomplished by developing strong external professional norms for teachers; developing organizational structures to intrinsically motivate teachers to engage in hard, uncertain work that typically accompanies fundamental change; creating deliberate processes that encourage reproduction of successes;

and creating structures that promote learning of new practices, together with incentive systems that reward teachers for engaging in these practices (Elmore, 1999).

Beyond these general considerations, some special challenges exist in transferring ICT-based innovations from one setting to another (Dede, 1998; Schofield & Davidson, 2002). These challenges revolve around the cost of technology, its rapid evolution, and the special knowledge and skills required by support staff. Dede (1998) suggests that leaders of school reform must change their ways of thinking about implementation and the assumptions that they hold. For example, rather than spending scarce resources on saturating schools with computers and neglecting other areas of need, he proposes a distributed learning model that leverages existing resources to orchestrate educational activities among classrooms, workplaces, homes, and community settings. Moreover, Schofield and Davidson (2002), in their 5-year study cited in Chapter 3, found that the staff of an Internet-based innovation in a school district had to build the technical expertise of the district's support staff in order for "partial institutionalization" of the innovation to occur. The project also encountered conflicts when the innovation spread to other schools because of the district's student Internet access policies, which ultimately shaped implementation of some of the innovation's original intents in the new schools.

With this overview of the innovation and the change process, we next turn to how sustainability and transferability were defined operationally for this study and then describe the methodology used to research the two key questions in this chapter.

SUSTAINABLE AND TRANSFERABLE CASES

As we mentioned in Chapter 2, an important goal of this study is to identify innovations that can be sustained and transferred. We now define these terms as they were implemented in the study and describe the cases we use in the analysis for this chapter.

SUSTAINABILITY AND TRANSFERABILITY DEFINED

Because the focus of the study is on innovation, we addressed the possibility that even though practices may otherwise be desirable, they may not yet have been transferred or even in place long enough to stand the test of time. Consequently, we defined one of the international criteria so as to select innovations for this study that were sustainable as well as transferable. That is, the case nomination should provide evidence or reasons to believe that an innovation is able to be sustained and transferred. If a particular innovation had not been in existence long enough to establish its longevity at a site, it was included in the study if it could be successfully argued that it had a strong potential to be sustained. If an innovation had not yet been transferred to another classroom or school, a case needed to be made that it had strong potential to be transferred.

Furthermore, sustainable innovations are those that are not so dependent upon any one individual—teacher or principal—that if the person left, the innovation would falter. Stated differently, an innovation should be robust enough so that others could step in and, with reasonable levels of training and practice, continue that innovation. Innovative practices were deemed transferable in this study if they could be implemented in other classrooms in the same school either at the same or a different level, or in other schools, school districts, or other jurisdictions within a given country, either at the same or a different level. These innovations should not require major changes in a local situation, which would be unreasonable to assume for typical schools. In this approach, "lighthouse cases"—special pilot projects that were provided with extraordinary resources—were not allowed unless a strong case could be made that the special resources would also be made available to other schools as part of a dissemination plan.

CASES INCLUDED IN THIS ANALYSIS

Sustainability and transferability were, together, one of four international criteria that national panels used to select cases for inclusion in the study. However, this criterion and one other—demonstrated student or teacher outcomes—were preferable criteria. Significant change and a central role for technology were the two essential criteria. Given the secondary level of emphasis for the sustainability and transferability criterion, not all of the innovations were equally compelling in this regard. An analysis of the cover sheets described in Chapter 2 (and included in Appendix B.2) indicated that out of the 174 case reports submitted by the National Research Coordinators (NRCs) of participating countries, 136 (or 78%) made a claim that the innovation had been sustained for more than 1 year. Of these, 130 provided evidence to back this claim, according to the members of the International Coordinating Committee (ICC) who read and coded the cases. However, only 76 (44%) of the reports claimed that the innovation had been transferred and only 71 presented supporting evidence.

Of the total, 59 were classified as having evidence of being both sustained and transferred. Of these 59, 53 (or 90% of the subset) had been sustained for 2 years or more, at the time of the data collection (2000–2001). However, the evidence of transfer presented in the case reports was often thin. While many reports referred to plans for transfer or provided ambiguous evidence, fewer than half the 59 cases had identified concrete instances where the innovation had actually been transferred.

This is itself a major finding of our study. That is, of 174 case reports of innovative practices that the national panels of 28 countries selected as worthy of emulating, only 59 (or 34%) of them presented evidence that they had been sustained and even minimum evidence that the innovation had been transferred or plans were in place to do so.

We chose this sample for our analysis in this chapter. At times, for the sake of brevity, we will simply refer to them as "the set of sustainable cases" or "the transferable cases." However, the reader should be aware that we are always referring to the same 59 cases that are both sustainable and transferable. Of the 28 countries participating in the Second Information Technology in Education Study (SITES) Module 2, 5 were not represented in the sample (France, Japan, Slovak Republic, Lithuania, Chinese Taipei) because none of their cases was classified as having evidence of both sustainability and transferability.

We selected these 59 cases because we felt that detailed analyses of these cases were most likely to provide us with insights into the reasons why innovative pedagogical practices using technology are sustained and transferred. We describe how we analyzed these case reports, but given the limitations of time and resources, we were not able to analyze in detail the cases that had not been sustained and transferred. Consequently, we cannot comment as much on why such cases have not (at least yet) been sustained and transferred.

GROUNDED THEORY APPROACH

A grounded theory approach (Glaser & Strauss, 1967; Strauss & Corbin, 1998) was taken in this chapter because our goal was to develop a model of sustainability and transferability derived from the cases we selected. This qualitative analysis approach provides a means to build from systematically gathered and analyzed data explanatory frameworks that specify relationships among concepts. Because grounded theory is developed from actual data, Strauss and Corbin (1998) maintain that the resulting theory is more likely to resemble "reality" and offer "insight, enhance understanding, and provide a meaningful guide to action" (p. 12).

Grounded theory researchers do not necessarily begin with a preconceived theory in mind; instead, they typically begin with an area of study and allow theory to "emerge" from their data. The research literature, however, can play an important role in stimulating questions during the analysis, directing the researcher to investigate concepts that otherwise may not have been considered, and confirming or pointing out where the literature is incorrect or overly simplistic (Strauss & Corbin, 1998). Our analysis was bounded and guided by the conceptual framework described in Chapter 1. This framework determined (1) the nature of the data that would be collected since interview questionnaires, classroom observation protocols, and document collection procedures were based on it; (2) the structure and topics addressed in the case reports; and (3) what contextual factors would be considered in the analysis as we derived our data coding schema a priori from it. More specifically, our work was informed by research related to sustainability and transferability reviewed at the beginning of this chapter.

We employed the constant comparative method to analyze the selected cases and build a theoretical model for sustainability, following the five steps outlined by Bodgan and Biklen (1998, pp. 67–68):

1. Look for key issues, recurrent events, or activities in the data that become categories of focus.

2. Search the data for more incidents of the categories of focus, with an eye to seeing the diversity of the dimensions under the categories.

3. Write about the categories being explored and attempt to describe and account for all the incidents in the data while continuing to search for new incidents.

4. Work with the data and emerging model to discover basic social processes and relationships.

5. Engage in sampling, coding, and writing as the analysis focuses on the core categories.

Although the constant comparative method is described as a series of steps, all activities go on at once and the researcher keeps doubling back to search for more data and do more coding. Throughout this process we used *ATLAS ti* qualitative software to assist with the data analysis. Relationships between categories were graphed using the Network View feature of *ATLAS ti*, which helped us visualize the emerging model. The final model on sustainability that resulted from our analysis is described in the next section.

Generally speaking, the same procedures were followed with the analyses of cases for transferability, but the data were inadequate to develop an explanatory model of transferability.

Nevertheless, we found sufficiently rich data to be able to describe factors that potentially aid in transferability.

A MODEL FOR SUSTAINABILITY OF CLASSROOM INNOVATION

The model of sustainability we developed from our analysis of our sample cases is illustrated in Figure 5.1. The model comprises two sets of conditions underlying sustainable innovative pedagogical practices using technology—one set we labeled Essential, the other Contributing. These are represented by "E" and "C," respectively, in links between factors in the figure. Essential conditions were defined as those that our analysis found necessary, but not sufficient, for innovations to be sustained. Evidence of these factors was found in all cases in our sample. Contributing conditions were those that we found facilitated the sustainability of innovations. These factors appeared in 50% or more of the cases, an arbitrarily chosen criterion that we believed justified their inclusion in the model.

Figure 5.1

EXPLANATORY MODEL FOR SUSTAINABILITY

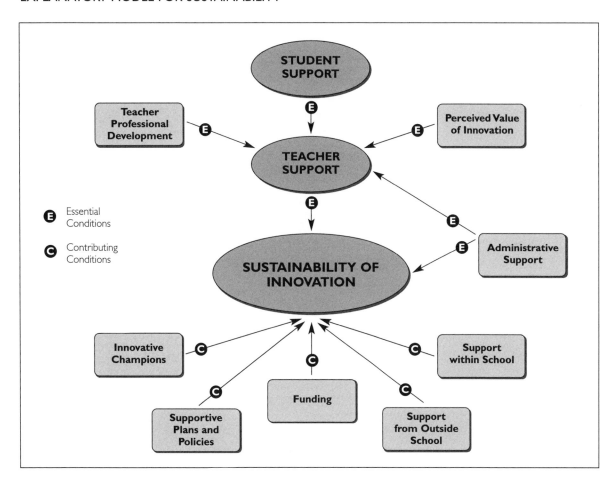

In our model the essential conditions for sustainability consist of support from the three main actors in any school innovation: the teacher, the principal, and the students. Most fundamental is teacher support, for without teacher support of the innovation, sustainability simply cannot occur. Directly related to this is teacher professional development for the innovation. It is important to note that teacher professional development should not necessarily be thought of in terms of formal courses because informal learning and learning on the job with peers can be equally, if not more, powerful. Principal support is crucial, too; however, the principal acts in more of a gatekeeper or facilitator role by taking either a neutral and passive stance toward the innovation or by actively encouraging and supporting it. The innovation could not exist, though, with a principal who is negative or discouraging. Students play a direct role in sustaining the innovation as well. If the innovation affects students positively—for example, in terms of improved achievement or attitudes—teachers tend to be motivated to continue with the innovation, look for ways to improve it, and improvise if resources are reduced. The remaining essential condition for an innovation to be sustained is that the innovation itself must be perceived by teachers to be of value—it must be something that makes eminent sense to teachers, be consistent with their beliefs about how children learn, and simply be a "good thing to do."

More diffuse are the contributing conditions for sustaining an innovation. We identified four main conditions in the model, but we make no claim that the list is exhaustive. Support for the innovation from others within the school and external to the school are two of the conditions. Inside support may come from other teachers not directly involved in the innovation, whereas outside support may come from peers, parents, school district officials, municipal leaders, or ministry of education personnel. Both groups of actors tend to provide recognition and validation of a teacher's efforts. Most innovations seem to have a "champion," an individual who provides leadership and direction to the initiative so that it is sustained. The innovation teacher may be the champion, or it may be a technology coordinator, another teacher, or the principal. Funding plays a hand in sustaining innovations, too. Many innovations are provided with extra start-up funds, and when this funding is inevitably withdrawn, the stronger innovations tend to survive when the essential conditions for sustainability are met. The final contributing condition for sustainability is the presence of schools, school districts, or national policies and planning and programs that support the innovation. While many innovations function successfully in the absence of policies or plans, those that have a supportive framework are judged to be more likely to endure. Supportive policies are discussed in this chapter and developed further in Chapter 6.

Overall, the factors represented in our model correspond to those identified by Fullan (2001a) and Rogers (1995) except for one—the support of students. While Fullan does make the point that students are important participants in the change process, he does not specifically mention them in his framework. As will be seen in the discussion in subsequent sections, Fullan's concept of need and Rogers's relative advantage, compatibility, and observability are directly relevant to our model. Not represented in our model is clarity (Fullan), complexity (Fullan; Rogers), and trialability (Rogers).

Our explanatory model for sustainable innovations should not be considered as definitive, however. It is grounded in our analysis of the previously described cases and hence represents the "best fit" to the cases. Nevertheless, we believe that it provides a starting point for discussion and conjecture about the reasons why some ICT-based innovations fail while others flourish. In the next section, we discuss in detail each of the conditions in the model and provide evidence supporting its inclusion in the model, beginning first with the essential conditions for sustainability.

BARRIERS

Notably absent from our model are issues of technical support and adequately reliable computer hardware, factors that are frequently cited in the literature as critical to the sustainability of innovations. Means and Olson (1997) found that teachers often cited a lack of access to technology and technical support as barriers to their use of ICT. Lack of equipment and inadequate teacher knowledge was also mentioned by principals in the SITES Module 1 study (Pelgrum & Anderson, 1999). Problems such as these were mentioned in reports of the SITES Module 2 cases as well. For example, a large majority of the cases (62%) mentioned the limitations of equipment or resources. Often there were not enough computers for all the students, or access to the equipment was limited by location (e.g., the computer lab) or by available time. In a smaller number of cases there were other problems involving teacher-related concerns (in 41% of the cases), such as an overworked schedule or limited computer skills, or student-related concerns (in 36% of the cases), such as inappropriate use of the Internet or off-task use of e-mail. Of the entire group, 30% of the cases mentioned insufficient technical support and the same percentage mentioned technical problems, such as unreliable equipment or slow Internet access. Unfortunately, we found that schools and teachers had invented very few solutions to these problems. More often than not, administrators and teachers were left to capitalize on opportunities and cope with limitations.

However, in the group of 59 cases we examined in detail the issues that were mentioned did not appear to be a significant threat to the sustainability of their innovation. Therefore, specific barriers, such as lack of equipment or technical support, were not included in the model. Of course, this "finding" is limited to the cases in our sample. That is, technical barriers were not identified as limitations by this small percentage of cases that were both sustained and transferred. Limitations of time and staff did not allow us to examine the many cases where there was not evidence of both sustainability and transfer. But in the cases we studied, we were struck by the ability of teachers and schools to overcome these barriers to sustain and transfer their innovative practices.

ESSENTIAL CONDITIONS FOR SUSTAINABILITY

TEACHER SUPPORT

Clearly, teachers need to support an innovation if it is to be sustained. As we shall see in Chapter 6, it is often the effort and commitment of individual teachers that result in successful innovation when ICT plans and policies are missing. Teachers are on the front line of implementing any innovation in the classroom. Without their support, no amount of special funding or principal encouragement is likely to make the innovation sustainable. As Fullan and Hargreaves (1996) state, "However noble, sophisticated, or enlightened proposals for change and improvement might be, they come to nothing if teachers don't adopt them and translate them into effective classroom practice" (p. 13).

All the cases we studied cited instances of how supportive teachers were of their innovations. Typical was a teacher in the NetLibris project in a Finnish primary school (FI005), Finland's stellar case, who said, "As a literature teacher I am very enthusiastic about this innovation. Literature is fantastic. This is how I can tell it to students, that literature is fantastic."

A Thai lower secondary science teacher (TH005) was so enthusiastic about the Web materials he developed for his students that he said, "I want to come to school early in the morning to try out what I think might interest the students."

In an Israeli upper secondary school (IL007), teachers and students worked together to design Web materials for courses in various disciplines. One teacher reported, "There is a feeling of pride in every discipline team. Teachers are proud to display the Web site, and to say: this is our site."

In another Israeli upper secondary school (IL010), teachers used the Internet to create a Peace Network that connected their students to Arab students. The researchers who wrote up this case commented that the key to the sustainability of the innovation was the teachers and their willingness and readiness to take part. The principal of this school commented that the teachers became "hooked" on the innovation and saw their commitment as one that would even transcend shortfalls in resources.

A Canadian primary school (CA002) was built as an institution where teacher reflection and experimentation and autonomous, authentic, and engaged student learning were to be part of everyday practice. This case was identified by Canadian researchers as their stellar case (see Chapter 7). The use of ICT throughout the curriculum was a major focus at the school. The source of teacher commitment to this project was, according to the researchers who wrote the report, "the professional and personal satisfaction they derived from being able to teach in what they found to be a more meaningful and effective manner, and from seeing the positive impact their work was having on students."

Many other cases cited the positive attitude of teachers as an essential element of sustainability. For example, the report for a primary school in The Netherlands (NL003) stated that the teachers were enthusiastic about the innovation, had taken ownership of it, and wanted to develop teaching materials even after the technology coordinator left the school. Teachers at an upper secondary school in the Philippine's (PH006)—that country's "stellar case"—were so positive about their innovation that they wanted it to continue even if the school's agreement with the Net Curricula, an external service provider, was terminated. Similarly, a project in a primary school in Germany (DE010) that used the Internet to connect with schools in Germany, Finland, Great Britain, France, and Poland had become so ingrained into the school's culture that teachers said they wanted to continue it even without funding and support from its sponsor, the European Union.

Often we found that teachers were supportive of the innovation even when it involved increased workload. One secondary teacher in Catalonia, Spain, reported, "I have spent many hours preparing the innovation but it has contributed to improve my methodology and human relationships." Of another Spanish case, a primary school (ES002), researchers reported:

> Time is another important demand to carry out successfully these innovative activities. Teachers at CEIP Eladi Homs [the innovative school] are ICT-competent and willing to continue with the innovation even if it is demanding because it is motivating and rewarding for both teachers and pupils.

Similarly, the sustainability of the FastTrack@School project in an upper secondary school in Singapore (SG006) depended on the willingness of a core group of teachers to voluntarily put in extra time and effort to develop Web-based content modules for physics and Chinese language instruction.

This level of effort can often limit the transfer of the innovation. While teachers directly involved in initiating innovations tend to go well beyond the call of duty, others may be reluctant to make this commitment. One Israeli teacher (IL007) commented:

> We are not free workers, ... pay us; ... until now, everything was done on a voluntary basis. We did not receive any hours for any of our work. This is the reason why teachers don't want to get involved in the project.

Where more than one teacher in a school is involved and committed to a sustained innovation, they typically share the same goals and vision. This was apparent in the Canadian primary school (CA002), cited previously. It was also evident in a lower secondary school in Norway (NO005), where a visual communication project spread across most of the school. Prior to the project, teachers were disenchanted with students' "information-seeking" activities on the Internet. However, when the idea of using iMovie video software for visual communication projects arose, they fully supported it as the kind of activity that would promote student "knowledge production" and involve students in project-oriented work, a pedagogy that all in the school highly valued.

We also noted this link between shared vision and sustainability in a lower secondary school in the United States (US010). A strong consensus among teachers and administrators was reported about the seamless use of ICT within teaching and learning. Teachers viewed this use of ICT as essential to improving students' academic performance.

In another case from the United States, the urban upper secondary school featured in Chapter 3 that used ICT to support whole language reform (US019), researchers reported:

> A striking feature of the school faculty was their shared understanding of the school's mission and purpose—their commitment to whole language and technology. Such complete acceptance is surprising in an already established staff (as compared to a staff hired to open a new school). This can be explained in part by the large ESL teacher workforce, which already embraced some of the pedagogical practices of whole language reform and the formal and informal professional development made available in the school and district.

Teacher support for the innovation does not emerge from a vacuum, however. We found that three factors—student support, the perceived value of the innovation, and professional development—play an instrumental role in gaining their support, as depicted in the sustainability model in Figure 5.1. In the next three sections we elaborate on these necessary factors for teacher support of innovations, beginning with student support.

STUDENT SUPPORT

Student support appears to be related to teacher support in an iterative manner. That is, as teachers see that students benefit positively from the innovation, they become motivated to continue and possibly enhance their practice. This relationship is clearly evident in a Chilean primary school (CL010), Chile's stellar case. In this case the mathematics teacher used tutorial software and visited the supermarket with children to teach math and thinking skills. The teacher observed that "the children had a fairly mechanical grasp of math. They knew numbers well; they knew how to add and subtract. But they knew nothing of logic." She felt compelled to address this difficulty and to "search hard for ways to make the work more attractive to the students." Using a suite of various software packages and tools, including the Internet, she developed a semester-long series of activities that proved successful in accomplishing her goals. Based on her initial experiences, the teacher subsequently refined the project the following year and helped teachers in five other classes adopt her innovation.

The science teacher in a Thai secondary school (TH005) commented on the response of students to his use of ICT: "The children want to attend class more than before. They are eager, enthusiastic, and want to use computers to search for knowledge. Sometimes, they discuss what they saw on the Internet at home."

All cases we examined contained comments that students were supportive of the innovations in their schools. In fact, the adjective "enthusiastic" was used repeatedly by report authors. Here are several illustrations of student enthusiasm:

> Students are really interested in literature, and they are very motivated, enthusiastic, and they learn easily. (FI005)

> Students simply say they love the innovation. (IL008)

> According to the students, the innovation has opened up new opportunities in interacting with their teachers and fellow students. They were not only completing the homework assigned by their teachers but also learning about their immediate world, using resources that are within their reach and leaving a personal stamp on their activities. (CL009)

> The positive response of all the pupils involved with the innovation is another positive point for [the innovation's] sustainability. (ES007)

A particularly touching statement comes from Federica, a fifth-grade student in an Italian primary school (IT002), where Web forums, e-mail, newsgroups, net-poll, chat, and Web pages were used to support communication and cooperation among children, teachers, and parents, both inside and outside the school. She summed up her experience with the project by saying, "School is so beautiful; what a pity that for us in the fifth-grade it will end soon."

On the whole we conclude that student support—and indeed enthusiasm—for the local innovation played an essential role in motivating teachers to continue to carry out and improve the innovation. We maintain that teachers want to do what is best for students to enhance their learning. If they believe that students are benefiting from and supporting a particular innovation, they in turn will be willing to devote the additional time and effort required to maximize the advantage brought on by the innovation. Metz (1993) provides a plausible explanation for a phenomenon like this in terms of teacher intrinsic rewards. She argues that there are so few extrinsic rewards gained by merit or persistent effort in teaching that teachers turn to intrinsic rewards for establishing job satisfaction. The most influential intrinsic reward comes from student cooperation and success. Therefore, teachers are bound to invest time and effort in activities that lead to student accomplishment.

PERCEIVED VALUE OF THE INNOVATION

Perceived value appears to directly influence teachers' desire to carry out an innovation. Beyond student support for an innovation, we found that teachers had to believe that what they were doing in the classroom had merit. Knowing that they were engaged in a very worthwhile activity, teachers approached their innovative practice with high levels of motivation and determination to sustain it, despite the inevitable setbacks and difficulties of implementing any ICT-based program.

This factor is a combination of what Rogers (1995) calls the "relative advantage" and "compatibility" of an innovation. In Rogers's terms an innovation will be adopted more rapidly if it is seen as better than what supersedes and it is compatible with the existing values, past experiences, and needs of the adopters. In Fullan's (2001a) terms the innovation will be adopted if there is a fit between the innovation and district's or school's needs.

Teachers in this study tended to express their views on the value of their innovations in terms of the how they fit with their students' needs. Teachers mentioned three types of student impact as the motivation for their efforts: (1) students' general life skills and attitudes, (2) ICT-specific skills, and (3) subject-specific skills.

General Impact

Beginning with the more generalized impact, we found that teachers felt that their innovation helped students develop skills that they would use throughout their lives. This was expressed by the physics teacher in the Philippines (PH006) who said, "Yes, students benefited from the innovation. The motivation is high. Leadership and communication skills are developed and enhanced."

Teachers at an upper secondary school in Israel (IL008) believed that their innovation supported students' acquisition of learning skills, inquiring skills, and the appropriate choice of tools. Similarly, in a secondary school in Thailand (TH003), researchers reported the following in regard to teachers' beliefs:

> The use of ICT is a way to prepare the students for their future careers, increase their achievement, encourage their cooperative learning, foster their independence, and develop their responsibility for self-learning. … Other benefits of the use of ICT in classroom are the students' increased interest in learning, confidence in expressing their opinions in the classroom, broadened horizon, being up to date, ability to work as a team and to apply the knowledge to daily living and to preparing for the future, and increased ability to understand difficult subject matters.

In another case report from a primary school in England (UK005), student benefits were succinctly described as follows: "Teachers noted that the children involved in the E-pals project developed improved attitudes to school work, better communications skills, increased motivation, and raised awareness of the world of work." In a primary school in Catalonia, Spain (ES001), the following was reported: "Both teachers and pupils agree that ICT motivates pupils and facilitates learning. Teachers stated that it is essential for their pupils' future professional development."

ICT Skills

It would hardly be a surprise that teachers engaged in the use of technology value innovations that develop student ICT skills. This is what we observed in a number of our 59 cases. This value is most prominently illustrated by a comment made by a teacher in the South African girl's primary school (ZA004) featured in Chapter 3: "I teach because technology in today's society is absolutely part and parcel of everything we do."

The physics teacher in the Philippines (PH006) commented that "students going to college become equipped with basic computer skills or if not they can find jobs through the net." His principal agreed: "It is very important to their learning and it would be very helpful in their future careers. The computer skills acquired can be of big help to a family business."

This position is supported by these excerpts from other case reports:

> Everybody agrees that it is good for the children to acquire computers skills. The staff is convinced that children take their work more seriously and in some cases can even be supported more effectively. (DE007)

> The use of ICT is regarded as an essential and necessary element of school activities. All students will learn basic knowledge of ICT, and it is largely integrated into learning. (FI001)

Subject Skills

The final category of perceived value is the teachers' belief that an innovation is one that will develop student subject matter competence. We found that cases which were sustained and transferred were more likely to report that students acquired subject matter knowledge (73% vs. 57%; $x^2 = 4.0$, $df = 1$, $p < .05$) and metacognitive skills (54% vs. 30%, $x^2 = 9.3$, $df = 1$, $p < .005$) than other cases. Given the nature of evidence on outcomes in the reports, this is just as likely to reflect teachers' and administrators' beliefs that student learning benefited from the innovation than to reflect actual student outcomes. But for our model it is this belief in the benefits to students that is important.

This was witnessed in the case of a primary school in Germany (DE007), where the teachers were convinced that children took their work more seriously and learning was more effective. This is evident from this statement from a language teacher at the school:

> Especially children with extremely low performance took great profit out of working with the computer. Children who were almost functionally illiterate devotedly wrote with the computer. Motivation is extremely important here. They suddenly liked to do things they had actually hated before and they had better results, too.

In a lower secondary school in Portugal (PT003), a number of math tutorial programs were used in a math laboratory called Net Mathict. Researchers in Portugal reported that teachers believed that their innovation developed students' mathematics skills:

> There were [reasons] for continuing the innovation, no longer as a mere pedagogical experiment but as a [routine] practice in the schools. ... The different people involved agree ... that project Net Mathict has introduced significant changes in the school, particularly as regards the teaching and learning of mathematics.

A Danish primary school (DK004) emphasizes the stimulation of the students' reading development in all grades. In the Reading Course, teachers used a software program called Work with Danish to support students' reading. The case report stated:

> The principal says that the students benefit from the Reading Course because they are able to work intensively with reading without being distracted. His impression is that the use of ICT is more beneficial to poor readers than to competent readers.

In a primary school in Italy (IT001) where students used ICT to write a Web-based magazine published for other schools and the community, the case report stated:

> For the school it is important to show and communicate the students' learning activities, as well as to foster a quick and [inexpensive] link among the schools of the outskirts and the centre. The edition of the magazine *Smoke Signals* improves the teaching of language (writing and reading).

The case report of a lower secondary school in Russia (RU002) that employed Geometer's Sketchpad stated:

> It appeared that even low-performing students became more interested in geometry and improved their outcomes. After that [the innovation teacher] started to use the facility in the regular course for geometry in Grades 5–9. The heart of innovation could be expressed in teacher's words: "Since the beginning of the experiment none of the geometric facts were merely presented to students, they discover them themselves. They discovered even more than is contained in the regular curriculum."

ICT was often seen as a central contribution to the impact of the innovation. In the words of a teacher of French in a secondary school in England (UK009) that used videoconferencing to connect foreign language students to students in France, "You do it in a technological way or don't do it. There isn't a nontechnological alternative."

However, the value of an innovation is not always immediately evident, and teachers may be skeptical until its value is demonstrated. For example, the English teacher in an upper secondary school in Spain (ES007) proposed that the school participate in the European Union Comenius and Socrates programs aimed at using the Internet to promote cross-cultural understanding. The report stated:

> The school board gave her all the support [she needed], but most of the teachers were a bit skeptical at the beginning and only the Catalan and Music teacher collaborated with her. When the first successful results appeared, many more teachers began to cooperate.

The point we want to emphasis is that teachers believed that their innovation was of value. Our contention is that teachers' beliefs led them to want to carry on with an innovation after initially trying it. Ultimately, teachers will question their beliefs if there is contradictory evidence, but this belief appears to be one of several necessary factors that lead teachers to persist with an innovation.

TEACHER PROFESSIONAL DEVELOPMENT

For any classroom innovation to be successful, teachers need to learn new skills, and, equally as important, they may need to unlearn beliefs about students or pedagogy that have dominated their professional careers (Darling-Hammond & McLaughlin, 1996). In addition, ICT-based innovations have unique professional development requirements. Such support may include hands-on technology use, a variety of learning experiences, ongoing technical assistance and support, and the learning of curriculum-specific software applications (NCREL, 2002). Thus, teacher professional development is at the heart of sustaining an innovation.

Our analysis supports this view and classifies professional development as an essential factor in the sustainability model. This is not just professional development related to ICT but to the pedagogical skills that are needed to integrate technology into teaching. Indeed, we found that cases which were sustained and transferred were much more likely than other cases to report that teachers acquired new pedagogical skills (68% vs. 51%, $x^2 = 4.3$, $df = 1$, $p < .05$).

However, in our model, we do not distinguish the manner in which teachers acquire the necessary knowledge and skills; it could be through preservice teacher education programs, formal professional development courses, learning in informal groups with colleagues, or self-study. Rather, we use the term *professional development* in the very broadest sense to indicate that teachers need to have or acquire ICT competencies and other related pedagogical knowledge and skills to implement sustainable technology-based innovations.

A variety of approaches to professional development was evident in the cases we studied. Most case reports described somewhat traditional ICT training workshops and courses run by outside experts. These were typically driven by formal national, district, or local school policies. For example, a private lower secondary school in Thailand (TH001) had allocated a budget for regular ICT workshops during school breaks. In these workshops there were expectations that all teachers would gain specific competencies, such as being able to search for information on the Internet.

These traditional approaches are often associated with national policies. National or provincial policies cited as having been influential in developing teacher skills included those in Catalonia, Spain (ES001); Chile (CL009); Latvia (LV005); and Thailand (TH004). Teachers in the cases we studied often participated in professional development courses or workshops that were supported by targeted funding from these policies. The professional development funding was often part of a larger budgetary allocation that was also for hardware and software.

Cases from some European schools (such as CZ002, LV005, and NL003) mentioned policies that either require or strongly urge teachers to acquire the European Computer Driving License (see **http://www.edcl.com**), which attests to their proficiency in ICT skills. In fact, the private professional secondary school in the Czech Republic (CZ002) featured in Chapter 3 reported receiving a special financial award for every teacher who was licensed. In the case of Denmark, the government has developed the Educational ICT Drivers License (see **http://www.skole-it.dk/**), which focuses on the pedagogical use and integration of ICT in educational contexts.

Less traditional approaches to professional development were apparent in other cases. For example, in the report of the science simulation project at a Korean lower secondary school (KR004), teachers had a range of professional learning opportunities available to them, and these were not uncommon in other schools we studied. They included graduate studies, participation in formal research projects, school-sponsored ICT training programs, teacher study groups, self-study, and individualized assistance.

A particularly creative school district policy was noted in a school in the United States (US010) where the district committed to a year-long, paid professional development experience for all of its middle school teachers. Unlike many one-size-fits-all teacher professional development experiences, the district gave teachers the choice to begin learning in the areas in which they felt most comfortable, whether it was in teacher-centered or student-centered uses of technology. The provision of flexibility in this policy and its connection to school implementation of ICT appeared to be the key to its success.

At the other U.S. school in this group (US019), one of the English teachers commented on the professional development opportunities at the school:

> They [the school district] have been bending over backwards trying to give people access to technology and courses, after school, … weekends paid, weekends with credit given, with increment credit given. So there were all kinds of incentives given to people to come in and to receive whatever they needed in the matter of tutoring.

Other teacher professional development approaches were evident in the cases we studied that were less formal and structured. These models focused on creating teacher-initiated cultures of teacher continuous learning. Case reports from both an upper secondary school in Israel (IL007) and a Canadian primary school (CA002) described the use of a "coaching model" for staff development. Here, teachers helped each other directly in the classroom or through teacher-led professional development workshops. In the Canadian school, the coaching model itself was sufficiently ingrained into the school's culture that it was "self-sustaining" and a particularly useful way of dealing with changes in teaching staff at the site.

At the previously cited U.S. secondary school (US010), both workshops and teacher reflection were part of the school culture. The case report contains this comment:

> At the school, the teachers meet in grade-level teams to discuss curriculum and other issues. These team interactions are in addition to bimonthly staff meetings and occasional "minimum days" when students are released early so teachers and staff can work together.

In an upper secondary school in Singapore (SG006) a similar collegial culture was reported:

> The innovation allowed teachers to be action researchers. It provided an avenue for teachers to try out different teaching approaches and see students' responses to teaching using Web content. This added variety to teaching. Teachers worked together and shared their teaching resources. … The new challenges of the innovation served as a glue to bond teachers closer together. There is quite a lot of sharing amongst us about how we should structure the [ICT learning experience to achieve our objectives].

These latter approaches are more consistent with current beliefs about professional development that emphasize teacher involvement in decisions about their professional development and long-term, school-based engagement in reflective communities of practice focusing on student learning and curriculum (e.g., Guskey, 1995; Hargreaves, 1995; Hiebert, Gallimore, & Stigler, 2002; Lieberman, 1996).

ADMINISTRATIVE SUPPORT

Support of the school administration, head teacher, or principal is an essential factor that contributes to sustainability in our model. Of the 59 cases in the sample that had evidence of sustainability and transferability, 7% had leaders classified on the case cover sheets as "neutral" toward the innovation, 66% were "supportive" but not directly involved, and 27% of the cases had leaders "actively involved" in the innovation. Of special note is that none resisted or discouraged the innovation in their schools. This is perhaps not too surprising because if the principal did not at least tacitly approve of the innovation it would be very difficult for it to flourish in a school.

Contrary to Fullan (2001a), who contends that principals must be active participants in innovation, our findings suggest that a principal can play a minimum role as "gatekeeper." The principal can sustain the innovation by approving of its existence and not undermining it. Fullan and Hargreaves (1996) emphasize this point when giving advice to school principals about leading successful school reform. They state that where leadership and school environments are persistently unsupportive, teacher efforts will be "slim, short-lived, or non-existent" (p. 84).

An example of the minimum level of support in our group of cases is the principal at a Finnish lower secondary school (FI007). This principal characterizes the small number of leaders who played a "neutral" role in their school's innovation. He apparently inherited the innovation from the previous principal, who was very actively involved. According to the case report, the current principal is "aware of the innovation and the innovation teacher does not experience resistance" from him. Another example of a neutral principal was found at the Russian school (RU002) where the Geometer's Sketchpad was used. In this case the principal said that he does not "prevent the innovation. But I cannot insist on [teachers participating] because they are overloaded with work." At the same time the principal acknowledged that changes "are coming, the demands of parents are growing, … In the near future, I suppose, they will insist on changing the teaching and learning practice."

In keeping with Fullan's (2001a) contention, most principals in our sample went beyond the minimum gatekeeper function to seek special resources for the innovation, explain and justify it to parents and senior school board or ministry of education officials, and encourage other teachers to take part in it. A small minority of principals went as far as being role models for teachers in the use of technology, or they provided visionary leadership in making the innovation come about.

There was considerable variability of involvement evident among these "supportive" principals. The principal of a German primary school (DE007), for instance, epitomizes the minimally supportive kind of leader who, according to the report, "takes a general interest in teachers' initiatives." Similarly, the principal of a secondary boy's school in China Hong Kong (CN009) "allowed new practices and innovation to occur in the school and did not interrupt [teachers] ... and he provided a liberal learning environment for the innovation to grow." A less passive role was also taken by the principal at a Catalonian primary school (ES001) who "follows her predecessor's philosophy, that is, she tries to facilitate and promote the implementation of collaborative projects and the use of ICT." The principal at an English secondary school (UK004) also played this kind of role since he saw himself being "a manager with a remit of facilitating, stimulating, and encouraging both staff and students to extract the full potential of individual students" by using the innovative database tracking system at his school.

More proactive was the principal at a South African girl's primary school (ZA004). The researchers in this case reported:

> The school is under the leadership of a principal who perceives herself as an instructional leader and a facilitator who treats staff as empowered professionals. She believes that her role is to create a safe and a happy environment that facilitates learning and innovation. She asserts, for example, that "I allowed the children and the teachers to virtually put a hold on what the normal timetable would be to run this project [the innovation]." She also promoted the project through the local press and by meeting with the relevant people regarding the project.

Similarly, the principal of a primary school in Singapore (SG001) saw herself as key in sustaining the school's digital art project. "What is my role?," she said. "To ensure that it [the innovation] goes on." The researchers in the case reported:

> She [arranged for the IT department head] to conduct training for teachers. ... The good working relationship the principal and the technology coordinator have with outside agencies contributes to the sustainability of Digital Art. The principal and the technology coordinator have got [a] very good partnership with [outside] service suppliers.

One might speculate that the supportive style of leadership is more likely than the passive neutral role to result in a sustainable innovation over a greater length of time. This would occur because supportive leaders would tend to lessen the burden on the classroom teacher by dealing with many of the external threats to sustainability, such as funding, upgrading hardware and software, and allocating sufficient teacher time to the innovation.

The third category, the actively involved leader, is frequently the visionary behind the school's innovation, identifies personally with the innovation, often persuades and cajoles others into adopting his or her vision, and demonstrates ICT skills. The founding principal at a Canadian primary school (CA002) appeared to be this kind of leader. In the report, he was described as "a brilliant and charismatic leader ... able through a series of public meetings and later work with the school council to assuage most of these concerns by explaining the goals, principles, and purposes ICT would serve in the school."

However, there may be risks that come with active involvement. This visionary ran into conflict with one of the school district officials and was removed a few years after the opening of the school. But the contrarian district official has also since left, and the principal's vision was sufficiently ingrained into the school's culture that it survived the transition to a new principal.

Another example of this leadership style was found at a private secondary school in the Philippines (PH006). The case study reported:

> The principal was very active and supportive in the integration of ICT in the school curriculum. According to the innovation teacher, "The key player in the innovation is our principal." ... She is a "hands-on leader" in the use of technology not only in her work as a principal (e.g., e-mail letters to teachers and external relations), but as one of the core faculty being trained by Net Curricula to give ICT training to the other teachers. She also acts as one of the school's [computer] system administrators trained by Net Curricula. Being a principal, she believes that she "should be knowledgeable about the innovation to be able to convince the parents and other teachers about the importance and benefits of the use of technology."

We saw similarities in the leader of a private girls' school, also in the Philippines (PH002), who was described as follows:

> The principal initiated the application of CAI [computer-assisted instruction], and it gained acceptance among the teachers. By taking the initiative, the principal demonstrated what leadership meant: providing support by encouraging teachers who would be the key implementers of the innovation, and believing in the pedagogical value of the technology by applying it in her work. The principal's philosophy [was]: "I cannot push as much unless I myself see its value. I cannot facilitate the learning process unless I'm a learner myself."

Much has been written about the need for strong, visionary leaders, particularly in the corporate world (Senge et al., 2000). In Chapter 4, we saw the role that a local vision played in schoolwide ICT-based innovation. However, Senge et al. cautions us that vision in a learning organization must not be only that of one person or a small group who imposes it on the rest of the organization. At best this situation commands compliance—not commitment. For commitment, a vision must be shared among all members of the organization, for only then will individuals be able to personally identify with it. We will return to this discussion in the next chapter when we examine the importance of a shared vision in local ICT policy and planning.

CONTRIBUTING CONDITIONS FOR SUSTAINABILITY

According to our analysis, the conditions we have described are necessary but not sufficient in order for an innovation to be sustained. But other factors make sustainability more likely. Our analysis of the cases identified five conditions that contribute to an innovation being sustained: (1) other support within the school, (2) support from outside, (3) having an innovation champion, (4) funding, and (5) supportive policy and planning conditions. We labeled these conditions as "contributing" because there was evidence that they facilitated sustainability, but they were not found in all sustainable cases. We will elaborate on these conditions in the next five sections.

OTHER SUPPORT WITHIN THE SCHOOL

When we refer to "other support" within the school as a contributing condition for sustainability, we are talking about effective, personal support and encouragement given to the innovation teachers by school colleagues. We hypothesize that peer recognition provides added encouragement for teachers to sustain their innovation. For example, in an ICT-based literature project in a secondary school in the Philippines (PH006), researchers reported:

> The innovation does not only serve as an instructional tool for teachers but it also created some positive impact on them by improving their self-confidence. The innovation teacher admitted in the interview that "we receive peer recognition from our fellow teachers and administrators." We learned from her that as an innovation teacher, she is selected to represent the school to the Annual Curricula Best Practices Symposium as teacher presenter.

The case report of a lower secondary school in Portugal (PT003) relates that the innovation was run by the "curricular department" that gained "recognition" inside the school for its innovative work. This recognition, in turn, acted as a "stimulus for the [math] teachers to continue their work."

Peer support is often associated with collaboration and teamwork. This aspect is reported in the case of a Catalonian primary school (ES001):

> As the school is small there are habitual coordination meetings among teachers implementing [the innovation at] the same level where they share project ideas and make arrangements to collaborate together, especially within the same cycle (2 consecutive school years). The two teachers directly involved in the innovation work still closer together. They often share classes, either both being in the same classroom with all the pupils or dividing the class into two groups and [each] taking half of the group. There are also at least three meetings per school year with the teachers implementing the innovation in the other schools.

When an innovation becomes part of the school culture, teachers who were the originators have their work validated by their peers and the school principal, which creates favorable conditions for the innovation to prosper. In a Danish primary and lower secondary school (DK004), researchers reported that "the teachers behind the Reading Course [the innovation] do not expect difficulties … having other teachers rendering the extra effort and time for preparing and carrying out the course. The course has become an institution in the school."

A similar situation was also evident in an Israeli secondary school (IL010), where researchers reported, "The fact that the Peace Network had become a part of the school folklore is evident when passing through the hallways. On the walls hang pictures of meetings between Jews and Arabs—and this affects uninvolved teachers as well."

Support from others in the school suggests that the innovation becomes more visible or has a higher profile than what one would normally expect of a classroom project. Indeed, the case reports frequently claimed that the innovations were highly recognized in the school and, many times, in the community. Rogers (1995) maintains that innovations that are easily seen and communicated to others are more likely to be adopted than those that are not, a concept discussed previously in this chapter as the "observability" of an innovation. Thus, the support from others may not only motivate innovation teachers to continue an innovation but may facilitate transfer as well.

SUPPORT FROM OUTSIDE THE SCHOOL

External recognition of the work in which teachers are engaged appears to contribute to the sustainability of an innovation. This factor, too, may be linked indirectly to Rogers's (1995) notion of observability described previously. In the cases we studied, external support came from a variety of sources including parents, local municipalities, school districts, private companies, agencies, universities, and ministries of education. The support of parents, however, was most prevalent and seemed to be particularly influential. In the Philippines, parents at the Filipino lower secondary school engaged in an ICT-supported literature course (PH006) showed their support of the innovation through voluntarily paying additional monthly technology fees. An e-mail message from a parent at this school made a significant enough impact on teachers that it was mentioned in the report:

> In fact, one parent showed recognition of the school's effort by sending an e-mail to the school's Web site. The parent (a mother) wrote: "As we face the global communication and as society becomes technologically capable, information technology is a prerequisite for all educational institutions. That's why I send this e-mail to express my deepest admiration to [the school] for its successful integration of technology in all subjects."

Many times, innovations in the sample had parental support from the beginning. But sometimes this support had to be earned, as described in the case of a visual communication project at a Norwegian lower secondary school (NO005):

> The parents are now very positive about the innovation. In the beginning they were very critical partly because they did not use a regular grade and evaluation system, and partly because they focused a lot on visual communication and less on written text. After some initial rounds of discussion the parent group is very supportive of the way the school is working. The main reason the parents explain is that they see that their children are much more motivated toward learning in school now than before.

In some cases, the school alumni were the source of outside support. At a secondary boys school in China Hong Kong (CN009), support from the school alumni was cited as contributing to the sustainability of their innovation because they "bring new ideas and insight to the students and help build a network community."

Beyond parents and alumni, cases reported outside support from school districts and local municipalities (e.g., ES007, DK005, IL007, US010) largely through the provision of ICT hardware, Internet access, and teacher training. Another important form of support was community recognition. For example, a local community in northern Italy recognized the Smoke Signals Project (IT001) in one of its primary schools by posting the project's logo on the community Web site and announcing that it had won a global award. This project is the stellar case from Italy featured in Chapter 7. At another Italian school—a secondary technical school (IT010)—a computerized self-learning center was given an award by the Italian Public Function Department for being one of the "most effective, innovative, and successful projects within public services."

Nongovernmental recognition and support came from several other sources, too. University support and validation of the teachers' work was evident at a primary school in Chile (CL004) that collaborated with the Pontifical Catholic University of Chile, a primary school in China Hong Kong (CN010) that worked with the University of China Hong Kong, and two Finnish schools (FI001 and FI002) that worked with the University of Helsinki and University of Turku, respectively.

In two other cases, international recognition motivated teachers to sustain their innovations. Teachers in the Reading via the Internet Project (DE009), Germany's stellar case, participated in the Comenius Project and were motivated by the positive comments received from colleagues in the Czech Republic, Sweden, and Hungary. Teachers and students in the Digital Art Project (SG001), Singapore's stellar case, were motivated by the fact that student paintings were sought after as gifts for local and foreign visitors at the Singapore Ministry of Education.

Finally, corporate support and participation was a contributing factor to the continuation of two projects. The E-Pals Project at an English primary school (UK005) was supported by the local employees from Ericsson Ltd. A particularly impressive case in this regard was Project PineLINK at a lower secondary school in the United States (US010). The goal of this project was to establish a community intranet that would provide courseware to students but access to parents of students, community members, and others. The project was funded by a federal challenge grant that was successful because it involved many partners, including companies such as Microsoft Corporation and the local cable service provider Cox Communications, as well as city, county, and state agencies and postsecondary education institutions.

INNOVATION CHAMPIONS

Many school innovations have "champions"—individuals who pioneer, advocate, defend, and advance the innovation in their schools and beyond. They are frequently charismatic individuals and risk-takers who throw their efforts behind the innovation to overcome obstacles and resistance (Howell & Higgins, 1990). These individuals are often key to the sustainability of their particular innovation. However, if the innovation is totally bound up in any one individual to the extent that no one else has the capability to offer it, the innovation will quickly fail if that individual leaves the school. Nevertheless, if the champion remains at the school the chances that the innovation will continue are excellent because of that person's dedication and commitment.

Not all schools that we studied had a champion, which suggests that they are a contributing factor to sustainability but not a prerequisite. The champions in our sample were principals, coordinators, or classroom teachers.

The principal of the Filipino secondary school (PH006) mentioned previously in this chapter, exemplifies the role of the champion principal. This principal set an example by using technology herself in her daily work and by participating in a specialized training session so that she would be able to assist other teachers in her school.

We observed this level of commitment and dedication in the project coordinator in a Portuguese secondary school (PT003). According to the school head, as reported by the researchers of this case, the project coordinator has been teaching for many years and her career testifies to her strong investment in her academic and professional training throughout her teaching life. Her interest in ICT goes back to the first national experiments in this field. The coordinator attaches great importance to that first contact with ICT, which was decisive in her future career. Later, she would work in teacher training, in the context of the first official programmes which promoted ICT in education. Nowadays, as project coordinator, she continues to do teacher training in this field.

In an Israeli secondary school (IL008), we noted the persuasive role champions can play in spreading the innovation. At this school the project coordinator, too, was the champion. According to the report:

> The pedagogical administrator of the school claims that "once there is someone who is hooked on the innovation that sweeps everyone away, it works." In the school there is such a person, and there are teachers willing to put in efforts. The Aviv [the innovation] coordinator is indeed the pioneer, and the camp follows her.

In the Comenius Project in the German primary school (DE009), the champion was a classroom teacher. Again, the champion's role in enticing others to be involved in the innovation is evident in the report, which states, "The usage of ICT in classes is fundamentally based on the commitment of one teacher who started the usage of the media in her class. Gradually, other teachers became fascinated by the application of ICT in teaching."

Clearly, the champion is a desirable individual to have in a school. Schools must exercise caution, however, not to rely exclusively on the champion to carry the load of the innovation. They need to make certain that the champion's expertise is shared among the school staff to ensure the innovation's long-term survival. As Fullan (2001b) cautions, "Deep and sustained reform depends on many, … not just the very few who are destined to become extraordinary." Reliance on champions alone results in "at best, episodic improvement followed by frustrated or despondent dependency" (pp. 1–2).

FUNDING

At first glance one might expect that funding would be listed as an essential factor in the sustainability model because of the ongoing costs of purchasing and supporting equipment. Indeed, almost all case reports bring up the issue of finances in relation to sustainability. But we came to realize that schools, despite the financial difficulties that most face, continue to innovate even in the face of adverse financial conditions. This is a testament to the dedication and determination of teachers and school leaders to do what they believe is best for their students. Therefore, we have listed financial issues as a contributing factor to sustainability rather than as a necessary condition.

Many of the sustainable cases in the subset we studied seem to rely on special grants, student fees, and fund-raising activities. Indeed, innovation leaders became masterful at pursuing local, national, and international funding opportunities from public and private sources to keep their projects alive. The key to long-term financial security, however, seems to lie in planning and setting local spending priorities.

A lower secondary school in the United States (US009) provides an excellent example of this strategy. The innovation in this school is part of an overall district strategy to integrate

ICT throughout the core curriculum. The school superintendent reframes the issue away from finances when he says, "I think it's a leadership question and an attitude question. ... So I don't think it's a big cost issue just to begin with." He continues on about the benefits of spending an additional $100 or $200 per student when schools are already spending several thousand dollars per student:

> We were spending $5,000 or $6,000 a kid with getting virtually no results, then for changing year round spending [by adding] about another $100 to $200 a child and getting significant results. ... The educational community ought to figure this one out. But they don't.

According to the case report, much of the sustainability of the innovation in this school was due to the district's reallocation of resources for technology and implementing cost-saving measures, such as strategic software purchases, tough negotiations with vendors, and the use of in-house maintenance.

Other cases (notably IL007 and PH006) describe the financial planning and priority-setting processes to sustain their innovation, but in less detail. In any case, setting spending priorities within schools and districts inevitably means that other initiatives or areas will not receive the funding they feel is due. The case report for a German primary school (DE007) raised this issue when a teacher not involved in the innovation made the accusation that 70,000 DM was being "squandered [on ICT] and there will be no penny left for the simplest repair of the [traditional] physics instruments." Clearly, leaders need to address resentment such as this; otherwise, their innovations could be undermined.

SUPPORTIVE POLICY AND PLANS

Pedagogical innovations can exist without being situated within a broader school, regional, or national plan; strong, motivated teachers will often innovate regardless of policies. This observation is supported by an analysis of the cover sheets for the 59 cases that showed evidence of both sustainability and transferability. Table 5.1 classifies cases according to whether they had a link to a national education policy or plan, to a national ICT policy or plan, or to a school ICT policy or plan. The strongest linkage to plans for sustainable and transferable cases was to a national ICT policy or plan: 86% were linked and, by implication, 14% were not. There were fewer linkages to other types of policies or plans. Therefore, we have included policy and planning as a contributing, rather than an essential, factor for sustainability in our model. Evidence for the contributions policy can make comes both from a comparison of the linkages of sustainable cases to the entire sample and from examination of statements made in the case reports themselves.

When the sustainable cases are compared to the entire sample, two differences stand out most markedly. First, 86% of the sustainable cases are linked to national ICT policies or plans, whereas only 66% of the remaining cases are linked. Second, 46% of the sustainable cases are linked to all three types of plans, while relatively fewer, 34%, of the remaining cases are linked in this way. The difference between the sustainable cases and the remaining cases on linkages to school ICT policies and plans is relatively modest (68% versus 60%), and there is no difference between groups for national educational policy or plans (61% for both). Although Chapter 6 provides a detailed analysis of policies for the entire set of cases, a brief examination of the sustainable cases linked to all three categories of policies or plans will be helpful in illuminating how policies and plans contributed to sustaining the innovations.

Table 5.1

NUMBER OF SUSTAINABLE CASES LINKED TO PLAN TYPE

Type of Link	NO. (%) OF SUSTAINABLE AND TRANSFERABLE CASES (n = 59)	NO. (%) IN REMAINING SET OF CASES (n = 115)
Link to national educational policy or plan	36 (61)	70 (61)
Link to national ICT policy or plan	51 (86)	76 (66)
Link to school ICT policy or plan	40 (68)	69 (60)
Link to all of the above	27 (46)	39 (34)

Sustainable Cases Linked to National ICT Policies

As will be seen in Chapter 6, national ICT policies tend to be aimed at educational reform, improving student skills and achievement, or developing student ICT competencies. Typically, the policies provide special funding for hardware, software, and network infrastructure in schools, and to a lesser extent for teacher professional development. These policies appeared to have a direct impact on sustaining innovations by providing schools with the necessary rationale and resources. For example, the case report for a secondary boys school in China Hong Kong (CN009) states:

> According to the IT team and the principal interviews, both the principal and teachers reported that the establishment of the Quality Education Fund and the Information Technology for Learning in a New Era 5-Year Strategy policy helped a lot in implementing the innovative practices in school. For example, the 5-year plan provided the initial IT training cost for teachers. Being one of the pilot schools, it had received additional funding for upgrading the infrastructure in school and for providing more computer access for the students. As the IT coordinator stated, "Under the national policy (5-year plan) it provides us with lots of resources, such as extra headcount (the IT coordinator) and the TSS system provides extra manpower. With the pilot school scheme extra funding is granted."

Similarly, in Thailand (TH005), the national policy was cited in the report as contributing to sustainability:

> The role of the National Education Act, B.E. 2542 (1999) should never be underestimated. It supports the school's policy regarding teacher development, the development of teaching-learning process, and ICT learning network, which in turns stimulates the development of innovations and contributes to its sustainability.

Another example of the impact of national ICT policy was the Connecting project of Escola das Carreiras (PT002). The case report described its connection to national policy as follows:

> There is a national support policy for the introduction and application of ICT in the educational process, expressed in several national programmes. The school has benefited from this policy, which has allowed it to acquire equipment to develop ICT-related projects.

Sustainable Cases Linked to National and Local Policies

The subset of 27 cases that linked to national education, national ICT, and school policies and plans are arguably in a stronger position to sustain their innovations because of their alignment to and support from local and national goals. Several examples of how cases link to the three kinds of plans will illustrate this. One is the secondary school laptop project described in the case report of a German secondary school (DE003). At the local level this school has a reputation for openness to innovation and a desire to move from "knowledge transmission and instruction-type lessons" toward "independent questions and learning by research" according to the principal. When the opportunity arose to acquire laptop computers from the national program for Systematic Integration of Media, Information and Communication, the staff members believed that ICT could be used in a way that would help them achieve their teaching objectives. As a result, the laptop project was established in all subject areas and for interdisciplinary work.

Another example of a sustainable innovation linked to local and national policies is described in the Interactive Toolkit for Mathematics Project at Makati Science High School (PH003). According to the case report, the school's mission includes the "pursuit of excellence in education, particularly in the fields of science and technology." Consistent with that mission it became a School of the Future, a government program that aimed at improving the quality of education through the use of modern technology. As part of the school's strategy to meet this challenge, it implemented ICT in various subject areas with a special focus on mathematics, science, and English. In addition to being linked to the national reform program and the school's mission, the innovation is connected to two other policies. One is the City of Makati Long-Term Development Plan, a comprehensive education program aimed at making the city a center of science and mathematics. Through the local school board the school receives special financial support to implement ICT-based teaching and learning. The other policy is the Department of Education, Culture and Sports framework for the implementation of ICT in school programs, which requires students to develop core knowledge, skills, and attitudes related to ICT. In part because of the interconnections with these various policies and programs, the school administrator confidently stated that "the innovation will go on even for the next 10 years."

These cases, particularly the latter case, illustrate how linkages to various levels of policies and plans can support an innovation. They lend further credence to Fullan's (1994) observation that neither top-down, centrally mandated school reforms nor grass-roots, bottom-up reform alone succeeds in the long run. He argues that a blended approach of centralized and decentralized reform will be the most effective in changing the core teaching and learning in schools.

TRANSFERABILITY OF INNOVATIONS

In the preceding sections we examined the essential and contributing factors relating to sustaining innovations and their interrelationships. Now we turn to the issue of transferability of innovations.

Many educational innovations begin as pilot projects aimed at reforming practice. The purpose of the pilot is to gain an understanding of the requirements, outcomes, implications, and value of the initiative. If the pilot proves sustainable and successful in meeting its goals, planners and policy makers next need to address the dilemma of how to scale up or transfer the innovation to other classrooms within the school, to other schools, or to both. This is a complex problem, for what works in one particular classroom or school may not necessarily function in another. Thus, there is a need to understand the underlying conditions that promote transferability or scalability of innovations. We explore some of these conditions from the perspective of the set of cases examined in this chapter.

As discussed at the beginning of the chapter, we selected for this analysis 59 case reports that had evidence supporting both sustainability and transferability. After a detailed reading of these cases, only 24 (41% of the subset) specifically identified the place where the innovation had been transferred. Of these, 10 had transferred within the school, 11 transferred beyond the school, and 3 transferred both within the school and beyond. The remaining 35 case reports were vague about the extent to which transfer had actually occurred, said the innovation was being "shared" with others but gave no specifics, or discussed transfer that was in process, such as the fact that other schools had set up an infrastructure for the innovation or they were training teachers in preparation for adopting the innovation. Evidence may be sparse because we were dealing with innovations that had often been in place for 2 years or less, and their transfer was at an even earlier state of progress.

Nevertheless, we were able to glean valuable data from both the 24 cases where transfer clearly had occurred and some from the 35 where it was ambiguous. The data did not allow us to develop a model for transferability, as we did for sustainability. What emerged from our analysis were four plausible factors that explain why transfer occurred in some of these cases:

- Infrastructure and resources
- The fit of the innovation
- Teacher support and preparation
- Plans and policies that encourage transfer

INFRASTRUCTURE AND RESOURCES

The demand for ICT resources and infrastructure varies considerably according to the nature of the innovation. Some innovations require only a few stand-alone computers in a classroom, whereas others may require that each student have an Internet-connected computer and multimedia peripherals. We saw a full range of situations in the cases we read.

The cases that are the easiest to transfer are those that draw on the equipment and infrastructure typically available to other schools in their areas. For example, the case report for a Canadian primary school (CA002) emphasized that its schoolwide innovation was accomplished by working within school district standard allotments for computer hardware, making it easier for others in the district to adopt the innovation.

A case report for an upper secondary school in Latvia (LV005) states:

> The school is ready to share this experience of integrative ICT use in physics and informatics with other secondary schools from Ogre region and also from other regions of Latvia. Taking into account that the government launched an investment program regarding ICT development in the schools of Latvia, there are no serious difficulties to transfer this practice to other schools.

The report for a primary school in Catalonia, Spain (ES001), stated that the Department of Education of Catalonia had equipped all its schools with sufficient ICT resources and conducted inservice teacher training courses, and that this facilitated transfer.

On the other hand, the absence of an adequate infrastructure is clearly a barrier to transferring some innovations, either to other teachers in the same school or to other schools. The costs involved with setting up an elaborate infrastructure can be significant. A number of the innovations described in this report simply may not be transferable in their present form to many chronically underfunded schools and school districts. Three accounts from case reports describe the obstacles to transferability that some innovations face:

> One of the reasons why the use of ICT hasn't increased even more is the fact that only half of the school building is equipped with multimedia computers with access to the Internet. Stand-alone PCs put up in the other part of the building are not linked to the school's intranet and can only be used for word-processing, spreadsheet, and learning software. Other primary schools also show an increasing interest in the use of ICT. They would certainly need to provide working conditions similar to those at the primary school we observed. A well-functioning intranet is as important as technical support and sufficient [inservice] training for the teachers. (DE007)

> This innovation is based on an infrastructure, which makes it possible to publish on the intranet of the school. This requirement must be realized in the infrastructure. Less important is the grouping of the computers: in clusters or in lines in a computer lab or other area of the school building. The management of the ICT-infrastructure requires a lot of knowledge from the technology coordinator. (NL003)

> The main problem of expanding the use of Storyline [the innovation] with integrated use of ICT is the lack of resources at the school. [There is] only one computer room, which is often reserved. "The problem is that we have a shortage of ICT resources. When more and more teachers see the opportunity ICT gives, we [will] have problems," said the innovation teacher. (NO008)

THE FIT OF INNOVATION

We found that Fullan's (2001a) concept of need and Rogers's (1995) concepts of relative advantage and compatibility were the most critical factors in our cases relating transferability concerning the nature of the innovation itself. As with sustainability, the transferability of an innovation depends on the extent to which it meets the needs of the adopting school, is seen as having an advantage over alternatives, and fits with current practices in important ways. It may be particularly difficult to make this fit apparent when transferring an innovation from one discipline or subject area to another.

A case described previously demonstrates this point. A secondary school in England (UK009) used videoconferencing in the teaching of foreign languages with considerable success. Other departments within the school had done some experimentation with it, too, but the case report points out that videoconferencing was not necessarily as useful for everyone because there were fewer perceived benefits:

> The head of ICT suggested their different departments had to "have a reason to do it; ... both people [participating in the videoconference] have to benefit from it" and the head teacher commented, "The rationale for use by others isn't as strong as it is for modern foreign languages."

The same point was reinforced in the case of a secondary school in Spain (ES003). The school reported that because its innovation (the Alteris program) dealt specifically with social studies, it would be difficult to transfer it to other subject areas. The teacher who created Alteris, however, was adapting it at the time so that it could be used in other areas and thus might be transferable in the future.

Transfer may also be difficult when the innovation must fit the needs of a very different school or population. The case report for the secondary school in the United States that used ICT to support whole language instruction (US019) states:

> The innovations undertaken at Elliot may not be best for another high school. There were a number of special circumstances that simply could not be duplicated. The demographic context is one example. Whole language reform may not have worked had the population not been 95% Latino, because the substantial base of ESL teachers would have been missing.

Teachers not involved in the BT Global Challenge Yacht Race in a South African girls school (ZA004) identified a barrier that needed to be overcome before that project could be expanded to other classes in the school. Apparently, these teachers began to resent the intrusion the project was making into regular instructional time and the temporary suspension of the school's normal timetable to carry out the project. Part of the problem stemmed from some teachers not being "properly informed" of the project, which resulted in negative attitudes toward it. Added to this was "professional jealousy sparked by the success of the project," which resulted in comments such as "the projects aren't educational." Although the principal and technology coordinator were trying to overcome these objections, they clearly had a problem on their hands in convincing these teachers to take part in the innovation the next time it was offered.

We see in these four illustrations that the innovation clearly has to be perceived as being more effective than what teachers are already doing, and it has to be consistent with their beliefs about how effective learning takes place before they are willing to spend the time and effort to adapt it to their classes. Other factors related to the nature of the innovation posited by Fullan (2001a) and Rogers (1995), such as its clarity, trialability, and complexity, did not surface in our data.

TEACHER SUPPORT AND PREPARATION

For an innovation to be successfully transferred to a new setting, teachers need to be supportive of the goals and approaches of the innovation and be prepared to possibly change their teaching practices. When discussing the transferability of innovation, educators often assume that teacher support and willingness to change are a given, and all that is necessary is some inservice training. But resistance from some quarters of a school should be expected, as we just saw in the South African case (ZA004).

Similarly, teachers in the Norwegian lower secondary school (NO005) were willing to use ICT in a limited way, but they were reluctant to fully engage in the visual communication project (the innovation) because of a belief that the quality of information on the Internet was lacking. According to the case report:

> Most teachers see the need to integrate ICT more in their learning activities with their students. … However, some teachers are more critical of the role of ICT and hesitate to include it too much in their projects. Mainly it is a cultural conflict in the sense that ICT is defined as containing a lot of bad-quality information.

We made the point in our previous discussion of teachers and sustainability that change is a difficult and incremental process. Resistance can be decreased when teachers are convinced that their current, successful practices can be improved by adopting a new ICT-based innovation; or, as Rogers (1995) states, they need to see the "relative advantage" of the innovation. To wit, "Some teachers may not endorse the benefits or importance of [ICT-based] innovations in teaching-learning, dismissing them as irrelevant," states the director of the ICT-supported art project in a Thai secondary school (TH003).

A powerful way of convincing teachers of the value of an innovation is for them to see the benefits it yields for students. This may be accomplished by having prospective adopters witness the innovation first hand. This was reported in a Norwegian lower secondary school (NO008), a Singaporean upper secondary school (SG006), and a Thai secondary school (TH002), the stellar case for this country, as well as in many other schools in our sample.

Once teachers are willing to adopt an innovation, the need for ongoing training and assistance is probably self-evident. But in support of the obvious, all cases we studied mentioned that teacher professional development was a key factor in facilitating transfer.

PLANS AND POLICIES THAT ENCOURAGE TRANSFER

Our cases evinced two forms of policies or plans that encouraged transference: those that focused primarily on infrastructure and equipment and those that were essentially pedagogical in nature. The focus on infrastructure and equipment is understandable because as we pointed out previously, it clearly is a prerequisite to certain kinds of innovation. Two case reports illustrate this emphasis:

> Concerning the transferability to other schools, the IT team members pointed out that all the schools in China Hong Kong are now being equipped with intranets and the network system under the 5-year IT policy. As the network system and the Internet access are the basic infrastructure required by the innovation, it would be easier to develop similar projects in other schools. (CN009)

There is also evidence to the expansion of the innovation to other local schools as well. The municipality is expected to allocate resources, to designate a municipal body centralizing all activities involving the Web sites and the supply of all necessary equipment and infrastructure to interested schools. The mayor is in favor of this course of action. Schools from across the country are interested in the innovation, intending to implement the idea. (IL007)

In the policy at a boys secondary school (TH005) in Thailand, we see a focus on making equipment and resources available to teachers:

> The policy that requires all teachers to produce at least one ICT material in the 2001 academic year gives an impetus to the transfer of innovations. According to the plan, laptop computers will be made available to every department for use in teaching. And overhead projectors will also be available in every classroom so that the teachers can use them in their teaching.

Other policies are more focused on pedagogical change; for example, the school district that is home to the ICT-based whole language project (US019) began with a systematic pedagogical plan to use whole language to improve the poor academic performance of the district's students, the vast majority of whom are nonnative English speakers. The district conducted formal and informal workshops to help teachers transform their language teaching methods. Then the district introduced thin client computer technology to support student literacy acquisition. The district developed a "five-stage model that supported teachers in becoming truly proficient in using new educational pedagogies."

A Chilean primary school (CL004) also began with a pedagogical vision. According to the case report, "The institution believes that the teaching-learning process must be motivating and meaningful for the students. For this reason, teachers strive to conduct classes that are active and stimulate the child to learn." The staff at the school developed the innovation, the Learning by Playing Program, and saw it as one way to realize the vision.

The salient point here is that a plan based on pedagogy is more likely to effectively communicate the educational intent of the innovation than a technocentric plan. The introduction of an innovation within the context of a pedagogical plan is more likely to make its "relative advantage" and "compatibility" clearer to teachers and promote its transfer. We will return to the discussion of such plans in the next chapter.

SUMMARY AND CONCLUSIONS

In this chapter we set out to answer these questions:

> *What are the contextual factors associated with the use of these innovations? Which factors seem to be present across different innovative pedagogical practices? Which factors are associated with different practices? What are the implications of contextual factors for the sustainability and transferability of these innovations?*

> *What are the barriers to using ICT in innovative ways? How are teachers overcoming these barriers? How do they cope with limited resources?*

Using grounded theory, we examined innovations in a sample of 59 cases that were classified in our cover sheet analysis as having evidence of being sustained and transferred to other settings within a school or beyond. First, it should be noted that this is itself an important finding of the study. That is, of the 174 cases submitted by the 28 participating countries, only 59 (or 34%) presented evidence that the innovations had been sustained for at least a year and transferred. Even at this level, the evidence for transfer was often sketchy. While this finding can be explained, in part, by the fact that we were specifically looking at "innovations" and, therefore, cases that were still in the process of development, it is of some concern to us that so few of these practices identified by national panels in each country would be so tenuous.

Beyond this finding, our analysis yielded a tentative model for sustainability, identified factors related to transferability, and identified some barriers to innovation. What emerged in our sustainability model were two sets of conditions: those that are essential and those that contribute to sustainability. The foremost essential requirement for sustainability in the model is teacher support of the innovation. It is often teacher commitment and effort that allows an innovation to prevail when nonessential conditions are lacking. Support from the school principal and students is also essential, as is the need for teachers to perceive innovation to be of value and for teacher professional development. The contributing characteristics in the model include the existence of support from others in the school and from external sources, innovation champions, funding, and supportive policies and plans. For transferability, we saw that four conditions appeared to facilitate its occurrence: (1) an adequate infrastructure and resources in the new setting to realize the innovation, (2) an innovation that is seen as relevant and applicable to the transferred setting, (3) teachers viewing the innovation to be of value to them in accomplishing their classroom goals, and (4) the presence of plans and policies that encourage the transfer of the innovation. The barriers to innovation that we found complement these factors.

CONTEXT, SUSTAINABILITY, AND TRANSFERABILITY

Overall, we agree with Fullan (2001a) that three categories of factors—characteristics of change, local characteristics, and external factors—affect the continuation of innovations. With regard to the characteristics of the change or innovation itself, we found in our analysis direct evidence of Fullan's *need* and for three of Rogers's (1995) five factors: *compatibility*, *relative advantage*, and *observability*. Stated in terms of the cases we studied, the innovation had to fit with the goals of the teacher and, better still, with those of the school (need) as well; teachers had to feel comfortable with the pedagogical approach used in the innovation (compatibility); teachers had to believe that students were benefiting more from the innovation than from past practices (relative advantage); and the recognition that came from the innovation being seen by others tended to motivate teachers to continue with it (observability).

Our findings do not suggest that the remaining factors of *clarity* (Fullan), *complexity* (Fullan; Rogers), or *trialability* (Rogers) are unimportant. We merely note that they did not emerge as being influential in the cases we studied. A possible reason for this may have to do with the design of our study, which took a "snapshot" of the innovation over a 1- to 2-week period, and the data collection procedures were unable to capture changes over time. Therefore, matters related to how clear the goals were, how complex the innovation was, and whether it could be experimented with in parts were not particularly influential.

As for the local characteristics of the innovation, the teachers, the principal, the school district, and the community all play roles in sustaining the innovation. As we have stated, teacher support is absolutely essential for classroom-based innovations to be successful. Teachers need to be supported in their professional learning. We saw a variety of professional development approaches in use. However, most common were traditional models of professional development based on "delivery" of technical skills to teachers, which current research suggests is not the most effective approach (e.g., Hiebert, Gallimore, & Stigler, 2002). Principals, at a minimum, needed only to tacitly approve of the innovation. Most principals, however, took a more proactive role, and we saw evidence of both the traditional visionary and the enlightened leaders described by Senge (1990). Direct involvement of communities and districts was relatively limited in our set of sustainable and transferable cases. They mostly gave only passive support to the innovation or, in the case of some districts, provided funding for the innovation. One characteristic not specifically raised in Fullan's (2001a) description of local characteristics, but significant in ours, is student support. While Fullan would not deny its importance, he does not specifically cite it as a factor affecting continuation of innovations, as our analysis does.

National ICT policy and plans typically provided funds for hardware, software, and network infrastructure in schools, and to a lesser extent for teacher professional development. Moreover, these policies provide an added rationale to support and give priority to local ICT-based innovation. A less common external factor we found was partnerships with universities and the private sector, although where partnerships were present they were cited as being critical to the success of the innovation.

Much of the foregoing discussion on the three categories of factors affecting sustainability also applies to our findings on transferability, which is not surprising given that transferability may be seen as implementing and sustaining an innovation in other settings. In addition, infrastructure and teacher incentives seemed to be factors influencing transferability that did not come up in our analysis of sustainability. While infrastructure did not emerge as a significant factor when we examined the cases from the perspective of sustainability, lack of infrastructure and lack of resources were clearly impediments to transferability. Finally, with regard to teacher incentives, our data support Elmore's (1996) position on the necessity of creating structures for teachers to see the benefits of adopting innovations and providing the support for them to engage in the new practice.

BARRIERS

Across all 174 case reports, a large variety of problems were cited as barriers to innovation. Often there were not enough computers or limited access to them; 62% of the cases mentioned the limitations of equipment or resources. A smaller number of case reports (41%) mentioned problems associated with teacher-related concerns, such as an overworked schedule or limited computer skills; and 36% mentioned student-related concerns, such as inappropriate use of the Internet or off-task use of e-mail. Of the entire group, 30% of the cases mentioned insufficient technical support and the same percentage mentioned technical problems, such as equipment problems or slow Internet access.

As mentioned in our discussion of sustainability, these issues that have been cited as serious problems in other research studies (Means & Olson, 1997; Pelgrum & Anderson, 1999) did not prove to be insurmountable in the 59 cases we studied. It did not seem that the schools in this group had come up with any special way to deal with these problems. Rather, their success in sustaining their innovations despite the problems seemed to result from a combination of muddling through (often at the expense of additional time and effort on the part of teachers) and taking advantage of opportunities, such as available funding programs. Consequently, barriers such as these did not make it into our model of sustainability, beyond their more positive complements, such as administrative support, funding, and supportive plans and policies.

The matter seemed quite different when it came to transfer. First, transfer was a more tenuous phenomenon than sustainability, even among these specially selected 59 cases. For many of the cases, transfer was still in progress. Consequently, we encountered more of the problems in the case reports. First, limitations in equipment and resources were particularly salient when it came to scaling up an innovation within a school or transferring it to another school. Other significant barriers to transfer were skeptical teachers who were not yet convinced of advantages of the innovation or its fit with goals and current practices. Related to this was the need for professional development or other means of demonstrating the advantages of the innovation and providing teachers with the skills that would allow them to use it successfully.

Policy makers will need to address these barriers—as well as our model for sustainability—when they develop plans to adopt and scale up the ICT-based innovative pedagogical practices that we examine in this book. It is policy to which we turn next.

local AND national

ICT POLICIES

By Richard M. Jones

INTRODUCTION

As the importance of technology has grown, ministries of education from all parts of the globe have established national goals and policies that identify a major role for information and communication technologies (ICT) in improving their education systems. Many of the countries that participated in the Second Information Technology in Education Study (SITES) Module 2 had established plans to promote the use of ICT in their schools. In previous chapters, we cited national policies in

Singapore, Finland, and the United States; and we will examine these policies in more detail in this chapter. We also refer the reader to a forthcoming book (Plomp, Anderson, Law, & Quale, in press) that details educational ICT policies for many of the other countries in this study.

Schools, too, have set local policies and developed plans related to ICT. A majority of the schools in half of the 26 countries that participated in SITES Module 1 reported that they had a written ICT policy or statement on the use of computers for educational purposes (Pelgrum & Anderson, 1999). More than 80% of the principals responding to the SITES Module 1 survey indicated that their policies focused on the "use of computers in the current school year"; this was the policy focus most often cited. The next most common policy issue was "plans for staff development with regard to ICT training." A majority of principals also mentioned policies related to the "use of computers in the forthcoming school years," "specifications for computer-related tasks and persons in charge," and "plans for software acquisition." "Plans to replace or upgrade hardware" and "policies related to the Internet" were most often mentioned by principals in upper secondary schools. At the same time, the principals in this study said that their policies had not yet been implemented, by and large.

This interest in policy is fortunate, given the findings mentioned in Chapter 5. Supportive policies and funding can be significant contributors to sustainability and transferability. Even more important—even essential—are professional development opportunities for teachers and the support of administrators, factors that also have policy implications. While national policies can—but often do not—result in change in classroom practices, it is local policies and support that seem to have the most immediate effect, at least when it comes to sustaining the innovation. Consequently, local policies and plans are of concern to us as well.

In this chapter, we examine the connections between the ICT-based innovative pedagogical practices that are the focus of this study and the local and national statements, plans, and programs that are the policy contexts for these innovations. Our goal is to derive implications for policy makers that can help them formulate more effective policies, those that are more likely to sustain and scale up the kinds of innovations that we have seen in this report.

The questions we address in our examination are:

Which local policies related to such things as staff development, student computer fees, facilities access, technical support, and other issues appear to be effective in supporting these innovations?

Which national telecommunications policies related to such things as school Internet access, equipment purchase, teacher training, and student Internet use seem to be effective in supporting innovative technology-based pedagogical practices?

In addressing these research questions, this chapter provides information about the existence and content of local and national ICT policies in the schools and countries that participated in the study. We describe the impact of local and national ICT policies on the innovative pedagogical practices, drawn from our 174 case reports. In Chapter 7, we discuss the implications of these findings—and those from the other chapters—for policy makers, teachers, and researchers.

POLICIES AND THEIR EFFECTS

Public policy can be seen as a "course of action or inaction chosen by public authorities to address a given problem or interrelated set of problems" (Pal, 2001, p. 2). The general nature of policy is that of a guide to action, a plan, or a framework designed to deal with problems or issues. Pal explains that there are three general elements of policy:

CHAPTER 6 | Local and National ICT Policies

164 | Technology, Innovation, and Educational Change—A Global Perspective

- Problem definitions

- General or specific policy goals that may be intermediate or ultimate and that are linked to the identified problems

- Policy instruments or means of addressing the problems and achieving the goals

As we saw in Chapter 1, one "problem" that has often driven the development of ICT policies in education is the massive societal and economic changes occurring as a result of the widespread use of technology in businesses, government, homes, and entertainment—changes associated with the knowledge economy and the information society. Policy makers are concerned about the implications of these changes for the kinds of skills and experiences students must have by the time they leave school. Policy makers are also concerned about the preparation students need as they enter the work world and become lifelong learners (OECD, 2001). In this chapter, we identify other problems addressed by policies and a variety of goals and instruments that have been used to address these problems.

Far too often, however, policies, goals, and instruments are disconnected from the changes in classroom practice that they are intended to effect (Cohen & Hill, 2001; McLaughlin, 1990). Policies are articulated but teachers are often not aware of the specifics of these policies or their goals. In turn, policies are implemented as programs, but often these programs are not effective in achieving change at the classroom level. Clearly, creating policies and programs that have an impact on the classroom practices of teachers and students is a major challenge that policy makers face.

Work done at the U.S. National Research Council (Weiss, Knapp, Hollweg, & Burrill, 2001) addresses this challenge in the context of education reform and national standards. This research identified three means, or "channels," by which policies can influence classroom practices. These are policies and programs that relate to:

- *Curriculum.* What teachers teach and students learn in the classroom is often influenced by curriculum goals and the instructional materials in which they are embedded. Policies can influence both the curricular goals and the instructional materials, and, in turn, classroom practice.

- *Teacher development.* Teachers' preparation and professional development influence what teachers know about their subject matter and pedagogical practices. Policies can influence the standards for teacher qualification and the inservice programs that are available to current teachers and, in turn, can change what happens in the classroom.

- *Assessment and accountability.* Assessment is the means of informing students, teachers, the public, and policy makers about student performance. Accountability links performance to consequential decisions about students, teachers, schools, or districts. Policies that link assessment to accountability and that provide resources to improve results can have a significant impact on classroom practice.

In a study of the effectiveness of state policy related to education reform in mathematics, Cohen and Hill (2001) found that a certain combination of these factors proved to be most powerful in affecting classroom practice. First, policies were most effectively implemented in classrooms where teachers had extended opportunities to learn policy-related materials. Rather than providing general reviews of policy statements or discussions of their implications, the most effective teacher development experiences were concrete, content-specific, and instructionally useable practices directly connected to policy. Second, Cohen and Hill found that substantive coherence among instruments of policy was also important. To be effective, policy statements and programs should be a coherent articulation among curriculum, assessment, and teacher development. Each of these components should go in the same direction to accomplish the same goals. Pal (2001) identifies three types of coherence or consistency in policy: internal consistency, in which problem definition, goals, and instruments are complementary; vertical consistency, in which the programs and actions undertaken are logically related to the policy; and horizontal consistency, in which what policy makers do in one field will not contradict what they do in another field.

Coherence is important, too, at the local level. Many recommendations for local ICT planning emphasize funding, the acquisition of equipment and software, technical support, and facilities (Anderson, 1996; National Center for Educational Statistics [NCES], 1998). However, Fishman and Pinkert (2001) emphasize the secondary nature of technology relative to curriculum and pedagogy when it comes to local policies and plans. They distinguish between *technology planning* and *planning for technology*. *Technology planning* focuses on the hardware, software, and support issues that arise as technology is introduced into the schools. But when *planning for technology*, a school begins not with technology but with the creation of a shared vision for teaching and learning enabled by technology. Next, the planning process focuses on teacher development. Beyond basic skills in technology use, professional development should focus on how teachers can use hardware and software to accomplish the vision. Next, teachers reshape the curriculum by looking for ways in which what and how they teach can be changed by the use of technology. The coherence between vision, teacher development, and the integration of ICT into the curriculum can increase the impact of local policy and planning on classroom practice.

Many of the case reports in our study mentioned links with local and national policies. Our goal in this chapter is to understand the nature of these connections and draw implications from what we learn for improvements in policy that can affect classroom practice.

LINKS WITH LOCAL AND NATIONAL POLICY

This chapter is not a traditional international comparative policy analysis. Such analyses typically start with a description of policies in each country in a certain policy area. They then move on to an analysis of the implementation of those policies and examine their relative impact on practice; for example, see the study by the OECD (2001). In the present study, we analyze policy from the perspective of practice, not practice from the perspective of policy. Policy is a context factor at the meso (local) or macro (national) level, as described in our conceptual framework (see Chapter 1). Consequently, we begin with innovative practices.

As part of the data collection for each innovation, teachers were asked questions about any linkages that might exist between their practices and local or national policies. Principals and technology coordinators were given the survey used in SITES Module 1. Administrators at the school and district levels (where there were such structures) were interviewed about policies and the impact the policies may have had on practices in their schools. The National Research Coordinators (NRCs) in each country examined local and national documents related to policy and plans, and the NRCs were asked to include policy considerations in their case reports (although the space allotted for these considerations was quite brief). When the International Coordinating Committee (ICC) read these reports, we used the cover sheet (see Chapter 2) to code each case for any links there might be between the innovation practices and local ICT policies or plans, national ICT policies, or national educational policies. In addition, the NRCs were also asked to supply us with summaries of the ICT policies in their countries. In many cases these summaries were the chapters prepared for a forthcoming book on the comparison of national ICT policies (Plomp, Anderson, Law, & Quale, in press).

The analyses in the following sections are based on an examination of these data sources. It should be noted that although a relatively small amount of space in the case reports was allocated to ICT policies, the NRCs were explicitly asked to address any policy issues relevant to each case. Consequently, the lack of a policy connection with an innovation was clearly no mere oversight.

A total of 174 case reports from 28 countries was submitted for SITES Module 2. According to the analysis of the cover sheets, 109 (63%) indicated a connection between the innovative pedagogical practices described in the case report and a local school policy or plan. Of the total, 127 (73%) of these reports indicated an explicit link between an innovative practice and national ICT policy, and 106 (61%) indicated a connection between the innovation and a national education policy other than one specific to ICT. A total of 94 case reports (about 54%) indicated that the innovation was linked to both a national and a school-level ICT policy, while only 15 case reports (9%) indicated that the innovation was not linked to policy at either level.

To understand the impact of policy on practice, we looked for patterns in the ways that innovative practices were connected to the local and national policies and plans that were cited in the case reports. In this chapter, we first examine the connections between ICT-based pedagogical innovations and local policies. Then we examine linkages with national policies.

LOCAL ICT POLICIES

There was a strong relationship between the local policies and changes in the classroom. Specifically, cases that reported links with local policies and plans were more likely to report that the innovations produced specific changes in teacher activities; 70% of the cases that had links to local policies mentioned these changes, while only 30% of those without links to local policies mentioned such changes (x^2 = 13.3, df = 1; $p < 0.001$). Teachers were also more likely to acquire new pedagogical and collaborative skills. While 74% of the cases linked to local policies reported teacher acquisition of new pedagogical skills, only 25% of those cases without such links reported it (x^2 = 14.4, df = 1; $p < 0.001$). While 77% of the cases with linkages reported teacher acquisition of new collaborative skills, only 23% reported this outcome when links with local policy were not present (x^2 = 8.3, df = 1; $p < 0.005$).

Student activities were also more likely to change when innovations were connected to local policies. While 76% of the cases with links to local policies and plans reported changes in student activities, only 24% reported changes without such links (x^2 = 4.9; df = 1, $p < .05$). Certain student outcomes were also more likely to be present in cases where there were connections to local policies. Specifically, students were more likely to acquire problem-solving skills, with 79% reporting this outcome in the presence of links to local policy and only 21% reporting this outcome otherwise (x^2 = 4.3, df = 1; $p < 0.05$). Also, 76% of the cases with links to local policy reported that students acquired metacognitive skills, while only 24% reported on such outcomes without these connections (x^2 = 8.4, df = 1; $p < 0.005$).

Countries differed in the likelihood that their cases were linked to local policies (see Table 6.1). All of the cases in China Hong Kong, Denmark, Korea, Japan, Latvia, the Philippines, Singapore, Thailand, Chinese Taipei, and England reported connections to local policies, although it should be noted that we received only one case report from Japan.

Clearly, local policy can have a significant impact on the classroom. The focus of the rest of this section is on examining the nature of this connection. Our analysis of the case reports suggests that the cases can be sorted into four broad categories, according to the objectives of local policies and plans. These categories are as follows:

- Cases linked to local ICT education reform policies or plans

- Cases linked to policies intended to improve student skills and achievement

- Cases linked to local policies intended to the develop ICT capacity

- Cases not linked to local policies

This categorization does not mean to imply that each case fits neatly into a single category. Some cases described links to several policies, and policies impacted cases in different and sometimes multiple ways. The cases referred to in this section and the next section on national policies are used as examples to illustrate the particular patterns that we found. The description of cases in each category is not meant to be exhaustive but illustrative.

CASES LINKED TO LOCAL EDUCATIONAL REFORM POLICIES

By "education reform" we mean that the school was engaged in a redesign of the educational goals and/or processes relative to traditional notions of school. Local plans were tightly linked to educational change in many of the innovations we examined. This is supported by the fact that a significant association existed between an innovation's connection with school plans and the likelihood that it was assigned to either the Information Management Cluster or the Student Collaborative Research Cluster (see Table C.5 in Appendix C). As described in Chapter 3, these clusters were more likely to involve significant changes in pedagogical practices, such as students' use of ICT to conduct research projects, solve problems, create products, and publish the results of their work. Specifically, all of the cases assigned to the Student Collaborative Research Cluster and 82% of the cases in the Information Management Cluster had links to school policies and plans, according to the cover sheet codes. However, only 60% of the cases in the Product Creation Cluster, 57% in the Tool Use Cluster, and 37% in the Outside Collaboration Cluster had links to local practice. We also noted in Chapter 4 that a local vision for ICT use was important in supporting school-wide curriculum change, and we noted in Chapter 5 that administrative support of at least a modest form was essential for the sustainability of an innovation.

Table 6.1

COUNTRY, LOCAL, AND NATIONAL POLICIES

Country	Total	CASE LINKED TO A SCHOOL ITC POLICY OR PLAN?		CASE LINKED TO A NATIONAL EDUCATION POLICY?		CASE LINKED TO A NATIONAL ICT POLICY?	
		Number	Percent	Number	Percent	Number	Percent
AU	5	3	60%	3	60%	2	40%
CA	7	5	71.4%	4	57.1%	1	14.3%
CL	7	3	42.9%	6	85.7%	6	85.7%
CN	9	9	100%	9	100%	9	100%
CZ	7	3	42.9%	0	0%	5	71.4%
DE	12	9	75%	4	33.3%	9	75%
DK	6	6	100%	6	100%	6	100%
ES	7	6	85.7%	0	0%	6	85.7%
FI	7	1	14.3%	1	14.3%	6	85.7%
FR	6	4	66.7%	5	83.3%	6	100%
IL	10	1	10%	5	50%	6	60%
IT	4	3	75%	3	75%	4	100%
JP	1	1	100%	1	100%	1	100%
KR	4	4	100%	4	100%	4	100%
LT	4	4	100%	3	75%	3	75%
LV	3	1	33.3%	0	0%	2	66.7
NL	9	6	66.7%	2	22.2%	6	66.7%
NO	11	6	54.5%	10	90.9%	9	81.8%
PH	6	6	100%	3	50%	3	50%
PT	4	1	25%	4	100%	4	100%
RU	2	1	50%	0	00%	0	0%
SG	6	6	100%	6	100%	6	100%
SK	6	1	16.7%	1	16.7%	3	50%
TH	5	5	100%	5	100%	5	100%
TW	3	3	100%	3	100%	3	100%
UK	6	6	100%	6	100%	6	100%
US	9	4	44.4%	7	77.8%	6	66.7%
ZA	8	1	12.5%	5	62.5%	0	0%
TOTAL	174		62.6%	106	61.9%	127	73%

Our analysis of the larger group of cases found that school policies and plans for reform were often framed as visions of what school learning should be like. An example of this is the Australian primary school engaged in the multimedia development project (AU002) described in Chapter 3. The principal of the school made this comment on the process used to create this local vision:

> A key starting point for the innovation was us thinking as a school where we need to go next with ICT because there had been a good investment with the infrastructure, the network and hardware, and some software, and so we did a visioning exercise as a staff where we looked at in 5 years time where is it that we want to be in terms of teaching and learning curriculum.

The resulting vision at this school was an increased use of teaching methodologies that are open ended and require higher-order thinking and problem-solving skills. Accompanying this was an expectation that more negotiation of the curriculum would occur with students, an increased emphasis on students working with others in teams, and students working more outside the classroom. Planning programs in this school explicitly integrated ICT into all aspects of the curriculum. Conversely, the explicit teaching of content was reduced. This resulted in local curriculum goals that used the potential of technology to:

- Change and improve the nature and quality of thinking and problem-solving processes.

- Support students to learn more about themselves and their world and to take action and make a difference locally and globally.

- Enhance the power and effectiveness of the message being communicated or the position argued.

- Improve students' critical engagement with and analysis of information being created and explored.

- Improve literacy and numeracy outcomes.

- Improve the independent and collaborative skills of all learners.

- Support students in learning how to learn.

Teamwork was a focus within the school for both students and staff, with attention to collaborative planning and shared responsibilities. As expressed in the preceding quotation from the principal, leadership within the school was highly supportive of experimentation and innovation, and the principal demonstrated trust in the ability of teachers and students to meet new challenges. The school provided teachers with both the training and the technical support they needed to implement change.

The case report for the primary School of the Future in Israel (IL003), mentioned in the previous three chapters, stated that the school's vision was one in which ICT was used to transform the relationship between students and knowledge. ICT was seen as a means of amplifying students' capabilities to deal with knowledge through the use of the Internet, e-mail, productivity tools, simulations, and the use of creation software throughout the curriculum. ICT-related projects were assessed by exams, portfolios, and follow-up personal notebooks at all grade levels. The report described the vision as a holistic plan that integrated several components:

- The physical structure and organization

- Professional teams that develop and adapt curricula

- The organization of teaching staff into 2-year "homes"

- The implementation of ICT in almost all disciplines

- A variety of teaching and learning methods

- An emphasis on self-studying and student responsibility

- The use of alternative assessment

Staff members were chosen on the basis of their acceptance of this vision. A school administrator commented on strides made toward implementing this vision: "Maybe the most evident achievement is that the teachers have become a learning community—not only students, but also teachers, learn in this school all the time. The school norms have become academic in nature, in that you can inquire about anything, doubt anything."

According to the report for this innovation, the vision permeated the school and influenced the use of ICT throughout the staff. ICT was seen as a way of improving the quality of learning and had a huge impact on the role of both students and teachers. The report also stated that the national ICT policy was connected to this local-level vision by:

- Supporting the creation of the school.

- Providing academic mentoring.

- Providing innovative pedagogy.

- Ensuring architecture that supports the innovative use of ICT.

The case report from Canada's stellar case (CA002), the primary school mentioned in Chapter 5, states that the school's vision is to make ICT an integral part of teaching and learning throughout its programs. The school was designed as a place where staff could rethink their teaching, where they could conduct action research, and where students could pursue inquiry-based, authentic, and self-directed learning. The use of ICT was seen as integral to this process. The school provided teachers with support for the development of this vision through teacher professional development where new practices were modeled and reflective discussions on the role of ICT in pedagogy and the curriculum took place. The school's vision is only remotely connected to the provincial government's ICT policy, which delineates a graduated curriculum of ICT competencies for various grade levels. In practice, however, this document is largely ignored by the staff at this school because teachers feel that their students' competencies go well beyond the requirements of the curriculum. The school's vision is focused on education reform rather than on the development of skills.

Common to these cases and others in this category is a clear and explicit vision of what education should be like in a school. This vision articulated specific changes in teaching and learning and a particular way in which technology could support these changes. However, as previously noted, these schools did not stop there. They enacted the vision with specific resources and support that allowed teachers and students to implement it. The China Hong Kong secondary school that is home to two of our innovative cases (CN005, CN009) is a good example of this support. The ICT vision and mission of this school is that technology is to provide a means for students and teachers to undergo self-learning. In service of this goal, the school set up a six-person ICT committee. An additional staff member was hired at the school to give committee members time to help their fellow teachers with technology. The role of the committee, as stated in the school's technology plan, was to:

- Enhance experience-sharing in information technology among staff members.

- Administer computer resources for the whole school.

- Advocate the appropriate use of the network service within the school.

- Computerize school work whenever appropriate.

- Collaborate with the academic committee in promoting the use of information technology in teaching.

- Support information technology education in liaison with various academic panels.

CASES LINKED TO LOCAL POLICIES INTENDED TO IMPROVE STUDENT SKILLS AND ACHIEVEMENT

In some schools, local policies and plans focused most specifically on the improvement of student skills and achievement in academic subjects. A number of case reports explicitly linked the use of ICT to these goals. The case of a Canadian inner-city primary school (CA004) provides an example. In this school, students used a variety of multimedia applications (e.g., digital cameras, scanners, HyperCard, HyperStudio) in language, social studies, science, and art to meet the stated achievement levels in the provincial curriculum. According to the case report, the vision of this school was:

> To promote a dynamic and equitable learning environment, to enhance student achievement, and to prepare students to be responsible citizens in the Canadian and global society through the implementation of information and computer technology.

The school developed a school technology plan, as well as a technology use plan, that served as the guiding principles for the innovation. The school technology plan consisted of school-based goals for teachers and students, objective strategies, and timelines for implementation. The technology use plan outlined the various skills that needed to be taught at each grade level and identified the application software to be used. The principal commented on her vision for the use of ICT: "We feel that this is going to give our students life chances in the 21st century that they might not ordinarily have had."

The innovation in a large English secondary school with many nonnative English-speaking students (UK004) used a database to set student performance targets and record and monitor student progress. According to the case report, the vision of the school was to encourage independent learning through ICT. The principal of this school saw his role as facilitating, stimulating, and encouraging both staff and students to extract the full potential of individual students. He saw the student-tracking innovation as the best way of achieving this because it meant that teachers could monitor the progress of students, gain an understanding of students' strengths and weaknesses, and identify ways of maximizing individual students' potential. One teacher involved in the innovation expressed the hope that the innovation would bring "more independent learning, open learning," and would help "students to take more responsibility for their own learning." Another teacher remarked, "My vision is of an 'anywhere, anytime' access to the curriculum for all of our students through electronic delivery. The course materials, activities, etc., would be supported by electronic tutoring and feedback."

A primary school in the United States (US006) had been opened 7 years earlier as a pilot site for a state extended-school-year requirement that was being considered at that time. District officials also decided to give the school a technology focus to match those of a middle school and a high school in the district. For 6 months prior to the school's opening, the school's faculty members met on Thursday evenings to conceptualize what they could achieve with technology and the extended school year. As a result, the school's mission was to help students reach their highest levels of achievement and foster their development as independent learners. The innovation in this case involved student use of technology in various classes and included the use of reference CD-ROMs, word processing, and presentation software for reports, and software for practice and remediation in areas such as vocabulary and math. Teachers used a range of instructional approaches rather than a specific one tied to the innovation. At times teachers used more traditional approaches, such as direct instruction, and at times they allowed students to explore topics more independently.

Since the focus of these cases was on the use of technology to support student achievement rather than on changing what students did or learned, the focus of the technology plans was on equipment and software and improving teachers' skill in their use. For example, teachers in the U.S. school (US006) met in grade-level groupings with the curriculum technology specialist and the network manager to discuss how specific pieces of software could be used with the state and district standards for learning. Teachers in the Canadian case (CA004) had released time to attend workshops on software, hardware, Web design, curriculum planners, and multimedia equipment.

CASES LINKED TO LOCAL POLICIES INTENDED TO DEVELOP ICT CAPACITY

In other cases, principals and teachers had a vision of what schools might be when enriched by technology; accordingly, their plans were focused on developing their ICT capacity. For example, a Norwegian upper secondary school (NO011) developed a special ICT strategy document that stated its vision of ICT in the school. First, the document described a well-developed infrastructure at the school; second, it focused on how ICT could be used as a tool for pedagogical activities and to motivate students and teachers; third, it described how ICT might work as a tool for administrative purposes. The principal commented, "An overall philosophy is that the PCs should be accessible in all classrooms and work-halls."

The vision in a Danish primary school (DK011) was that the students and the teachers would become competent at integrating ICT in their learning and education. To develop the necessary ICT skills, the school specified goals for what the students would need to master at each grade level. The school's ICT action plan provided guidelines for the integration of ICT into the curriculum. However, the focus was on ICT rather than on educational change. The local municipality had an ICT curriculum whose goal was that students develop and acquire the most advanced information and communication technologies.

The Danish case was typical of many schools. Schools often wanted to increase not only their hardware and networking capacity but also the technological capacities and skills of their teachers and students. There were many examples of this type of vision, including the following:

- A primary school in the Slovak Republic (SK011) expressed a vision for ICT in which students would learn to work with ICT and teachers would apply information or demonstrate ICT resources in their lessons.

- A Finnish upper secondary school (FI003) held the vision that ICT would belong naturally to the everyday work of the school and ICT could be applied in every subject.

- In a German secondary school (DE006) the vision of the school consisted of making computers and the Internet available in each of its current classrooms and completely equipping at least two classrooms of a planned new building.

- The principal and teachers in a French lower secondary school (FR003) shared the vision that ICT development in school must involve all teachers and all disciplines and not rely on a single ICT team.

The vision of a secondary school in Singapore (SG004), mentioned in Chapter 4, was to prepare pupils for a future in which technology would be pervasive in the culture. As a consequence, the goals of its innovation—Project I—were to use ICT to:

- Facilitate independent and innovative learning and teaching.

- Initiate and induct the whole school community to become thinking, independent, global citizens.

- Provide opportunities for borderless or distance learning beyond the confines of the school and even beyond Singapore.

In all of these cases, technology-based visions motivated administrators and staff to seek equipment and ICT resources and integrate these into their teaching and learning.

CASES NOT LINKED TO LOCAL POLICIES

Of the 174 case reports, 65 (37%) made no connection between the innovation and a local policy or plan. A number of these case reports indicated that a single teacher or group of teachers working together initiated the school innovation, with little or no impact from the school-level ICT policy. For example, the case report for a primary school in France (FR002) indicated that the school's innovation was initiated by a teacher with a passion for computers and that this innovation occurred without a school policy. The teacher felt that there was a need for technology in the school and initiated a program to meet that need. Since there was no specific ICT policy at the school, the teacher used available resources to create collaborative learning experiences for the students without it.

Similarly, in a primary school in Portugal (PT002) a teacher initiated the innovation to meet the school's particular need—its geographical isolation was affecting students' educational and personal development. The teacher took this need into account when determining how to meet the national curriculum goals. Thus, the innovation was connected to national policy, although local policies and plans played no part in it. The innovation was part of a national project to connect isolated schools through the network. Thus, ICT became a way to contribute to student achievement and expose students to a variety of educational experiences. This project helped the school develop its infrastructure and helped this particular teacher develop ICT skills. However, even though these national policies played a role in the innovation, school staff believed that the innovation was mainly teacher initiated.

Generally, the case reports from Latvia stated that the innovations in these schools were teacher initiated. In this country, ICT was often seen as a tool to improve the quality of instruction. Schools had an informal vision of learning and occasionally a focus on ICT, but for the most part no school-level ICT policies influenced the development of these innovations. For example, the case report for one Latvian secondary school (LV002) stated that a group of teachers developed the school's innovation to use ICT as a source of information for different topics in the geography curriculum without the benefit of a written school ICT plan.

The final case we will mention is the Global Challenge Yacht Race project (ZA004) in the primary school in South Africa, which was discussed in Chapters 3 and 5. There was no written ICT policy in this school. In this case, the innovative teacher, who was also the technology coordinator, was the prime mover behind the project. This case is typical of many where no local policy existed. Of the 65 projects that made no connection to local plans, 36 were connected to national, state, regional, or international projects; and 22 had connections to business, industry, a university, or a government project. Indeed, Table 3.5 (Chapter 3 Appendix) shows that projects assigned to the Outside Collaboration Cluster were least likely to be linked to a local policy. Apparently, these external projects often gave shape and structure to the local activities, in lieu of a local policy or plan, as well as providing additional resources or support that allowed the project to succeed.

SUMMARY OF LOCAL POLICY CONNECTIONS

The preceding examples indicate that school-level ICT policies can affect the innovative use of technology in the school. About 63% of the cases in this study were linked in some way to a school policy or plan. Cases that were linked to local policy were more likely to be associated with changes in teacher practices and their acquisition of new pedagogical and collaborative skills. Linkages with local policy were also more likely to be associated with students' acquisition of problem-solving and metacognitive skills, as reported in the case write-ups.

These schools often had a clear focus and vision of the role of technology in attaining education reform, increasing student achievement, or developing ICT capacity. The connection between technology plans and education reform seemed particularly productive. In these cases, school plans articulated a change in the curricular goals of students and approaches that teachers might take to accomplish these goals. These approaches were also connected to specific resources such as pedagogical training for teachers and hardware and software that might help teachers accomplish these goals. These cases seem closest to what Fishman and Pinkert (2001) call "planning for technology"—rather than "technology planning"— where the use of technology is planned around shared visions of teaching and learning that are enabled by technology and a plan for technology that can realize this vision.

Technology planning is more characteristic of schools that are focused on developing their technology capacity. In these cases, school plans describe the hardware and software resources that are desirable and the technological skills that are expected of their teachers and students in order to use the technology. Some schools use these capabilities to focus on increasing students' achievement in academic subjects.

Then there were those case reports that did not connect innovations to local plans; this was so for about 37% of the cases. Here the initiative and effort of individual teachers or groups of teachers prevailed. Sometimes these efforts were shaped by an outside project or coupled with outside resources, such as additional equipment or technical support from a university or cooperating business. These factors often compensated for the lack of a local plan and helped the innovation succeed.

NATIONAL ICT POLICIES

As mentioned previously, 127 (73%) of the 174 case reports in this study described an explicit link between the innovation and national ICT policy; 106 (61%) indicated a connection between the innovation and a national education policy other than one specific to ICT. A total of 89 (51%) reports described a connection to both national ICT policies and education policies.

Countries differ not only in whether they have specific policies addressing ICT but in the extent to which they apply central control over their educational systems. France, Singapore, and Thailand, for example, have centralized policies and instruments that influence the curriculum, instructional materials, assessment, and teacher training. Other countries, such as Canada, Germany, Spain, and the United States, are federal or more decentralized systems, with control of education delegated to provinces or states and local levels. Consequently, it is not surprising that cases in certain countries were more likely to mention linkages with national ICT or educational policies. Table 6.1 shows the percentage of cases from each country that was linked to a national ICT policy or plan. All of the cases in China Hong Kong, Denmark, France, Italy, Japan (only 1 case submitted), Korea, Portugal, Singapore, Thailand, Chinese Taipei, and England cited links to a national ICT policy or plan. So, too, did all of the cases in China Hong Kong, Denmark, Japan, Korea, Portugal, Singapore, Thailand, Chinese Taipei, and England cite links to a national education policy. Table 6.1 shows that cases were connected to national ICT policies, national education policies, and local policies for all of the cases in the following countries: China Hong Kong, Denmark, Korea, Singapore, Thailand, Chinese Taipei, and England.

These policies played an important role in the innovations we studied. For example, while 50% of the cases connected to national ICT policies were transferred to other classrooms or schools, only 17% of the cases without such a connection were transferred (x^2 = 15.08; df = 1, $p < .001$). Also, cases that cited connections with national ICT policies were more likely to be associated with changes in student classroom activities. Table 6.2 shows that while 76% of the cases that cited a link to national ICT policies reported changes in student classroom activities, only 24% of the cases reported student changes without citing links to national ICT policies (x^2 = 4.9; df = 1, $p < .05$). Table 6.2 also shows that cases connected to national educational policies were more likely to show change in teacher classroom activities; 66% of the cases with connections to education policies showed such changes, as opposed to 34% without such connections ($x^2 = 5.2$; $df = 1$, $p < .05$). Cases were more likely to report that teachers acquired new pedagogical skills when the cases were also linked to national education policies, with 63% reporting such changes when linked to education policies and only 47% reporting such changes otherwise ($x^2 = 4.4$; $df = 1$, $p < .05$).

Table 6.2

NATIONAL POLICIES AND TEACHER AND STUDENT ACTIVITIES

		TEACHER ACTIVITIES CHANGED		STUDENT ACTIVITIES CHANGED	
		YES	NO	YES	NO
Link to National ICT Policy	Yes	96 (74.4%)	31 (68.9%)	112 (76.2%)	15 (55.6%)
	No	33 (25.6%)	14 (31.3%)	35 (23.8%)	12 (44.4%)
Link to National Educational Policy	Yes	85 (65.9%)	21 (46.7%)	94 (64.0%)	12 (44.4%)
	No	44 (34.1%)	24 (35.3%)	53 (36.0%)	15 (55.6%)

In this section, we examine the ways that national policies are linked to and influence the innovations we studied. As with local policies, our analysis of the SITES Module 2 case reports sorted them into four broad categories according to the objectives of the national policies and the ways cases were linked to them. These categories are:

◆ Cases linked to national educational reform policies.

◆ Cases linked to national policies intended to improve student skills and achievement.

◆ Cases linked to national policies intended to develop ICT capacity.

◆ Cases not linked to national policies.

As with local policies, this categorization does not mean to imply that each case fits neatly into a single category; some cases displayed characteristics of more than one category. Policies often had multiple purposes, and cases were connected to them in multiple ways. Similarly, when a case in a country was placed in one of the above categories, all of that country's cases did not necessarily belong to that same category. Although, as previously noted, the category patterns differed from country to country, not all schools or all innovations were equally influenced by these policies.

CASES LINKED TO NATIONAL EDUCATION REFORM POLICIES

Cases in this category had a link to a national ICT policy that was part of a larger effort to change the education system. That is, reform was intended to change the goals and/or means of education. These cases often included a formal education reform document. Such a national ICT policy either was part of or referenced a national education policy related to reform; thus, the introduction or use of ICT was seen as an opportunity and resource to support reform. In this category, innovations were directly influenced by these policies.

For example, Singapore's current national ICT policy, the Masterplan for IT in Education, is also connected to education reform. The goal of the policy is to integrate ICT in education as a strategy to meet the challenges of the 21st century, as described in Box 6.1. As part of the plan, schools are provided with the funding, hardware, software, infrastructure, training, and technical support to attain this goal. They also reduced the content in the national curriculum by 10% to 30% to accommodate ICT use and the infusion of thinking skills. In addition, all Singapore schools are fully networked (with both intranet and Internet access). The case report for the Virtual Gallery Project (SG002), featured in Chapter 3, states that these policies and other supporting factors allowed the school's innovation to "take off." The innovation involved the use of a virtual gallery to facilitate the sharing of teaching and learning resources at the school. Teachers posted their lesson materials in this gallery, and students posted their assignments and projects. Both could update or enhance content as required. This initiative was supported by the government's policies, and, in turn, the innovation met the national educational goal of integrating ICT in education to assist students in preparing for their future.

Chile's national ICT policy was designed to support that country's education reform. From the mid-1990s, Chile has been implementing a major curriculum reform intended to decentralize decision making. The government's ICT initiative, known as Enlaces, is an important component of the reform; accordingly, ICT is specifically integrated into the country's educational reform document. The aim of the ICT policy is to integrate these technologies as learning and teaching resources for all students and teachers. One of the key objectives of the policy is to increase equity in educational opportunity for all Chilean students. The government provides a number of programs to implement this policy, including programs to supply schools with appropriate hardware, software, Internet access, teacher training, and technical and pedagogical support. The centrally defined curriculum specified how technology should be used, and the government's aim is to integrate technology as a learning-teaching resource. A great emphasis is placed on teacher training and the development of a technical assistance network to ensure that all participants in the educational process use ICT tools.

The case report for the Mi Lugar Project in a Chilean secondary school (CL009) states that the national policy was a strategic ally in attaining the school's goals. Resources and support obtained from the government allowed the school to focus on its needs and develop a program to integrate technology into a range of curriculum subjects, one of the national policy objectives. Similarly, the case report for the Virtual Orchestra Project in an upper secondary school (CL003) indicates that the national policy created the conditions for the innovation to take place in the school. Hardware and software was provided to the school as part of the national ICT initiative, and teachers used the resources to develop interdisciplinary projects and promote collaborative work between different subject areas, meeting one of the national ICT objectives.

Thailand's comprehensive national ICT policy is also connected to that country's Education Reform Act, developed in 1999. The reform policy moves the education system toward learner-centered pedagogy and strives to increase the overall quality of schools and teachers. The ICT policy provides a vision for a new way of teaching. Under this policy, teachers are encouraged to use pedagogical approaches, such as project-based and inquiry learning, that get students actively involved in their own learning. Technology is an important part of this policy. To implement the policy, the government provides technology and resources to the schools, including teacher training; monitors the schools' quality and the teachers' management and administration skills; and uses benchmarks to evaluate all of these components.

| Box 6.1 | NATIONAL POLICY IN SINGAPORE |

Singapore is an island nation with approximately 24,000 teachers and 480,000 students in primary and secondary schools. In Singapore, decision making in national policy matters is centralized at the Ministry of Education, whose main role is to establish education goals and develop a coordinated education plan for schools. Generally, the ministry provides guidelines for curriculums, textbook use, and assessment. Within this broad national framework of policies and guidelines, schools develop and implement their own programs to meet local needs.

In 1997, Singapore initiated a plan called Masterplan for IT in Education to incorporate ICT into the school system (Ministry of Education, Singapore, 1997). This US$1.2 billion project provides a national blueprint for the use of ICT in all schools and aims to create an ICT-enriched school environment for every child. The intent is that through the use of ICT, children will become equipped with the learning, creative-thinking, and communication skills needed to produce a "workforce of excellence" for the future.

The goals of the Masterplan are to:

• Enhance linkages between the school and the world around it.

• Enhance creative thinking, lifelong learning, and social responsibility.

• Generate innovative processes in education.

• Promote administrative and management excellence in the education system.

The implementation of the Masterplan involves four elements: curriculum and assessment, content and learning resources, teacher development, and physical and technological infrastructure. ICT is used to help shift learning toward a better balance between the acquisition of factual knowledge and mastery of concepts. Schools have been given an annual budget for educational software, and a central clearinghouse of educational software has been set up at the Ministry. A program for teacher training in the use of ICT in teaching has been established, with 60 experienced teachers and department heads serving as coaches across the country. These coaches visit schools to train and help teachers incorporate ICT-facilitated learning strategies into their teaching practice through lesson demonstrations, modeling, and hands-on activities. National standards for ICT infrastructure have been set, calling for student-computer and teacher-computer ratios of 2:1, and stipulating that students must have access to ICT and the Internet in all learning areas of the school. On average, each school has about 300 PCs as well as IT peripherals such as digital cameras, scanners, data loggers, electronic microscopes, classroom management systems, laser printers, and projection systems. Teachers' purchase of PCs is also subsidized by the Ministry. In addition, the Ministry is seeking to improve the physical environment for teaching and learning and has initiated a program for rebuilding and improving existing schools at a cost of about US$2.8 billion.

In 2002, Singapore unveiled its Masterplan 2 to consolidate and build on the achievements of Masterplan 1. The new Masterplan adopts a more systemic and holistic approach in which all the key pieces—curriculum, assessment, instruction, professional development, and school culture—are integrated and addressed. The intended outcomes for the plan include the following: pupils will use technology effectively for active learning; connections will be enhanced among curriculum, instruction, and assessment; teachers will use technology effectively for professional and personal growth; and there will be active research on technology in education.

The case report for the physics project (TH005) mentioned in Chapter 3 states that the Education Reform Act has affected the management, administration, and teaching-learning policies of this secondary school.

But in this school and others in Thailand, it is the principal who helps turn the Reform Act into practice. The case report states:

> The administrators play an important role in defining the vision and involving the community in formulating school policies as well as directing the teaching-learning in alignment with the school's vision, particularly where the use of technology in education is concerned.

The school's vision, in this case, focused on promoting academic and technological excellence, and administrators made sure that teachers had the resources and training they needed to implement the project in their classrooms. Similarly, the innovation in a Thai lower secondary school (TH003) combines local with national resources to effect change, as described in the previous chapter.

Lithuania's extensive national ICT policy, the Strategy for Information and Communication Technology Implementation, is also connected to educational reform. ICT implementation includes all elements and areas of education and influences the concept of education and the teaching system. Among other things, the strategy aims to implement the principle of lifelong learning; guarantee the right of all students to become technologically literate; provide schools with hardware, systems, and software; expand teacher training centers; and ensure that teachers have ICT literacy and skills and apply them to their teaching methods. The case report for a Lithuanian secondary school (LT001) states that the school obtained computer resources as a result of this national policy. The school also participated in a range of government-initiated projects specifically to obtain computer resources. This participation resulted in the expansion of the school's ICT resources, the development of the school network, and the organization of ICT inservice training for teachers. The innovation, applying ICT in the teaching and learning of fine arts theory and the history of art, was developed specifically to meet the goals of the national policy.

In a similar way, Korea's national ICT policy is connected to the broader concept of education reform. In 1995 the Ministry of Education implemented a school reform plan that ensures that anyone who wishes to study can study anytime and anywhere. In 1998 the government declared a campaign titled Education Vision 2002: Establishment of New Culture for Schools. The campaign focused on ICT as a way to promote this new school culture. As part of the implementation of the national policy, a number of schools were designated as ICT model schools to promote research and evaluation of teaching and learning strategies using ICT. The case report for a Korean lower secondary school (KR003) states that participating in this project provided the school with research and infrastructure aids, leading to the development of the school's innovation. Additional funding, computer resources, and training came from the Ministry of Education when the school was designated a model school. Now teachers from other schools are encouraged to visit the school to obtain new teaching techniques they can use.

Like Korea, a major goal of Norway's educational policy is that all students have the right to an education, regardless of where they live. Norway's national curriculum and ICT plan support the use of ICT in the classroom through the integration of technology in all subject areas. The curriculum supports project-oriented pedagogy across different subjects, providing schools with a framework for implementing the use of technology. In Norway a large number of small schools have inadequate resources. Lack of government funding threatened the closure of many of these schools. Technology has become a way of survival and ensures that students can live at home during their schooling years. The case report for a rural primary school in Norway (NO003) describes how the innovation (videoconferencing between two schools) allowed the teachers in the two schools to support and supplement each other. The innovation ensured the survival of both schools. The innovation was facilitated by—and helped attain—the national policy goal of ensuring every student's right to an education.

CASES LINKED TO NATIONAL POLICIES INTENDED TO IMPROVE STUDENT SKILLS AND ACHIEVEMENT

Some countries see ICT as a mechanism to improve the education system they currently have rather than as a tool to reform the education system. Cases associated with this category are linked to national ICT policies that focus specifically on improving the learning of students in terms of skills and achievement.

In the United States, the primary responsibility for education rests with the states and local school districts. Policy and programs at the national level try to influence education by challenging the states and their school systems to perform at a higher level. ICT policy in the United States is consistent with this role (see Box 6.2). Many states, in turn, have a goal of improving student achievement and see ICT as a means of attaining this goal. This is the case in California, where the principal of a lower secondary school acknowledged its influence on the innovation (US010) in her school:

> It [the standards and accountability movement in California] is a tremendous influence. It dominates our conversation. There is no question about that. It's something the state is saying—this is what our expectations are as a school. That carries a lot of weight.

The innovation in this school was developed with funding from the U.S. Department of Education's Technology Innovation Challenge Grant Program and resources from corporate partners that participated in the proposal. With the help of the federal grant, the district provided the school with an ICT infrastructure, training, and technology support. The school used these resources to develop strategies to improve students' academic performance in reading and mathematics, thereby meeting the state goals. In this case, the national goal of improving student achievement was supported and achieved at the school level through the use of ICT.

In Australia, as in the United States, curriculum frameworks are developed at the state as well as local levels, and in support of a nationally agreed-upon statement of goals. Those frameworks describe plans with goals for student achievement, as well as parameters that teachers use to design their own teaching. With regard to the implementation of ICT in schools, Australian states provide funding for hardware, software, and resource support for ICT in schools. The focus of these policies is to integrate ICT into all aspects of learning, which in turn promotes the innovative use of computers in the classroom. The goals of the national ICT plan are that students become confident, creative, and productive users of technology and that schools integrate ICT into their operations to improve student achievement.

| Box 6.2 | NATIONAL POLICY IN THE UNITED STATES |

The United States has approximately 2.9 million teachers and 33 million primary and secondary students. The education system is decentralized; much of the decision making resides with the state and local education authorities. The function of the U.S. Department of Education is to assure access to equal educational opportunity for every individual; to complement the efforts of states and the local school systems; and to promote improvements in the quality and usefulness of education through federally supported research, evaluation, and sharing of information.

In 1996, the Department of Education released a report called *Getting America's Students Ready for the 21st Century: Meeting the Technology Literacy Challenge*. In this report the department presented a vision for the 21st century in which all students would be technologically literate and better prepared for the demands of the new American economy. The report defined four concrete goals:

- All teachers in the nation will have the training and support they need to help students learn by using computers and the information superhighway.

- All teachers and students will have modern multimedia computers in their classrooms.

- Every classroom will be connected to the information superhighway.

- Effective software and online learning resources will be an integral part of every school's curriculum.

In 1999, the department undertook a strategic review and revision of the national educational technology plan. The result was five new goals:

- All students and teachers will have access to information technology in their classrooms, schools, communities, and homes.

- All teachers will use technology effectively to help students achieve high academic standards.

- All students will have technology and information literacy skills.

- Research and evaluation will improve the next generation of technology applications for teaching and learning.

- Digital content and networked applications will transform teaching and learning.

In support of these goals, the Department of Education set up several programs. Key among them was the Technology Innovation Challenge Grant Program. For 6 years, between 1995 and 2001, the program supported partnerships among educators, business and industry, and other community organizations to develop innovative strategies that integrated technology into standards-based curricula. The program funded 100 projects designed to:

- Develop standards-based curricula in a wide range of subjects.

- Provide professional development for teachers.

- Increase student access to technology and online resources.

- Provide technology training and support for parents in low-income areas.

- Devise techniques for assisting teachers in developing computer-based instruction.

- Create strategies for accelerating the academic progress of at-risk children via technology.

- Develop new approaches to measuring the impact of educational technology on student learning.

Schools adopt learning paradigms using ICT to achieve these goals. The case report for a primary school in the state of South Australia (AU002) states that as a result of the national policies, ICT has been integrated into all aspects of the curriculum and has helped the school meet the national goal of improving student skills and achievement.

In England, achievement standards are set at the national level. The student-tracking database project (UK004) mentioned previously in this chapter, was influenced by national policy as well as local plans. The government has sets standards and targets for student achievement and numbers of students achieving certain levels of attainment (expressed as the percentages of students achieving specific levels in formal tests at age 11 and in accreditation at 16+). These are published for state primary and secondary schools. As part of the innovation, the school sets targets for individual students that will enable them to reach their full potential as well as contribute to the overall school performance data. The case report states:

> By providing detailed information about the ongoing performance of each individual student, the tracking system allows teachers to set realistic targets for each student and to take account of their different ability levels when preparing both courses and lessons. Thus, the system provides teachers with more detailed information about all the students in their teaching groups, which helps them to plan and deliver their lessons more effectively. It also benefits students because their teachers have more detailed knowledge of their performance across subjects and can take into account individual students' strengths and weaknesses when allocating specific work.

CASES LINKED TO NATIONAL POLICIES INTENDED TO DEVELOP ICT CAPACITY

Many countries have national policies specifically or primarily focused on ICT infrastructure and human ICT capacity rather than on educational change or student achievement per se. These policies may include building the hardware and networking infrastructure in schools, developing students' ICT-related skills, improving teacher competencies with ICT, or integrating ICT into all subject areas. The focus, therefore, is primarily on ICT itself. The cases in this category, then, are linked to national policies related to developing ICT capacity.

Some countries tie the development of ICT capacity to a larger set of national needs or a vision of what society will be like if technological resources are used wisely. Finland has developed ICT strategies to help create an information society in that country (see Box 6.3). This policy influenced the innovation in an upper secondary school (FI003) described in Chapter 3. This school created a line of study called Information, Technology, and Media, which was composed of 26 different courses, from which every student in the program had to choose 16. The program included technical courses such as programming, data structures, and multimedia, as well as nontechnical courses such as creative writing, social psychology, and media criticism. The students in the program became highly skilled, and a collaborative culture evolved in which students assisted teachers in their use of ICT. The program was directly linked to the Ministry of Education's information strategies.

| Box 6.3 | NATIONAL POLICY IN FINLAND |

Finland has approximately 48,000 teachers and 700,000 primary and secondary students. The school system is decentralized. Every school writes its own curriculum, developed in accordance with discussions among teachers and parents and based on very general guidelines from the National Board of Education. As a result, school curricula may be quite diverse across the country. Like other Nordic countries, local and municipal authorities in Finland have a prominent role to play in education and culture by organizing activities and providing services. Finnish education is funded by two sources: the state, which covers two-thirds of the public education expenditure, and the municipalities where the schools are located, which cover the remaining one-third of the cost. Primary and secondary school students receive free tuition, teaching and learning materials; school meals; and, where necessary, accommodations and school transportation.

During the 1990s, the national strategy was to develop ICT in education as part of the country's policy of building a Finnish information society. Since the mid 1990s, the specific information strategies of the Ministry of Education have included the National Strategy on Education, Training and Research (1995); Towards a Culture-Oriented Information Society (1996); and Information Strategy for Research and Education for the years 2000–2004 (1999). Among the goals of these policy statements is a focus on the following:

- Moving from a "once-and-for-all" training to lifelong learning.

- Providing basic information society skills for all.

- Ensuring that teachers achieve a high level of professional skills.

- Securing the development of information products and services.

- Building education and research networks into an open, global network.

- Developing learning-centered approaches that focus on collaboration, individual styles of learning, learning difficulties, alternative ways of learning, and multidisciplinary approaches to learning.

From 1996 through 1999, the Ministry of Education introduced a program called Information Finland, which helped schools purchase computers, link to international information networks, promote the introduction of ICT as a tool for teaching and learning, and carry out inservice training for teachers. The program's aim was for all schools to be connected to the networks by the year 2000 and for all teachers to be using ICT-based tools in their teaching. The purpose of the inservice training program was to provide educators with the knowledge and skills needed to reform the pedagogical practices in their schools, especially with regard to collaborative teaching and learning, networking, and teamwork. The program also produced instructional materials that are available on the Internet.

The training of teaching personnel has been planned in three steps: knowledge about the common uses of a computer and general productivity software; skills in using ICT for educational purposes, including the World Wide Web environment and groupware; and specialized knowledge, such as content-specific and professional applications, as well as the production of digital learning materials.

Denmark's national ICT policy, the Act on the Folkeskole, states that schools are to create opportunities for students to develop ICT skills and ICT is to be integrated into all school subjects. Danish national ICT policy also connects ICT to education reform. But the government's intent in emphasizing ICT in education is that the Danish education system should be among the 5–10 best in the world in this area. Investments in ICT have two main purposes: to improve the quality of education and to give students the ICT qualifications they need in the present and future society. To attain these goals, government regulations specify the grade level at which ICT should be introduced to students and describe general ICT skills and competencies to be obtained by the end of Grades 3, 6, and 9, as well as by the time of graduation. Other mechanisms to implement the government's policy included connecting all schools to an ICT network, making teacher training in the use of ICT a priority, and ensuring that ICT is a focus for all school boards. The case report for a Danish primary school (DK004) indicated that its school-level innovation was developed to meet the national requirement of creating opportunities for students to develop skills and competencies in the use of ICT in all subject areas. The school focused on training teachers in ICT to ensure that students had the required ICT skills and that ICT was integrated into all subjects. This focus was connected to the national ICT policy of developing ICT capacity.

The Netherlands' national ICT policy also focuses on developing ICT capacity. The government provides schools with a general framework for ICT policies. In this country, the use of ICT is seen as a social trend, and that trend is the main impetus for schools to integrate ICT into teaching practice. The government provides general aims, ensures the right conditions, and provides encouragement. However, it is up to the individual schools to determine how to use ICT to improve education. Schools are given money to implement the policy and are free to use it as they wish. The national ICT policy includes the following provisions:

- Teacher ICT skills, expectations, training, evaluation of skills, and money to upgrade skills

- Software and support to meet curriculum standards

- Connecting all schools to a network

The ultimate goal is to integrate ICT into teaching practice. The Vanguard Schools is a national program of model schools that demonstrate for other schools in the country how to use computers in the classroom. A number of case reports from The Netherlands (e.g., NL002, NL003, NL008, NL013, NL017, and NL025) indicated that these schools were participants in the Vanguard Schools project and consequently received additional ICT resources (computers, network and Internet access, and training) to stimulate the development of innovations in these schools and to integrate ICT into teaching activities. Teachers visit these schools and others in the Vanguard Schools project to see how to integrate ICT into their classroom teaching. The case report for a Dutch primary school (NL003) states that being connected to the government's network, part of the national ICT policy, facilitated the school's innovation of teaching students a range of ICT skills. Similarly, another primary school (NL002) cited the Vanguard Schools as important to its use of computers for curriculum content and for developing student ICT skills.

Chinese Taipei's ICT policies focus primarily on ICT rather than on educational change. These policies include:

- Providing hardware and software

- Improving Internet access

- Improving information education

- Using ICT resource centers

- Describing best practices integrating ICT

- Enhancing teachers' ICT competencies

The Ministry of Education also released a new curriculum requiring that ICT be integrated into each subject area. The Ministry specifies the schools' requirements in terms of computer lab equipment and provides Internet access, hardware, and software resources. Ministry policy also addresses best practices and teacher competencies and ensures that ICT is integrated into the curriculum. A teacher from a lower secondary school (TW003) stresses the importance of these national policies at the school level:

> Evaluation of the effectiveness of using ICT in school by the Ministry of Education had the most powerful impact on school. Everyone was learning ICT-related knowledge and skills at that time. The principal was no exception.

The case report from another lower secondary school (TW006) in Chinese Taipei states that the Ministry's policy of providing schools with ICT hardware and resources led to the development of the school's innovation, the use of technology to learn geography. These cases support the view that the country's national ICT policy is primarily a means of developing ICT capacity.

The goal of the Czech Republic's national ICT policy is that when students leave school they be sufficiently computer literate. To implement this policy, the government focuses on ICT resources and training at the school level, developing ICT capacity. In fact, the amount of funding a school receives is dependent on the number of teachers in the school that pass the national computer literacy test. The belief here is that if teachers are ICT literate, students will become more computer literate. Student computer skills are specified in the national policy, as well as provisions for all schools to be connected to the Internet and be adequately equipped. The impact of this policy is shown in the case report on a Czech upper secondary school (CZ002). The report states that the national policy ensured that the school had full-time ICT coordinators and sufficient connection to the Internet to allow for increased use of technology in the classroom. As mentioned in Chapter 3, the school's innovation involved designing Web sites for local villages that included all the materials available to the public by law (for example, decrees, minutes, maps, transportation, and history). The goal of the innovation was that students develop their ICT skills in order to use them in the working world after school.

CASES NOT LINKED TO NATIONAL POLICIES

Of the 174 cases in this study, only 39% did not mention a connection between their innovation and national education policy; only 27% lacked a connection with national ICT policy.

Only 30 cases (17%) were not linked to a national ICT policy or an education policy. However, half of these cases were supported by local policies or plans.

There are various reasons for disconnections between schools and the national policies that do exist. Some schools in our study were private schools, such as the Filipino primary school (PH005) cited in Chapter 3, and were disconnected from national policies for that reason. Some cases without a connection to national policy came from countries with federal systems. An example is the U.S. primary school (US006) mentioned previously in this chapter, which constructed a school policy to use ICT to improve student achievement. The Filipino and U.S. cases were similar to several others that lacked a connection to a national policy but did have a link to local policy. Another is a lower secondary school in Australia (AU001). The focus of this school was on strategic planning to integrate information and communication technology into the classroom and into the learning programs. The school invested much money in resources to ensure that it remained at the forefront of the new technological developments that aimed to enhance learning opportunities for its students. In these schools, the lack of connection to national policy was compensated by local policies and plans.

Only 15 schools out of the 174 mentioned neither a link to national policy nor a connection at the local level. This is not to say that no national policy existed in these cases; rather, such a policy, if it existed, did not play a role in the innovation. The existence of a national policy was cited as important by several case reports from Chile, as mentioned previously in this chapter. However, the case report from a subsidized private primary and secondary school (CL007) in Chile does not make strong connections to either national or local policies. The case report states:

> The project was begun in 1999 on the personal initiative of the teacher in charge, as a result of the knowledge she gained from a professional course on the use of information systems in education, as well as an invitation extended to the school to participate in the ThinkQuest international competition. To support this participation, an elective Computer-Based English Workshop was created. The students in this elective course used spoken, and especially written, English at various levels, corresponding to their increasing facility with the language. Educational software, productivity tools, electronic mail, and the Internet were used in the course. Its methodology was based on cooperative work among the students as well as interaction with students in foreign schools involved in the ThinkQuest competition.

The initiative and effort of this teacher are typical of many cases we read, but such efforts are particularly important in the absence of national policies or local plans that support the use of ICT. This was also the case for teachers in a lower secondary school (SK008) in the Slovak Republic, where resources for ICT were quite scarce. In this innovation, students participated in a European-Union–sponsored environmental and health project that encouraged them to care for the environment. Thanks to outside sponsors, the school obtained five computers, which were installed in the computer laboratory and used by the students during club activities. The teachers also gradually learned to use this technology. As part of the project, students collected, identified, photographed, and scanned different kinds of healing plants. Students used ICT tools to access various kinds of text and graphic information related to their reports. Teachers coordinated and planned for the fieldwork with students, prepared worksheets for students, and assessed student work. They showed students how to use various tools and a scanner to digitize the photographs from their fieldwork.

Similarly, an innovation in a Czech secondary school (CZ005) relied on the enthusiasm of a teacher and his students to succeed. The original intention of the IT teacher was to share his enthusiasm for film and video with his students. His project was focused on the activities connected to video processing and filming, but it also involved other areas of the school. In this voluntary project, the teacher worked with a group of enthusiastic students on a variety of multimedia activities that included the school magazine. The main person behind the project was the teacher who initiated and led it. He gradually became an advisor and an assistant who cooperated with the students on their voluntary projects. The teacher reported, "The most important fact is that the students organize everything by themselves. They know what it is about and it leads them towards independent work."

In conclusion, even though the vast majority of the countries have a national ICT policy, a number of cases either do not mention such a policy or indicate that the innovation occurred without a direct connection to a national ICT policy. Often, the innovations in these cases were teacher initiated. Most often, these efforts were supported by local school plans and policies and/or external resources. Other innovations required few resources and additional teacher effort.

SUMMARY OF CONNECTIONS WITH NATIONAL POLICIES

The large majority of cases reported connections with either national ICT policies or education policies. As has been described, there were different types of national ICT policies and programs. The policies themselves included a wide range of information, including the following:

- ◆ Visions of a changed education system or society, in general, that are enriched by technology

- ◆ Descriptions of student and teacher ICT competencies

- ◆ Required ICT resources, including software, hardware, Internet connections, and technical support

The programs that accompany these policies would sometimes provide the following:

- ◆ Equipment, software, or network connections

- ◆ Teacher training in ICT skills or curriculum integration

- ◆ Curriculum materials or software connected to the curriculum

- ◆ Evaluation of student achievement, teacher skills, and school effectiveness

- ◆ Funding for any of the above

These policies supported innovations by linking them to education reform, fostering efforts to increase student achievement, and building the technological capacity of schools and the capabilities of teachers and students. Cases that were connected to national education policies were more likely to report changes in teachers' activities in the classroom. Cases that were linked to national ICT policies were more likely to mention changes in students' activities in the classroom.

SUMMARY AND CONCLUSIONS

In this chapter we addressed these questions:

Which local policies related to such things as staff development, student computer fees, facilities access, technical support, and other issues appear to be effective in supporting these innovations?

Which national telecommunications policies related to such things as school Internet access, equipment purchase, teacher training, and student Internet use seem to be effective in supporting innovative technology-based pedagogical practices?

While research elsewhere has often found disconnections between policies and classroom practice (Cohen & Hill, 2001; McLaughlin, 1990), our research found many connections. A large majority (63%) of the case reports for the innovations in our study mentioned that innovations were influenced by local policies and plans. A large proportion of cases also mentioned links with national ICT policies (73% of the cases) and education policies (61% of the cases).

In addition, cases that cited connections to local policies and plans were more likely to report changes in teacher classroom activities and the outcomes of both teachers (new pedagogical skills and collaborative skills) and students (problem-solving skills and metacognitive skills). In Chapter 5, we identified administrative support and teacher professional development—factors associated with local policy—as essential to the sustainability of the innovations we studied.

Cases that mentioned links with national education policies were more likely to cite changes in teacher activities in the classroom; those that mentioned connections with national ICT policies were also more likely to mention changes in student classroom activities. Our analysis in Chapter 5 found that funding and supportive policies, such as those at the national level, were important contributors to sustained practice. Cases that were linked to national ICT policies were also more likely to show evidence that they were transferred to other sites.

The few cases that were not linked to either local or national policies seemed to be voluntary innovations, ones that required few resources, or ones that disproportionately relied on the initiative and energy of individual teachers.

Granted, we studied a specially selected and particularly innovative set of cases that were, perhaps, more likely to be affected by policy than the ordinary classroom. Nonetheless, these special cases help us understand not only how teachers can use technology to implement innovative practices but also how schools, districts, and ministries of education can formulate effective policies that support these innovations.

We found that national and local statements and plans supported similar policy goals. Policies at both levels supported innovations that used ICT to reform education, improve student performance, and increase ICT capacity. But policies and programs at these two levels served different and complementary functions. The coordination of policies at the two levels could be a particularly powerful force for innovation.

NATIONAL ICT AND EDUCATIONAL POLICIES

At the national level, ICT policies stated broad visions of the way ICT could change education (as in Singapore and Finland) or improve student achievement (as in the United States). Some policies set goals and challenges for states and schools to accomplish. These goals were related to the development of ICT capacity or skills in teachers and students (as in the case of Denmark). On occasion, ICT policies were connected to education policies that specified new ways of teaching (as in Thailand) or specific goals for student performance (as in England). Occasionally these policies were mentioned in case reports as motivations for the innovation.

But more often, policies and programs at the national level were cited as enabling forces that allowed the innovation to happen. The primary function of national policies and programs was to provide schools with funds or resources that addressed schools' needs for equipment, networking, and teacher professional development. Case reports often stated that the innovations succeeded because they received hardware, software, and teacher training as a result of national policies and programs. This was so for cases in Chinese Taipei, Korea, Lithuania, Singapore, Thailand, and many other countries. Some countries provided free access to the Internet (as in Chinese Taipei, Denmark, and Singapore), sometimes in partnership with telecommunications providers to do so (as in Chile). A case in the Czech Republic (CZ002) mentioned the important function of a national program in supplying the school with a full-time technology coordinator.

In some countries, it was important for the national policies to support the development of educational software coordinated with the curriculum. This was particularly so where languages are used that are not common in the international software marketplace, such as Thai and Catalan.

Finally, programs in several countries, such as Korea and The Netherlands, identified model schools that use ICT in their classrooms. Several of the innovations in this study were picked from among such model schools. These national programs would encourage and support visits to these schools by teachers from other schools to observe their innovative practices.

LOCAL POLICIES AND PLANS

Like national policies and plans, one of the functions of local policies was to provide a vision of ways to use ICT. However, the difference is that local visions were much more specific and tied to what happened in the classroom than were state or national policies. For example, the vision in the Australian primary school (AU002) was one in which teaching methodologies were open ended and required higher-order thinking and problem-solving skills. The vision in an English secondary school (UK004) was one in which students took more responsibility for their learning, and ICT provided them with anywhere, anytime access to curriculum materials. In some cases, principals and teachers had visions of using technology in specific ways to change how they taught and how students learned. Others had visions of all students achieving at their potential, and some had visions of their schools and classrooms enriched by technology.

These visions were sometimes expressed in personal terms as a "mission" or "philosophy" of the principal or a teacher. At other times, as in the case of schools in Australia (AU002), Israel (IL003), and the United States (US006), the administration and staff worked together to create a shared vision of what they wanted the school to be. Sometimes these local visions, missions, and philosophies drew on broad, national statements for their inspiration. But detailed, personal, and often shared local visions were cited more often than national visions as the motivation for the concrete plans and actions of administrators and teachers.

This was another important function of local efforts; schools converted these local visions into specific plans and actions that had immediate implications for classroom practice. In these cases, the staff articulated specific goals related to the vision and guidelines to support this vision, as illustrated by the Australian (AU002) and Danish (DK011) primary schools cited previously. Principals allocated equipment and other resources to accomplish the vision. Often these resources included equipment and network access; but human resources were important, too, as in China Hong Kong, where the IT committee in a secondary school helped teachers in two innovative cases from that country (CN005 and CN009), and in the Canadian primary school where peer mentors supported each other's practice (CA002).

Teachers' professional development experiences were also an important—even essential—part of local plans and efforts. These professional development experiences were sometimes very extensive; in the Israeli primary school (IL003) mentioned previously, the staff received 900 hours of ICT training over 3 years that included courses, private sessions, and self-study. Professional development sometimes included pedagogical training and the integration of ICT into the curriculum, but most often it focused on ICT training. This training was often associated with national policies that provided resources for teacher professional development, as in Catalonia, Spain (in ES001); Chile (in CL009); Latvia (in LV005); and Thailand (in TH004).

As mentioned in the previous chapter, a variety of approaches to professional development was evident in the cases we studied. Training was often conducted in formal workshops. But much of it was conducted informally, for example, through regular gatherings of teachers who shared their experiences and advice, as in the case of a U.S. school (US006) where subject-area teachers regularly met to review specific software packages relative to student performance goals in their subjects. Informal professional development was particularly important in cases that involved connections between the use of ICT and education reform. Here, development was focused on specific applications of ICT to classroom practices, as in the case of the Canadian primary school (CA002) where staff got together once a week to share best practices and conduct critical discussions of teaching.

In our analysis at the local level, policies specifically related to student fees and computer access did not emerge, but other local policies and plans did have an important impact on innovation. Local policy makers could affect classroom practice by expressing a detailed vision for ICT use, converting these visions into concrete action plans, allocating technical and human resources to the innovation, and providing teacher professional development focused on classroom practice. These policies and plans can have impacts on education reform, improved student achievement, and increased ICT capacity of schools.

COORDINATED LOCAL AND NATIONAL POLICIES

Of the 174 cases we studied in SITES Module 2, 94 case reports (about 54%) indicated the innovation was linked to both a national education or ICT policy and a school-level ICT policy. Policy makers and researchers agree that when national and local policies and plans are coherent, or at least consistent, they are more likely to have an impact on classroom practice.

Pal (2001) identifies three types of coherence or consistency in policy:

◆ Internal consistency, in which problem definition, goals, and instruments are complementary.

◆ Horizontal consistency, in which what policy makers do in one field or agency does not contradict what is done in another.

◆ Vertical consistency, in which the programs and actions undertaken are logically related to the policy.

Consistency is perhaps easiest to achieve when educational systems are highly centralized, as in Singapore. In such countries, education ministries can achieve internal consistency by expressing a coherent vision in which the problems facing schools and society in general are clearly articulated, and by proposing ICT solutions that address these problems. They can achieve horizontal consistency by coordinating the efforts of various departments around problems and their solutions. In this regard, ministries can make sure that the various channels by which policies influence classroom practices are coordinated. They can construct curriculum, teacher development, assessment and accountability policies, and instruments that have the same general goals and reinforce each other. Ministries can also create vertical consistency by ensuring that local policies and plans are synchronized with national policy and by ensuring that schools have the resources needed to carry out these policies. National plans that encourage initiative on the part of principals can achieve a top-down, bottom-up coordination around the goals for ICT use in schools.

However, many countries have federal or decentralized educational systems. In these cases, vertical consistency or coherence of policy is quite rare, in the view of Cohen and Hill (2001). This is partly due to the fragmentation of educational governance and the lack of coordination between levels. Reforms may be formed at the national and state level but may not be consistent. By the time policies have worked their way though the various levels to the district and school, any coherence that existed often breaks down. As a result, teachers who try to promote new ideas and engage in new practices may not receive the required level of support from their principals or districts, and the principals and districts may not in turn receive support from their teachers.

With decentralized systems or in countries moving toward decentralization, internal and horizontal consistency become even more important. Because the connection between levels is less strong in these countries, it is more important that the communications that schools and teachers do receive are consistent. In this regard the role of state or provincial policy makers is crucial. In their study of effective reform policies at the state level, Cohen and Hill (2001) found that internal consistency among policy instruments had an important influence on the success of reforms. The authors contend that "policies that aim to improve teaching and learning depend on complex chains of causation. Making the policies work depends both on their elaboration and on connecting the links in those chains" (p. 8). They found that in cases where policy had an impact on classroom practice,

> policymakers took steps to create such consistency at the state level. They developed curricular frameworks that set out the aims and direction for the changes. … They used those frameworks to evaluate commercial … texts, in an effort to guide the creation of … materials that could improve teaching and learning. And they used the frameworks to guide creation of new state assessments that were

designed to test students' performance on the sorts of tasks that the curriculum and frameworks specified. Reformers also used the frameworks to guide development of instruments of practice, like new … curriculum units for students and teachers. (p. 7)

When national and state policies and instruments are coherent and backed by necessary resources, school administrators and teachers can plan for technology in ways that maximize change. They can extend these policies to create local visions of what teaching and learning can be like when enriched by technology. They can distribute resources to teachers and classrooms in ways that support the policies. And, most importantly, they can create extended professional development experiences in which policies have direct implications for teacher and student pedagogical practices using ICT. In these situations, national, state, and local policies and plans can work together to maximize educational change and improvement and the impact of technology on teachers and students.

stellar cases OF technology-supported

PEDAGOGICAL INNOVATIONS

By Ronald E. Anderson

INTRODUCTION

The Second Information Technology in Education Study (SITES) Module 2 was a qualitative study of innovative pedagogical practices using technology. The study produced 174 case studies from 28 participating countries from Europe, Asia, North America, South America, and Africa. We used a case selection procedure (described in Chapter 2) that combined both international and local considerations. National research teams used standard instruments and protocols to collect data and wrote up their case reports using a common format. Our primary goal in Chapters 3–6 was to analyze these case reports or subgroups of them to look for trends across cases and answer the research questions that drove

this study. The approach to qualitative analysis we used in these chapters is what Stake (1995) refers to as an *instrumental* approach. By this he means that the case studies using this approach are not examined for their unique or special qualities but for the knowledge that might be gained relative to a general question, issue, or problem—this is its instrumental nature. Stake contrasts this approach to one he calls *intrinsic*, in which cases are studied for their own special or unique status relative to the purpose of the study. Analysis in this approach focuses on the people, events, and issues that characterize the case rather than on the underlying trends or generalizations that might be derived from them.

While Chapters 1–6 use the instrumental approach, there are certainly reasons to look at these cases for their own sake. As mentioned in Chapter 2, the cases in this study were selected after an extensive consideration of selection criteria and potential candidates. Criteria and candidates were considered by national panels in each country, together consisting of 241 members, including researchers, ministry officials, business people, administrators, teachers, and even some students. Many cases were considered that were not ultimately selected. Researchers in each country spent 1 to 2 weeks at each case study site and collected data from principals, teachers, students, and parents. They observed classes and analyzed teacher and student materials. The case reports that made it through the selection process are definitely worth considering on their unique merits. To a large extent, the schools and classrooms described in these case reports are models for other schools and teachers in their respective countries and elsewhere in the world. They certainly warrant the use of an intrinsic analytic approach.

However, with 174 cases it was not possible for us to examine each of them in the way that the intrinsic approach requires. This chapter is our attempt to feature a small number of stellar cases.

This analysis consists of summaries of 22 cases, each one selected as special, or stellar, by one of 22 National Research Coordinators (NRCs). Table 7.1 gives a list of the countries that submitted stellar case selections, along with the case numbers and brief titles of the cases. Because these cases were selected as outstanding by the NRCs, they are in some sense exemplary and worthy of review, and this discussion provides such a review. Without a doubt these 22 cases are stimulating and rich with unique features. This short report cannot describe this smaller number of cases in depth, but we hope that other researchers will find the cases worthy of further investigation.

Each NRC was invited to select a case he or she considered to be in some sense the most outstanding national case. However, no criteria were specified for what constituted an outstanding or stellar case. Instead, each NRC was asked to provide written reasons for his or her selection. Some NRCs went to their National Panel of Experts for their advice on the criteria and the selection. When they submitted their selections, not every NRC supplied a clarification of the criteria. Those who did, however, cited their national selection criteria for all cases, saying that their stellar cases best met those criteria. A few NRCs gave explicit new criteria they used in selecting their stellar cases. These criteria were used in this discussion to highlight specific aspects of those cases.

Some NRCs did not submit cases for this consideration. Some felt that each case was unique and stellar in its own way. Others felt that it was difficult to choose one among the many they had studied. A few NRC members did not provide a reason for not submitting a case.

As mentioned previously, the methodological orientation we used to analyze these cases is *intrinsic* in its approach. In our analyses we focus on the special qualities of the cases themselves. Every attempt has been made to represent what really happened in the schools. We are necessarily limited to the case reports supplied by the NRCs, since we could not go back to the schools for additional information or clarification.

This summary of the cases begins with an overview of the schools, the innovations, and the ICT used. This material is summarized in Tables 7.1 to 7.3. The first table identifies the cases, the second gives school demographics and a summary of the ICT involved, and the third summarizes the pedagogies used in each innovation. After summarizing the demographics, the discussion will focus on the innovations and the ICT used.

Table 7.1

STELLAR CASES: COUNTRIES, CASE NUMBERS, AND TITLES

COUNTRY	CASE NUMBER	BRIEF CASE TITLE
Australia	AU004	Constructivist Teaching with ICT
Canada	CA002	Creating a Learning Community
Chile	CL010	Working Recreationally with Math
China, Hong Kong	CN003	Cyber Art Project
Czech Republic	CZ003	School Library as Multimedia Center
Germany	DE009	Luring into Reading via the Internet
Spain, Catalonia	ES005	Roots: To Share among Schools Using ICT
Finland	FI005	Netlibris Literature Circles
France	FR005	A Trip to Rome
Israel	IL013	The Salt Flat Project
Italy	IT001	Smoke Signals
Lithuania	LT004	Information Skills through Project-Based Learning
Latvia	LV001	ICT in Foreign Language
Netherlands	NL017	Code Name Future
Norway	NO006	Crossing the Antarctic
Phillippines	PH006	Filipino Literature in Motion
Portugal	PT001	Image in Movement
Singapore	SG001	Digital Art
Slovakia	SK011	Let's Sing Together CD-ROM
Thailand	TH002	Learning to Compose Poems with ICT
England	UK010	Challenge 2000
United States	US014	Future High School

OVERVIEW OF THE SCHOOLS

Out of the 22 stellar cases, 9 were primary schools, 4 were schools with all grades from preschool through Grade 12, and the remaining were secondary schools or a subset thereof (see Table 7.2.). In the majority of instances, but not all, the grades of the innovation were a smaller subset of grades. The sizes of the schools varied widely, ranging from 100 students to more than 3,000. The curricular subjects involved in the innovations are given in Table 7.2, which shows that there was considerable diversity among the innovations: about half of them addressed either almost all subjects or a multidisciplinary learning activity.

The range of ICT access for students was enormous, varying from one Internet-networked computer per student to more than 50 students per computer, many without Internet access. In fact, in quite a number of cases the student-computer ratio was higher than 25 students per computer for the school as a whole. Every school had some kind of local network and at least one point of access to the Internet; and all schools had a variety of software installed on their computers, called "various" in Table 7.2. The pedagogies involved in the innovation, given in Table 7.3, will be discussed later.

Many of the innovations themselves defy analytical description, in that 22 separate categories are needed to completely capture the exceptional qualities of these educational programs. As an example of the distinctive character of many of these cases, consider this description from the NRC's discussion of Smoke Signals, the case from Italy:

> The stellar case (IT001) from Italy, named Smoke Signals, has a Web site at **http://www.sanremonet.com/scuole/segnali/index.htm**. The name Smoke Signals was borrowed from early American Indians who used smoke and a variety of primitive signals to communicate with distant communities. Because some of the eight primary school communities resided in remote mountains, the idea of a telematic or electronic magazine made sense as a way to share experiences. This idea appealed to the teachers and other staff when they started the project 6 years ago because they thought it could stimulate a wide variety of pedagogical activity. Each classroom in each of the eight schools is expected to construct stories, which can include pictures, drawings, and other materials, for the e-newspaper. One of the 12 sections of their periodical is reserved for preschoolers to share their drawings and other artifacts. The articles, sent via e-mail to the editorial staff, arise from everyday school activities. Writing an article; reading what others have drafted; discussing the different essays; and using a computer to produce, send, or upload hypertext are familiar activities for these students; they [the activities] are part of the daily curriculum. The most obvious result is the regular e-mail exchange between the schools, the management of documentation, and the possibility to take part in similar initiatives. The growing culture of expertise in e-mail and Web publishing has led to other networked projects including links with disabled students and links to classrooms in other counties.

Table 7.2

STELLAR CASES: COUNTRY, SCHOOL TYPE AND SIZE, AND SUMMARY OF ICT USED

CASE NUMBER	SCHOOL TYPE, GRADES	GRADES OF INNOVATION	SCHOOL SIZE	SUBJECT(S)	SUMMARY OF ICT USED
AU004	P–12	P–10	1,100	Cross Curriculum	5–6 computers in each classroom, one point of Internet access; e-mail and wide range of software for investigation
CA002	Primary	K–8	437	Almost All	100 computers in clusters and a tech room; Web and various software
CL010	Primary	4	837	Math	12 computers in computer lab; educational games and various software
CN003	Primary	4–6	1,000+	Art	110 computers in 2 labs; 35 laptops; 15 airport wireless hubs; most computers with Internet access
CZ003	Secondary	10–12	300+	Multiple, Info, Civics	2 labs with 32 PCs with Internet access; 1 PC for video work
DE009	Primary	1, 3, 4	620	Languages, Misc.	50+ computers, some with Internet access; 1 computer per classroom; e-mail, productivity software
ES005	Primary (5 Schools)	4–6	100+	History, Geography, Misc.	10 computers, Internet access; multimedia production and various software
FI005	K–12	All	700+	Lit., Languages, Info.	95 computers; various software for collaboration and e-mail
FR005	Upper Sec.	10	900	Languages, Hist., Geog.	200 computers, Internet access plus various software
IL013	7–12	7–12	380	Multiple	53 computers in 3 labs and elsewhere, all in LANs with Internet access; various software
IT001	P–5 (8 Schools)	P–5	650	Multiple	8+ computers, at least 1 per school; Web access using FrontPage; various software
LT004	1–12	5–11	1,365	Multiple, Biology, Info.	25 computers, most in labs; various peripherals and software
LV001	1–12	10–12	1,200	Foreign Languages, Hist.	23 computers, all with Internet access; various software
NL017	Lower Secondary	7	620	Multiple, Geography	64 computers, most networked; proxy server; various software
NO006	Lower Secondary	8	315	Math, Earth, Foreign Languages	20 (estimated) computers, 6 in library, others in classrooms; various software
PH006	Secondary	9	2,060	Most, Languages	55 computers, 15 in LAN with Internet access; various software
PT001	Primary	3–4	150	Art	8 computers, video equipment; video production software, e.g., Director 7
SG001	Primary	K–6	2,500	Art, Some Language	80 computers in 3 labs, plus an art room with 12 iMacs, most with Internet access and various software
SK011	1–9	3	600	Music, Art, Info.	12 PCs with sound card and software plus 1 with I-access and various software
TH002	Secondary	7–12	3,328	Native Language	87 computers with 62 networked; e-mail; Internet access; various software
UK010	Primary	6	347	Mostly Multiple	27 computers, 10 in studio; all networked with various software (also a number of older computers)
US014	10–12	10–12	240	All	1 computer for each student; all have Internet access and various software

Table 7.3

STELLAR CASES AND THEIR MAJOR PEDAGOGIES

CASE NUMBER	PRINCIPAL PEDAGOGIES USED IN INNOVATION
AU004	Constructivism; learning community model; group collaboration; large projects; peer assessment
CA002	Learning community model; many student-led, long-term inquiry projects, many of which are cross-disciplinary; alternative assessments; server space for collaborative work
CL010	Active learning and problem solving; tutorials and learning games; collaborative work; peer grading
CN003	Digital drawing and painting to teach aesthetic sense and creativity; collaboration with another class in a very different city; peer tutors; self and peer assessment
CZ003	Project learning; distance learning; collaborative learning; ICT integrated
DE009	Projects; groups; multidisciplinary problems; collaboration with students and teachers in other European schools and with an expert
ES005	Large projects; collaboration; research and presentation skills
FI005	Student-centered work (empowerment); collaboration; peer assessment
FR005	Information search; research; collaboration
IL013	Projects; information search; collaboration; networking with Jordanian school community; some students trained for "computer trustee" role; Web site construction and maintenance by students
IT001	Student-produced Web "telematic magazine" for a "circle" of 8 schools; giving voice to students; group subprojects; self-assessment
LT004	Projects; information skill development; peer assessment
LV001	Projects; group work; Internet-based research
NL017	Cross-curricular projects; pair collaboration; large Internet search project; multimedia presentations; alternative assessment of independence, creativity; no textbook
NO006	Large project; networking; virtual field trip; alternative assessment
PH006	Projects; multimedia presentation
PT001	Teams of both students and teachers; cinematic animation projects for motion arts curriculum
SG001	ICT to learn multiple forms of drawing and painting, color and brush choices; assessing and describing digital art
SK011	Digital sound production to refine singing and learn music principles; digital audio recording, editing, and publishing; student collaboration in musical production; ICT integration
TH002	Poetry construction in Thai; evaluations in groups; peer grading; ICT integration; tutorials with testing; sharing work via the Web
UK010	Cross-curriculum projects and problem solving; groups working on large projects for depth; research and information handling; presentations; implicit learning community
US014	Constructivist emphasis on past student experience; implicit learning community model; long projects, some with collaboration; self-assessments; Web-based sharing of all course info

The key to the success of this award-winning project seems to be the way the teachers and staff have integrated their e-magazine activities with their curricular goals, while giving the students the responsibility of producing the communications. Perhaps the most important outcome of the innovation is that, as one teacher put it, "It gives voice to the children." While school district personnel did not use the following phrases to describe their effort, the personnel at this somewhat remote school district have discovered on their own the benefits of a "student-centered school learning organization."

OVERVIEW OF THE PEDAGOGY

We have found that any given innovation is likely to utilize diverse pedagogies concurrently. Nonetheless, the majority of pedagogies were philosophically compatible and characterizable in terms like "authentic instruction" or "student-centered learning," including such instructional methods as project learning, inquiry, alternative assessment, and collaborative learning.

While any collection of innovations by definition is unlikely to be categorizable to a great degree of satisfaction, we have divided these innovations into groups to simplify the process of summarizing them. It is our intent that this grouping will highlight the essential features of the stellar cases; to this end, some of the cases could be discussed in more than one grouping.

NETWORKED CULTURES AND COMMUNITIES (DE, ES, IL, IT)

The case from Italy that we have already summarized illustrated those stellar cases that were structured around networked communities. A similar type of innovation was selected as stellar by Catalonia, Spain. What was accomplished is particularly impressive, given the scarcity of resources in the community and the minimal level of ICT.

Italy's Stellar Case

The Catalonian project (ES005), called Roots, is a collaborative multimedia project of five primary schools in five little villages within the same rural, mostly farming region. These five schools belong to a ZER (Rural School Area) that provides technical and teacher development support. A typical participating school had two teachers, two classrooms, 20 students, and two computers. The project was done primarily in the classroom, with students in Grades 4 to 6. The student tasks were to research the geography, history, and culture of their village, including such things as songs, legends, and families, using a diversity of methods such as interviews, library research, digital photography, and a variety of Web searches. Field trips also were provided. The students generally worked in pairs; they were expected to write multimedia documents reporting their research, using word-processing and presentation software. They also worked together to produce a multimedia report for their Web site. While the students were working, they shared intermediate documents via e-mail with students in the other schools. These activities promoted electronic as well as face-to-face collaborations among students, between students and teachers, and between students and community experts. Teachers integrated the student work on the project into their teaching of geography, history, science, and language. Two key elements were collaboration among the teachers across schools and the cooperation from the community. The project's potential transferability is very high. The school's Web site is **http://ww.xtec.es/centres/c5008108**. The potential transferability of this work is very high.

Another rural school setting is represented by Israel's stellar case, featuring the development of a major Web site dealing with the surrounding salt flats.

Israel's Stellar Case

The stellar case chosen to represent Israel's cases, called ICT in Environmental Studies (IL013), was conducted in the upper grades (7–12) of the Maale Shaharut K–12 school. Located in the Southern Negev desert, the innovation is exemplified by the Salt Flat project, a major Web site development project. The innovation involved the 380 students in the upper grades and a variety of project-based activities and independent studies fostering independent learning. All of the students and teachers participate in these projects, including the collaboration that resulted in the development of the school's Web site. Leading much of the work of this project were "computer trustees," students who have received an 80-hour ICT training course. In both its pedagogical and technical aspects, the Web site serves as a dynamic learning center for the whole school; its most elaborate part deals with the salt flat that surrounds the school. This Web learning center contains projects by students, a bank of geographical and historical textual and visual materials, learning activities, links to relevant Web sites, and sections for special education and immigrant students. The Web site was a semifinalist in the ThinkQuest competition; it can be viewed at **http://library.thinkquest.org/C004132/plain/indexE.html**. Students from many disciplines contributed to the site through classes in biology, earth science, computers, art, and language. Students in turn can use the data from this site for other projects. The international border divides the salt flat between Jordan and Israel, so collaboration between the students and Jordanian students in the village of Rah'me resulted in joint products.

The collaboration between students in this area of major, long-term conflict is striking and worthy of greater attention. Another case that is best described as an example of networked cultures took place in Germany, where students in a primary school maintained e-mail interaction with students from three other countries.

Germany's Stellar Case

Germany's stellar case (DE009) was an innovation in a primary school of 620 students in a little Bavarian town. This innovation, called Luring into Reading through the Internet, involved a literature project in third- and fourth-grade language classes. Students in these classes collaborated with students in four other schools, three of which were in other countries; the Czech Republic, Sweden, and Hungary. The primary goal of the innovation was "to stimulate students' pleasure in reading and to advance creative writing." The participating students used computers to write texts and communicated with the other students by e-mail. The innovation focused on the subject of fairy and legendary tales and was part of an interdisciplinary class. While the emphasis was on the German language, the subjects of science, social studies, textile design, and art were also integrated into the program. Typical activities began with an assignment randomly picked from a collection of fairy-tale index cards. These assignments were then done by students on their own or as partners in small working groups. Possible assignments included writing a new fairy tale, rearranging an already existing fairy tale, modifying a fairy tale into a radio drama, creating comic figures from fairy tales, creating fairy-tale poems, or sewing dresses for fairy-tale figures. First, the students had to come up with conceptual ideas on how they wished to do their assignments. They could write these ideas on paper by hand. The students were free to choose a method to use in their respective assignments; some students wrote their texts on a computer, while others created forms with paper or cardboard. The exchange with an author of children's books underlines the seriousness of the activity and enhances the learning process. Students exchanged letters with pen pals at other participating schools. At the end of the lesson, they presented the result of their work to the whole class. The teachers reported that in the program the students wrote much more than usual and paid more attention to the style and readability of their stories. This international exchange broadened both the cultural views of the students and the teachers' repertoire of methods. The students worked on their tasks with greater seriousness, knowing that the results would be shared with other schools.

Taken together, these cases demonstrate that very different types of cultures and communities can be bridged with curricular projects utilizing e-mail communication. Their potential impact is great, though difficult to quantify.

VIRTUAL FIELD TRIPS (CN, FR, NO, UK)

Innovations in this category tend to resemble those of networked communities; however, their unique contribution is that they typically combine e-mail interaction with another community (or with experts). The first two examples from this category actually featured real field trips, where the students traveled to another cultural system. We call them Virtual Field Trips because students spent most of their learning time at a distance from the home school.

China Hong Kong's Stellar Case

The stellar case selected by China Hong Kong's team was called the Cyber Art project (CN003). It was located in a primary school of more than 1,000 students, but only Grades 4–6 participated in the innovation. The innovation took up about 25% of the classroom time allocated for the art curriculum. The goals were to cultivate students' creativity, to develop their aesthetic sense, to promote new ways of learning and teaching art with multimedia, to extend the learning space beyond the classroom, and to motivate students to do more and better artwork. Students used laptop computers and art-related software such as Painter Classics and Art Dabbler to create artwork within both the art lessons and extracurricular activities. These digital art activities gave students the advantage of quickly experiencing the effects of different painting media and various special effects. Fifteen wireless AirPort transmitters had been installed around the school so that students could access the Internet from most areas of the school with their laptops. Most of the time Internet access was not needed, so the students were able to take the laptops to draw or paint outdoors, in art galleries, and on an extended field trip to Beijing. The program involved 770 students and 17 teachers, but a group of 35 students exhibiting greater talents in art were selected by their teachers for participation in the extracurricular activities. These 35 selected students travelled to Beijing for a collaborative event with the Beijing students.

During their 4-day trip they sketched with Mainland China students, learned Chinese painting from these students, taught them how to sketch with the laptops, and critiqued each other's work. Thus, the students learned to collaborate in several new ways, but most of all they experienced a largely new culture and identified how they could learn from and collaborate with each other across cultural lines.

France's stellar case involved travel to another country but lacked face-to-face contact with a "sister" classroom. It also differed from China Hong Kong's stellar case in that the students were at the secondary rather than the primary level, and the subjects of study were language and history rather than art.

France's Stellar Case

The stellar case of France (FR005) took place in the Louise Michel secondary school, which has 900 students and is located in an inner suburb of Paris. The students, most of whom have a foreign origin, come from underprivileged cultural and social circles. Students involved in the innovation belonged to two classes in the 10th grade. These classes were chosen because of the involvement of the two history and geography teachers in the project for several years. Fifty students and six teachers were involved in this innovation in 2001, and about the same number during the prior 3 years. The innovation was built around a trip to Rome (Italy) during a week in April 2001. For the entire year preceding the trip, students planned and prepared for the trip, focusing on two different disciplines: French and history. The subject chosen for the 2000–2001 school year was cinema. Students had to view several relevant films and build files about them. Another assignment was to write the scenario for a short piece of fiction. The students also had to prepare a trip diary, before, during, and after the trip itself. In this innovation ICT contributed to students' research, document writing (journey diary, scenario), and additional activities, including film production and the creation of Web site pages. The project took place during the entire school year and began with the retrieval research step and the writing of the fiction scenario during the trip. At the same time, students did research on the films, analyzing images and comparing files about films. ICT, which was used in all the activities, added an innovative and motivating dimension to the project.

The next two summaries describe instances of truly virtual field trips. Norway's innovation utilized various activities to build upon the long journey of two women Antarctic explorers.

Norway's Stellar Case

Norway's stellar case consisted of eighth-grade students taking a virtual field trip by electronically following the progress of two women explorers as they crossed the Antarctic. The innovation took place in a junior secondary school and was part of a wider program at the school that consists of various projects and activities.

The school had 315 students and about 20 computers with Internet access. The effective focus of the innovation was "to make a dream come true." It started in October 1999 when two explorers presented their ideas for an education program connected to their 2000–2001 Antarctica expedition. A special database was developed that anyone could use to follow the expedition. The school had a special arrangement with one of the explorers whereby students would have direct interaction with her before, during, and after the expedition. The objective was to get both factual and research-based information as well as information of a more personal nature about the experiences of the two women in Antarctica. For instance, the students were assigned the task of writing an essay about their "secret dream," translating it into English, and then exchanging their dream stories with students in other countries. They did not get as much response from students in other countries as they expected, but the responses they did get produced learning experiences about cultural differences and exchanges. The innovation provided a variety of different types of knowledge for the students, including knowledge about their school as an institution, about real journalists, and, of course, about Antarctica and numerous scientific processes and issues. Some of the students produced a Web page on the virtual field trip that was followed by 3,000 visitors per week during the expedition.

England's case involved younger students than those in the Norway case, but the pedagogical focus also appears to be broader. Not only did the English innovation concentrate on collaborations of various types, it also required students to solve problems across a wide spectrum of the curriculum, which was designed to yield benefits from a variety of student-centered pedagogies.

England's Stellar Case

England's stellar case (UK010) was a primary school in which year 6 students (10 to 11 year olds) actively utilized a virtual field trip to engage in collaborative, cross-curricular problem solving. Forty-four of the schools' 347 students participated in the innovation, which consisted of students working in groups of 4 to 7 to solve puzzles and problems presented monthly on the Challenge 2000 Web site and set in the context of a journey around the world in a hot air balloon. The work extended across many different areas of the curriculum, including history, language, geography, music, and mathematics, as well as developing ICT skills. Students used the Internet extensively for research as well as drawing on other sources; the teacher supported the students but did not lead the activities. As the balloon passed through various countries, questions and activities were used to increase cultural awareness among the students. In some cases this required the students to contact an expert for specialist information, for example, to obtain a translation of a text presented in Arabic. For the entire year, 1 hour per week of class time was devoted to the innovation. These activities were all consistent with the school's vision of a learning community where teachers were committed to reflective and innovative teaching methods. Teachers and students identified the following positive impacts of the innovation: motivation to learn, improved self-discipline, improved attendance, improved ICT skills, better general knowledge, independent learning, and improved self-confidence and effective teamwork. Because Challenge 2000 was available via the Internet, students in other schools and other countries also used the resource.

Taken together these four cases show how student travel, either virtual or real, can be highly productive pedagogically, provided that considerable attention is given to exercises and activities that support the instructional objectives.

PIONEERING PROJECTS OF TEACHERS

While all of the stellar cases were to some extent pioneered by teachers, in some cases the teacher or teachers were the only or the major driving force behind the project. For instance, in Chile and the Philippines the innovations seemed to revolve around the effort of one or two teachers.

Chile's Stellar Case

Chile's stellar case (CL010) is a fourth-grade mathematics class transformed with a diversity of ICT applications. It is situated in Juan Seguel Elementary School, which is located in a low-income area and serves over 800 students. The school had only 12 computers, which were located in a lab. The innovation, pioneered by a math teacher in 1999, was intended to find a method to enable students to solve math logic problems on their own, i.e., in a less mechanical way. The program proved to be a dynamic and flexible learning experience that included introductory exercises for logic, numerals, and geometric logical thought, and other related subjects. Several games and other educational software were used. Students received exercise guides linking the software activities to the curriculum. The math teacher prepared the exercise guides, selected the software, and conducted pretests and posttests to measure the program's impact. She instructed students not only in math content but also in the particular skills needed in the use of the software and electronic informational resources. Students visited the computer lab accompanied by their math teacher. They divided into groups to work together on solving games on the computer or worked at the classroom tables with the learning guides for 3 hours per week. While the project was designed for a math class, the approach has since been transferred to a science class. The pioneering teacher did not have any special resources to design and develop the initial innovation; however, since then it has been transformed into a project for the national Program for Educational Improvement, in which the innovation was made available as a model for other schools to consider.

The Philippines' case has some parallels.

The Philippine's Stellar Case

The Philippines' stellar case (PH006), called Filipino Literature in Motion, is another example of an innovation led by a single teacher. The school had an enrollment of 2,060 students and was a private, coeducational secondary school about 2 driving hours from Manila. The class where this innovation took place had 56 students who were 14 to 15 years old. The innovation consisted of using computers to teach poetry as part of the third year of classes in Filipino language and literature. (The students' first language is Tagalog.) Instead of the traditional recitation of a poem, the students worked in groups of 6 or 7 to do various assigned activities or construct products. Each group's contribution culminated with a PowerPoint presentation of images and other representations that the group had produced. Some of the tasks given to the groups required Web-based searches. Before the group activity began, the teacher gave a multimedia presentation, developed in the Philippines, using animations and sounds in PowerPoint. This innovative activity was spread over two class periods and repeated once or twice during the quarterly term. Not only did this instructional unit allow students to learn through constructing products collaboratively, but the teacher's role also shifted toward one of helping and collaborating with the students."

This innovation was especially significant because the teacher's innovation helped substantially to counteract large class size and limited resources, both of which are prevailing conditions of education in the Philippines.

Thailand's stellar case is similar to that of the Philippines in some respects.

Thailand's Stellar Case

Thailand's researchers selected a poetry composition project (TH002) at a very large, 3,328-student secondary school that had 87 computers, most of which were networked with Internet access. A Thai language teacher, seeking to minimize boredom and increase motivation for seventh-grade students, developed a series of CAI programs to teach students how to compose poems. The students select the assignments of their preference from the predefined Web sites. In this learning method, the students either pair up or form groups with the classmates of their choice. At least two students have to share one computer, but they help each other do exercises or answer questions. In the process, they have to talk over their differing views to arrive at an agreement. Teacher-student communication takes place on the Web Board developed by the teacher. It is here that the students choose a picture to compose a poem. The group members are the first to comment and score the work. To hone their skills, the students can use ICT to study verses at **www.thai.net/bunga/poem.html**, then individually compose verses for submission to the innovation teacher by e-mail. According to the innovation teacher, using ICT not only contributes to better understanding of the content but also effects changes among the students. Seeing their works on the Internet (**www.thai.net/greenpink/ep04.html**) gives the students a sense of pride.

In some instances a team consisted of an ICT teacher working with a non-ICT teacher, as the next two stellar cases reveal.

Lithuania's Stellar Case

In Lithuania, the stellar case (LT004) selected was project-based learning at the Paneve'ys 'Vyturys' Secondary School. Although the innovation was implemented among the 800 students in Grades 5–11, the school served 1,365 students in 12 grades. The innovation consisted of two sequential student activities: (1) learning information skills during lessons on natural science and history in the fifth grade, and (2) doing project work in other subjects such as history and math in Grades 5–11. Two teachers, one in informatics and the other in history or natural science, work together to design integrated lessons. During these lessons, students learn skills in finding, organizing, evaluating, and presenting information, and learn to perform project tasks creatively on their own or in groups. The teachers propose various themes for projects and coordinate student work. The work performed by students is assessed from different perspectives. When assessing the work, more attention is paid to the skills (especially information), the process, and the results of the work than to subject knowledge. Project work and information skills are not graded. Students and project supervisors discuss the assessment method and criteria, describing them in a project contract. Students participate in the assessment as well; they evaluate their work and its process, write reviews on their friends' work, and engage in other assessment activities. The implementation of the innovation has influenced the organization of traditional lessons. Teachers now apply the project method more widely during their lessons and hold more integrated lessons. Also, student work is now assessed from several different perspectives.

The next stellar case, an innovation in Slovakia (SK011), was so successful that many schools have adopted it.

Slovakia's Stellar Case

This innovation was called Let's Sing Together on CD-ROM. For this activity third-grade students recorded the songs they sang, entered notes, composed songs, and replayed their own songs, all with the help of ICT. The students not only became familiar with a variety of music but they also learned how to use ICT to actively compose songs. Second-grade students have a compulsory computer science curriculum, which helps to prepare them for the year-long ICT-based music and art instruction. The primary school where this innovation took place had 18 computers. In the innovation students worked either in pairs or in larger teams like those in professional recording studios. The teacher of the class provided two to four lessons per week over an entire year and was assisted by a music teacher and an informatics teacher. The year ended with the students' production of an audio CD with their own songs as well as songs from several of the other 26 schools where similar projects were underway. While the innovation resulted in a number of beneficial outcomes for the students, the staff viewed it as establishing that "music lessons could be taught in a computer lab."

Another stellar case from Latvia, in Eastern Europe, shares a number of similar characteristics.

Latvia's Stellar Case

Latvia selected a foreign language innovation (LV001) as its stellar case. The innovation was implemented in Grades 10–12 in a 1,200-student school, with Grades 1–12 sharing 23 computers, all with Internet access. In 1999, the English-as-a-foreign-language teacher began using ICT as a tool to teach Grade 12 students. These students were assigned to search independently for information in English on the Internet or CD encyclopaedia. They were also expected to use ICT to assemble the information and write their reports in English. Those students who had computers at home were encouraged to expand their work after school and on the weekend, bringing their work to school on a floppy disk. In some instances the students worked in pairs. They also were encouraged to help each other with technical issues and other problems. While these pedagogical activities might not seem new or unusual in Western Europe, the students considered them highly innovative because traditionally they had experienced a strict segmentation between informatics instruction and the rest of the curriculum.

In Singapore, the last site profiled in this section, the teachers shared and helped each other in improving their work so extensively that they would be best described as having professional communities.

Singapore's Stellar Case

Singapore selected Digital Art (SG001) as its stellar case. This innovation was pioneered by a teacher several years ago in order to make art more appealing. The work of this teacher was supported by the school's professional community, which included a "cluster focus group" of teachers that encouraged innovation and sharing in the school. The school is a large, 2,500-student primary school with 80 computers, including a 12-iMac art room. Students also can use computers located in corridors and the library. In this program the students learn multiple forms of drawing and painting, color and brush choices, and how to describe and evaluate digital art. In a typical lesson, the teacher first triggers the interest of her students by showing them examples of a particular art form. Students are then given time to surf the Web, visiting virtual museums and art galleries to find more examples. Next, the teacher introduces the task and demonstrates how a software application (Kid's Studio or Crayola Art) can be used to achieve the effects of different art techniques. The innovation is now being transferred to all grade levels within the school. In some classes, students are paired according to their abilities, with the more ICT-savvy students helping the less proficient ones. The teachers also train "leader helpers" to assist them in the lessons. Expansion of the innovation is strongly supported by parents and staff as well as the Ministry of Education. A teacher reports that "students are excited about creating digital art. They show initiative and take on greater responsibilities for their own learning." Students frequent the computer room during their free time to work on their own digital art. Samples of student work are displayed at the school's Web site. These amazingly creative and sophisticated samples include batik painting, water color, calligraphy, Chinese digital painting, posters, repeated patterns, picture composition, and portraits.

Several other sites with impressive professional communities will be noted in the last grouping, called Schoolwide Innovations.

LARGE CROSS-CURRICULAR PROJECTS

Several cases demonstrate intriguing projects that went beyond one or two subjects but fell short of schoolwide curricular reform; these we have called Large Cross-Curricular Projects. One such project was provided by the Czech Republic.

The Czech Republic's Stellar Case

Gymnazium Humpolec, site of the stellar case CZ003, is a state secondary school serving eight grades of more than 300 children aged 12–19. Its Web site is http://www.gymhu.cz/. Its mission is to prepare students to enter universities; students must qualify for admission by examination. The innovation, the School Libraries as Multimedia Centers (SLAM) project, has, however, only one computer dedicated to video processing, so the Multimedia Center is virtual. Students can access library information and other resources from one of the 32 computers located in two computer laboratories. The SLAM project symbolizes a significant reform—a new organizational model oriented toward open or project learning, a variety of distance learning activities, and lifelong learning. These activities include the worldwide Globe project, the Peace in Time project, and the House 2012 project, in which a group of students had to reflect on a future house and plan the details of design, finance, and construction. The Globe science activity yielded publicity because the girls' biology team, called the Ladybirds, won a prize for the data they contributed. The SLAM project also included the construction of a videoconferencing and production facility, as well as a new online book-management system for the library. SLAM made it possible to expand Internet access to the school as a whole; many teachers took advantage of this expansion to develop projects with teachers in other schools. Ironically, what is officially defined as innovative for the outside world is only somewhat innovative and probably has less pedagogical impact than a variety of Internet-based instructional projects only tangentially related to this one.

It is probably much more common than has been recognized in the educational literature to find that when funding is desired for instructional improvement or reform, it has to be raised under some other banner. Perhaps most noteworthy about this case was the ability of the school community to produce some degree of pedagogical progress in spite of some major obstacles, such as the inability of the school to afford a librarian or a full-time ICT coordinator.

The next case, from The Netherlands, is clearly an exemplary instance of a large cross-curricular innovation.

The Netherlands's Stellar Case

The case selected as stellar for The Netherlands (NL017) was called Codename Future because students were assigned the challenge of thinking and writing about improving the future. This 7-week project for lower secondary education was cross-curricular, textbook replacing, and Web-based. It was implemented in the first year (Grade 7), where students worked in pairs on the project. They were expected to work in stages to develop a plan, draw up questions, carry out the plan, and finally report about their findings by means of a PowerPoint presentation. Information about the topics and links to other relevant Web sites were available on the project's password-protected Web site (**http://www.codenamefuture.nl**). The students used a logbook with instructions and notes for each stage. The project is accessible to all schools for secondary education in The Netherlands. The school started the project with a pilot in the 2000–2001 school year. The information technology teacher supported the other two teachers in the use of ICT in the project because the other two did not have much experience with it. At the end, students gave a presentation of their activities while the other students participated in the assessment. The students used ICT in several ways: to get instructions, to find basic information on each of the 30 social topics for the future, to search the Internet, and to use e-mail to get help. They also used non-ICT means, such as telephone interviews and questionnaires. The teachers believe that this innovation has been useful not only in developing knowledge of ICT and the subjects covered but also in improving study skills and lifelong learning in general. The innovation as implemented encouraged students to be creative and take responsibility for their own learning.

Students from The Netherlands work on the Codename Future project.

The last case in this group is not as broadly cross-curricular as the others; however, it clearly linked art with the ICT work generally associated with the informatics curriculum.

Portugal's Stellar Case

In Portugal's stellar case (PT001) all primary school students in the third and fourth years worked in small groups throughout the school year to develop small cinema projects. The project was called Image in Movement: Young Cartoon Directors. The students used ICT for the entire process of producing an animation, including image capturing and script design. A major pedagogical focus was upon skills in plastic expression and in the critical evaluation of audiovisual messages. Art was one of five subjects in the curriculum; the ICT-based animation activity was allocated 2 hours per week for the entire year. Each classroom was guided by a three-teacher team consisting of (1) the main teacher of the class, (2) the teacher-coordinator who gave assistance primarily with the ICT, and (3) the teacher in charge of "visual and technological education, who helped with plastic and visual expression." The latter two teachers came into the classroom for the weekly 2-hour session. The students generally worked in groups on their animation projects. The students learned to use Director and Premier software in order to produce animations. Some of the resulting animations were extraordinary for 10 year olds.

SCHOOLWIDE INNOVATIONS

The following case in Australia is typical of the stellar cases that addressed schoolwide reform.

Australia's Stellar Case

Woodcrest College, site of stellar case AU004, is a state school serving preschool students through Grade 10, with Grades 11 and 12 to be added in 2004. The school opened in 1998 and is located near Brisbane, Australia. It serves culturally diverse students and has grown from 300 to 1,100 students in 4 years. The innovation studied at this site consists of an instructional program where the shared vision was that of staff and students functioning together as a learning community, with a constructivist philosophy and heavy utilization of collaboration and ICT to achieve the vision. Accordingly, the Woodcrest model is a learning community with ICT used across the whole school and the entire curriculum. Classes are multiage across 2-year levels called stages, and the students remain with their teacher or teachers for 2 years. Their curriculum, which includes English, mathematics, and integrated studies, is based upon the state-specified learning outcomes and stresses higher-level thinking skills. In integrated studies, students complete eight units of work, which are really rich learning tasks, over each 2-year period. Students work in groups on these rich learning tasks and present their work as completed projects, called Quality Products, to wider forums of parents and members of the community. ICT is used as a tool for investigation and as a medium for the presentation of completed work. Woodcrest College was chosen as the second Apple Classrooms of Tomorrow (ACOT) school in Australia. The school has more than 300 Apple Mac computers, 5 to 6 of which are located in each classroom. The Internet and a large variety of application software are available for students and teachers to use. Despite the heavy use of ICT in learning activities, the equipment and the Internet are defined as just two of the many resources available for learning. Some of the weekly teachers' meetings are devoted to ways of using ICT. New teachers are paired with teaching partners with more ICT experience. Teacher support related to ICT includes a full-time technical support officer and two full-time technology coordinators. Teachers find that their roles include that of colearner, designer, guide, and observer. School administrators cultivate community support by sharing details of the children's learning experience. They show parents how students love learning, attributing part of this outcome to the students' ICT-supported experiences, which are purposely selected to optimize motivation and engagement.

Finland's stellar case is associated more specifically with literature and poetry. However, reading skills, from primary to upper secondary levels, were the main beneficiaries of this innovation; therefore, it is included here with other schoolwide innovations.

Finland's Stellar Case

The research team in Finland chose Netlibris Literature Circles (FI005) as its stellar case. Actually the team studied two schools, one a primary and the other a secondary school, both of which were located in the city of Espoo and both of which were involved in the innovation. Currently, schools from eight communities in different parts of the country are participating in Netlibris, with a total of 700 students and 50 teachers involved. The innovation started at the primary level; its basic aim was to integrate reading and computer use, with both individual and cooperative learning. Now, Netlibris is an umbrella term for three different literature circles: Matilda, for 7- to 12-year-old students; Sinuhe, for 12- to 15-year-old students; and Odysseia, for 15- to 20-year-old students. Students select books to read from a list of books on the Web, read the books they have chosen, keep a "reader response journal" or reading diary on the Web, and discuss the books in a Web-based discussion environment. Every month or two, face-to-face meeting events are scheduled. Locations for these meetings of students from many different communities are arranged so as to relate to the books that the students have chosen. Teachers who are educated in Netlibris principles act as tutors, meeting once a week with the reading circles. Otherwise the students work independently in their Web-based activities. Students can share their feelings and opinions about books with other students. The goal is quality discussion based on the readers' own reading experiences. Students read the books and write the reading diaries in their free time. The general goal is to encourage and challenge the good readers so that they can read more and different books and also share their reading experiences with other book lovers. Both students and teachers seemed to think that this innovation accomplished its goals and was a successful example of student-centered teaching.

Canada's stellar case is a primary school that experienced major reform with apparent great success.

Canada's Stellar Case

The Canadian team selected Mountview (CA002) as its stellar case. Mountview is a primary K–8 school with 437 students sharing 137 fully networked computers and using them in almost all of their subjects. The ambitious schoolwide innovation began with a principal-led planning team defining their vision of Mountview as "an institution where teacher reflection, risk-taking, and experimentation in the furtherance of more autonomous, authentic, and engaged student learning was to be part of everyday practice." ICT was to be infused throughout the reform to help realize its goals. A major component of the program was a research and professional development center at the school (the Galileo Centre), which not only provided staff development but also coordinated the infusion of ICT with constructivist modes of practice into the curriculum. Consultants and master teachers were given release time to enable them to provide long-term, situated, in-class support. The use of ICT is now widespread in the school, with most teachers and their students accessing it daily for a range of purposes. Several teachers are doing virtually no direct teaching and instead have students take the lead in developing inquiry questions of interest on curriculum topics; these questions then become themes for major student projects that can continue over several weeks and encompass all subject areas. The criteria used for project assessment are frequently mutually developed with students and do not always involve quantitative grading. Fully networked with Internet connectivity, students worked with advanced, professional-level ICT tools such as Office, Astound, Photoshop, and Internet Explorer. No tutorial or other educational software was available. Children as young as 7 and 8 years were seen developing animations to accompany stories they had written or coding HTML for a new page they were creating for the school's Web site. Many projects were cross-disciplinary, incorporating elements from both the math and science and the humanities and arts disciplines, and often were directly relevant to the local community. Both shared and private (password accessed) server storage space was available to students; they used the shared space for their collaborative work.

Most noteworthy about this major school reform was that it was accomplished without special funding or other special resources. This is definitely not true of the last case, which is from the United States, an innovation in an upper secondary school that obtained generous amounts of special funding that enabled it to achieve a range of major changes.

The United States' Stellar Case

New Tech High School (US014) serves the last two grades of secondary school in a small city in northern California. The school is 6 years old and has grown from 200 to 240 students. There is at least one computer with Internet access for every student. This high school represents an unusually innovative design in terms of curriculum, school layout, and relationships with business and community. Technology is embedded in every aspect of the school's activities and culture. The underlying philosophy of the instructional program is to educate students in capabilities most essential to the 21st century, especially problem solving, project construction, knowledge management, and teamwork. Students spend a major part of every day using computers because most of their assignments are projects requiring educational technology applications. Teachers interact daily with students, parents, and colleagues via the school intranet. Instructors store most of their assignments and course materials on the computer system; students access these and turn in their work by computer. Teachers and students have e-mail accounts and access to Lotus Notes, which allows them to create databases and store class work in a portfolio for teacher and peer review. The construction of the school building is modeled after high-performance organizations, in that the classrooms have glass rather than solid walls and the students work at desk areas that resemble offices more than classrooms. Most classes are interdisciplinary and team taught, and students' work often requires them to serve as team members on a project. Nearly 95% of the students attend college within 2 years of graduation. New Tech High has established a reputation for innovation and high productivity with frequent visitors from all over the world.

CONCLUSIONS

Taken together, these cases offer a rich collection of mostly verbal images of communities where innovation survived and had an impact. Each case was selected because its school community, despite pressures from old traditions and rigid institutions, was able to produce what appeared to be a valuable contribution to learning. Of course, each innovation has to be evaluated within the national and local culture in which it thrived. The case reports provide considerable context in which to begin to understand what was going on in each case and what its impact will be.

Perhaps diversity is the outstanding characteristic of these cases. The cultural, demographic, policy, and technological contexts of these cases are all highly diverse. A wide variety of types of ICT was utilized in these 22 cases, although every school had at least one level of access to the Internet and most integrated that access into their innovations. Significantly, ICT, regardless of its configuration, played a more or less key supportive role in each case.

Any collection of innovations is, by definition, unlikely to be categorizable to a great degree of satisfaction. Furthermore, we found that any given innovation was likely to utilize diverse pedagogies concurrently. For instance, a high-level, group problem-solving project might incorporate a lower-level, computer-based tutorial. Most pedagogies were philosophically more compatible and characterizable in terms such as "authentic instruction" or "student-center learning," including such instructional methods as project learning, inquiry, alternative assessment, and collaborative learning. It is impressive that the pedagogical approaches had such commonalities, given their highly diverse contexts.

One pattern that emerged would seem at first glance to be an anomaly—more than half of the stellar cases focused on either a fine art or a language. It would seem that this pattern stems from a desire by school staff members to select subjects for ICT innovation that students would find exciting and enjoyable. Such subjects make good demonstration projects that may encourage teachers in other disciplines to try to follow suit. This pattern may also stem from the fact that art and writing are areas where creativity in producing concrete results is possible without many years of education. From a constructivist point of view there is much to be said for such an apparent payoff. This apparent anomaly is surely suggestive for future research.

While we have learned much from these cases and there is great potential for transferring many of their innovations to other sites, some gaps remain in the information needed to fully understand the cases and to replicate them in other locations. While these cases offer a wealth of information about student and teacher outcomes from the innovations, most of them are based on subjective reports of the teachers and staff, who all have some degree of vested interest. The outcome patterns and profiles need to be researched systematically by a variety of methods and assembled for critique and review in order to build a solid base of knowledge about the conditions that produced different types of impact.

Second, we need to know more about the essential conditions for the replication of the types of innovation represented by these cases. Such knowledge will require the use of a variety of qualitative and quantitative, if not experimental, methods over a sustained period of time. Unfortunately, this does not yet appear to be an area of high priority in educational research related to ICT.

Finally, Chapter 6 approached the matter of policy from the perspective of the individual cases rather than an overall policy analysis. This was intentional in order to focus on the innovations themselves. Nevertheless, policy is extremely important in the matter of ICT investment, programs, and implementation. We hope that subsequent studies will more deeply analyze national ICT policies and the role they play in the success of stellar innovations.

CHAPTER 8

summary AND implications

FOR ICT-BASED EDUCATIONAL CHANGE

By Robert B. Kozma

INTRODUCTION

The Second Information Technology in Education Study (SITES) Module 2 was motivated by dramatic global economic and social changes, as well as the consequent increase of investment that policy makers have made in equipping schools and connecting them to the Internet. Many national and multinational agencies have acknowledged massive economic changes—referred to as the knowledge economy—in which the creation, distribution, and use of knowledge is both an engine and a product of economic growth. A parallel social change is the widespread use of information and communication technologies (ICT) and the potential these have to make education and health care more widely available, foster cultural creativity and productivity, increase democratic participation, and promote social integration—what is sometimes called the information society. Employees in the knowledge economy need to search for relevant information, interpret and analyze data, and work with teams distributed across space or time. Citizens must be able to use ICT to access information, create cultural artifacts, and communicate effectively with others if they are to benefit from the information society. These social and economic developments also require that people be able to acquire new skills in response to changing circumstances, assess their own learning needs and progress, and learn throughout their lifetime—what is referred to as lifelong learning.

Educational policy documents have referenced these global economic and social developments and used them to justify significant investments in educational ICT. Much of this investment has been focused on purchasing computers and hooking schools to the Internet. The goal has been to use ICT to prepare students for participation in the global knowledge economy and information society. Early classroom studies have documented the kinds of changes in pedagogy and curriculum that can be made when ICT is integrated into classroom practice. SITES Module 1 found that such changes—referred to as the emerging pedagogical paradigm—are beginning to occur in many countries around the world.

SITES Module 2 was designed as an in-depth, qualitative examination of the findings from SITES Module 1. Specifically, the study was designed to examine innovative pedagogical practices using technology. We drew on a conceptual framework that positions ICT within layered contexts of classroom (micro), school and community (meso), and national (macro) factors. Drawing on this framework, we derived a set of research questions, methods, procedures, and instruments for the study. Our goal was to conduct classroom case studies within participating countries that would address a set of questions in four different categories.

ICT AND INNOVATIVE CLASSROOM PRACTICES

What are the ICT-based pedagogical practices that countries consider to be innovative? How are these innovative practices similar and different from one country to another?

What new teacher and student roles are associated with innovative pedagogical practices using technology? How are these innovations changing what teachers and students do in the classroom? How do they affect patterns of teacher-student and student-student interactions?

How do these practices change the classroom? In what ways does the use of ICT change the organization of the classroom, extend the school day, break down the walls of the classroom, and involve other actors (such as parents, scientists, or business people) in the learning process?

What capabilities of the applied technologies support innovative pedagogical practices? How do these capabilities shape the practices they support?

ICT AND THE CURRICULUM

How do these practices change curriculum content and goals? What impact do these practices have on student competencies, attitudes, and other outcomes? Have they changed what students are learning and what teachers need to learn? Have they changed the ways student outcomes are assessed?

ICT IN THE SCHOOLS

What contextual factors are associated with the use of these innovations? Which factors seem to be present across different innovative pedagogical practices? Which ones are associated with different practices? What are the implications of contextual factors for the sustainability and transferability of these innovations?

What are the barriers to using ICT in these innovative ways? How are teachers overcoming these barriers? How do they cope with limited resources?

ICT POLICIES

Which local policies related to staff development, student computer fees, facilities access, technical support, and other issues appear to be effective in supporting these innovations?

Which national telecommunications policies related to such things as school Internet access, equipment purchase, teacher training, and student Internet use seem to be effective in supporting these innovations?

DESIGN OF THE STUDY

The study generated 174 case studies of ICT-based innovative pedagogical practice from the 28 participating countries. These cases were selected after an extensive review process that involved national panels composed of 241 researchers, ministry officials, administrators, computer coordinators, teachers, and other experts. The national panels used a common set of international criteria to select their cases. However, panels were allowed to modify the international criteria (with review of the International Coordinating Committee, or ICC) when it was appropriate to the national context. The criteria specified that cases be selected in which there was a change in classroom practice (i.e., changes in the activities or roles of teachers and students, instructional materials, assessment, or the delivered curriculum). The change also had to be supported by technology, it had to have an impact on student and teacher outcomes, and it had to be sustainable and transferable. In addition, each panel was required to specify a local definition for "innovative."

The thoughtfulness and effort by a wide range of participants who contributed to the selection process is a testament to the importance of these cases and significance of our findings for policy and practice. These cases were not meant to represent typical practice in a country. Rather, they represent the aspirations that each country has for the use of ICT to change and improve education. The cases represent models of ICT-supported innovative pedagogical practices that teachers in other schools and other countries can use to improve teaching and learning.

Once these cases were selected, national research teams used standard instruments and protocols to collect a variety of data from multiple sources for each case. These included questionnaires from principals and technology coordinators; individual interviews with administrators and teachers; focus group interviews with teachers, students, and parents; classroom observations; and documents, such as teacher lesson plans and student products. These data were analyzed using standard guidelines, and case reports were written for each case, using a common format. This distributed effort was coordinated by the ICC, which was also responsible for quality monitoring. A number of policies and procedures were put into place to assure the high quality of data and case reports.

The ICC used a mixture of qualitative and quantitative methodologies to analyze the 174 case reports. Each case was read by one of the ICC members and characterized using a cover sheet coding scheme (see Appendix B.2) that was based on the project's conceptual framework and research questions. These codes were used to analyze trends in the data related to classroom practices, curricular change, school contexts, and local and national policies. Individual cases were identified and examined in more detail to understand the nature of the trends.

SUMMARY OF FINDINGS

To address each set of research questions, we analyzed a special subset or subsets of cases that seemed best suited to the nature of the question. We summarize our findings in the following sections.

ICT AND INNOVATIVE CLASSROOM PRACTICES

Our primary focus in SITES Module 2 was the examination of innovative pedagogical practices using technology, practices that might help students meet the requirements of the knowledge economy and the information society. The stellar cases described in Chapter 7 give a sense of the range of the innovations we examined. We saw innovations in primary, lower secondary, and upper secondary schools. ICT was used to support pedagogical innovations in subjects that ranged from mathematics and biology to language and art. Several were integrated throughout all the subjects. The pedagogical innovations included project-based learning and investigations, collaborative learning, and the construction of digital products.

In our cross-case analysis of 174 ICT-supported classroom practices in Chapter 3, we found eight clusters or patterns of practices that created useful distinctions among types of cases. These clusters included the Tool Use Cluster, which was distinguished primarily by the high use of productivity tools and e-mail. The Student Collaborative Research Cluster was a much more complex pattern characterized primarily by students collaborating with each other in their classes to conduct research and analyze data. Various ICT tools were used to support this collaboration and research. Teachers lectured, advised students, created structure for their students, and monitored their results. In the Information Management Cluster, also a complex pattern, ICT was used to support the search for information, the creation of products, the monitoring of students, and planning. Students searched for information, solved problems, published their results, and assessed themselves and each other; and teachers created structure and designed materials. As the name implies, the Teacher Collaboration Cluster was characterized primarily by teachers collaborating with students, their colleagues in the school, and others outside the school. Students picked their own tasks, and ICT was used to support the creation of products. Students collaborated with others outside the school, and ICT supported this communication in the Outside Collaboration Cluster. In the Product Creation Cluster, students designed products and used ICT to support this process, while teachers created structure and gave advice. The use of tutorial software for tutoring, drill, and practice was the distinguishing feature of the Tutorial Cluster. Finally, the eighth cluster was an Undefined Cluster, distinguished primarily by the lack of a unique pattern of practice.

While this cluster analysis created distinctions among groups of cases, there was much commonality among them. In a large majority of cases across different countries and clusters, teachers and students engaged in a common set of innovative pedagogical practices supported by technology. This is a major finding of the study. In the 174 cases we studied, teachers stepped back from their role as knowledge provider to advise students (90% of all cases), create structure for student activities (80%), and monitor student progress (76%), as indicated by our coding of the cover sheets. Students collaborated with others in their classes (83% of the cases) and searched for information (74%). E-mail (68% of all cases) and productivity tools (78%) were used, and ICT supported the search for information (77%)

and communication (55%). We call this core set of practices the Student Collaboration Model. We also identified three other pedagogical models that cut across clusters and augmented this core model.

In the Product Model, both teachers (56% of all cases) and students (61%) created products. Typically, teachers collaborated with their colleagues (59%) in this effort, and students published the results of their work (66%). They used multimedia (52%) in addition to the e-mail and productivity tools of the core model, and this ICT supported product creation. In a third pedagogical model—the Student Research Model—students conducted research (39% of all cases) and solved problems (33%) while using Web resources (71%) and local area networks (41%), along with multimedia, productivity tools, and e-mail, to support product creation and planning (26%). In the Outside Collaboration Model, students collaborated with outside actors (26% of all cases) and other students in the class to create products and publish results. Teachers also collaborated with peers in this model (59%).

It was when the core Student Collaboration Model was augmented by other practices that certain teacher and student outcomes were more likely to be reported in the cases. The Student Collaborative Research and Information Management Clusters—those clusters that combined both the core Student Collaboration Model and the Student Research Model—were associated with teacher acquisition of new pedagogical skills. These clusters were also associated with student acquisition of ICT skills, problem-solving skills, and team or collaborative skills.

The Information Management and Teacher Collaboration Clusters—those exhibiting the Product Model along with the core Student Collaboration Model—were associated with teacher acquisition of collaborative skills. Beyond this, the Information Management Cluster—the only cluster to participate in both the Student Research and the Product Models, as well as the core Student Collaboration Model—was associated with student acquisition of communication skills and information-handling skills, as reported in the case studies. These more complex pedagogical models and their combinations seem to be most likely to result in the kinds of activities and skills that are required in the knowledge economy and the information society.

In many cases, we saw ICT-supported practices that reorganized the classroom such that students worked with each other on projects that cut across subject domains. Teachers also collaborated with each other, in many cases. In this regard, ICT is beginning to break down some of the traditional barriers within the classroom. But we saw few cases in which teachers and students connected and collaborated with others outside the classroom. In most of these cases, the communication was with other teachers and students. Very few innovations involved collaboration with scientists, professors, and business people. Far fewer cases connected parents to the classroom. It is still rare that ICT is being used to break down the schoolhouse walls, even in these innovative classrooms around the world.

ICT AND THE CURRICULUM

The knowledge economy and information society also have implications for what is taught in schools. As part of our study we examined how innovative pedagogical practices were associated with changes in the curriculum—the goals of education and the way the curriculum was organized. In our analysis of ICT and the curriculum, we looked at changes in the intended goals of the curriculum, the implementation of the curriculum, and the extent to which this implementation realized the goals in terms of student and teacher outcomes. We also examined how these goals were assessed and the role of ICT in supporting these various changes.

First, we found that innovations were evenly distributed across the primary (34% of the cases), lower secondary (36%), and upper secondary (35%) grades. A wide variety of subjects, including math (21%), natural science (physics, 13%; chemistry, 5%; biology, 25%; and earth science, 14%), social science (history, 16%; civics, 13%), language arts (mother tongue, 32%, foreign languages, 24%), and creative arts (20%), were represented. Only 21% of the innovations involved informatics, while 28% were cross-curricular.

In our analysis of the 174 cases, we found that only 27% of the case reports described new content and 37% described new goals. Most of the curriculum changes involved a reorganization of the current content (68% of the cases), and 36% involved a reallocation of time for the innovation. Because we were specifically looking at the role that ICT could play in supporting significant curriculum change, we identified only 32 cases, or 18% of the 174 total cases, in which both the goals or content of the curriculum changed and ICT added value to these changes. This is a significant finding in itself.

Nonetheless, we examined this group of cases for things we might learn about how ICT might be used best to support such changes. We found that the group of 32 cases varied with regard to curricular focus; 11 had a Single-Subject Curricular Focus, 13 had a Thematic Curricular Focus, and 8 had a Schoolwide Curricular Focus.

Our in-depth analysis of these case reports found that curriculum change was less often related to providing new content and more often related to achieving new goals or offering existing content in a different way. These changes in goals differed among the three patterns. The cases with a Single-Subject Curricular Focus often described improvements of the teaching of content and concepts, particularly a more in-depth coverage of current content. Cases with a Thematic Curricular Focus described new goals that were considered important for the information society. The cases in this pattern often referenced information management and lifelong learning goals. In order to realize these goals, curriculum content was delivered in a different way and cross-curricular and thematic approaches to the curriculum were adopted. The cases with a Schoolwide Curricular Focus emphasized new goals, particularly those that fostered student responsibility for their own learning. The innovations in this group were strongly aligned with a vision of the school that held student independence and responsibility for their own learning in high regard.

Student activities were rather similar in all three curricular patterns: students created products or carried out a research project. In most cases across the three groups, students collaborated during their project work and part of the project involved searching for information. In the Single-Subject Curricular Focus, students were often involved in tasks requiring problem solving. In the other two patterns, students published or presented results. In a number of cases, students were involved in self-assessment or peer assessment. In many innovations with a Schoolwide Curricular Focus, students picked their own tasks. In all three groups, teachers advised and guided students while providing structure and keeping track of students' progress. In cases with a Schoolwide Curricular Focus, teacher collaboration was common. In innovations with a Single-Subject Curricular Focus, teachers also mediated content and prepared (sometimes ICT-based) materials for students.

The organization of these learning activities was very different in each of the three groups. In cases with a Schoolwide Curricular Focus students participated in the innovation during the whole school day. There were major changes in the organization of the curriculum that included team teaching and extensions of the classroom and school boundaries. In cases with a Thematic Curricular Focus, subject boundaries were crossed and this often had implications for the organization of content. In cases with a Single-Subject Focus, students worked primarily in one course.

In all three curricular patterns, changes in assessment practices were observed. In cases with a Single-Subject Curricular Focus and a Thematic Curricular Focus, more emphasis was placed on formative assessment over summative assessment only. Teachers gave students more feedback about their progress or feedback more often during the execution of activities. In some innovations students assessed their own or their peers' work, in addition to being assessed by the teacher. Summative assessments often focused on students' products rather than only on paper-and-pencil tests. In the Schoolwide Curricular Focus, new assessment systems were adopted in which formative and summative assessment were integrated and, in some cases, supported by ICT.

Across the 174 cases, we noted that the primary impact of the innovations was on student (75% of the cases) and teacher (63%) acquisition of ICT skills, as reported in the case write-ups. They were also related to student acquisition of positive attitudes toward learning (68%) and the acquisition of subject matter knowledge (63%) and collaboration skills (63%). Teacher acquisition of new pedagogical skills was also reported in 57% of the cases.

Across the three patterns of curriculum change in the group of 32 cases, students were motivated by the innovation and the innovation improved their self-esteem. Students also acquired ICT skills in all three patterns, although a little less so for cases with a Thematic Curricular Focus. These ICT skills were learned within the content and activities of school subjects. In all three groups, students acquired collaborative skills, although a little less so in cases with a Single-Subject Curricular Focus. In cases with a Thematic Curricular Focus or a Schoolwide Curricular Focus, students also acquired communication skills. Subject matter knowledge was an important student outcome in cases with a Single-Subject Curricular Focus. The subject matter outcomes for cases with a Schoolwide Curricular Focus were often in compliance with national curriculum requirements. Cases with a Thematic Curricular Focus were associated with student acquisition of information-handling skills, while cases with a Single-Subject Curricular Focus were associated with student acquisition of metacognitive skills.

Common outcomes for teachers in all three patterns were the development of a positive attitude toward the innovation and the acquisition of ICT skills. The development of pedagogical skills was an important teacher outcome in many innovations in all three patterns but appeared particularly important in the innovations that had a Single-Subject Curricular Focus. Cases with a Thematic Curricular Focus or a Schoolwide Curricular Focus were associated with teachers' acquisition of collaborative skills.

Our analysis showed that the role of ICT differed to some extent among the three curricular patterns. In cases with a Single-Subject Curricular Focus, specialized software and subject-specific Web environments supported a more in-depth coverage of curriculum content that seemed to foster student understanding of subject matter. In cases with a Thematic Curricular Focus, ICT supported curricular change that helped students master new goals in preparation for participation in the knowledge economy and the information society. Students in these cases used generalized productivity tools and digital resources that cut across disciplinary boundaries and helped students acquire information-handling skills that prepare them for these societal changes. In cases with a Schoolwide Curricular Focus, ICT was integrated throughout the curriculum to help students take more responsibility for their own learning.

In general, the change in ICT-supported curriculum and assessment that we saw was relatively rare and often quite modest. We noted that such changes are often limited by national policy when it determines the content to be taught and how it is to be examined. From our analysis, it appears that for the most part national policies are not yet in place that can mobilize ICT in support of significant curriculum change and education reform.

THE SCHOOL CONTEXT, SUSTAINABILITY, AND TRANSFERABILITY OF INNOVATIONS

Pedagogical innovation takes place in the context of a number of school factors that include the support of colleagues and administrators and existence of resources that might influence its success. Any of these factors could have an impact on the ability to sustain an innovation and scale it up or transfer it to other classrooms or other schools. In this study, we examined innovations in a sample of 59 cases that provided evidence of being sustained and transferred to other classrooms within the school or beyond. We felt that by understanding the school contexts associated with innovations that succeeded and flourished we might be able to provide insights into how other innovations might also be sustained and transferred.

First, 75% of the 174 cases reported that the innovation had been sustained for at least a year and provided some evidence that this was so. But only 41% provided evidence that the innovation had been or was being transferred. It is an important finding that of the 174 cases that were submitted by the 28 participating countries, only 59 (or 34%) presented evidence that the innovations had been both sustained and transferred. Even with this group, the evidence for transfer was often sketchy. This is particularly surprising since such evidence was a recommended criterion for selection of innovative cases. The finding can be explained, in part, by the fact that these cases were innovative and still in the process of development. However, the evidence also suggests—as does the research literature—that it is difficult to sustain and scale up innovations in schools. This further suggests that understanding the cases where it does happen would be particularly important to policy makers and practitioners.

Our analysis of the 59 cases yielded a tentative model for sustainability composed of two sets of conditions: those that are essential and those that contribute to sustainability. The foremost essential requirement for sustainability is teacher support of the innovation. We found that it was often the energy and commitment of teachers that kept an innovation going. Student support is essential, primarily as a motivation for teachers' efforts, and thus contributes to teacher support. Perceived value is also essential. Increases in student subject matter knowledge and metacognitive skills were more likely to be reported in the 59 cases than in other cases. These benefits contribute to the teachers' perception of the value of the innovation—and thus their support—as do other benefits, such as student acquisition of technology skills. Teacher professional development is also essential because it increases the teachers' ability to support and implement the innovation. We found many cases where teachers in the 59 cases were provided not only with traditional workshops but also with nontraditional forms of development, such as peer study groups. This training includes the ICT skills that are necessary for using technology as well as the pedagogical skills needed to integrate it into the classroom. In fact, the 59 cases were much more likely to report that teachers acquired new pedagogical skills than were the rest of the cases. Administrator support is essential not only because it contributes to teacher support but also because it is a direct enabler of the innovation.

Beyond these essential factors, others contributed to sustainability and increased the likelihood of success. These contributing factors included the existence of support from others in the school and from external sources, innovation champions, funding, and supportive policies and plans. Particularly important was the connection with national ICT plans that provided resources that often enabled the innovation to succeed.

Transfer was more problematic for even these successful cases. Indeed, only 24 of the 59 cases identified a specific place where the innovation had been transferred, while others mentioned plans that were being implemented. Again, these innovations were often in an early state of development, and many of them were in the process of being transferred to other settings. But this result attests to the further difficulties that transfer has for innovation. Specifically, our findings suggest that transfer is dependent on an adequate infrastructure and resources in the new setting. Also the innovation must be seen as relevant and applicable to the transferred setting. Teachers must perceive the value of the innovation for accomplishing their classroom goals. Plans and policies also need to be in place that encourage the transfer of the innovation.

Barriers played an interesting role in our results. Barriers, such as the lack of equipment and technical support, are often cited in research studies as being significant impediments to success. In the 59 cases we studied, these factors did not emerge as barriers. Granted, this was a specialized group of cases. But it was not because these problems were not mentioned—they were. Lack of equipment and other resources was often identified as a problem in the case reports. Rather, this problem did not seem to keep the innovation from being sustained. We did not find that schools came up with special solutions. The innovations succeeded despite the problems because of a combination of teacher effort and their ability to take advantage of opportunities that arose.

Transfer was a different matter; we encountered more problems and barriers in this regard. Limitations in equipment and resources were particularly salient when it came to scaling up an innovation within a school or transferring it to another school. Other significant barriers to transfer were skeptical teachers who were not yet convinced of advantages of the innovation or its fit with goals and current practices. Related to this was the need for professional development or other means of demonstrating the advantages of the innovation and providing teachers with the skills that would allow them to use it successfully.

ICT AND LOCAL AND NATIONAL POLICY

Of the 174 cases in the study, 109 (63%) indicated a connection between the innovative pedagogical practices and a local school policy or plan. These policies had a direct impact on the classroom. Cases that were linked to local policy were more likely to be associated with changes in teacher practices and their acquisition of new pedagogical and collaborative skills. Linkages with local policy were also more likely to be associated with students' acquisition of problem-solving and metacognitive skills.

Of the total, 127 (73%) indicated a link with a national ICT policy, and 106 (61%) were linked to a more general national education policy. A total of 94 case reports (about 54%) indicated that the innovation was linked to both a national and a school-level ICT policy, while only 15 case reports (9%) indicated that the innovation was not linked to policy at either level.

To understand the impact of policy on practice, we looked for patterns in the ways that innovative practices were connected to the local and national policies and plans, as they were cited in the case reports. That is, we came at our analysis from the perspective of practice rather than from the perspective of policy. Since there is often a gap between policy and practice, we wanted to start by examining successful innovations and look at the links they cited with local and national policies.

We found that national and local policies and plans supported similar policy goals. Policies at both levels supported innovations that used ICT to reform education, improve student performance, and increase ICT capacity. But local and national policies served different and complementary functions.

One of the functions of local policy was to articulate a vision of ways to use ICT in the school. These local visions were sometimes collaboratively crafted, shared visions; but sometimes they represented the aspirations of a single person. They were often quite specific and tied to what would happen in the classroom. Some principals and teachers had visions of using technology in specific ways to change how teachers taught and how students learned. Others had visions of all students achieving at their potential. Some had visions of their schools and classrooms enriched by technology.

Another function of local policies was to convert these visions into specific plans and actions that had immediate implications for classroom practice. Principals allocated equipment and other resources to accomplish the vision. Teachers' professional development experiences were also an important—indeed, essential—part of local plans and efforts. These professional development experiences were sometimes very extensive and ranged from formal workshops to regular informal meetings and peer mentoring. They included both ICT skills training and pedagogical training on the integration of ICT into the curriculum.

ICT and education policies at the national level supported innovations by linking them to education reform, fostering efforts to increase student achievement, and building the technological capacity of schools and the capabilities of teachers and students. Cases that were connected to national education policies were more likely to report changes in teachers' activities in the classroom. Cases that were linked to national ICT policies were more likely to mention changes in students' activities in the classroom.

National policies and plans also stated visions. But at the national level, these were broad visions of the way ICT could change education or improve student achievement. Some policies set goals and challenges related to the development of ICT capacity or skills in teachers and students for states and schools to accomplish. In a few countries, ICT policies were also connected to education policies that specified new ways of teaching or specific goals for student performance. The primary function of national policies and programs was to provide schools with funds or resources that addressed schools' needs for equipment, networking, and teacher professional development. In some countries, it was important for the national policies to support the development of educational software coordinated with the curriculum, particularly when noncolonial languages were involved. Some programs identified outstanding ICT schools that others could use as models for change.

When local policies were lacking, national policies were particularly important to the innovation. Conversely, when national policies and resources were not available, local policies filled in. National and local policy working together was particularly powerful. But in the 15 cases linked to neither local nor national policy, the initiative depended on the effort of individual teachers or groups of teachers. Teacher support and effort were important in all cases but particularly so when the influence of policy was lacking. Sometimes these teachers' efforts were shaped by an outside project or coupled with outside resources, such as additional equipment or technical support from a university or cooperating business. These factors often compensated for the lack of policy and helped the innovation succeed.

IMPLICATIONS

We believe these research findings have important implications for educational change supported by ICT. In the following sections we describe implications for teachers, school administrators, policy makers, and multinational and nongovernmental organizations, as well as for our fellow researchers.

IMPLICATIONS FOR TEACHERS

Several classroom studies (Means & Olson, 1997; Means, Penuel, & Padilla, 2001; Sandholtz, Ringstaff, & Dwyer, 1997; Schofield & Davidson, 2002) have found a range of ways that teachers are using ICT to change their classroom practices. SITES Module 1 (Pelgrum & Anderson, 1999) established that these changes are happening worldwide. The results of our analysis of classroom practices in Chapter 3 extend this research to provide teachers with several graduated alternative models or organized patterns of practices for using ICT in their classes.

"Guide on the side, not sage on the stage" is a common phrase used to describe the teacher's role in the new student-centered classroom. However, this metaphor does not itself provide teachers with much guidance for their new role. Our models begin to provide teachers with some of the details and options. In a large majority of the classrooms we studied, teachers structured students' activities, guided their students' work, and monitored their progress, while students collaborated with others in their classes and used ICT to search for information—what we called the Student Collaboration Model. Several of our case studies provide vivid images of how teachers played an active role in the student-centered, ICT-based classroom. That is, one way to use ICT would be to let students work together while using e-mail and productivity tools to search for information. The teacher could prepare the activity by structuring the task and then serve only as an advisor or guide. While the pairs or teams of students take on the primary responsibility for their work, the teacher could circulate among the students to monitor their work and provide feedback on their success. This pattern of practice is illustrated in many of our cases, including the Creanimate project (CN006), where groups of lower secondary students in China Hong Kong used graphics software to explore creativity in art, and the Roots project (ES005), in

Catalonia, Spain, where teams of primary students in rural schools worked together to create Web sites about their villages.

While the Student Collaboration Model provides a good beginning or entry point for ICT-based classroom practice, a number of projects, including those previously mentioned, used ICT in more complex ways. Merely having students work together to search the Web seems to be insufficient in bringing about significant educational change. When other components were added to the Student Collaboration Model, outcomes were more likely to change. For example, in the Product Model, teachers collaborated with their colleagues to design materials and their students created products and published the results of their work. ICT tools, including multimedia, supported their product creation. Using the Product Model, teachers could go beyond the search for information to emphasize the creation of products in their classes. Teachers could collaborate with their peers on the creation of ICT classroom materials, as did a cross-disciplinary group of upper secondary science teachers in France (FR006) who developed materials related to satellite imaging of scientific data, and two upper secondary fine arts teachers in Lithuania (LT001) who worked with the informatics teacher to incorporate ICT into their course. Students could also work in pairs or groups, using a variety of multimedia, productivity, and e-mail tools to search for information, create products, and publish their work, which was the case for upper secondary students in the Hypertext Development project in the Slovak Republic (SK003). These students worked with teachers to develop Web materials for their courses, as did the very young children in a Canadian primary school (CA002) who developed animations and Web pages for stories they wrote.

In the Student Research Model, students not only collaborated with others in their class to search for information, they also conducted research and solved problems. Here again, teachers designed materials, structured student activities, provided them with guidance, and monitored their progress. ICT tools, e-mail, multimedia, and Web resources were used to support the search for information, communication, and product creation. These ICT resources were also used to support planning related to these more complex tasks. This model was associated with teacher acquisition of new pedagogical skills and also student acquisition of ICT skills, problem-solving skills, and team or collaborative skills. The combination of the Product Model and the Student Research Model, a pattern found in the Information Management Cluster, was associated with student acquisition of communication skills and information-handling skills, as reported in the case studies.

Using the Student Research Model, teachers could employ ICT to design more complex research and problem-solving tasks to support students' inquiry. Teachers could design materials and research problems themselves, as did the South African upper secondary teachers for the Theme Day project (ZA008) or the primary teacher in the Philippines who developed material for her integrated science course (PH005); or they could find structured materials on the Web, as did the teachers in the Australian primary school (AU002) who integrated the Jason project (www.jasonproject.org) into their science class. In the course of such projects, students could use multimedia and Web resources connected to local area networks, as they did in the Singapore Virtual Gallery project (SG002) and the multimedia development project in Australia (AU002). Teachers could use ICT to support their own planning and that of their students, as happened in the Virtual Gallery project (SG002) and the Exploring Live Physics project (CN005).

Alternatively, teachers could focus on breaking down the boundaries of the classroom and providing students with access to outside experts or students and teachers from schools in other parts of the world. This is the Outside Collaboration Model. Teachers might want to connect students to real-world events and activities, as in the Information, Technology, and Media program in Finland (FI003), where upper secondary students who became highly skilled in ICT worked with university faculty and local companies. In the Antarctic project in Norway (NO006), students communicated with explorers crossing Antarctica.

Teachers might also use outside connections to foster cross-cultural understanding, as did primary teachers in Denmark (DK007) who had their students work with students on the Faeroe Islands to compare geography, climate, and culture, and as did teachers in Germany (DE010) who had their students communicate with students in four other countries to compare consumer behavior of adolescents. To these ends, students could work together in groups, using e-mail and productivity tools, to communicate with outside actors such as students and teachers in other countries, scientists or explorers, or potential employers.

IMPLICATIONS FOR SCHOOL ADMINISTRATORS

While we found a lot of pedagogical change in our study, it was relatively rare that significant curricular change occurred, and, for the most part, few of the innovations had been sustained for a period of time and transferred elsewhere. Yet requirements of the knowledge economy and information society imply the addition of new skills and goals for the curriculum, such as the ability of students to manage their own learning, handle information, collaborate, and solve problems. And a major challenge for policy makers and local administrators is to take innovative practices and scale them up so as to impact the entire school or education system. When projects were successfully sustained and transferred and when the curriculum was significantly changed, the school context often played a significant—indeed, essential—role. Our findings in this regard have implications for the strategies and policies of school district administrators and principals.

Administrative support is essential for the success of an innovation, both direct support for the innovation and support for innovative teachers, as we saw in Chapter 5. At a minimum the principal or school administrator in our successful cases provided tacit support for the innovation. But more often, principals were proactive, either by creating an environment supportive of ICT-based change, as in the primary school in Catalonia, Spain (ES001), and an upper secondary school in England (UK004), or by providing resources to the project, as in a South African girl's primary school (ZA004) and a primary school in Singapore (SG001). In some cases the principal got more directly involved in the innovation. This was the case with a principal of a secondary school in the Philippines (PH006) who used technology regularly herself, was a participant in workshops related to the innovation, and advocated the innovation with teachers and parents. Supportive plans and policies also contributed to the success and transfer of the innovations we analyzed.

Curriculum change also has important implications for the school context and administrators. In the cases we analyzed in Chapter 4, thematic change—change that involved the use of ICT to bridge the boundaries of school subjects—was often associated with new goals considered important to the information society and with student acquisition of new skills such as collaboration, communication, and information handling. Some examples of these innovations include Project Region (CZ002), where students in a Czech secondary school worked with officials in local villages to create Web sites that contained information on local history, laws, places of interest, and accommodations. This project combined history, civics, and geography. In Smoke Signals, an electronic newspaper project in an Italian primary school (IT001), the learning of ICT skills was combined with reading and writing skills. These kinds of projects require teacher coordination and administrative support to make at least minor adjustments in the curriculum.

An even more active role for the principal and supportive local policies and plans seems required for schoolwide curriculum change. Innovations of this sort are closely connected to a school's vision. For example, in the Future High School (US014) the vision was to prepare students to excel in an information-based, technology-advanced society. For an Israeli primary school (IL003) the vision was to develop autonomous learners. For a Norwegian lower secondary school (NO005), it was to develop responsibility in students.

We also saw an important role for school vision and for the principal in our analysis of local policy in Chapter 6, particularly when it came to policies tied to educational reform. An important function of local policy was to articulate a vision of ways to use ICT in the school and convert these visions into classroom-based actions. These visions were sometimes collaboratively forged, shared visions and were often tightly tied to resource allocation and teacher professional development designed to realize the vision. This shared vision could be the basis for mutual support among teachers, a factor that contributes to the long-term success of an innovation, as we saw in Chapter 5. A vivid example of this systematic approach to local planning was seen in a primary school in Australia (AU002), where staff collaborated on a 5-year vision for the school, and in Israel's School of the Future (IL003), where the vision was to transform the relationship between students and knowledge.

Fishman and Pinkard (2001) provide a practical model that can be used by local administrators to create an environment that supports ICT-based innovation. Called the Planning for Technology Model, it proposes that a school begin not by building a technology plan but by creating a shared vision for teaching and learning that is enabled by technology. This might involve structured exercises in which teachers create scenarios to depict what learning would look like in their ideal classroom when technology is available. By exchanging and jointly elaborating on these individual visions, a teaching staff can work with the principal to come up with a common vision and a plan to realize it. Next, the planning process focuses on teacher development and making the needed technology available. Professional development should focus on hardware and software skills, as well as the pedagogical skills needed to enact the vision. Principals should avoid what Fishman and Pinkard call "false equity," in which technology is either centralized in one place or doled out to every teacher merely to minimize staff conflict. Rather, resources should be allocated in a way that is most likely to accomplish the vision. The next step in the model is to look for ways in which technology can be strategically used to fit into and reshape the curriculum. An important part of the process is the creation of a set of benchmarks that allow administrators and staff to monitor their progress toward accomplishing their shared vision.

Teacher professional development also plays an essential role in the success of the innovation, as we saw in Chapter 5. In some of our cases the professional development experiences were quite extensive, as we saw in an Israeli primary school (IL003) where the staff received 900 hours of ICT training over 3 years, and in a lower secondary school in the United States (US010) where teachers had a year-long paid professional development experience. The staff development experiences in our cases ranged from formal workshops and graduate studies to informal opportunities that included peer-coaching, classroom observation, and ongoing team meetings focused on the use of ICT in the classroom. However, for the most part, teacher professional development was still "delivered" to teachers and it emphasized technology skills. Our study and the literature suggest that the most effective professional development occurs on the job when teachers learn from each other and have a voice in determining their professional needs. We recommend that principals formulate policies and practices that reflect this. These informal experiences can create an environment of continuous development and shared support, as in the Australian primary school (AU002) and the Canadian stellar case (CA002). An important goal of any professional development program should be to tie new ICT skills and classroom practices to the school vision. This type of professional development might be particularly important for innovations with a thematic focus, where changes require collaboration across subject areas, and for schoolwide change, where it is equally important.

IMPLICATIONS FOR STATE AND NATIONAL POLICY MAKERS

Many of the innovations we examined were linked to either national education policy, national ICT policy, or both. We believe our study has a lot to say to national policy makers. We base these implications on the connections not only on what we saw between policy and the innovations in our study but also on what we did not see.

In our analysis of successful innovations, as well as our analysis of national policies, it was clear that policy played an important role in sustaining and transferring these innovations. These ICT and education policies often provided a broad vision of the way ICT could change education or improve student achievement. Singapore, the United States, and Finland provide us with some examples of national visions. These broad visions were sometimes cited by school administrators as a source of inspiration for the local, more specific visions they constructed with their staff. The second function of national policies and programs was to provide schools with funds or resources that schools could draw on to implement their innovations. The programs supplied or funded equipment, networking, and teacher professional development. Programs in some countries also supported the development of educational software coordinated with the curriculum. These policies and programs enabled a large majority of the innovations we saw, and this is an important finding from this study.

Policy makers often expect to see returns of ICT investment that constitute major changes in education. The development of pedagogical changes we saw that engaged students in knowledge creation, product development, investigation, and problem solving can be considered the first return on these investments. These findings argue for continued funding and the investment of resources that enable schools to institute ICT-based pedagogical change.

However, there were many things we did not see or did not see often that are frequently mentioned as goals in policy documents. For example, we did not see many innovations that were both sustained and transferred. Policy makers hope to see a significant "ripple effect" as a consequence of their investments such that successful projects will pass quickly and efficiently to other classrooms and schools. Policy documents that tie education to the needs of the knowledge economy describe new skills that imply new goals and outcomes for education related to students' skills in metacognition, information handling, problem solving, and working in teams. Despite pedagogical practices that engaged students in activities related to these skills, we did not see many innovations that reflected these new goals in the curriculum. Consequently, relatively few cases reported that students acquired problem-solving skills, information-handing skills, or metacognitive skills.

Nor did we did see much in the way of collaboration or connection with outside actors. When there was outside collaboration, it was most often with other teachers and students. Many policy documents see the connection of classrooms with the real world as a way to prepare students for the knowledge economy and information society.

Finally, we saw very few innovations that provided particular benefits to groups of students with special needs, such as those of low socioeconomic status or ethnic or language minorities. Documents that describe the benefits of the information society often focus the role that ICT can play in developing social integration and the inclusion of individuals with special needs. While these various goals have been articulated in the policy documents, for the most part they have not been realized in the schools. Consequently, policy makers need to go beyond the grand visions for the use of ICT in education and implement more specific practice-based programs by which these policies will affect schools and classrooms.

A report generated by the U.S. National Research Council (Weiss, Knapp, Hollweg, & Burrill, 2001) identified three channels by which policies can influence classroom practices: curriculum, teacher development, and assessment and accountability. These channels provide policy makers with mechanisms by which they can use ICT to make more dramatic changes in education.

First, we mentioned that the existence of a national curriculum was often a major constraint on the kinds of changes teachers could make with regard to the goals and content of their instruction. Countries committed to planning for the knowledge economy and information society need to go beyond the incorporation of ICT skills into their curriculum and explicitly incorporate skills related to information management, knowledge creation, investigation, and collaboration into the content and goals of their curricular frameworks. Several cases in our analysis that had a Thematic Curricular Focus integrated ICT into and across various subject matters, such as science, civics, reading, and writing. However, it is quite likely that teachers will not take these new goals seriously until they appear in state or national curriculum standards or frameworks. In Singapore, the national curriculum was reduced by 10% or more to accommodate new ICT and the infusion of thinking skills. A principal in the United States (US010) characterized the influence that national or, in this case, state standards can have on the work of schools and teachers. Standards are, the principal remarked, "a tremendous influence. It dominates our conversation. There is no question about that. It's something the state is saying; this is what our expectations are as a school. That carries a lot of weight."

Second, as mentioned in the previous section, teacher professional development is essential to sustained success. The important role played by principals in ICT-development would suggest that professional development for administrators is also wise. In our cases, resources that came from national policies and programs were often cited as important sources of teacher professional development opportunities related to ICT. However, not all teacher development is effective in implementing policy-based change. Cohen and Hill (2001) identify teacher professional development practices that are particularly effective in connecting policy with classroom practice. These are extensive professional development experiences that focus directly on the implementation of policies in classroom activities. Countries that would like to increase the impact of ICT on educational change should concentrate on the support of such policy-focused professional development programs and instructional materials that help teachers integrate ICT-based change into their classroom activities. Professional development for principals might focus on ways to help them build local visions and a community supportive of innovation.

Third, assessment also constrains what it is that teachers can do in their classrooms. Means, Penuel, and Quellmalz (2001) point out that a major barrier for ICT-based education change is the lack of congruence between the goals of student-centered practices and the standardized tests commonly used for national assessments and examinations. Policy makers who want to see more return on their ICT investment need to consider the means by which that return is measured. Unless assessments are revised to incorporate new goals and content, such as information management, problem-solving, communication, and collaboration skills, policy makers will not be able to measure, let alone see, returns on their investments. Means, Penuel, and Quellmalz provide some examples of how ICT can be used to support such changes in assessment. When students are assessed with such instruments and teachers are held accountable for performance (and this accountability is supported with resources and rewards), dramatic change can be expected. These new kinds of assessments can also be used in the classroom to address the frustration that teachers in our study expressed about the inability to adequately measure student outcomes related to their innovations.

Congruence between different components of the educational system is also a theme struck by Cohen and Hill (2001) when they discuss effective impact of policy on classroom practice. Not only must curriculum, teacher professional development, and assessment change in order to realize the ICT-based promise for education, but these changes also must be aligned. Curriculum must reflect new goals and content, teachers must be trained in how to use ICT to incorporate these new goals and content in their classes, and assessments must be designed that measure the attainment of these new skills.

In addition to this congruence between goals and the instruments used to accomplish them—what Pal (2001) calls *internal consistency*—there needs to be *vertical consistency* between different levels of the system. Indeed, in our policy analysis a majority of the cases cited the influence of both national and local policies and plans on their innovations. However, there were few cases that specifically mentioned the alignment of these policies. We featured a few of the exceptions. For example, a Singapore primary school that was the source of the Virtual Gallery project (SG002) had a vision expressed in the school's motto, which is, in part, "Fire the imagination: To innovate and to create." This school received equipment, networking, and teacher training that allowed it to implement some of the pedagogical practices that resulted in its assignment to the Information Management Cluster in Chapter 3. These practices, in turn, contributed to Singapore's national goal of enhancing creative thinking, lifelong learning, and social responsibility. In the U.S. case (US010) the school district received a major grant from the U.S. Department of Education to foster the use of ICT in support of student achievement. The State of California had developed a set of standards and expectations for schools, and the primary school in this case report used these ICT resources obtained from the grant to help achieve its goal of increasing student achievement on the state standards-based test. Finally, the secondary school in Finland (FI003) had a vision in which ICT belonged naturally to students' everyday work, while the national policy expressed a vision for increasing the ICT capabilities of schools and students in support of Finland's Information Society. Part of the policy is to ensure that every school has a strategy for use of ICT in education. The innovation was part of the school's strategy.

This top-down, bottom-up congruence between national and local policies and programs is especially challenging for decentralized systems. At the top, the vision articulated for the use of ICT in schools needs to be detailed and inspirational enough to have some impact on the nation's education system; at the same time, the vision needs to be open enough to provide states, provinces, districts, and schools with the latitude needed to craft a more specific vision responsive to local needs and conditions. In the many nations that have federal or decentralized education systems it is probably even more important that there be coordination among national agencies and programs—what Pal (2001) calls *horizontal coherence*—so that there is a unified message that helps bridge the vertical gap. This requires coordination between ICT policy and education policy within the ministry or department of education. It may also involve the coordination between the ministry of education and the ministries of telecommunications, science, and labor, as well as coordination among programs within these ministries.

Here is a final policy implication or, perhaps, admonition: Innovation that is sustained and scaled up is likely to require sustained support. There is nothing in our findings that would encourage a policy maker to believe in the "ripple effect." Our analysis of successful innovations indicates that ongoing funding and supportive policies contribute to the continuation of innovations and that infrastructure, resources, and supportive policies facilitate their transfer. But there are continuing costs associated with these needs. Until it gets to the point when these innovations become institutionalized in the education system and in school budgets, their continuation, and especially their transfer, is likely to require exceptional support and investment from national and state sources.

IMPLICATIONS FOR MULTINATIONAL AND NONGOVERNMENTAL ORGANIZATIONS

We believe our study also has implications for foreign assistance programs and multinational and nongovernmental agencies (NGOs) and foundations. There are implications of two sorts. The first has to do with the digital divide between nations (United Nations Development Program, 1999). The ICC made a significant effort to include developing and economically distressed countries from Eastern Europe, Latin America, and Africa in SITES Module 2. We were successful in receiving funding from an anonymous donor that allowed us to support the participation of five Eastern European countries. However, we were not able to find funding for the participation of countries in Latin America and Africa. Nonetheless, Chile and South Africa participated with their own funding.

We found many exciting innovations in South Africa, Chile, the Czech Republic, the Slovak Republic, Lithuania, Latvia, and the Russian Federation that lead us to believe that ICT holds promise for developing and economically distressed countries. Our experience in this study, as well as our work for the World Bank (Kozma & McGhee, 2000; McGhee & Kozma, 2001) and the work of others (Blurton, 1999; Orsin, 1998; Wright, 2000) lead us to believe that teachers in developing countries can use even limited ICT resources to change how they teach and how students learn in ways that are not significantly different from those of the more developed countries. These changes can contribute both to the improvement of educational systems and to the integration of these countries into the knowledge economy and information society.

However, special help is needed. There are five types of funding and technical support that NGOs could provide to help developing and economically distressed countries build their ICT capacity in education.

1. Of course, help is needed in developing basic infrastructure. This help could focus on the development and deployment of less expensive equipment, such as the Simputer (**http://www.simputer.org**)—the handheld, networked computer developed in India specifically for the needs of developing countries. Because telecommunications are both unreliable and inaccessible for schools in many underdeveloped countries, help is particularly important in building the networking infrastructure that will allow teachers and students in these countries to connect with the rest of the world. The World Links for Development program (**http://www.world-links.org/english/**) has designed a series of low-cost plans for connecting these schools to the Internet, but technological developments are necessary that will allow these schools to have high-bandwidth access.

2. As in developed countries, teacher training is important. Unfortunately, developing countries have less access to the technically skilled manpower needed for this training. Schools often have to compete with large companies for the limited manpower that exists. Foreign aid or NGO assistance could be useful in securing and developing the technical expertise schools need. However, it is equally important that this teacher professional development be focused on pedagogical skills as well as ICT skills.

3. NGOs and multinational organizations can assist developing countries at a policy level as well. It is vitally important that any developments at the school level fit into an overall national educational policy. At the same time, the introduction of ICT into the school system could be an opportunity to change educational policy related to curriculum, assessment, and teacher training. These policies would have to be customized to the national goals and resources of the country rather than transplanted from developed countries. These countries may find helpful advice from other developing countries that are more experienced in the use of ICT but that also face some of the same problems. We found such expertise in our colleagues from Chile, who have had considerable experience in developing and deploying the Enlaces program and coordinating it with national policy. Undoubtedly, there is other indigenous expertise in developing and distressed countries. NGO funding could support connections between this emerging expertise and the needs in other countries.

4. Many developing countries and ethnic communities within these countries are faced with a lack of content in their own language and culture. NGOs can play an important role in supporting the development of such content for the Web. Schools and teachers can make a significant contribution to this development. In many of the cases we studied, teachers and students developed educational content that was placed on the Web for others to use. A good example of this is the case of the Hypertext Development project in the Slovak Republic (SK003), where technologically savvy upper secondary students worked with teachers to develop content for their courses. Another example is Project Region in the Czech Republic (CZ002), where secondary students worked with local municipalities to place content on the Web related to local history, places of interest, and local ordinances. A particularly poignant case was the Roots project (ES005) in Catalonia, Spain, in which primary school children from five rural schools collected multimedia materials in the Catalan language about their local

villages and customs, including folktales and songs from their grandparents that were in danger of being lost. Support for such content development can help bridge the language and cultural divide, as well as the digital divide that confronts developing countries and regions.

5. Finally, NGOs could also support research studies that examine the use and impact of ICT within developing countries. Such funding would contribute to the development of indigenous research capacity and also allow studies within these countries to be tailored to meet their specific needs and conditions.

A second type of implication our study has for multinational and nongovernmental agencies has to do with the use of ICT to support cross-national, cross-cultural, and global projects on the Web. There were relatively few projects in our study that helped teachers break down the boundaries of the school. When these types of projects did exist they often fostered cross-cultural communication, as was the case in Chile (CL002), where lower secondary students compared differences in food, tourist attractions, and national news with adults in Belgium who were taking a Spanish course. Another example is the Peace Network (IL010) in Israel, where Jewish and Arab students were exchanging views and trying to understand each other. Several case reports from European countries (CZ002, DE009, DE010, ES002, ES007, FI004, IT010, NL008, NO004) mentioned the Comenius project, which is supported by the European Commission and aims at promoting international contact and the sense of a European community within the European Union. Such international projects are difficult to mount and coordinate for individual countries, let alone individual teachers and schools. Multinational and nongovernmental agencies can play an important role in launching, supporting, and giving credibility to such projects. International Web-based projects not only can promote social and cultural integration—one of the goals expressed for the information society—but also can contribute to deeper student understanding of international and global issues, such as world or regional peace, sustainable growth, and environmental protection.

IMPLICATIONS FOR RESEARCHERS

We make our last set of recommendations to our fellow researchers, including our colleagues at the International Association for the Evaluation of Educational Achievement (IEA). SITES Module 2 has a number of acknowledged limitations that can be addressed by future research, including SITES Module 3. By intent, this study looked at a highly selective set of schools and classrooms. Within these classrooms we found certain patterns of innovative pedagogical practice using ICT and certain associations with contextual factors. Subsequent research can build on our findings in significant ways.

First, there is a need to conduct studies of representative samples of schools and classrooms to see the extent to which these patterns are used throughout the educational system. Since the cases in our study are "innovative," it is quite likely that there are relatively few classrooms that are currently using them, at least in some countries. Consequently, these large-scale representative studies would be most informative if they were longitudinal, tracking the trends in ICT use over time. The findings from SITES Module 2 provide information that can be used to design more precise indicators of classroom practice that go beyond the "emerging pedagogical paradigm" to look at specific, alternative pedagogical models for ICT use. These studies could also look more systematically at the relationship between these patterns of ICT-supported pedagogical practices and other contextual factors, such as grade level, subject area, teacher preparation, school environment, and socioeconomic factors, for example, number of computers in the home.

Second, an important policy need is to systematically establish the impact of these innovations on student and teacher outcomes. Our study relied on self-reports and other locally available information to get some sense of the impact of these innovations. Our results are suggestive of the kinds of impacts that these innovations are having. But the nature of our evidence is insufficient for evaluation and policy needs. More precise measures of student achievement are needed that can examine the impact of ICT-based innovations, and other research designs are needed to establish causality. Large-scale correlational or quasi-experimental studies could provide stronger evidence of the relationship between certain uses of ICT and certain student and teacher outcomes. These large-scale studies could be complemented by controlled experiments or more extensive qualitative classroom studies that examine these relationships in a more fine-grained way so as to establish causal mechanisms. We provide a note of caution, however. The research question should not be "what impact does ICT have on learning or student achievement?" Our study makes it clear that ICT is not an unvariegated treatment; there are different kinds of ICT and a variety of ways ICT can be used in the classroom. We provide initial evidence that these different patterns are likely to have different outcomes. But more importantly, we show that ICT use is embedded in patterned sets of pedagogical practice. The "dependent variable" should not be the extent of use of ICT or even the kinds of ICT used. Rather it should be the particular sets of patterns of pedagogical practice and ICT use considered together. Our study provides considerable detail about the different kinds of patterns that could be examined and the various outcomes that could be measured.

A third research implication of our study has to do with the kinds of measures that are needed to establish the impact of ICT-supported pedagogical practice. As mentioned in our discussion of policy, the standardized tests currently used to measure student achievement are not likely to measure the kinds of skills often associated with innovative, ICT-based pedagogical practice and needed to prepare students for the knowledge economy and information society. We recommend the development of measures and scoring rubrics to assess not only ICT skills but also information management, problem-solving, communication, and collaboration strategies and skills. These measures should be embedded in complex, authentic tasks of the sort that students are likely to encounter as employees in the knowledge economy and citizens of the information society. In these performance assessments students should use ICT to conduct investigations and produce products within and across subject matter areas, as they did in the innovative classrooms we studied. Such assessments would provide standard measures that could be used to compare and contrast not only outcomes associated with different patterns of ICT-based pedagogical practice but also differences and similarities in schools within and across countries.

Finally, we encourage secondary analysis of the data from this study. A significant amount of funding and effort went into the collection of data, its analysis, and the writing of the case study reports. We have put the results of this effort on the Web (**www.sitesm2.org**) as a searchable database of the 174 case studies. The search engine is based on the cover sheet coding system used for the cross-case analysis in Chapters 3–6. We encourage other researchers to examine these data and conduct further research.

ICT-SUPPORTED EDUCATIONAL CHANGE AND THE GLOBAL CONTEXT

We began this book and this chapter with a reference to the emerging knowledge economy and information society, global developments that have motivated policies and investments related to educational ICT around the world. We end this chapter by examining the assumptions behind these policies and providing a counterpoint.

Without doubt, these economic and social trends are global. However, these trends have not equally benefited everyone within and across all nations, as we have already mentioned. Nor has everyone responded to these trends in the same way. Responses of different countries to these developments have depended on their local values, histories, cultures, and conditions. For example, Nobel Laureate Joseph Stiglitz, former senior vice president and chief economist at the World Bank and current professor of economics at Columbia University, describes a very different response that many Asian countries have taken to the globalization of trade. While the United States and the United Kingdom urge the deregulation of markets as means to drive economic development, the governments of many Asian countries take a more active role in creating, shaping, and guiding markets, including promoting the use of new technologies (Stilitz, 2002). Asian companies also take more responsibility for the social welfare of their employees than do most companies in the United States. At the same time, Stiglitz is critical of the policies of Western governments and intergovernmental agencies, such as the International Monetary Fund, for their unwillingness to take such differences into account. Specifically, he is concerned about policies that press many developing countries to open their trade and financial markets when these countries do not yet have the necessary regulatory infrastructure in place, and to exercise fiscal constraints at the expense of social policies and programs.

Similarly, Arnove and Torres (1999) discuss the dialectic between global and local forces in education. They point out that the global forces that drive education change are modified and, in some cases, even transformed to meet local ends and values. Our intent was to accommodate this dialectic in our case selection procedures by allowing each country to provide its own definition of "innovative" and to propose modifications in the international criteria that reflected local concerns. We also provided for national differences in our analysis of national policies. In this regard, perhaps the most interesting finding to emerge from our analysis is the pronounced pattern of pedagogical practices found in many Asian countries relative to other countries, and the policies associated with these practices. As reported in Chapter 3, a disproportional number of cases from Singapore, the Philippines, Thailand, and Chinese Taipei were assigned to the Information Management Clusters and Student Collaborative Research Clusters. These are the more complex patterns of the student-centered pedagogical practices that use ICT. Also, in Chapter 6 we reported the strong connection between national policy and local policy in Asian countries. This finding attests to the growing importance of student-centered practices in Asia, particularly when compared to the findings from SITES Module 1 that elaborated on the traditional classroom practices of Asian countries. These national patterns attest to the global but variegated nature of the trends in our findings and the need to accommodate national and cultural differences, as well as similarities, in international comparative research and policy analysis.

Likewise, the global nature of these trends prompts us to question the narrowness of assumptions upon which they are based. Spring (1998) claims that policies linking education solely to economic development are based on the assumption that this development will result in an increased demand for a better trained workforce. This demand will, in turn, result in improved education that will contribute to political and social development. According to Spring, these assumptions do not take into account alternative value structures, particularly those that assign a premium to learning for its own sake and the role this plays in personal and social development. Lifelong learning need not be motivated only by the need for continuous retraining in response to a constantly changing labor market. As an alternative to a knowledge economy or an information society, Spring advocates the importance of a *learning society*, echoing the main theme of a 1972 UNESCO report (Faure et al., 1972). In this view, it is the privileged value given to learning that motivates continual personal and social development rather than the indirect value it has in contributing to economic development or social integration. We mention this alternative position only to advocate that researchers and policy makers alike keep their minds open to the full range of ways that education—and the evolving power and capability of ICT—can contribute to the betterment of humankind.

REFERENCES

A

Anderson, L. (1996). *Guidebook for developing an effective instructional technology plan.* Starkville, MS: National Center for Technology Planning.

Anderson, R., & Ronnkvist, A. (1999). *Computer presence in American schools and classrooms, TLC Report 2.* http://www.crito.uci.edu/tlc/findings/computers_in_american_schools/

Arnove, R., & Torres, C. (1999). Introduction: Reframing comparative education—The dialectic of the global and the local. In R. Arnove & C. Torres (Eds.), *Comparative education: The dialectic of the global and the local* (pp. 1–23). New York: Rowman & Littlefield.

B

Beaton, A., Mullis, I., Martin, M., Gonzales, E. Kelly, D., & Smith, T. (1996). *Mathematics achievement in the middle school years: IEA's Third International Mathematics and Science Study.* Chestnut Hill, MA: TIMSS International Study Center.

Becker, H., Ravitz, J., & Wong, Y. (1999). *Teacher and teacher-directed student use of computers and software.* Irvine, CA: Center for Research on Information Technology and Organizations.

Behrmann, M. (1998). Assistive technology for young children in special education. In C. Dede (ed.), *Learning with technology. 1998 Yearbook of the Association for Supervision and Curriculum Development* (pp. 73–93). Alexandria, VA: ASCD.

Bereiter, C. (2002). *Education and mind in the knowledge age.* Mahwah, NJ: Erlbaum.

Berends, M., Bodilly, S., & Kirby, S. (2002). *Facing the challenges of whole-school reform: New American Schools after a decade.* Santa Monica, CA: RAND (MR-1498-EDU).

Berman, E. (1999). The political economy of educational reform in Australia, England and Wales, and the United States. In R. Arnove & C. Torres (Eds.), *Comparative education: The dialectic of the global and the local* (pp. 257–282). New York: Rowman & Littlefield.

Black, P., & Wiliam, D. (1998). Assessment and classroom learning. *Assessment in Education, 5*(1), 7–74.

Blurton, C. (1999). *New directions in ICT use in education.* Paris: UNESCO.

Bogdan, R., & Biklen, S. K. (1998). *Qualitative research for education: An introduction to theory and methods* (3rd ed.). Boston: Allyn and Bacon.

Bransford, J., Brown, A., & Cocking, R. (2000). *How people learn: Brain, mind, experience, and school.* (Expanded ed.). Washington, DC: National Academic Press.

Brown, A., & Campione, J. (1994). Guided discovery in a community of learners. In K. McGilly (Ed.), *Classroom lessons: Integrating cognitive theory and classroom practice* (pp. 229–270). Cambridge, MA: MIT Press.

Bucur, M., & Eklof, B. (1999). Russia and Eastern Europe. In R. Arnove & C. Torres (Eds.), *Comparative education: The dialectic of the global and the local* (pp. 371–392). New York: Rowman & Littlefield.

C

Chan, C., Burtis, J., & Bereiter, C. (1997). Knowledge building as a mediator of conflict in conceptual change. *Cognition and Instruction, 15*(1), 1–40.

Cognition and Technology Group at Vanderbilt. (1997). *The Jasper Project: Lessons in curriculum, instruction, assessment, and professional development.* Mahwah, NJ: Lawrence Erlbaum Associates.

Cohen, D., & Hill, H. (2001). *Learning policy: When state education reform works.* New Haven, CT: Yale University Press.

Collis, B. (Ed.) (1993). *The ITEC Project: Information technology in education and children.* Paris: UNESCO.

Creswell, J. (1998). *Qualitative inquiry and research design: Choosing among five traditions.* Thousand Oaks, CA: Sage.

Cuban, L. (2001). *Oversold and underused: Computers in classrooms.* Cambridge, MA: Harvard University Press.

D

Dalin, P. (1973). *Case studies of educational innovation: Strategies for innovation in education* (Vol. IV). Paris: CERI/OECD.

Dalin, P. (1978). *Limits of educational change.* New York: St. Martin's Press.

Dalin, P. (1994). *How schools improve: An international report.* London: Cassell.

Darling-Hamilton, L., & McLaughlin, M. W. (1996). Policies that support professional development in an era of reform. In M. W. McLaughlin & I. Oberman (Eds.), *Teacher learning: New policies, new practices* (pp. 202–218). New York: Teachers College Press.

De Corte, E. (1993). *Psychological aspects of changes in learning supported by informatics.* Paper presented at the meeting on Informatics and Changes in Learning, Gmunden, Austria.

Dede, C. (1998). The scaling-up process for technology-based educational innovations. In C. Dede (Ed.), *Learning with technology. 1998 Yearbook of the Association for Supervision and Curriculum Development* (pp. 199–215). Alexandria, VA: ASCD.

Dede, C. (2000). Emerging influences of information technology on school curriculum. *Journal of Curriculum Studies, 32*(2), 281–303.

Dertouzos, M., & Gates, B. (1998). *What will be: How the new world of information will change our lives.* New York: Harper.

Drucker, P. (1994). *New realities in government and politics/in economics and business/in society and world view.* New York: Harper.

E

Elmore, R. F. (1996). Getting to scale with good educational practice. *Harvard Educational Review, 66*(1), 1–26.

Elmore, R. F., Peterson, P. L., & McCarthey, S. J. (1996). *Restructuring in the classroom: Teaching, learning, and school organization.* San Francisco: Jossey-Bass.

European Commission. (1997). *Teaching and learning: Towards the learning society.* Brussels: Author.

European Commission (2000). *eEurope: An information society for all*. Brussels: Author.

European Commission (2001a). *Basic indicators on the incorporation of ICT into European educational systems*. Brussels: Author.

European Commission (2001b). *The eLearning action plan: Designing tomorrow's education*. Brussels: Author.

F

Faure, E. (1974). *Learning to be: The world of education today and tomorrow*. Paris: UNESCO.

Faure, E., Herrera, F., Kaddoura, A., Lopes, H., Ptrovsky, A., Rahnema, M., & Ward, F. (1972). *Learning to be: The world of education today and tomorrow*. Paris: UNESCO.

Fishman, B., & Pinkard, N. (2001). Bringing urban schools into the information age: Planning for technology vs. technology planning. *Journal of Educational Computing Research, 25*(1), 63–80.

Fullan, M. (1994). *Coordinating top-down and bottom-up strategies for educational reform*. Retrieved September 25, 2002, from **http://www.ed.gov/pubs/EdReformStudies/SysReforms/fullan1.html**

Fullan, M. (1999). *Change forces: The sequel*. Philadelphia, PA: Falmer Press.

Fullan, M. (2001a). *Leading in a culture of change*. San Francisco: Jossey-Bass.

Fullan, M. (2001b). *The new meaning of educational change* (3rd ed.). New York: Teachers College Press.

Fullan, M., & Hargreaves, A. (1996). *What's worth fighting for in your school?* New York: Teachers College Press.

Fuller, B., & Clarke, P. (1994). Raising school effects while ignoring culture? Local conditions and the influence of classroom tools, rules and pedagogy. *Review of Educational Research, 64*(1), 119–157.

G

Gage, N. (1989). The paradigm wars and their aftermath: A "historical" sketch of research on teaching since 1989. *Educational Researcher, 18*(7), 4–10.

Glaser, B., & Strauss, A. (1967). *The discovery of grounded theory*. Chicago: Aldine.

Gordin, D. N., & Pea, R. D. (1995). Prospects for scientific visualization as an educational technology. *Journal of the Learning Sciences, 4*(3), 249–279.

Guskey, T. R. (1995). Professional development in education: In search of the optimal mix. In T. R. Guskey & A. M. Huberman (Eds.), *Professional development in education: New paradigms and practices* (pp. 114–132). New York: Teachers College Press.

H

Hamel, J. (1993). *Case study methods*. Newbury Park, CA: Sage.

Harel, I., & Papert, S. (1991). *Constructionism*. Norwood, NJ: Ablex.

Hargreaves, A. (1995). Development and desire: A postmodern perspective. In T. R. Guskey & A. M. Huberman (Eds.), *Professional development in education: New paradigms and practices* (pp. 9–34). New York: Teachers College Press.

Henderson, A., & Berla, N. (1994). *A new generation of evidence: The family is critical to student achievement*. Washington, DC: National Committee for Citizens in Education.

Hiebert, J., Gallimore, R., & Stigler, J. W. (2002). A knowledge base for the teaching profession: What would it look like and how can we get one? *Educational Researcher, 31*(5), 3–15.

Howe, K., & Eisenhart, M. (1990). Standards for qualitative (and quantitative) research: A prolegomenon. *Educational Researcher, 19*(4), 2–9.

Howell, J. M., & Higgins, C. A. (1990). Champions of technological innovations. *Administrative Science Quarterly, 35*(2), 317–341.

Huberman, M. (1992). Critical introduction. In M. Fullan (Ed.), *Successful school improvement*. Buckingham: Open University Press, and Toronto: OISE Press.

K

Kankaanranta, M., & Linnakyla, P. (in press). Cross-national policies and practices on ICT in education: Finland. In T. Plomp, R. Anderson, N. Law, & A. Quale (Eds.), *Cross-national ICT policies and practices in education*. Greenwich, CT: Information Age Publishing.

Kozma, R. (1991). Learning with media. *Review of Educational Research, 61*(2), 179–212.

Kozma, R. (1994). Will media influence learning? Reframing the debate. *Educational Technology Research and Development, 42*(2), 7–19.

Kozma, R., & McGhee, R. (1999). *World Links for Development: Accomplishments and challenges. Monitoring and Evaluation Annual Report: 1998–1999*. Menlo Park, CA: SRI International.

Kozma, R., & Schank, P. (1998). Connecting with the 21st century: Technology in support of educational reform. In C. Dede (Ed.), *Technology and learning*. Washington, DC: American Society for Curriculum Development.

L

Law, N., Yuen, H., Ki, W., Li, S., Lee, Y., & Chow, Y. (2000). *Changing classrooms: A study of good practices in using ICT in Hong Kong schools*. China Hong Kong: Centre for Information Technology in School and Teacher Education, University of Hong Kong.

Lieberman, A. (1996). Practices that support teacher development: Transforming perceptions of professional learning. In M. W. McLaughlin & I. Oberman (Eds.), *Teacher learning: New policies, new practices* (pp. 185–201). New York: Teachers College Press.

Light, P. C. (1998). *Sustaining innovation: Creating nonprofit and government organizations that innovate naturally*. San Francisco: Jossey-Bass.

Linn, M. C. (1997). Learning and instruction in science education: Taking advantage of technology. In D. Tobin & B. J. Fraser (Eds.), *International handbook of science education* (pp. 372–396). The Netherlands: Klewer.

Louis, K., & Miles, M. (1991). *Improving the urban high school: What works and why*. New York: Teachers College Press.

M

Marsh, C. J., & Willis, G. (1999). *Curriculum. Alternative approaches, ongoing issues* (2nd ed.). Upper Saddle River, NJ: Prentice-Hall.

Martin, M., Rust, K., & Adams, R. (1999). *Technical standards for IEA studies*. Amsterdam: International Association for the Evaluation of Educational Achievement.

McGhee, R., & Kozma, R. (2000). *World Links for Development: Accomplishments and challenges. Monitoring and Evaluation Annual Report: 1999–2000*. Menlo Park, CA: SRI International.

McLaughlin, M. (1990). The Rand Change Agent Study revised: Macro perspectives and micro realities. *Educational Researcher, 19*(9), 11–16.

McLaughlin, M. (1993). What matters most in teachers' workplace context? In J. Little & M. McLaughlin (Eds.), *Teacher's work: Individual, colleagues, and contexts* (pp. 97–123). New York: Teachers College Press.

Means, B., & Olson, K. (1997). *Technology's role in education reform: Findings from a national study of innovating schools*. Washington, DC: U.S. Department of Education, Office of Educational Research and Improvement.

Means, B., Penuel, W., & Padilla, C. (2001). *The connected school: Technology and learning in high school*. San Francisco: Jossey-Bass.

Means, B., Penuel, W., & Quellmalz, E. (2001). Developing assessments for tomorrow's classrooms. In W. Heineke & J. Willis (Eds.), *Methods of evaluating educational technology*. Greenwich, CT: Information Age Publishing.

Merriam, S. (1998). *Qualitative research and case study applications in education*. San Francisco: Jossey-Bass.

Metz, M. H. (1993). Teachers' ultimate dependence on their students. In J. W. Little & M. W. McLaughlin (Eds.), *Teacher's work: Individuals, colleagues, and contexts* (pp. 104–136). New York: Teachers College Press.

Miles, M., & Huberman, A. (1994). *Qualitative data analysis* (2nd ed.). Thousand Oaks, CA: Sage.

Ministry of Education, Finland (1999). *Education, training and research in the information society: A national strategy for 2000–2004*. Olso, Norway: Ministry of Education.

Ministry of Education, Singapore (2002). *Masterplan 2.* **http://www.moe.gov.sg/edumall/mp2/mp2_overview.htm**

Ministerio de Educación, Republica de Chile. (1998). *Reform in progress: Quality education for all*. Santiago, Chile: Ministerio de Educación.

N

National Center for Educational Statistics [NCES]. (1998). *Technology @ your fingertips: A guide to implementing technology solutions for education agencies and institutions*. Washington, DC: U.S. Department of Education.

National Center for Educational Statistics [NCES]. (2001). *The nation's report card: Science 2000*. Washington, DC: National Center for Educational Statistics.

Northern Central Regional Educational Laboratory [NCREL]. (2002). *Critical issue: Providing professional development for effective technology use.* Retrieved July 28, 2002, 2002, from **http://www.ncrel.org/sdrs/areas/issues/methods/technlgy/te1000.htm**

O

Office of the National Education Commission. (1999). *National Education Act of B.E. 2542.* Bangkok: Kurusapa Ladprao Press.

Organization for Economic Co-operation and Development [OECD]. (1996). *The knowledge-based economy.* Paris: Author.

Organization for Economic Co-operation and Development [OECD]. (1998). *Education policy analysis.* Paris: OECD, Centre for Educational Research and Innovation.

Organization for Economic Co-operation and Development [OECD]. (1999). *Knowledge management in the learning society.* Paris: Author.

Organization for Economic Co-operation and Development [OECD] (2000). *Knowledge management in the learning society.* Paris: Author.

Organization for Economic Co-operation and Development [OECD] (2001a). *Education policy analysis.* Paris: Author.

Organization for Economic Co-operation and Development [OECD] (2001b). *Learning to change: ICT in schools.* Paris: Author.

Orsin, L. (1998). *Computers in education in developing countries: Why and how.* Washington, DC: The World Bank.

P

Pal, L. A. (2001). *Beyond policy analysis: Public issue management in turbulent times.* Scarborough, Ontario, Canada: Nelson Thomson Learning.

Papert, S. (1980). *Mindstorms: Children, computers, and powerful ideas.* New York: Basic Books.

Pelgrum, W., & Anderson, R. (1999). *ICT and the emerging paradigm for lifelong learning.* Amsterdam: International Association for the Advancement of Educational Achievement.

Pelgrum, W., & Plomp, T. (2002). Indicators of ICT in mathematics: Status and covariation with achievement measures. In A. E. Beaton & D. F. Robitaille (Eds.), *Secondary analysis of the TIMSS data.* Dordrecht: Kluwer Academic Press.

Peters, T. (1997). *The circle of innovation.* New York: Knopf.

Plomp, T., Anderson, R., Law, N., & Quale, A. (in press). *Cross-national ICT policies in education.* Greenwhich, CT: Information Age Publishing.

Plomp, T., & Loxley, W. (1993). *The contribution of international comparative assessment to curriculum reform.* Paper presented at the OECD conference on the Curriculum Redefined, Paris.

Plomp, T., Ten Brummelhuis, A., & Rapmund, R. (1996). *Teaching and learning for the future* (Report of the Committee on Multimedia in Teacher Training [COMMITT] to the Netherlands Minister of Education). The Hague: Sdu.

President's Committee of Advisors on Science and Technology [PCAST]. (1997). *Report to the President on the use of technology to strengthen K–12 education in the United States.* Washington, DC: Office of Science and Technology Policy. Available:**http://www.whitehouse.gov/WH/EOP/ OSTP/NSTC/PCAST/k-12ed.html**

President's Information Technology Advisory Committee [PITAC]. (1999). *Information technology research: Investing in our future.* Arlington, VA: National Coordination Office for Computing.

R

Ragin, C. (1987). *The comparative method: Moving beyond qualitative and quantitative strategies.* Berkeley, CA: University of California Press.

Ravitz, J., Becker, H., & Wong, Y. (2000). *Constructivist-compatible beliefs and practices among U.S. teachers.* Irvine, CA: Center for Research on Information Technology and Organizations.

Riel, M. (1998). Teaching and learning in the educational communities of the future. In C. Dede (Ed.), *Learning with technology: ASCD Yearbook 1998.* Alexandria, VA: Association for Supervision and Curriculum Development.

Rogers, E. (1995). *Diffusion of innovations* (4th ed.). New York: Free Press.

S

Salomon, G. (1991). Transcending the qualitative-quantitative debate: The analytic and systemic approaches to educational research. *Educational Researcher, 20*(6), 1018.

Samoff, J. (1999). No teacher guide, no textbooks, no chairs: Contending with crisis in African education. In R. Arnove & C. Torres (Eds.), *Comparative education: The dialectic of the global and the local* (pp. 393–432). New York: Rowman & Littlefield.

Sandholtz, H., Ringstaff, C., & Dwyer, D. (1997). *Teaching with technology: Creating student-centered classrooms.* New York: Teachers College Press.

Scardamalia, M., & Bereiter, C. (1991). Higher levels of agency for children in knowledge-building: A challenge for the design of new knowledge media. *Journal of the Learning Sciences, 1*(1), 37–68.

Scardimalia, M., & Bereiter, C. (1994). Computer support for knowledge-building communities. *Journal of the Learning Sciences, 3*(3), 265–384.

Schank, R. C., Fano, A., Bell, B., & Jona, M. (1994). The design of goal-based scenarios. *Journal of the Learning Sciences, 3*(4), 305–346.

Schofield, J., & Davidson, A. (2002). *Bringing the Internet to school: Lessons from an urban district.* San Francisco: Jossey-Bass.

Senge, P. M. (1990). *The fifth discipline: The art and practice of the learning organization.* New York: Doubleday/Currency.

Senge, P., Cambron-McCabe, N., Lucas, T., Smith, B., Dutton, J., & Kleiner, A. (2000). *Schools that learn.* New York: Doubleday.

Shavelson, R., & Towne, L. (2001). *Scientific inquiry in education.* Washington, DC: National Academy Press.

Soros, G. (2002). *On globalization.* New York: Public Affairs.

Spring, J. (1998). *Education and the rise of the global economy*. Mahwah, NJ: Erlbaum.

Stake, R. (1995). *The art of case study research*. Thousand Oaks, CA: Sage.

Stigliz, J. (1999). *Public policy for a knowledge economy*. Washington, DC: The World Bank Group.

Stiglitz, J. (2002). *Globalization and its discontents*. New York: Norton.

Stoll, L., & Fink, D. (1996). *Changing our schools*. Buckingham: Open University Press.

Strauss, A., & Corbin, J. (1990). *Basics of qualitative research: Grounded theory procedures and techniques*. Newbury Park, CA: Sage.

Su, Z. (1999). Asian education. In R. Arnove & C. Torres (Eds.), *Comparative education: The dialectic of the global and the local* (pp. 329–344). New York: Rowman & Littlefield.

T

Tashakkori, A., & Teddlie, C. (1998). *Mixed methodology: Combining qualitative and quantitative approache*s. Thousand Oaks, CA: Sage.

Taylor, R. (1980). *The computer in the school: Tutor, tool, tutee*. New York: Teachers College Press.

Thurow, L. (1999). *Building wealth: The new rules for individuals, companies, and nations*. New York: HarperCollins.

Trotter, A. (Ed.) (1998). Technology counts 1998: Putting school technology to the test (special report). *Education Week, 18*(5). Available: **http://www.edweek.com/sreports/tc98/**

Tucker, M., & Codding, J. (1998). *Standards for our schools: How to set them, measure them, and reach them*. New York: Jossey-Bass.

U

United Nations Development Program [UNDP]. (1999). *Globalization with a human face*. New York: United Nations.

U.S. Census Bureau. (2001). *Home computers and use of the Internet in the U.S.: August 2000*. Washington, DC: Author.

U.S. Department of Education. (1996). *Getting America's students ready for the 21st century: Meeting the technology literacy challenge*. Washington, DC: U.S. Government Printing Office.

U.S. Department of Education. (2000). *E-learning: Putting a world-class education at the fingertips of all children*. Washington, DC: U.S. Government Printing Office.

V

Van Den Akker, J. J. H., Keursten, P., & Plomp, T. (1992). The integration of computer use in education. *International Journal of Curriculum Research, 17*, 65–76

Van Velzen, W., Miles, M., Eckholm, M., Hameyer, U., & Robin, D. (1985). *Making school improvement work*. Leuven, Belgium: ACCO.

Venezky, R., & Davis, C. (2002). *Quo vademus? The transformation of schooling in a networked world*. Paris: OECD.

Voogt, J., & Odenthal, L. (1999). *Met het oog op de toekomst: een studies naar innovatief gebruik van ICT in het onderwijs. [With a view to the future: A study of innovative use of ICT in education].* Enschede, The Netherlands: University of Twente, Faculty of Educational Science and Technology.

W

Weiss, I., Knapp, M., Hollweg, K., & Burrill, G. (2001). *Investigating the influence of standards: A framework for research in mathematics, science, and technology education.* Washington, DC: National Research Council.

Wenglinski, H. (1998). *Does it compute? The relationship between educational technology and student achievement in mathematics.* Princeton, NJ: Educational Testing Service.

World Bank. (1998). *Latin America and the Caribbean: Education and technology at the crossroads.* Washington, DC: Author.

Wright, C. (Ed.). (2000). *Issues in education and technology: Policy guidelines and strategies.* London: Commonwealth Secretariat.

Y

Yeo, H., Kan, E., & Tham, Y. (in press). Cross-national policies and practices on ICT in education: Singapore. In T. Plomp, R. Anderson, N. Law, & A. Quale (Eds.), *Cross-national ICT policies and practices in education.* Greenwich, CT: Information Age Publishing.

Yin, R. (1994). *Case study research: Design and methods* (2nd ed.). Thousand Oaks, CA: Sage.

APPENDIX A

SITES MODULE 2 PERSONNEL

SITES Module 2 International Coordinating Committee (ICC)

United States	Robert B. Kozma (Study Director) Raymond McGhee
Canada	Ronald D. Owston Richard M. Jones
The Netherlands	Willem J. Pelgrum Joke M. Voogt

SITES Module 2 International Steering Committee (ISC)

United States	Ronald Anderson (Cochair) Chris Dede
The Netherlands	Tjeerd Plomp (Cochair)
China Hong Kong	Nancy Law
Norway	Jan Peter Stromsheim
Japan	Ryo Watanabe

SITES Module 2 National Research Coordinators (NRCs)

Australia	John Ainley
Canada	Douglas Hodgkinson
Chile	Enrique Hinostroza Andrea Guzman
China Hong Kong	Nancy Law
Chinese Taipei	Cheng-Chih Wu Guey-Fa Chiou
Czech Republic	Borivoj Brdicka
Denmark	Inge Bryderup
England	Sue Harris
Finland	Marja Kankaanranta Päivi Häkkinen
France	Catherine Regnier
Germany	Renate Schulz-Zander
Israel	David Mioduser Rafi Nachmias

Italy	Renata Picco
	Roberto Melchiori
Japan	Katsuhiko Shimizu
	Taro Numano
Korea	Myong Sook Kim
	Sung Heum Lee
Latvia	Andris Grinfelds
Lithuania	Lina Markauskaite
The Netherlands	Gerard Doornekamp
Norway	Ola Erstad
Philippines	Ester B. Ogena
	Filma G. Brawner
Portugal	Gertrudes Amaro
	Helena Henriques
Russia	Alexander Lesnevsky
Singapore	Khee-Shoon Teo
	Wee-Haur Pek
	Yoke-Chun Tham
Slovakia	Viera Blahová
South Africa	Sarah Howie
	Andrew Paterson
Spain, Catalonia	Carme Amorós Basté
	Fina Grané Mas
	Jordi Saura Valls
Thailand	Pornpun Waitayangkoon
United States	Ronald Anderson
	Sara Dexter

COUNTRIES PARTICIPATING IN THE SITES AND OECD STUDIES

COUNTRY (Letter codes used for M2 Cases)	SITES M1	SITES M2	OECD STUDY*
Australia [AU]		✔	✔
Belgium (French)	✔		
Bulgaria	✔		
Canada [CA]	✔	✔	✔
Chile [CL]		✔	
China Hong Kong [CN]	✔	✔	
Chinese Taipei [TW]	✔	✔	
Cyprus	✔		
Czech Rep [CZ]	✔	✔	
Denmark [DK]	✔	✔	✔
England [UK]		✔	✔
Finland [FI]	✔	✔	✔
France [FR]	✔	✔	✔
Germany [DE]		✔	✔
Hungary	✔		✔
Iceland	✔		
Israel [IL]	✔	✔	✔
Italy[IT]	✔	✔	✔
Japan [JP]	✔	✔	✔
Korea [KR]		✔	✔
Latvia [LV]	✔	✔	
Lithuania [LT]	✔	✔	
Luxembourg	✔		✔
The Netherlands [NL]		✔	✔
New Zealand	✔		
Norway [NO]	✔	✔	✔
Philippines [PH]		✔	
Portugal [PT]		✔	✔
Russian Fed [RU]	✔	✔	
Singapore [SG]	✔	✔	✔
Slovak Rep [SK]	✔	✔	
Slovenia	✔		
South Africa [ZA]	✔	✔	
Spain (Catalonia) [ES]		✔	
Thailand [TH]	✔	✔	
United States [US]		✔	✔

* Only countries participating both in the OECD study and either SITES study are included. There were a total of 23 countries participating in the OECD case study project.

SITES MODULE 2 CASE WRITE-UP COVER SHEET

GENERAL

Country: _____

Case Number: (from the Case Nomination Form) _____

(N; %)

   1. Students' Grade Levels

       ☐   a. Primary (60; 34.5%)

       ☐   b. Lower secondary (62; 35.6%)

       ☐   c. Upper secondary (61; 35.1%)

MESO LEVEL

   2. Does the case report suggest a link to a school ICT policy or plan?

      ☐ Yes   ☐ No

      (109; 62.6 %)   (65; 37.4%)

   3. Who else, outside the school, was directly involved in the application of the innovation? (tick all that apply)

       ☐   a. Parents (15; 8.6%)

       ☐   b. Students and/or teachers from other schools (35; 20.1%)

       ☐   c. Scientific or higher education institutions (16; 9.2%)

       ☐   d. Business and industry (23; 13.2%)

       ☐   e. Government agencies (8; 4.6%)

       ☐   f. No outside involvement (100; 57.5%)

   4. How would you characterize the leadership style of the school's principal? (tick most appropriate)

       ☐   Active involvement in the innovation (53; 30.5%)

       ☐   Supportive but not directly involved (112; 64.4%)

       ☐   Neutral (8; 4.6%)

       ☐   Against the innovation (1; 0.6%)

MACRO LEVEL

5. Does the case report suggest a link to a national (or state/province in decentralized countries) education policy or plan (other than ICT plan)?

   ☐ Yes   ☐ No

   (106; 60.9%)   (68; 39.1%)

6. Does the case report suggest a link to a national (or state/province in decentralized countries) ICT policy or plan?

   ☐ Yes   ☐ No

   (127; 73.0%)   (47; 27.0%)

7. Is the innovation part of either of these outside activities? (tick all that apply)

   ☐   a. National, state, or regional projects (66; 37.9%)

   ☐   b. International projects (18; 10.3%)

   ☐   c. No outside involvement (96; 55.2%)

THEMATIC ANALYSIS OF THE INNOVATION

C1. Curriculum, Content, Goals, and Assessment

8. How many subject matter areas (all together in the school) are involved in the innovation? (tick most appropriate)

   ☐   One specific subject (51; 29.3%)

   ☐   A few subjects (65; 37.4%)

   ☐   All (or almost all) subjects (56; 32.2%)

   ☐   No response (2; 1.2%)

9. In what subject matter areas did the classroom observations of the innovation take place? (tick all that apply)

   ☐   a. Mathematics (37; 21.3%)

   ☐   b. Physics (23; 13.2%)

   ☐   c. Chemistry (9; 5.2%)

   ☐   d. Biology/life science (43; 24.7%)

   ☐   e. Earth science (24; 13.8%)

   ☐   f. Language/mother tongue (56; 32.2%)

   ☐   g. Foreign language(s) (42; 24.1%)

   ☐   h. Creative arts (music, visual arts) (35; 20.1%)

   ☐   i. History (28; 16.1%)

   ☐   j. Civics (23; 13.2%)

   ☐   k. Economics (10; 5.8%)

   ☐   l. Geography (25; 14.4%)

    ☐   m. Vocational subjects (**14; 8.1%**)

    ☐   n. Computer education/informatics (**36; 20.7%**)

    ☐   o. Multidisciplinary projects or activities (**49; 28.2%**)

10. Does this case describe changes in the curriculum related to: (tick all that apply)

    ☐   a. Content (**47; 27.0%**)

    ☐   b. Goals other than ICT skills and/or "normal" subject-related skills (**65; 37.4%**)

    ☐   c. The organization of content (i.e., the curriculum is organized differently) (**119; 68.4%**)

    ☐   d. Allocation of time for the innovation (**63; 36.2%**)

11. Does this case describe alternative assessment procedures (e.g., portfolio assessment, self- or peer assessment, authentic assessment, etc.)?

☐ Yes   ☐ No

(**105; 60.3%**)   (**69; 39.7%**)

C2. Teacher Practices and Outcomes

12. Does this case contain an explicit statement that the activities of the teacher have changed due to the innovation?

☐ Yes   ☐ No

(**129; 74.1%**)   (**45; 25.9%**)

13. What type of activities did the innovation teachers carry out? (tick all that apply)

    ☐   a. Lecture (**43; 24.7%**)

    ☐   b. Advise or guide students (**156; 89.7%**)

    ☐   c. Create structure for student activity (**140; 80.5%**)

    ☐   d. Design and prepare instructional materials (**100; 57.5%**)

    ☐   e. Monitor and/or assess student performance (**132; 75.9%**)

    ☐   f. Collaborate with students (**42; 24.1%**)

    ☐   g. Collaborate with colleagues (**102; 58.6%**)

    ☐   h. Collaborate with actors outside the class (**40; 23.0%**)

14. Does this case describe the impact(s) of the innovation on the teacher(s) in terms of: (tick all that apply)

    ☐   a. Acquisition of new pedagogical skills (**99; 56.9%**)

    ☐   b. Acquisition of ICT skills (**110; 63.2%**)

    ☐   c. Acquisition of collaborative skills (**61; 35.1%**)

    ☐   d. Development of positive attitudes toward the teaching profession (**37; 21.3%**)

    ☐   e. Negative outcomes (**13; 7.5%**)

C3. Student Practices and Outcomes

15. Does this case contain an explicit statement that the activities of the students have changed due to the innovation?

☐ Yes ☐ No

(147; 84.5%) (27; 15.5%)

16. What type of activities did the innovation students carry out? (tick all that apply)

☐ a. Perform drill-and-practice tasks (23; 13.2%)

☐ b. Perform research projects (68; 39.1%)

☐ c. Search for information (128; 73.6%)

☐ d. Solve problems (58; 33.3%)

☐ e. Manipulate/interpret data in tables/charts/graphs (38; 21.8%)

☐ f. Publish and present results (115; 66.1%)

☐ g. Design and create products (106; 60.9%)

☐ h. Collaborate with others (145; 83.3%)

☐ i. Collaborate with actors outside the class (45; 25.9%)

☐ j. Assess own/peers' performance (53; 30.5%)

☐ k. Pick their own tasks (70; 40.2%)

17. Does this case describe the impact(s) of the innovation on the students in terms of: (tick all that apply)

☐ a. Acquisition of new subject matter (knowledge and/or skills) (109; 62.6%)

☐ b. Acquisition of ICT skills (131; 75.3%)

☐ c. Acquisition of communication skills (69; 39.7%)

☐ d. Acquisition of problem-solving skills (33; 19.0%)

☐ e. Acquisition of information-handling skills (50; 28.7%)

☐ f. Acquisition of team/collaborative skills (109; 62.6%)

☐ g. Acquisition of metacognitive skills (67; 38.5%)

☐ h. Development of positive attitudes toward learning and/or school (119; 68.4%)

☐ i. Outcomes for different groups of students (35; 20.1%)

☐ j. Negative outcomes (33; 19%)

18. Was the innovation especially beneficial for any of these special student groups: (tick all that apply)

☐ a. Ethnic or language minorities (11; 6.3%)

☐ b. Students of low socioeconomic status (13; 7.5%)

☐ c. Low-ability students or students at risk of failure (20; 11.5%)

☐ d. Learning disabled, handicapped, or other special needs students (9; 5.2%)

   ☐   e. Girl students (6; 3.4%)

   ☐   f. Gifted students (8; 4.6%)

   ☐   g. No special group of students is specifically targeted (128; 73.6%)

C4. Kinds of Technology and Ways They Are Used

19. Which are the technologies used in this innovation? (tick all that apply)

   ☐   a. Laptop computers (28; 16.1%)

   ☐   b. Local area network (including wireless networks) used as a key part of the innovation (71; 40.8%)

   ☐   c. E-mail, Internet, conferencing software, or listservs (118; 67.8%)

   ☐   d. Educational Web resources (123; 70.7%)

   ☐   e. Productivity tools (e.g., Word, Excel, Access, PowerPoint, etc.) (136; 78.2%)

   ☐   f. Web design tools (59; 33.9%)

   ☐   g. Collaborative environments (16; 9.2%)

   ☐   h. Photography, video, multimedia software (91; 52.3%)

   ☐   i. Simulations, microcomputer-based laboratories (22; 12.6%)

   ☐   j. Tutorial or drill-and-practice software (31; 17.8%)

   ☐   k. Course management systems (e.g., Learning Space, Blackboard) (11; 6.3%)

20. Where does the innovation take place? (tick all that apply)

   ☐   a. Location outside of school (48; 27.6%)

   ☐   b. Location in school but outside of regular classroom, library, or computer lab (31; 17.8%)

   ☐   c. In the regular classroom, library, or computer lab (163; 93.7%)

21. What kinds of ICT practices were used in the innovation? (tick all that apply)

   ☐   a. Tutorial or drill-and-practice software for instruction (31; 17.8%)

   ☐   b. E-mail or other communication tools to support communication (96; 55.2%)

   ☐   c. Web browsers or CD-ROMs to search for information and other resources (134; 77.0%)

   ☐   d. Software packages to create products or presentations (139; 79.9%)

   ☐   e. Software or the Internet to support student collaborative activities (30; 17.2%)

   ☐   f. Software to perform simulations or modeling for research or experimentation (23; 13.2%)

   ☐   g. ICT to monitor/assess student work (39; 22.4%)

   ☐   h. ICT to plan and organize instruction (46; 26.4%)

22. Was there added value specifically claimed for ICT in the innovation? (tick all that apply)

☐ a. ICT supports student practice (activity or assignment) not otherwise possible/likely (**134; 77.0%**)

☐ b. ICT supports teacher practice not otherwise possible/likely (**57; 32.8%**)

☐ c. ICT associated with student outcome (**114; 65.5%**)

☐ d. ICT associated with teacher outcome (**29; 16.7%**)

☐ e. ICT supports educational change/reform (**43; 24.7%**)

☐ f. ICT supports a change in the curriculum (**28; 16.1%**)

☐ g. ICT saves money/resources/increases efficiency (**36; 20.7%**)

☐ h. ICT provides resources that would not otherwise be available (**80; 46.0%**)

☐ i. ICT changes the time/structure of school/classroom (**47; 27.0%**)

☐ j. ICT performs important functions in support of student learning (provides feedback, monitors progress, gives guidance, etc.) (**53; 30.5%**)

☐ k. ICT inhibits undesirable activities/outcomes (**11; 6.3%**)

☐ l. ICT associated with (stimulates, facilitates) parents involvement or commitment (**11; 6.3%**)

C5. Problems and Solutions Related to the Innovation

23. Does this case describe problems and/or solutions in carrying out the innovation in terms of: (tick all that apply):

	TICK IF PROBLEM IS MENTIONED	TICK IF SOLUTION IS MENTIONED
a. Resources and equipment	☐ 108; 62.1%	☐ 28; 16.1%
b. Technical support	☐ 48; 27.6%	☐ 13; 7.5%
c. Pedagogical support	☐ 21; 12.1%	☐ 8; 4.6%
d. Teacher-related issues	☐ 71; 40.8%	☐ 28; 16.1%
e. Student-related issues	☐ 62; 35.6%	☐ 20; 11.5%
f. Curriculum-related issues (including lack of time in the curriculum to include the innovation)	☐ 41; 23.6%	☐ 6; 3.4%
g. Issues related to support for the innovation (from teachers, parents, administrators, etc.)	☐ 47; 27.0%	☐ 17; 9.8%
h. Technical problems (e.g., hardware, phone lines, network)	☐ 52; 29.9%	☐ 11; 6.3%
i. Policies (e.g., national, state, or local policies work against the innovation)	☐ 9; 5.2%	☐ 1; 0.6%
j. Organizational-related issues (including limitations of time for teachers to work on the innovation)	☐ 73; 42.0%	☐ 24; 13.8%

C6. Sustainability

24. Does the case specifically state that the innovation has been sustained over time (i.e., more than one year)?

☐ Yes   ☐ No

(136; 78.2%)   (38; 21.8%)

25. If yes, is supportive evidence given? (n = 136)

☐ Yes   ☐ No

(130; 95.6%)   (6; 4.4%)

C7. Transferability

26. Does the case specifically state that the innovation has been transferred to other classes within the school or other schools?

☐ Yes   ☐ No

(76; 43.7%)   (98; 56.3%)

27. If yes, is there supportive evidence given? (n = 76)

☐ Yes   ☐ No

(71; 93.2%)   (5; 6.6%)

APPENDIX C

TABLES

Table C.4.1

CLUSTER AND GRADE LEVEL—PRIMARY

	CLUSTER (Frequency/Column Percent)								
	Tool Use	Student Collaborative Research	Information Management	Teacher Collaboration	Outside Communication	Product Creation	Tutorial	Undefined	Total
Not checked	11	11	15	16	17	20	3	20	113
	78.6	78.6	68.2	84.2	63.0	57.1	25.0	74.1	66.5%
Checked	3	3	7	3	10	15	9	7	57
	21.4	21.4	31.8	15.8	37.0	42.9	75.0	25.9	33.5%
Total	14	14	22	19	7	35	12	27	170
Row percent	8.2%	8.2%	12.9%	11.2%	15.9%	20.6%	7.1%	15.9%	

	DF	Value	Prob
Chi-Square	7	16.0271	0.0249

Table C.4.2

CLUSTER AND GRADE LEVEL—LOWER SECONDARY

	CLUSTER (Frequency/Column Percent)								
	Tool Use	Student Collaborative Research	Information Management	Teacher Collaboration	Outside Communication	Product Creation	Tutorial	Undefined	Total
Not checked	11	5	10	13	21	23	9	17	109
	78.6	35.7	45.5	68.4	77.8	65.7	75.0	63.0	64.1%
Checked	3	9	12	6	6	12	3	10	61
	21.4	64.3	54.6	31.6	22.2	34.3	25.0	37.0	35.9%
Total	14	14	22	19	27	35	12	27	170
Row percent	8.2%	8.2%	12.9%	11.2%	15.9%	20.6%	7.1%	15.9%	

	DF	Value	Prob
Chi-Square	7	12.526	0.0845

Table C.4.3

CLUSTER AND GRADE LEVEL—UPPER SECONDARY

	CLUSTER (Frequency/Column Percent)								
	Tool Use	Student Collaborative Research	Information Management	Teacher Collaboration	Outside Communication	Product Creation	Tutorial	Undefined	Total
Not checked	5	11	18	8	15	27	12	14	110
	35.7	78.6	81.8	42.1	55.6	77.1	100	51.9	64.7%
Checked	9	3	4	11	12	8	0	13	60
	64.3	21.4	18.2	57.9	44.4	22.9	0.0	48.2	35.3%
Total	14	14	22	19	27	35	12	27	170
Row percent	8.2%	8.2%	12.9%	11.2%	15.9%	20.6%	7.1%	15.9%	

	DF	Value	Prob
Chi-Square	7	25.261	0.0007

Table C.5

CLUSTER AND SCHOOL ICT POLICY

	CLUSTER (Frequency/Column Percent)								
	Tool Use	Student Collaborative Research	Information Management	Teacher Collaboration	Outside Communication	Product Creation	Tutorial	Undefined	Total
Yes	8	14	18	10	10	21	8	17	106
	57.1	100	81.8	52.6	37.0	60.0	66.7	63.0	62.4%
No	6	0	4	9	17	14	4	10	64
	42.9	0.0	18.2	47.4	63.0	40.0	33.3	37.0	37.6%
Total	14	14	22	19	27	35	12	27	170
Row percent	8.2%	8.2%	12.9%	11.2%	15.9%	20.6%	7.1%	15.9%	

	DF	Value	Prob
Chi-Square	7	20.4842	0.0046

Table C.6.1

CLUSTER AND OUTSIDE INVOLVEMENT—PARENTS

	CLUSTER (Frequency/Column Percent)								
	Tool Use	Student Collaborative Research	Information Management	Teacher Collaboration	Outside Communication	Product Creation	Tutorial	Undefined	Total
Not checked	13	13	20	17	21	34	10	27	155
	92.9	92.9	90.9	89.5	77.8	97.1	83.3	100	91.2%
Checked	1	1	2	2	6	1	2	0	15
	7.1	7.1	9.1	10.5	22.2	2.9	16.7	0.0	8.8%
Total	14	14	22	19	27	35	12	27	170
Row percent	8.2%	8.2%	12.9%	11.2%	15.9%	20.6%	7.1%	15.9%	

	DF	Value	Prob
Chi-Square	7	11.273	0.1271

Table C.6.2

CLUSTER AND OUTSIDE INVOLVEMENT—STUDENTS FROM OTHER SCHOOLS

	CLUSTER (Frequency/Column Percent)								
	Tool Use	Student Collaborative Research	Information Management	Teacher Collaboration	Outside Communication	Product Creation	Tutorial	Undefined	Total
Not checked	12	14	22	14	12	28	12	23	137
	85.7	100	100	73.7	44.4	80.0	100	85.2	80.6%
Checked	2	0	0	5	15	7	0	4	33
	14.3	0.0	0.0	26.3	55.6	20.0	0.0	14.8	19.4%
Total	14	14	22	19	27	35	12	27	170
Row percent	8.2%	8.2%	12.9%	11.2%	15.9%	20.6%	7.1%	15.9%	

	DF	Value	Prob
Chi-Square	7	35.2959	<.0001

Table C.6.3

CLUSTER AND OUTSIDE INVOLVEMENT—SCIENTIFIC OR HIGHER EDUCATION INSTITUTIONS

	CLUSTER (Frequency/Column Percent)								
	Tool Use	Student Collaborative Research	Information Management	Teacher Collaboration	Outside Communication	Product Creation	Tutorial	Undefined	Total
Not checked	14	14	21	16	19	34	11	25	154
	100	100	95.5	84.2	70.4	97.1	91.7	92.6	90.6%
Checked	0	0	1	3	8	1	1	2	16
	0.0	0.0	4.6	15.8	29.6	2.9	8.3	7.4	9.4%
Total	14	14	22	19	27	35	12	27	170
Row percent	8.2%	8.2%	12.9%	11.2%	15.9%	20.6%	7.1%	15.9%	

	DF	Value	Prob
Chi-Square	7	19.2785	0.0074

Table C.6.4

CLUSTER AND OUTSIDE INVOLVEMENT—BUSINESS OR INDUSTRY

	CLUSTER (Frequency/Column Percent)								
	Tool Use	Student Collaborative Research	Information Management	Teacher Collaboration	Outside Communication	Product Creation	Tutorial	Undefined	Total
Not checked	11	12	19	14	24	34	12	24	150
	78.6	85.7	86.4	73.7	88.9	97.1	100	88.9	88.2%
Checked	3	2	3	5	3	1	0	3	20
	21.4	14.3	13.6	26.3	11.1	2.9	0.0	11.1	11.8%
Total	14	14	22	19	27	35	12	27	170
Row percent	8.2%	8.2%	12.9%	11.2%	15.9%	20.6%	7.1%	15.9%	

	DF	Value	Prob
Chi-Square	7	9.5924	0.2129

Table C.6.5

CLUSTER AND OUTSIDE INVOLVEMENT—GOVERNMENT AGENCIES

	CLUSTER (Frequency/Column Percent)								
	Tool Use	Student Collaborative Research	Information Management	Teacher Collaboration	Outside Communication	Product Creation	Tutorial	Undefined	Total
Not checked	14 100	14 100	22 100	18 94.7	24 88.9	33 94.3	11 91.7	26 96.3	162 95.3%
Checked	0 0.0	0 0.0	0 0.0	1 5.3	3 11.1	2 5.7	1 8.3	1 3.7	8 4.7%
Total **Row percent**	14 8.2%	14 8.2%	22 12.9%	19 11.2%	27 15.9%	35 20.6%	12 7.1%	27 15.9%	170

	DF	Value	Prob
Chi-Square	7	5.4444	0.6059

Table C.6.6

CLUSTER AND OUTSIDE INVOLVEMENT—NO OUTSIDE INVOLVEMENT

	CLUSTER (Frequency/Column Percent)								
	Tool Use	Student Collaborative Research	Information Management	Teacher Collaboration	Outside Communication	Product Creation	Tutorial	Undefined	Total
Not checked	6 42.9	3 21.4	4 18.2	10 52.6	25 92.6	12 34.3	2 16.7	8 29.6	70 41.2%
Checked	8 57.1	11 78.6	18 81.8	9 47.4	2 7.4	23 65.7	10 83.3	19 70.4	100 58.8%
Total **Row percent**	14 8.2%	14 8.2%	22 12.9%	19 11.2%	27 15.9%	35 20.6%	12 7.1%	27 15.9%	170

	DF	Value	Prob
Chi-Square	7	42.7197	<.0001

Table C.7

CLUSTER AND PRINCIPAL'S SUPPORT FOR INNOVATION

	CLUSTER (Frequency/Column Percent)								
	Tool Use	Student Collaborative Research	Information Management	Teacher Collaboration	Outside Communication	Product Creation	Tutorial	Undefined	Total
Active involvement in the innovation	7 50.0	6 42.9	8 36.4	7 36.8	11 40.7	5 14.3	4 33.3	5 18.5	53 31.2%
Supportive but not directly involved	7 50.0	8 57.1	14 63.6	12 63.2	12 44.4	29 82.9	8 66.7	18 66.7	108 63.5%
Lack of support	0 0.0	0 0.0	0 0.0	0 0.0	4 14.81	1 2.86	0 0.0	4 14.81	9 5.3%
Total Row percent	14 8.2%	14 8.2%	22 12.9%	19 11.2%	27 15.9%	35 20.6%	12 7.1%	27 15.9%	170

	DF	Value	Prob
Chi-Square	21	29.7294	0.0976

Table C.8

CLUSTER AND NATIONAL EDUCATION POLICY

	CLUSTER (Frequency/Column Percent)								
	Tool Use	Student Collaborative Research	Information Management	Teacher Collaboration	Outside Communication	Product Creation	Tutorial	Undefined	Total
Yes	10 71.4	12 85.7	17 77.3	10 52.6	13 48.2	20 57.1	9 75.0	12 44.4	103 60.6%
No	4 28.6	2 14.3	5 22.7	9 47.4	14 51.9	15 42.9	3 25.0	15 55.6	67 39.4%
Total Row percent	14 8.2%	14 8.2%	22 12.9%	19 11.2%	27 15.9%	35 20.6%	12 7.1%	27 15.9%	170

	DF	Value	Prob
Chi-Square	7	13.3732	0.0635

Table C.9

CLUSTER AND NATIONAL ICT POLICY

	CLUSTER (Frequency/Column Percent)								
	Tool Use	Student Collaborative Research	Information Management	Teacher Collaboration	Outside Communication	Product Creation	Tutorial	Undefined	Total
Yes	9	10	16	14	19	30	9	16	123
	64.3	71.4	72.7	73.7	70.4	85.7	75.0	59.3	72.4%
No	5	4	6	5	8	5	3	11	47
	35.7	28.6	27.3	26.3	29.6	14.3	25.0	40.7	27.6%
Total	14	14	22	19	27	35	12	27	170
Row percent	8.2%	8.2%	12.9%	11.2%	15.9%	20.6%	7.1%	15.9%	

	DF	Value	Prob
Chi-Square	7	6.0127	0.5383

Table C.10.1

CLUSTER AND OUTSIDE ACTIVITIES—NATIONAL, STATE, OR REGIONAL PROJECTS

	CLUSTER (Frequency/Column Percent)								
	Tool Use	Student Collaborative Research	Information Management	Teacher Collaboration	Outside Communication	Product Creation	Tutorial	Undefined	Total
Not checked	7	13	18	11	11	20	5	20	105
	50.0	92.9	81.8	57.9	40.7	57.1	41.7	74.1	61.8%
Checked	7	1	4	8	16	15	7	7	65
	50.0	7.1	18.2	42.1	59.3	42.9	58.3	25.9	38.2%
Total	14	14	22	19	27	35	12	27	170
Row percent	8.2%	8.2%	12.9%	11.2%	15.9%	20.6%	7.1%	15.9%	

	DF	Value	Prob
Chi-Square	7	19.5732	0.0066

Table C.10.2

CLUSTER AND OUTSIDE ACTIVITIES—INTERNATIONAL PROJECTS

	CLUSTER (Frequency/Column Percent)								
	Tool Use	Student Collaborative Research	Information Management	Teacher Collaboration	Outside Communication	Product Creation	Tutorial	Undefined	Total
Not checked	12	13	21	17	21	31	12	25	152
	85.7	92.9	95.5	89.5	77.8	88.6	100	92.6	89.4%
Checked	2	1	1	2	6	4	0	2	18
	14.3	7.1	4.6	10.5	22.2	11.4	0.0	7.4	10.6%
Total	14	14	22	19	27	35	12	27	170
Row percent	8.2%	8.2%	12.9%	11.2%	15.9%	20.6%	7.1%	15.9%	

	DF	Value	Prob
Chi-Square	7	6.8222	0.4476

Table C.10.3

CLUSTER AND OUTSIDE ACTIVITIES—NO OUTSIDE INVOLVEMENT

	CLUSTER (Frequency/Column Percent)								
	Tool Use	Student Collaborative Research	Information Management	Teacher Collaboration	Outside Communication	Product Creation	Tutorial	Undefined	Total
Not checked	7	2	5	9	22	16	6	10	77
	50.0	14.3	22.7	47.4	81.5	45.7	50.0	37.0	45.3%
Checked	7	12	17	10	5	19	6	17	93
	50.0	85.7	77.3	52.6	18.5	54.3	50.0	63.0	54.7%
Total	14	14	22	19	27	35	12	27	170
Row percent	8.2%	8.2%	12.9%	11.2%	15.9%	20.6%	7.1%	15.9%	

	DF	Value	Prob
Chi-Square	7	25.2343	0.0007

Table C.11

CLUSTER AND NUMBER OF SUBJECT AREAS INVOLVED

	CLUSTER (Frequency/Column Percent)								
	Tool Use	Student Collaborative Research	Information Management	Teacher Collaboration	Outside Communication	Product Creation	Tutorial	Undefined	Total
One specific subject	5	8	7	6	4	5	4	10	49
	35.7	57.1	31.8	31.6	14.8	14.3	33.3	37.0	28.8%
A few subjects	2	1	3	8	16	20	6	8	64
	14.3	7.1	13.6	42.1	59.3	57.1	50.0	29.6	37.6%
All (or almost all) subjects	7	5	12	5	7	8	2	9	55
	50.0	35.7	54.6	26.3	25.9	22.9	16.7	33.3	32.4%
No response	0	0	0	0	0	2	0	0	2
	0.0	0.0	0.0	0.0	0.0	5.7	0.0	0.0	1.2%
Total	14	14	22	19	27	35	12	27	170
Row percent	8.2%	8.2%	12.9%	11.2%	15.9%	20.6%	7.1%	15.9%	

	DF	Value	Prob
Chi-Square	21	41.0705	0.0055

Table C.12.1

SUBJECT AREAS OF THE INNOVATIONS—MATHEMATICS

	CLUSTER (Frequency/Column Percent)								
	Tool Use	Student Collaborative Research	Information Management	Teacher Collaboration	Outside Communication	Product Creation	Tutorial	Undefined	Total
Not checked	11	13	16	14	21	32	5	21	133
	78.6	92.9	72.7	73.7	77.8	91.4	41.7	77.8	78.2%
Checked	3	1	6	5	6	3	7	6	37
	21.4	7.1	27.3	26.3	22.2	8.6	58.3	22.2	21.8%
Total	14	14	22	19	27	35	12	27	170
Row percent	8.2%	8.2%	12.9%	11.2%	15.9%	20.6%	7.1%	15.9%	

	DF	Value	Prob
Chi-Square	7	15.39	0.031

Table C.12.2

SUBJECT AREAS OF THE INNOVATIONS—PHYSICS

	CLUSTER (Frequency/Column Percent)								
	Tool Use	Student Collaborative Research	Information Management	Teacher Collaboration	Outside Communication	Product Creation	Tutorial	Undefined	Total
Not checked	14	11	20	12	25	32	12	22	148
	100	78.6	90.9	63.2	92.6	91.4	100	81.5	87.1%
Checked	0	3	2	7	2	3	0	5	22
	0.0	21.4	9.1	36.8	7.4	8.6	0.0	18.5	12.9%
Total	14	14	22	19	27	35	12	27	170
Row percent	8.2%	8.2%	12.9%	11.2%	15.9%	20.6%	7.1%	15.9%	

	DF	Value	Prob
Chi-Square	7	16.76	0.019

Table C.12.3

SUBJECT AREAS OF THE INNOVATIONS—CHEMISTRY

	CLUSTER (Frequency/Column Percent)								
	Tool Use	Student Collaborative Research	Information Management	Teacher Collaboration	Outside Communication	Product Creation	Tutorial	Undefined	Total
Not checked	14	14	20	17	24	34	12	26	161
	100	100	90.9	89.5	88.9	97.1	100	96.3	94.7%
Checked	0	0	2	2	3	1	0	1	9
	0.0	0.0	9.1	10.5	11.1	2.9	0.0	3.7	5.3%
Total	14	14	22	19	27	35	12	27	170
Row percent	8.2%	8.2%	12.9%	11.2%	15.9%	20.6%	7.1%	15.9%	

	DF	Value	Prob
Chi-Square	7	6.2789	0.5076

Table C.12.4

SUBJECT AREAS OF THE INNOVATIONS—BIOLOGY / LIFE SCIENCE

	CLUSTER (Frequency/Column Percent)								
	Tool Use	Student Collaborative Research	Information Management	Teacher Collaboration	Outside Communication	Product Creation	Tutorial	Undefined	Total
Not checked	11	11	15	14	18	30	8	21	128
	78.6	78.6	68.2	73.7	66.7	85.7	66.7	77.8	75.3%
Checked	3	3	7	5	9	5	4	6	42
	21.4	21.4	31.8	26.3	33.3	14.3	33.3	22.2	24.7%
Total	14	14	22	19	27	35	12	27	170
Row percent	8.2%	8.2%	12.9%	11.2%	15.9%	20.6%	7.1%	15.9%	

	DF	Value	Prob
Chi-Square	7	4.48	0.723

Table C.12.5

SUBJECT AREAS OF THE INNOVATIONS—EARTH SCIENCE

	CLUSTER (Frequency/Column Percent)								
	Tool Use	Student Collaborative Research	Information Management	Teacher Collaboration	Outside Communication	Product Creation	Tutorial	Undefined	Total
Not checked	13	14	18	12	23	33	10	24	147
	92.9	100	81.8	63.2	85.2	94.3	83.3	88.9	86.5%
Checked	1	0	4	7	4	2	2	3	23
	7.1	0.0	18.2	36.8	14.8	5.7	16.7	11.1	13.5%
Total	14	14	22	19	27	35	12	27	170
Row percent	8.2%	8.2%	12.9%	11.2%	15.9%	20.6%	7.1%	15.9%	

	DF	Value	Prob
Chi-Square	7	14.01	0.051

Table C.12.6

SUBJECT AREAS OF THE INNOVATIONS—LANGUAGE / MOTHER TONGUE

	CLUSTER (Frequency/Column Percent)								
	Tool Use	Student Collaborative Research	Information Management	Teacher Collaboration	Outside Communication	Product Creation	Tutorial	Undefined	Total
Not checked	9 64.3	13 92.9	12 54.6	13 68.4	16 59.3	24 68.6	7 58.3	22 81.5	116 68.2%
Checked	5 35.7	1 7.1	10 45.5	6 31.6	11 40.7	11 31.4	5 41.7	5 18.5	54 31.8%
Total **Row percent**	14 8.2%	14 8.2%	22 12.9%	19 11.2%	27 15.9%	35 20.6%	12 7.1%	27 15.9%	170

	DF	Value	Prob
Chi-Square	7	9.65	0.209

Table C.12.7

SUBJECT AREAS OF THE INNOVATIONS—FOREIGN LANGUAGE(S)

	CLUSTER (Frequency/Column Percent)								
	Tool Use	Student Collaborative Research	Information Management	Teacher Collaboration	Outside Communication	Product Creation	Tutorial	Undefined	Total
Not checked	9 64.3	13 92.9	18 81.8	15 79.0	13 48.2	27 77.1	11 91.7	22 81.5	128 75.3%
Checked	5 35.7	1 7.1	4 18.2	4 21.1	14 51.9	8 22.9	1 8.3	5 18.5	42 24.7%
Total **Row percent**	14 8.2%	14 8.2%	22 12.9%	19 11.2%	27 15.9%	35 20.6%	12 7.1%	27 15.9%	170

	DF	Value	Prob
Chi-Square	7	16.92	0.018

Table C.12.8

SUBJECT AREAS OF THE INNOVATIONS—CREATIVE ARTS

	CLUSTER (Frequency/Column Percent)								
	Tool Use	Student Collaborative Research	Information Management	Teacher Collaboration	Outside Communication	Product Creation	Tutorial	Undefined	Total
Not checked	10	13	17	14	23	29	11	19	136
	71.4	92.9	77.3	73.7	85.2	82.9	91.7	70.4	80.0%
Checked	4	1	5	5	4	6	1	8	34
	28.6	7.1	22.7	26.3	14.8	17.1	8.3	29.6	20.0%
Total	14	14	22	19	27	35	12	27	170
Row percent	8.2%	8.2%	12.9%	11.2%	15.9%	20.6%	7.1%	15.9%	

	DF	Value	Prob
Chi-Square	7	5.88	0.554

Table C.12.9

SUBJECT AREAS OF THE INNOVATIONS—HISTORY

	CLUSTER (Frequency/Column Percent)								
	Tool Use	Student Collaborative Research	Information Management	Teacher Collaboration	Outside Communication	Product Creation	Tutorial	Undefined	Total
Not checked	12	13	17	13	22	29	12	24	142
	85.7	92.9	77.3	68.4	81.5	82.9	100.0	88.9	83.5%
Checked	2	1	5	6	5	6	0	3	28
	14.3	7.1	22.7	31.6	18.5	17.1	0.0	11.1	16.5%
Total	14	14	22	19	27	35	12	27	170
Row percent	8.2%	8.2%	12.9%	11.2%	15.9%	20.6%	7.1%	15.9%	

	DF	Value	Prob
Chi-Square	7	7.74	0.356

Table C.12.10

SUBJECT AREAS OF THE INNOVATIONS—CIVICS

	CLUSTER (Frequency/Column Percent)								
	Tool Use	Student Collaborative Research	Information Management	Teacher Collaboration	Outside Communication	Product Creation	Tutorial	Undefined	Total
Not checked	13 92.9	13 92.9	17 77.3	16 84.2	23 85.2	30 85.7	10 83.3	25 92.6	147 86.5%
Checked	1 7.1	1 7.1	5 22.7	3 15.8	4 14.8	5 14.3	2 16.7	2 7.4	23 13.5%
Total **Row percent**	14 8.2%	14 8.2%	22 12.9%	19 11.2%	27 15.9%	35 20.6%	12 7.1%	27 15.9%	170

	DF	Value	Prob
Chi-Square	7	3.67	0.817

Table C.12.11

SUBJECT AREAS OF THE INNOVATIONS—ECONOMICS

	CLUSTER (Frequency/Column Percent)								
	Tool Use	Student Collaborative Research	Information Management	Teacher Collaboration	Outside Communication	Product Creation	Tutorial	Undefined	Total
Not checked	13 92.9	14 100	21 95.5	17 89.5	24 88.9	32 91.4	12 100	27 100	160 94.1%
Checked	1 7.1	0 0.0	1 4.6	2 10.5	3 11.1	3 8.6	0 0.0	0 0.0	10 5.9%
Total **Row percent**	14 8.2%	14 8.2%	22 12.9%	19 11.2%	27 15.9%	35 20.6%	12 7.1%	27 15.9%	170

	DF	Value	Prob
Chi-Square	7	5.95	0.545

Table C.12.12

SUBJECT AREAS OF THE INNOVATIONS—GEOGRAPHY

	CLUSTER (Frequency/Column Percent)								
	Tool Use	Student Collaborative Research	Information Management	Teacher Collaboration	Outside Communication	Product Creation	Tutorial	Undefined	Total
Not checked	12 85.7	13 92.9	19 86.4	14 73.7	22 81.5	28 80	12 100	25 92.6	145 85.3%
Checked	2 14.3	1 7.1	3 13.6	5 26.3	5 18.5	7 20.0	0 0.0	2 7.4	25 14.7%
Total **Row percent**	14 8.2%	14 8.2%	22 12.9%	19 11.2%	27 15.9%	35 20.6%	12 7.1%	27 15.9%	170

	DF	Value	Prob
Chi-Square	7	7.01	0.428

Table C.12.13

SUBJECT AREAS OF THE INNOVATIONS—VOCATIONAL SUBJECTS

	CLUSTER (Frequency/Column Percent)								
	Tool Use	Student Collaborative Research	Information Management	Teacher Collaboration	Outside Communication	Product Creation	Tutorial	Undefined	Total
Not checked	10 71.4	13 92.9	21 95.4	17 89.5	22 81.5	35 100	12 100	26 96.3	156 91.8%
Checked	4 28.6	1 7.1	1 4.6	2 10.5	5 18.5	0 0.0	0 0.0	1 3.7	14 8.2%
Total **Row percent**	14 8.2%	14 8.2%	22 12.9%	19 11.2%	27 15.9%	35 20.6%	12 7.1%	27 15.9%	170

	DF	Value	Prob
Chi-Square	7	16.94	0.018

Table C.12.14

SUBJECT AREAS OF THE INNOVATIONS—COMPUTER SCIENCE / INFORMATICS

	CLUSTER (Frequency/Column Percent)								
	Tool Use	Student Collaborative Research	Information Management	Teacher Collaboration	Outside Communication	Product Creation	Tutorial	Undefined	Total
Not checked	10 71.4	14 100	18 81.8	16 84.2	19 70.4	26 74.3	10 83.3	22 81.5	135 79.4%
Checked	4 28.6	0 0.0	4 18.2	3 15.8	8 29.6	9 25.7	2 16.7	5 18.5	35 20.6%
Total Row percent	14 8.2%	14 8.2%	22 12.9%	19 11.2%	27 15.9%	35 20.6%	12 7.1%	27 15.9%	170

	DF	Value	Prob
Chi-Square	7	6.62	0.470

Table C.12.15

SUBJECT AREAS OF THE INNOVATIONS—MULTIDISCIPLINARY PROJECTS

	CLUSTER (Frequency/Column Percent)								
	Tool Use	Student Collaborative Research	Information Management	Teacher Collaboration	Outside Communication	Product Creation	Tutorial	Undefined	Total
Not checked	7 50.0	11 78.6	16 72.7	15 79.0	20 74.1	19 54.3	10 83.3	23 85.2	121 71.2%
Checked	7 50.0	3 21.4	6 27.3	4 21.0	7 25.9	16 45.7	2 16.7	4 14.8	49 28.8%
Total Row percent	14 8.2%	14 8.2%	22 12.9%	19 11.2%	27 15.9%	35 20.6%	12 7.1%	27 15.9%	170

	DF	Value	Prob
Chi-Square	7.00	12.44	0.087

Table C.13.1

CLUSTER AND CURRICULUM CHANGE—CHANGE IN CONTENT

	CLUSTER (Frequency/Column Percent)								
	Tool Use	Student Collaborative Research	Information Management	Teacher Collaboration	Outside Communication	Product Creation	Tutorial	Undefined	Total
Not checked	9	8	18	11	20	27	10	21	124
	64.3	57.1	81.8	57.9	74.1	77.1	83.3	77.8	72.9%
Checked	5	6	4	8	7	8	2	6	46
	35.7	42.9	18.2	42.1	25.9	22.9	16.7	22.2	27.1%
Total	14	14	22	19	27	35	12	27	170
Row percent	8.2%	8.2%	12.9%	11.2%	15.9%	20.6%	7.1%	15.9%	

	DF	Value	Prob
Chi-Square	7	6.6668	0.4644

Table C.13.2

CLUSTER AND CURRICULUM CHANGE—CHANGE IN GOALS

	CLUSTER (Frequency/Column Percent)								
	Tool Use	Student Collaborative Research	Information Management	Teacher Collaboration	Outside Communication	Product Creation	Tutorial	Undefined	Total
Not checked	11	11	17	8	16	20	10	14	107
	78.6	78.6	77.3	42.1	59.3	57.1	83.3	51.9	62.9%
Checked	3	3	5	11	11	15	2	13	63
	21.4	21.4	22.7	57.9	40.7	42.9	16.7	48.2	37.1%
Total	14	14	22	19	27	35	12	27	170
Row percent	8.2%	8.2%	12.9%	11.2%	15.9%	20.6%	7.1%	15.9%	

	DF	Value	Prob
Chi-Square	7	12.6305	0.0816

Table C.13.3

CLUSTER AND CURRICULUM CHANGE—CHANGE IN ORGANIZATION OF CONTENT

	CLUSTER (Frequency/Column Percent)								
	Tool Use	Student Collaborative Research	Information Management	Teacher Collaboration	Outside Communication	Product Creation	Tutorial	Undefined	Total
Not checked	7 50.0	1 7.1	1 4.6	3 15.8	8 29.6	14 40.0	5 41.7	14 51.9	53 31.2%
Checked	7 50.0	13 92.9	21 95.5	16 84.2	19 70.4	21 60.0	7 58.3	13 48.2	117 68.8%
Total **Row percent**	14 8.2%	14 8.2%	22 12.9%	19 11.2%	27 15.9%	35 20.6%	12 7.1%	27 15.9%	170

	DF	Value	Prob
Chi-Square	7	22.7434	0.0019

Table C.13.4

CLUSTER AND CURRICULUM CHANGE—CHANGE IN ALLOCATION OF TIME

	CLUSTER (Frequency/Column Percent)								
	Tool Use	Student Collaborative Research	Information Management	Teacher Collaboration	Outside Communication	Product Creation	Tutorial	Undefined	Total
Not checked	9 64.3	6 42.9	10 45.5	10 52.6	15 55.6	29 82.9	9 75.0	19 70.4	107 62.9%
Checked	5 35.7	8 57.1	12 54.6	9 47.4	12 44.4	6 17.1	3 25.0	8 29.6	63 37.1%
Total **Row percent**	14 8.2%	14 8.2%	22 12.9%	19 11.2%	27 15.9%	35 20.6%	12 7.1%	27 15.9%	170

	DF	Value	Prob
Chi-Square	7	14.1519	0.0485

Table C.14

CLUSTER AND ALTERNATIVE ASSESSMENTS

	CLUSTER (Frequency/Column Percent)								
	Tool Use	Student Collaborative Research	Information Management	Teacher Collaboration	Outside Communication	Product Creation	Tutorial	Undefined	Total
Yes	9 64.3	9 64.3	20 90.9	10 52.6	14 51.9	21 60.0	5 41.7	13 48.2	101 59.4%
No	5 35.7	5 35.7	2 9.1	9 47.4	13 48.2	14 40.0	7 58.3	14 51.9	69 40.6%
Total **Row percent**	14 8.2%	14 8.2%	22 12.9%	19 11.2%	27 15.9%	35 20.6%	12 7.1%	27 15.9%	170

	DF	Value	Prob
Chi-Square	7	13.3215	0.0647

Table C.15

CLUSTER AND CHANGE IN TEACHER ACTIVITIES

	CLUSTER (Frequency/Column Percent)								
	Tool Use	Student Collaborative Research	Information Management	Teacher Collaboration	Outside Communication	Product Creation	Tutorial	Undefined	Total
Yes	8 57.1	13 92.9	20 90.9	16 84.2	18 66.7	25 71.4	7 58.3	18 66.7	125 73.5%
No	6 42.9	1 7.1	2 9.1	3 15.8	9 33.3	10 28.6	5 41.7	9 33.3	45 26.5%
Total **Row percent**	14 8.2%	14 8.2%	22 12.9%	19 11.2%	27 15.9%	35 20.6%	12 7.1%	27 15.9%	170

	DF	Value	Prob
Chi-Square	7	11.956	0.102

Table C.16.1

CLUSTER AND TEACHER OUTCOMES—ACQUISITION OF NEW PEDAGOGICAL SKILLS

	CLUSTER (Frequency/Column Percent)								
	Tool Use	Student Collaborative Research	Information Management	Teacher Collaboration	Outside Communication	Product Creation	Tutorial	Undefined	Total
Not checked	4	2	6	6	11	15	8	22	74
	28.6	14.3	27.3	31.6	40.7	42.9	66.7	81.5	43.5%
Checked	10	12	16	13	16	20	4	5	96
	71.4	85.7	72.7	68.4	59.3	57.1	33.3	18.5	56.5%
Total	14	14	22	19	27	35	12	27	170
Row percent	8.2%	8.2%	12.9%	11.2%	15.9%	20.6%	7.1%	15.9%	

	DF	Value	Prob
Chi-Square	7	28.1402	0.0002

Table C.16.2

CLUSTER AND TEACHER OUTCOMES—ACQUISITION OF ICT SKILLS

	CLUSTER (Frequency/Column Percent)								
	Tool Use	Student Collaborative Research	Information Management	Teacher Collaboration	Outside Communication	Product Creation	Tutorial	Undefined	Total
Not checked	8	1	5	8	12	13	4	13	64
	57.1	7.1	22.7	42.1	44.4	37.1	33.3	48.2	37.6%
Checked	6	13	17	11	15	22	8	14	106
	42.9	92.9	77.3	57.9	55.6	62.9	66.7	51.9	62.4%
Total	14	14	22	19	27	35	12	27	170
Row percent	8.2%	8.2%	12.9%	11.2%	15.9%	20.6%	7.1%	15.9%	

	DF	Value	Prob
Chi-Square	7	11.9622	0.1018

Table C.16.3

CLUSTER AND TEACHER OUTCOMES—ACQUISITION OF COLLABORATIVE SKILLS

	CLUSTER (Frequency/Column Percent)								
	Tool Use	Student Collaborative Research	Information Management	Teacher Collaboration	Outside Communication	Product Creation	Tutorial	Undefined	Total
Not checked	12	9	9	7	19	24	9	22	111
	85.7	64.3	40.9	36.8	70.4	68.6	75.0	81.5	65.3%
Checked	2	5	13	12	8	11	3	5	59
	14.3	35.7	59.1	63.2	29.6	31.4	25.0	18.5	34.7%
Total	14	14	22	19	27	35	12	27	170
Row percent	8.2%	8.2%	12.9%	11.2%	15.9%	20.6%	7.1%	15.9%	

	DF	Value	Prob
Chi-Square	7	19.2365	0.0075

Table C.16.4

CLUSTER AND TEACHER OUTCOMES—DEVELOPMENT OF POSITIVE ATTITUDES

	CLUSTER (Frequency/Column Percent)								
	Tool Use	Student Collaborative Research	Information Management	Teacher Collaboration	Outside Communication	Product Creation	Tutorial	Undefined	Total
Not checked	13	11	15	16	20	27	11	20	133
	92.9	78.6	68.2	84.2	74.1	77.1	91.7	74.1	78.2%
Checked	1	3	7	3	7	8	1	7	37
	7.1	21.4	31.8	15.8	25.9	22.9	8.3	25.9	21.8%
Total	14	14	22	19	27	35	12	27	170
Row percent	8.2%	8.2%	12.9%	11.2%	15.9%	20.6%	7.1%	15.9%	

	DF	Value	Prob
Chi-Square	7	5.308	0.6224

Table C.16.5

CLUSTER AND TEACHER OUTCOMES—NEGATIVE OUTCOMES

	CLUSTER (Frequency/Column Percent)								
	Tool Use	Student Collaborative Research	Information Management	Teacher Collaboration	Outside Communication	Product Creation	Tutorial	Undefined	Total
Not checked	13	13	19	17	26	31	12	26	157
	92.9	92.9	86.4	89.5	96.3	88.6	100	96.3	92.4%
Checked	1	1	3	2	1	4	0	1	13
	7.1	7.1	13.6	10.5	3.7	11.4	0.0	3.7	7.6%
Total	14	14	22	19	27	35	12	27	170
Row percent	8.2%	8.2%	12.9%	11.2%	15.9%	20.6%	7.1%	15.9%	

	DF	Value	Prob
Chi-Square	7	4.2419	0.7515

Table C.17

CLUSTER AND CHANGE IN STUDENT ACTIVITIES

	CLUSTER (Frequency/Column Percent)								
	Tool Use	Student Collaborative Research	Information Management	Teacher Collaboration	Outside Communication	Product Creation	Tutorial	Undefined	Total
Yes	12	13	21	18	22	31	9	18	144
	85.7	92.9	95.5	94.7	81.5	88.6	75.0	66.7	84.7%
No	2	1	1	1	5	4	3	9	26
	14.3	7.1	4.6	5.3	18.5	11.4	25.0	33.3	15.3%
Total	14	14	22	19	27	35	12	27	170
Row percent	8.2%	8.2%	12.9%	11.2%	15.9%	20.6%	7.1%	15.9%	

	DF	Value	Prob
Chi-Square	7	12.4417	0.0869

Table C.18.1

CLUSTER AND STUDENT OUTCOMES—ACQUISITION OF NEW SUBJECT MATTER KNOWLEDGE

	CLUSTER (Frequency/Column Percent)								
	Tool Use	Student Collaborative Research	Information Management	Teacher Collaboration	Outside Communication	Product Creation	Tutorial	Undefined	Total
Not checked	7 50.0	4 28.6	4 18.2	5 26.3	12 44.4	15 42.9	5 41.7	12 44.4	64 37.6%
Checked	7 50.0	10 71.4	18 81.8	14 73.7	15 55.6	20 57.1	7 58.3	15 55.6	106 62.4%
Total **Row percent**	14 8.2%	14 8.2%	22 12.9%	19 11.2%	27 15.9%	35 20.6%	12 7.1%	27 15.9%	170

	DF	Value	Prob
Chi-Square	7	7.5418	0.3747

Table C.18.2

CLUSTER AND STUDENT OUTCOMES—ACQUISITION OF ICT SKILLS

	CLUSTER (Frequency/Column Percent)								
	Tool Use	Student Collaborative Research	Information Management	Teacher Collaboration	Outside Communication	Product Creation	Tutorial	Undefined	Total
Not checked	7 50.0	0 0.0	1 4.6	5 26.3	3 11.1	11 31.4	4 33.3	11 40.7	42 24.7%
Checked	7 50.0	14 100	21 95.5	14 73.7	24 88.9	24 68.6	8 66.7	16 59.3	128 75.3%
Total **Row percent**	14 8.2%	14 8.2%	22 12.9%	19 11.2%	27 15.9%	35 20.6%	12 7.1%	27 15.9%	170

	DF	Value	Prob
Chi-Square	7	21.9871	0.0026

Table C.18.3

CLUSTER AND STUDENT OUTCOMES—ACQUISITION OF COMMUNICATION SKILLS

	CLUSTER (Frequency/Column Percent)								
	Tool Use	Student Collaborative Research	Information Management	Teacher Collaboration	Outside Communication	Product Creation	Tutorial	Undefined	Total
Not checked	9 64.3	9 64.3	6 27.3	9 47.4	19 70.4	19 54.3	12 100	20 74.1	103 60.6%
Checked	5 35.7	5 35.7	16 72.7	10 52.6	8 29.6	16 45.7	0 0.0	7 25.9	67 39.4%
Total **Row percent**	14 8.2%	14 8.2%	22 12.9%	19 11.2%	27 15.9%	35 20.6%	12 7.1%	27 15.9%	170

	DF	Value	Prob
Chi-Square	7	23.3032	0.0015

Table C.18.4

CLUSTER AND STUDENT OUTCOMES—ACQUISITION OF PROBLEM-SOLVING SKILLS

	CLUSTER (Frequency/Column Percent)								
	Tool Use	Student Collaborative Research	Information Management	Teacher Collaboration	Outside Communication	Product Creation	Tutorial	Undefined	Total
Not checked	12 85.7	9 64.3	12 54.6	14 73.7	23 85.2	33 94.3	11 91.7	25 92.6	139 81.8%
Checked	2 14.3	5 35.7	10 45.5	5 26.3	4 14.8	2 5.7	1 8.3	2 7.4	31 18.2%
Total **Row percent**	14 8.2%	14 8.2%	22 12.9%	19 11.2%	27 15.9%	35 20.6%	12 7.1%	27 15.9%	170

	DF	Value	Prob
Chi-Square	7	21.5834	0.003

Table C.18.5

CLUSTER AND STUDENT OUTCOMES—ACQUISITION OF INFORMATION-HANDLING SKILLS

	CLUSTER (Frequency/Column Percent)								
	Tool Use	Student Collaborative Research	Information Management	Teacher Collaboration	Outside Communication	Product Creation	Tutorial	Undefined	Total
Not checked	12 85.7	10 71.4	11 50.0	12 63.2	23 85.2	19 54.3	11 91.7	24 88.9	122 71.8%
Checked	2 14.3	4 28.6	11 50.0	7 36.8	4 14.8	16 45.7	1 8.3	3 11.1	48 28.2%
Total **Row percent**	14 8.2%	14 8.2%	22 12.9%	19 11.2%	27 15.9%	35 20.6%	12 7.1%	27 15.9%	170

	DF	Value	Prob
Chi-Square	7	21.113	0.0036

Table C.18.6

CLUSTER AND STUDENT OUTCOMES—ACQUISITION OF COLLABORATIVE SKILLS

	CLUSTER (Frequency/Column Percent)								
	Tool Use	Student Collaborative Research	Information Management	Teacher Collaboration	Outside Communication	Product Creation	Tutorial	Undefined	Total
Not checked	8 57.1	3 21.4	2 9.1	5 26.3	10 37.0	9 25.7	8 66.7	18 66.7	63 37.0%
Checked	6 42.9	11 78.6	20 90.9	14 73.7	17 63.0	26 74.3	4 33.3	9 33.3	107 63.0%
Total **Row percent**	14 8.2%	14 8.2%	22 12.9%	19 11.2%	27 15.9%	35 20.6%	12 7.1%	27 15.9%	170

	DF	Value	Prob
Chi-Square	7	28.7935	0.0002

Table C.18.7

CLUSTER AND STUDENT OUTCOMES—ACQUISITION OF METACOGNITIVE SKILLS

	CLUSTER (Frequency/Column Percent)								
	Tool Use	Student Collaborative Research	Information Management	Teacher Collaboration	Outside Communication	Product Creation	Tutorial	Undefined	Total
Not checked	10 71.4	6 42.9	11 50.0	10 52.6	21 77.8	20 57.1	9 75.0	19 70.4	106 62.4%
Checked	4 28.6	8 57.1	11 50.0	9 47.4	6 22.2	15 42.9	3 25.0	8 29.6	64 37.6%
Total **Row percent**	14 8.2%	14 8.2%	22 12.9%	19 11.2%	27 15.9%	35 20.6%	12 7.1%	27 15.9%	170

	DF	Value	Prob
Chi-Square	7	9.6515	0.2092

Table C.18.8

CLUSTER AND STUDENT OUTCOMES—DEVELOPMENT OF POSITIVE ATTITUDE

	CLUSTER (Frequency/Column Percent)								
	Tool Use	Student Collaborative Research	Information Management	Teacher Collaboration	Outside Communication	Product Creation	Tutorial	Undefined	Total
Not checked	7 50.0	5 35.7	4 18.2	4 21.1	10 37.0	12 34.3	4 33.3	9 33.3	55 32.4%
Checked	7 50.0	9 64.3	18 81.8	15 79.0	17 63.0	23 65.7	8 66.7	18 66.7	115 67.6%
Total **Row percent**	14 8.2%	14 8.2%	22 12.9%	19 11.2%	27 15.9%	35 20.6%	12 7.1%	27 15.9%	170

	DF	Value	Prob
Chi-Square	7	5.5392	0.5945

Table C.18.9

CLUSTER AND STUDENT OUTCOMES—OUTCOMES FOR DIFFERENT GROUPS OF STUDENTS

	CLUSTER (Frequency/Column Percent)								
	Tool Use	Student Collaborative Research	Information Management	Teacher Collaboration	Outside Communication	Product Creation	Tutorial	Undefined	Total
Not checked	11 78.6	10 71.4	16 72.7	15 79.0	22 81.5	30 85.7	11 91.7	20 74.1	135 79.4%
Checked	3 21.4	4 28.6	6 27.3	4 21.1	5 18.5	5 14.3	1 8.3	7 25.9	35 20.6%
Total **Row percent**	14 8.2%	14 8.2%	22 12.9%	19 11.2%	27 15.9%	35 20.6%	12 7.1%	27 15.9%	170

	DF	Value	Prob
Chi-Square	7	3.6494	0.8192

Table C.18.10

CLUSTER AND STUDENT OUTCOMES—NEGATIVE OUTCOMES

	CLUSTER (Frequency/Column Percent)								
	Tool Use	Student Collaborative Research	Information Management	Teacher Collaboration	Outside Communication	Product Creation	Tutorial	Undefined	Total
Not checked	11 78.6	10 71.4	11 50.0	16 84.2	22 81.5	30 85.7	12 100	26 96.3	138 81.2%
Checked	3 21.4	4 28.6	11 50.0	3 15.8	5 18.5	5 14.3	0 0.0	1 3.7	32 18.8%
Total **Row percent**	14 8.2%	14 8.2%	22 12.9%	19 11.2%	27 15.9%	35 20.6%	12 7.1%	27 15.9%	170

	DF	Value	Prob
Chi-Square	7	22.3368	0.0022

Table C.19.1

CLUSTER AND BENEFITS FOR SPECIAL GROUPS—ETHNIC OR LANGUAGE MINORITIES

	CLUSTER (Frequency/Column Percent)								
	Tool Use	Student Collaborative Research	Information Management	Teacher Collaboration	Outside Communication	Product Creation	Tutorial	Undefined	Total
Not checked	12 85.7	14 100	22 100	18 94.7	24 88.9	31 88.6	11 91.7	27 100	159 93.5%
Checked	2 14.3	0 0.0	0 0.0	1 5.3	3 11.1	4 11.4	1 8.3	0 0.0	11 6.5%
Total **Row percent**	14 8.2%	14 8.2%	22 12.9%	19 11.2%	27 15.9%	35 20.6%	12 7.1%	27 15.9%	170

	DF	Value	Prob
Chi-Square	7	8.2683	0.3095

Table C.19.2

CLUSTER AND BENEFITS FOR SPECIAL GROUPS—STUDENTS OF LOW SOCIOECONOMIC STATUS

	CLUSTER (Frequency/Column Percent)								
	Tool Use	Student Collaborative Research	Information Management	Teacher Collaboration	Outside Communication	Product Creation	Tutorial	Undefined	Total
Not checked	13 92.9	13 92.9	22 100	17 89.5	27 100	32 91.4	9 75.0	24 88.9	157 92.4%
Checked	1 7.1	1 7.1	0 0.0	2 10.5	0 0.0	3 8.6	3 25.0	3 11.1	13 7.6%
Total **Row percent**	14 8.2%	14 8.2%	22 12.9%	19 11.2%	27 15.9%	35 20.6%	12 7.1%	27 15.9%	170

	DF	Value	Prob
Chi-Square	7	9.9082	0.1938

Table C.19.3

CLUSTER AND BENEFITS FOR SPECIAL GROUPS—LOW ABILITY OR STUDENTS AT RISK OF FAILURE

	CLUSTER (Frequency/Column Percent)								
	Tool Use	Student Collaborative Research	Information Management	Teacher Collaboration	Outside Communication	Product Creation	Tutorial	Undefined	Total
Not checked	11 / 78.6	13 / 92.9	21 / 95.5	17 / 89.5	23 / 85.2	31 / 88.6	11 / 91.7	24 / 88.9	151 / 88.8%
Checked	3 / 21.4	1 / 7.1	1 / 4.6	2 / 10.5	4 / 14.8	4 / 11.4	1 / 8.3	3 / 11.1	19 / 11.2%
Total **Row percent**	14 / 8.2%	14 / 8.2%	22 / 12.9%	19 / 11.2%	27 / 15.9%	35 / 20.6%	12 / 7.1%	27 / 15.9%	170

	DF	Value	Prob
Chi-Square	7	3.1543	0.8704

Table C.19.4

CLUSTER AND BENEFITS FOR SPECIAL GROUPS—LEARNING DISABLED

	CLUSTER (Frequency/Column Percent)								
	Tool Use	Student Collaborative Research	Information Management	Teacher Collaboration	Outside Communication	Product Creation	Tutorial	Undefined	Total
Not checked	14 / 100.0	14 / 100	19 / 86.4	17 / 89.5	26 / 96.3	33 / 94.3	12 / 100	26 / 96.3	161 / 94.7%
Checked	0 / 0.0	0 / 0.0	3 / 13.6	2 / 10.5	1 / 3.7	2 / 5.7	0 / 0.0	1 / 3.7	9 / 5.3%
Total **Row percent**	14 / 8.2%	14 / 8.2%	22 / 12.9%	19 / 11.2%	27 / 15.9%	35 / 20.6%	12 / 7.1%	27 / 15.9%	170

	DF	Value	Prob
Chi-Square	7	6.6118	0.4704

Table C.19.5

CLUSTER AND BENEFITS FOR SPECIAL GROUPS—GIRLS

	CLUSTER (Frequency/Column Percent)								
	Tool Use	Student Collaborative Research	Information Management	Teacher Collaboration	Outside Communication	Product Creation	Tutorial	Undefined	Total
Not checked	13 92.9	14 100	21 95.5	19 100	27 100	34 97.1	11 91.7	26 96.3	165 97.0%
Checked	1 7.1	0 0.0	1 4.6	0 0.0	0 0.0	1 2.9	1 8.3	1 3.7	5 3.0%
Total Row percent	14 8.2%	14 8.2%	22 12.9%	19 11.2%	27 15.9%	35 20.6%	12 7.1%	27 15.9%	170

	DF	Value	Prob
Chi-Square	7	4.1604	0.7611

Table C.19.6

CLUSTER AND BENEFITS FOR SPECIAL GROUPS—GIFTED STUDENTS

	CLUSTER (Frequency/Column Percent)								
	Tool Use	Student Collaborative Research	Information Management	Teacher Collaboration	Outside Communication	Product Creation	Tutorial	Undefined	Total
Not checked	13 92.9	14 100	22 100	17 89.5	26 96.3	34 97.1	12 100	26 96.3	164 96.5%
Checked	1 7.1	0 0.0	0 0.0	2 10.5	1 3.7	1 2.9	0 0.0	1 3.7	6 3.5%
Total Row percent	14 8.2%	14 8.2%	22 12.9%	19 11.2%	27 15.9%	35 20.6%	12 7.1%	27 15.9%	170

	DF	Value	Prob
Chi-Square	7	5.0762	0.6507

Table C.19.7

CLUSTER AND BENEFITS FOR SPECIAL GROUPS—NO SPECIAL GROUP

	CLUSTER (Frequency/Column Percent)								
	Tool Use	Student Collaborative Research	Information Management	Teacher Collaboration	Outside Communication	Product Creation	Tutorial	Undefined	Total
Not checked	5	1	4	5	9	10	5	6	45
	35.7	7.1	18.2	26.3	33.3	28.6	41.7	22.2	26.5%
Checked	9	13	18	14	18	25	7	21	125
	64.3	92.9	81.8	73.7	66.7	71.4	58.3	77.8	73.5%
Total	14	14	22	19	27	35	12	27	170
Row percent	8.2%	8.2%	12.9%	11.2%	15.9%	20.6%	7.1%	15.9%	

	DF	Value	Prob
Chi-Square	7	6.4852	0.4844

Table C.20.1

CLUSTER AND LOCATION OF INNOVATION—OUTSIDE OF SCHOOL

	CLUSTER (Frequency/Column Percent)								
	Tool Use	Student Collaborative Research	Information Management	Teacher Collaboration	Outside Communication	Product Creation	Tutorial	Undefined	Total
Not checked	11	12	17	10	16	29	11	19	125
	78.6	85.7	77.3	52.6	59.3	82.9	91.7	70.4	73.5%
Checked	3	2	5	9	11	6	1	8	45
	21.4	14.3	22.7	47.4	40.7	17.1	8.3	29.6	26.5%
Total	14	14	22	19	27	35	12	27	170
Row percent	8.2%	8.2%	12.9%	11.2%	15.9%	20.6%	7.1%	15.9%	

	DF	Value	Prob
Chi-Square	7	12.2283	0.0933

Table C.20.2

CLUSTER AND LOCATION OF INNOVATION—IN SCHOOL BUT OUTSIDE OF REGULAR CLASSROOM OR COMPUTER LAB

	CLUSTER (Frequency/Column Percent)								
	Tool Use	Student Collaborative Research	Information Management	Teacher Collaboration	Outside Communication	Product Creation	Tutorial	Undefined	Total
Not checked	11	13	20	11	20	31	12	22	140
	78.6	92.9	90.9	57.9	74.1	88.6	100	81.5	82.4%
Checked	3	1	2	8	7	4	0	5	30
	21.4	7.1	9.1	42.1	25.9	11.4	0.0	18.5	17.6%
Total	14	14	22	19	27	35	12	27	170
Row percent	8.2%	8.2%	12.9%	11.2%	15.9%	20.6%	7.1%	15.9%	

	DF	Value	Prob
Chi-Square	7	14.9199	0.037

Table C.20.3

CLUSTER AND LOCATION OF INNOVATION—IN REGULAR CLASSROOM

	CLUSTER (Frequency/Column Percent)								
	Tool Use	Student Collaborative Research	Information Management	Teacher Collaboration	Outside Communication	Product Creation	Tutorial	Undefined	Total
Not checked	1	1	0	3	1	2	0	3	11
	7.1	7.1	0.0	15.8	3.7	5.7	0.0	11.1	6.5%
Checked	13	13	22	16	26	33	12	24	159
	92.9	92.9	100	84.2	96.3	94.3	100	88.9	93.5%
Total	14	14	22	19	27	35	12	27	170
Row percent	8.2%	8.2%	12.9%	11.2%	15.9%	20.6%	7.1%	15.9%	

	DF	Value	Prob
Chi-Square	7	6.4349	0.49

Table C.21.1

CLUSTER AND VALUE ADDED BY ICT—SUPPORTS STUDENT PRACTICES

	CLUSTER (Frequency/Column Percent)								
	Tool Use	Student Collaborative Research	Information Management	Teacher Collaboration	Outside Communication	Product Creation	Tutorial	Undefined	Total
Not checked	4	1	1	2	5	8	8	11	40
	28.6	7.1	4.6	10.5	18.5	22.9	66.7	40.7	23.5%
Checked	10	13	21	17	22	27	4	16	130
	71.4	92.9	95.5	89.5	81.5	77.1	33.3	59.3	76.5%
Total	14	14	22	19	27	35	12	27	170
Row percent	8.2%	8.2%	12.9%	11.2%	15.9%	20.6%	7.1%	15.9%	

	DF	Value	Prob
Chi-Square	7	25.72	0.0006

Table C.21.2

CLUSTER AND VALUE ADDED BY ICT—SUPPORTS TEACHER PRACTICES

	CLUSTER (Frequency/Column Percent)								
	Tool Use	Student Collaborative Research	Information Management	Teacher Collaboration	Outside Communication	Product Creation	Tutorial	Undefined	Total
Not checked	13	8	7	11	16	26	7	25	113
	92.9	57.1	31.8	57.9	59.3	74.3	58.3	92.6	66.5%
Checked	1	6	15	8	11	9	5	2	57
	7.1	42.9	68.2	42.1	40.7	25.7	41.7	7.4	33.5%
Total	14	14	22	19	27	35	12	27	170
Row percent	8.2%	8.2%	12.9%	11.2%	15.9%	20.6%	7.1%	15.9%	

	DF	Value	Prob
Chi-Square	7	27.6124	0.0003

Table C.21.3

CLUSTER AND VALUE ADDED BY ICT—ASSOCIATED WITH STUDENT OUTCOMES

	CLUSTER (Frequency/Column Percent)								
	Tool Use	Student Collaborative Research	Information Management	Teacher Collaboration	Outside Communication	Product Creation	Tutorial	Undefined	Total
Not checked	5 35.7	4 28.6	4 18.2	7 36.8	11 40.7	14 40.0	3 25.0	11 40.7	59 34.7%
Checked	9 64.3	10 71.4	18 81.8	12 63.2	16 59.3	21 60.0	9 75.0	16 59.3	111 65.3%
Total **Row percent**	14 8.2%	14 8.2%	22 12.9%	19 11.2%	27 15.9%	35 20.6%	12 7.1%	27 15.9%	170

	DF	Value	Prob
Chi-Square	7	4.7275	0.6932

Table C.21.4

CLUSTER AND VALUE ADDED BY ICT—ASSOCIATED WITH TEACHER OUTCOMES

	CLUSTER (Frequency/Column Percent)								
	Tool Use	Student Collaborative Research	Information Management	Teacher Collaboration	Outside Communication	Product Creation	Tutorial	Undefined	Total
Not checked	12 85.7	9 64.3	15 68.2	17 89.5	24 88.9	29 82.9	11 91.7	25 92.6	142 83.5%
Checked	2 14.3	5 35.7	7 31.8	2 10.5	3 11.1	6 17.1	1 8.3	2 7.4	28 16.5%
Total **Row percent**	14 8.2%	14 8.2%	22 12.9%	19 11.2%	27 15.9%	35 20.6%	12 7.1%	27 15.9%	170

	DF	Value	Prob
Chi-Square	7	10.8364	0.1459

Table C.21.5

CLUSTER AND VALUE ADDED BY ICT—SUPPORTS EDUCATIONAL REFORM

	CLUSTER (Frequency/Column Percent)								
	Tool Use	Student Collaborative Research	Information Management	Teacher Collaboration	Outside Communication	Product Creation	Tutorial	Undefined	Total
Not checked	12	8	11	15	22	21	12	26	127
	85.7	57.1	50.0	79.0	81.5	60.0	100	96.3	74.7%
Checked	2	6	11	4	5	14	0	1	43
	14.3	42.9	50.0	21.1	18.5	40.0	0.0	3.7	25.3%
Total	14	14	22	19	27	35	12	27	170
Row percent	8.2%	8.2%	12.9%	11.2%	15.9%	20.6%	7.1%	15.9%	

	DF	Value	Prob
Chi-Square	7	25.8557	0.0005

Table C.21.6

CLUSTER AND VALUE ADDED BY ICT—SUPPORTS CURRICULAR CHANGE

	CLUSTER (Frequency/Column Percent)								
	Tool Use	Student Collaborative Research	Information Management	Teacher Collaboration	Outside Communication	Product Creation	Tutorial	Undefined	Total
Not checked	13	7	16	15	24	32	11	25	143
	92.9	50.0	72.7	79.0	88.9	91.4	91.7	92.6	84.1%
Checked	1	7	6	4	3	3	1	2	27
	7.1	50.0	27.3	21.1	11.1	8.6	8.3	7.4	15.9%
Total	14	14	22	19	27	35	12	27	170
Row percent	8.2%	8.2%	12.9%	11.2%	15.9%	20.6%	7.1%	15.9%	

	DF	Value	Prob
Chi-Square	7	19.3387	0.0072

Table C.21.7

CLUSTER AND VALUE ADDED BY ICT—SAVE MONEY OR INCREASE EFFICIENCY

	CLUSTER (Frequency/Column Percent)								
	Tool Use	Student Collaborative Research	Information Management	Teacher Collaboration	Outside Communication	Product Creation	Tutorial	Undefined	Total
Not checked	11 78.6	12 85.7	18 81.8	14 73.7	20 74.1	31 88.6	8 66.7	22 81.5	136 80.0%
Checked	3 21.4	2 14.3	4 18.2	5 26.3	7 25.9	4 11.4	4 33.3	5 18.5	34 20.0%
Total **Row percent**	14 8.2%	14 8.2%	22 12.9%	19 11.2%	27 15.9%	35 20.6%	12 7.1%	27 15.9%	170

	DF	Value	Prob
Chi-Square	7	4.3928	0.7336

Table C.21.8

CLUSTER AND VALUE ADDED BY ICT—PROVIDES RESOURCES NOT OTHERWISE AVAILABLE

	CLUSTER (Frequency/Column Percent)								
	Tool Use	Student Collaborative Research	Information Management	Teacher Collaboration	Outside Communication	Product Creation	Tutorial	Undefined	Total
Not checked	9 64.3	4 28.6	5 22.7	9 47.4	15 55.6	20 57.1	10 83.3	19 70.4	91 53.5%
Checked	5 35.7	10 71.4	17 77.3	10 52.6	12 44.4	15 42.9	2 16.7	8 29.6	79 46.5%
Total **Row percent**	14 8.2%	14 8.2%	22 12.9%	19 11.2%	27 15.9%	35 20.6%	12 7.1%	27 15.9%	170

	DF	Value	Prob
Chi-Square	7	20.4295	0.0047

Table C.21.9

CLUSTER AND VALUE ADDED BY ICT—CHANGES TIME OR STRUCTURE OF SCHOOL

	CLUSTER (Frequency/Column Percent)								
	Tool Use	Student Collaborative Research	Information Management	Teacher Collaboration	Outside Communication	Product Creation	Tutorial	Undefined	Total
Not checked	10	5	8	17	21	31	11	23	126
	71.4	35.7	36.4	89.5	77.8	88.6	91.7	85.2	74.1%
Checked	4	9	14	2	6	4	1	4	44
	28.6	64.3	63.6	10.5	22.2	11.4	8.3	14.8	25.9%
Total	14	14	22	19	27	35	12	27	170
Row percent	8.2%	8.2%	12.9%	11.2%	15.9%	20.6%	7.1%	15.9%	

	DF	Value	Prob
Chi-Square	7	37.1486	<.0001

Table C.21.10

CLUSTER AND VALUE ADDED BY ICT—SUPPORTS STUDENT LEARNING PROCESSES

	CLUSTER (Frequency/Column Percent)								
	Tool Use	Student Collaborative Research	Information Management	Teacher Collaboration	Outside Communication	Product Creation	Tutorial	Undefined	Total
Not checked	12	7	8	15	18	31	8	20	119
	85.7	50	36.4	79.0	66.7	88.6	66.7	74.1	70.0%
Checked	2	7	14	4	9	4	4	7	51
	14.3	50	63.6	21.1	33.3	11.4	33.3	25.9	30.0%
Total	14	14	22	19	27	35	12	27	170
Row percent	8.2%	8.2%	12.9%	11.2%	15.9%	20.6%	7.1%	15.9%	

	DF	Value	Prob
Chi-Square	7	23.0581	0.0017

Table C.21.11

CLUSTER AND VALUE ADDED BY ICT—INHIBITS UNDESIRABLE ACTIVITIES

	CLUSTER (Frequency/Column Percent)								
	Tool Use	Student Collaborative Research	Information Management	Teacher Collaboration	Outside Communication	Product Creation	Tutorial	Undefined	Total
Not checked	13	11	18	18	27	35	11	26	159
	92.9	78.6	81.8	94.7	100	100	91.7	96.3	93.5%
Checked	1	3	4	1	0	0	1	1	11
	7.1	21.4	18.2	5.3	0.0	0.0	8.3	3.7	6.5%
Total	14	14	22	19	27	35	12	27	170
Row percent	8.2%	8.2%	12.9%	11.2%	15.9%	20.6%	7.1%	15.9%	

	DF	Value	Prob
Chi-Square	7	14.9176	0.0371

Table C.21.12

CLUSTER AND VALUE ADDED BY ICT—ASSOCIATED WITH PARENT INVOLVEMENT

	CLUSTER (Frequency/Column Percent)								
	Tool Use	Student Collaborative Research	Information Management	Teacher Collaboration	Outside Communication	Product Creation	Tutorial	Undefined	Total
Not checked	12	13	19	19	26	34	10	26	159
	85.7	92.9	86.4	100	96.3	97.1	83.3	96.3	93.5%
Checked	2	1	3	0	1	1	2	1	11
	14.3	7.1	13.6	0.0	3.7	2.9	16.7	3.7	6.5%
Total	14	14	22	19	27	35	12	27	170
Row percent	8.2%	8.2%	12.9%	11.2%	15.9%	20.6%	7.1%	15.9%	

	DF	Value	Prob
Chi-Square	7	8.104	0.3235

Table C.22

CLUSTER AND SUSTAINABILITY

	CLUSTER (Frequency/Column Percent)								
	Tool Use	Student Collaborative Research	Information Management	Teacher Collaboration	Outside Communication	Product Creation	Tutorial	Undefined	Total
Yes	9 64.3	10 71.4	20 90.9	14 73.7	19 70.4	27 77.1	11 91.7	23 85.2	133 78.2%
No	5 35.7	4 28.6	2 9.1	5 26.3	8 29.6	8 22.9	1 8.3	4 14.8	37 21.8%
Total **Row percent**	14 8.2%	14 8.2%	22 12.9%	19 11.2%	27 15.9%	35 20.6%	12 7.1%	27 15.9%	170

	DF	Value	Prob
Chi-Square	7	7.3299	0.3954

Table C.23

CLUSTER AND TRANSFERABILITY

	CLUSTER (Frequency/Column Percent)								
	Tool Use	Student Collaborative Research	Information Management	Teacher Collaboration	Outside Communication	Product Creation	Tutorial	Undefined	Total
Yes	3 21.4	5 35.7	10 45.5	10 52.6	13 48.2	14 40.0	7 58.3	11 40.7	73 42.9%
No	11 78.6	9 64.3	12 54.6	9 47.4	14 51.9	21 60.0	5 41.7	16 59.3	97 57.1%
Total **Row percent**	14 8.2%	14 8.2%	22 12.9%	19 11.2%	27 15.9%	35 20.6%	12 7.1%	27 15.9%	170

	DF	Value	Prob
Chi-Square	7	5.3637	0.6157